THE ROYAL VICTORIANS

King Edward VII,
His Family and Friends

By the same author

THE ROYAL VICTORIANS

King Edward VII,
His Family and Friends

CHRISTOPHER HIBBERT

J. B. LIPPINCOTT COMPANY
Philadelphia and New York

All illustrations except those otherwise attributed have been
reproduced by gracious permission of Her Majesty the Queen.

U.S. Library of Congress Cataloging in Publication Data

Hibbert, Christopher, birth date
  The royal Victorians.

  Bibliography: p.
  Includes index.
  1. Edward VII, King of Great Britain, 1841-1810.
I. Title.
DA567.H5   941.082'3'0924 [B]   75-46507
ISBN-O-397-01111-3

For Henry and Angela

Contents

List of Illustrations

Sections of photographs follow pages 84 and 180.

Author's Note and Acknowledgements

A new study of King Edward VII seems to demand some apology, not to say warning. When I first began to write it the King was not such a well-known figure as he has since become. But a popular television series and several recent biographies have combined to ensure that the outlines of the story contained in the following pages will already be familiar to many of their readers. I have, however, not been deflected from my original purpose, which was to present a fresh study of Edward VII based on as much new material as I was able to assemble, and to add as many unknown or little-known details to the portrait of the man whose career has been so conscientiously chronicled by Sir Sidney Lee and so ably described by Sir Philip Magnus. I have covered again some well-trodden fields; but even those readers who know them well will, I hope, be rewarded by discovering some clumps of hitherto disregarded clover amidst the familiar grass.

I wish to thank her Majesty the Queen for gracious permission to reproduce material from the photograph collections in the Royal Archives.

For allowing me to consult their family papers and other unpublished material I am most grateful to the Duke of Devonshire and the Trustees of the Chatsworth Settlement, the Duke of Richmond and Gordon, the Duke of Northumberland, the Duke of Wellington, the Duke of Westminster, the Marquess of Salisbury, the Earl of Clarendon, the Earl of Rosebery, Viscount Downe, Lord Carrington, Lord Armstrong, Sir William Gordon Cumming and Brigadier Llewellen Palmer.

For helping me with the relevant papers I want to thank Mr T.S. Wragg, the Duke of Devonshire's librarian; Mr D. Legg-Willis, House Manager at Goodwood, and Mrs Patricia Gill, West Sussex County Archivist; Mr D.P. Graham and the staff of the Northumberland Estates Office; Miss Joan Wilson, the Duke of Wellington's librarian; Mr G. Acloque of the Grosvenor Estate Office; Dr J.F.A. Mason, Librarian of Christ Church, Oxford, who had charge of the Salisbury Papers; the Keeper of Western

Manuscripts and his staff at the Bodleian Library, Oxford, in whose care are the Clarendon Papers and photocopies of the Lincolnshire Papers; Mr Patrick Cadell of the Department of Manuscripts, National Library of Scotland, where the Rosebery and Gordon Cumming Papers have been deposited, and Mr M.Y. Ashcroft of the County Record Office, Northallerton, in whose care are the Downe Papers.

I have also made use of the Londonderry Papers and the Earl Grey Papers at Durham; the Filmer, Chilston and Knollys Manuscripts at Maidstone; the Asquith, Sandars and Acland Papers at the Bodleian, Oxford; the papers of Lord Crewe and Lord Hardinge of Penshurst and the manuscript diaries of Joseph Romilly at Cambridge University Library; the Minto, Haldane, Elibank and Combe Papers at Edinburgh; the Cadogan Papers in the House of Lords Record Office; the Manchester Collections at Huntingdon; the King Papers at Cambridge; the Henniker and Cranworth Collections at Ipswich; the Desborough Papers at Aylesbury; the Gibbs Papers at Oxford; and the Wharncliffe Correspondence at Sheffield.

I would, accordingly, like to express my thanks for their help to Mr J. Keith-Bishop and the staff of the Durham County Record Office; Mr J. E. Fagg and Dr J.M. Fewster of the Department of Palaeography and Diplomatic, University of Durham; Dr F. Hull, the Kent County Archivist; Mr A.E.B. Owen, Under-librarian at Cambridge University Library; Miss L.E. Thomas, Assistant Archivist at the County Record Office, Huntingdon; Mr J.M. Farrar, the Cambridgeshire County Archivist; Mr W.R. Serjeant, of the Ipswich and East Suffolk Record Office; Mr E.J. Davis, Buckingham County Archivist; Miss S.J. Barnes of the Oxfordshire Record Office; and Mr John Bibbington of the Sheffield City Libraries.

I have also to acknowledge the generous help of Messrs Holden, Scott & Co. and Messrs Rollit, Farrel & Bladen, solicitors of Hull; Mr E.A. Bellamy, Librarian at the National Motor Museum, Beaulieu; Miss Màiri Macdonald of the Harrowby Manuscripts Trust; Mr Hugh H. Cundey of Messrs Henry Poole & Co. (Savile Row) Ltd; Mrs Mollie Travis, Archivist at Broadlands; Dr Frank Taylor of the John Rylands Library, Manchester; Mrs J. Percival, Archivist at University College, London; Mr J.M. Collinson of the Leeds City Libraries; and the County Archivists and their staffs at Newcastle upon Tyne, Carlisle, Beverley, Barnsley, Winchester, Chester, Warwick, Taunton, Norwich, Lincoln, Guildford, Gloucester, Reading, Hertford and Northampton. I am further grateful to Mr E.J. Priestley, Assistant Keeper of the Merseyside County Museums, Liverpool.

I would also like to thank the Hon. Georgina Stonor; the Earl of Crawford and Balcarres; Lord Barnard; Lord Montagu; Lord Hastings; Lady Hamilton; Sir Roualeyn Cumming-Bruce; Captain Gordon Fergusson; Lord Hardinge of Penshurst; Mr E.H. Cornelius, Librarian of the Royal College of Surgeons of England; Sir Robin Mackworth-Young, the Queen's Librarian; the Librarian of New Scotland Yard; Mr C.H. Graves of Messrs Davies & Son; Mr Philip Howard; Mr David Higham; Dr A.J. Salmon; Miss Elaine Mallett of the Lord Chamberlain's Office; Mr. F.G. Lintott of Messrs H. Huntsman & Sons Ltd; Mrs. Lucy Pinney; and Miss Frances Dimond, Assistant Registrar, the Royal Archives.

I am most grateful also to Mrs Stewart Ryan for reading newspapers for me in the Newspaper Library at Colindale, and to Mrs Joan St George Saunders for working for me in the British Museum, the Public Record Office and the House of Lords Record Office.

The Chef du Cabinet du Préfet de Police in Paris kindly made arrangements for me to see the police dossiers on the King's movements and activities when he was in France; and I am much indebted to Mme Jeanne Harburger of the Bureau des Archives at the Préfecture de Police for her help when I was in Paris.

For their help in a variety of ways I am also deeply indebted to Mr Godfrey Whitelock, Mr R.H. Owen, Mrs John Rae and Mrs Maurice Hill.

Finally I want to say how grateful I am to Mr George Walker and Mr Hamish Francis for having read the proofs and to my wife for having compiled the detailed index.

The text is not documented in the usual way; but the reader curious to discover the source of any previously unpublished material will be able to find it in the notes at the back of the book.

C.H.

Part I

PRINCE OF WALES
1841-1901

1
'Poor Bertie'

In many things savages are much better educated than we are.

Within a few months of the birth of her first child, Queen Victoria discovered herself to be pregnant again. And by the early autumn of 1841 she was feeling thoroughly out of sorts. It was not only that she was often sick and nearly always depressed, that she viewed the prospect of another delivery with both trepidation and distaste; she had had to say good-bye to her beloved Prime Minister, Lord Melbourne, a parting that had distressed her deeply, and there now seemed a danger that she might lose the Princess Royal, too. For 'Pussy', so fat and healthy a baby at first, was becoming thin and pale, fretful and peevish. The Queen shut her mind to the fear that there was any real danger; but the weakness of the child fussed and worried her much. She felt 'very wretched ... low and depressed'.

On more than one occasion in October there had been a sudden fear that the birth of her second baby might be premature, so that when the pains returned on 8 November, the Queen thought at first that this was another 'false alarm'. The new Prime Minister, Sir Robert Peel, was coming to dinner the following evening and she decided not to put him off. The next day, however, there could be no further doubt. 'My sufferings were really very severe,' the Queen later recorded. 'And I don't know what I should have done, but for the great comfort and support my beloved Albert was to me during the whole time. At last at twelve m[inutes] to eleven, I gave birth to a fine large Boy ... It was taken to the Ministers for them to see.'

The ministers were delighted to see so obviously robust a baby, and so was the country at large. No heir had been born to a reigning monarch since the appearance of George III's first child, almost eighty years before; and this new birth led royalists to hope that the monarchy, which the young Queen was once more making respectable and popular, was secure from a decline into its recent disrepute. Salutes were fired, crowds gathered in the streets to cheer and sing 'God Save the Queen', and the Prime Minister made reference to the nation's enthusiasm in a speech at the Guildhall, which was decorated

3

for the occasion with illuminated letters spelling 'God save the Prince of Wales'. *The Times* described the 'one universal feeling of joy which ran throughout the kingdom'. 'What a joy!' wrote the boy's grandmother, the Duchess of Kent, expressing a common opinion. 'Oh God, what a happiness, what a blessing!'

Nowhere was his arrival more welcome than in the palace nursery, for he was not the least trouble. Healthy, fair and fat, 'a wonderfully large and strong child', he smiled readily, digested his food without trouble, and made those gurgling, crowing noises so pleasing to the ears of nursemaids. His mother was very pleased with the look of him, with his 'very large dark blue eyes', his 'finely formed but somewhat large nose' and his 'pretty little mouth'.

'What a pretty boy!' the people called out when they saw him being taken to be inspected by the Duke of Wellington at Walmer Castle. 'Bless his little face! . . . Show him! Turn him this way! . . . How like his father!'

To his mother, indeed, the resemblance to his father was his principal virtue. And when, on 25 January, he was baptized in St George's Chapel, Windsor, by the Archbishop of Canterbury, honoured with a christening cake eight feet wide, and given the names Albert Edward, the Queen decided that the best thing about 'the Boy' was that he now had his dear father's name. She had refused to heed Lord Melbourne's advice that Edward, 'a good English appellation', might precede Albert, 'which had not been so common nor so much in use since the Conquest'. The child was 'to be called *Albert* and Edward [was] to be his second name'—and that was that. But the name was far from enough: he must be made to resemble his father in every way; any tendency to infantile vice must be rigorously suppressed; any hints that he might, if left unchecked, grow up like his mother's wicked uncles must be carefully watched so that the necessary steps could be taken to counter so appalling, so calamitous a development. 'You will understand how fervent are my prayers, and I am sure everybody's must be, to see him resemble his father in *every, every* respect, both in body and mind,' the Queen wrote to her Uncle Leopold, King of the Belgians; 'I hope and pray he may be like his dearest papa.'

The nursery in which 'the Boy's' growth was so anxiously observed was under the supervision of Mrs Southey, a worthy, old-fashioned fogey who declined to make any concessions to modern ideas and still wore a wig. But while Mrs Southey, who had been recommended by the Archbishop of Canterbury, had been considered adequate enough when there was but one child to look after, she was not a suitable person to deal with the added responsibility of two. She went out too often, leaving her charges in the care of underlings inclined to squabble. She was not sufficiently firm or vigilant enough to ensure that the strict rules of the nursery were observed: that the two children must never be left alone for an instant; that no unauthorized person must ever be admitted to see them; that there must not be the slightest variation in the daily routine without prior consultation with the parents. It was felt that a lady of high birth would be better suited to superintend the nursery, to control the tantrums of the Princess Royal and to report intelligently upon the development of the Prince of Wales. And so, after consultation with various advisers, this most important post was offered to Lady Lyttelton, eldest daughter of the second Earl Spencer and widow of the third Baron Lyttelton.

The choice was a fortunate one. Lady Lyttelton was a gifted woman, understanding, good-natured and sensible. 'Princessy', as she called her elder charge, did not take to her at first, screaming with 'unconquerable horror' when she arrived; and thereafter, though bawling less, treating her new governess with a kind of irritable reserve which was finally overcome by Lady Lyttelton's patience and tact. With the Prince of Wales, who appeared to like her from the beginning, Lady Lyttelton had no such problems. He continued to flourish, remaining constantly in 'crowing spirits' and in the best and calmest of tempers. He looked people full in the face through his 'large clear blue eyes'.

This early stage of placid equanimity did not, however, last long. As his sister grew stronger in health and less fractious in temper, she was also recognized to be extremely sharp and quick-witted. Precociously forward, active, animated, 'running about and talking a great deal', she was, at the same time, 'all gracefulness and prettiness', in the opinion of Lady Lyttelton; and in that of her mother's half-sister, Princess Feodora, an 'irresistible . . . treasure . . . a darling child'. The Prince of Wales, on the contrary, was becoming increasingly difficult. At the age of two he was considered to be 'as forward as the majority of children of his age', if 'no more'; but the next year —although 'very handsome' and 'most exemplary in politeness and manner', 'bowing and offering his hand beautifully, besides saluting *à la militaire*—all unbidden'—he was considered 'very small in every way . . . not articulate like his sister, but rather boyish in accent [and] altogether backward in language'. Two years later Lady Lyttelton had cause to complain of his being 'uncommonly averse to learning' and requiring 'much patience from wilful inattention and constant interruptions, getting under the table, upsetting the books and sundry other *anti-studious* practices'. By the age of five he was causing the 'greatest distress' to his French governess, Mlle Hollande.

His father neither now nor later troubled to conceal the fact that Victoria, the Princess Royal, was his favourite child. When he came into the nursery his eye alighted upon her with pleasure. He loved to play bricks with her and to put her on his knee while he played the organ; but in the contemplation of his son his countenance became troubled and apprehensive. The Queen also seemed to prefer her daughter to her son and spent far more time with her, always helping her with her Sunday lesson which the little boy was left to do on his own. One day he asked her 'to do his little Sunday lesson with *him* sometimes'; and the Queen admitted to having been 'much touched' by this, as though she had previously been quite unaware of his need of her attention.

He began to stammer; and his sister teased him for it, imitating him, driving him to fury. One afternoon they had 'a tremendous fight' when brought down to their parents' room; so the next day they were brought down separately but, the one being taken into the room before the other had been led away, they fell to quarrelling again.

It was worse when other children were born; and when they, too, proved to be brighter than the Prince of Wales, who was now known as 'Bertie' rather than 'the Boy'. Princess Alice was born in 1843, Prince Alfred the following year, Princess Helena in 1846. And Bertie—still a pretty boy 'but delicate looking' in Lord Macaulay's opinion—found it quite impossible to maintain the intellectual lead he ought to have had over them. By the time he was six he had already been overtaken by Princess Alice, who was not only more than eighteen months younger than himself but who was 'neither studious nor so clever as the Princess Royal'.

The Queen could but hope that in time the child would improve; and, for the moment, she comforted herself with the discovery that once they were out of the distasteful 'frog stage', as she called it, children could be good company. She enjoyed playing games with them, rowdy games like blind-man's-buff and fox-and-geese, and quieter ones like beggar-my-neigh-bour. She danced quadrilles with the Prince of Wales as her partner, and on summer evenings she went for little walks with him and helped him to catch moths. She watched him rehearse plays with his brothers and sisters under the direction of their conscientious father, who made them 'say their parts over and over again'. 'Children,' she decided, 'though often a source of anxiety and difficulty are a great blessing and cheer and brighten up life.'

By the time she made this entry in her journal, a detailed plan of education for the children had been drawn up by their father and set down by him and the Queen in a memorandum dated 3 January 1847. The younger children were to be placed in a separate class from the two elder, who were to begin their more advanced lessons in February. Particular attention was to be paid in these lessons to English, arithmetic and geography; and an hour each day was to be devoted to both German and French. The Queen herself was to give religious instruction to the Princess Royal; but the Prince's education in this subject was to be entrusted to Lady Lyttelton and her assistant governess, Miss Hildyard. Miss Hildyard was also to supervise the children's daily prayers which they were required to repeat kneeling down. If the governesses wished to make any alterations in the syllabus, or to propose outings, rewards or punishments, the Queen must always be consulted in such matters.

Lady Lyttelton herself did not believe in the severe punishment of young children as one was *'never sure'* that it was fully understood by the culprits 'as belonging to the naughtiness'. But Prince Albert believed that physical chastisement was on occasions necessary to secure obedience. Even the girls were whipped and required to listen to lengthy admonishments with their hands tied together. At the age of four Princess Alice received 'a real punishment by whipping' for telling a lie and 'roaring'. The Prince of Wales, of course, received even harsher treatment; but there was no improvement in his behaviour. His stammer did not improve, his sudden rages grew more violent and prolonged.

Occasional doubts were expressed about the suitability of so strict and unvarying a regime for a child of the Prince's temperament. Even his parents' influential and masterful friend and adviser, Baron Stockmar, who joined their anxious discussions and submitted a series of memoranda on the Prince's education while supporting the view that the strictest discipline was necessary, gave it as the opinion of one who had been trained as a doctor that a system of continuous study and organized pursuits 'if fully carried into effect and especially in the earlier years of the Prince's life would, if he were a sprightly boy, speedily lead to a cerebral disease, and if he was constitutionally slow, induce inevitable disgust'.

The parents were not convinced. The ghosts of King George IV and his brothers seemed to hang continually about the room where the worried discussions between the parents and their advisers took place. Not many years before, members of the government had been harassed by fears that the discontent of the English people might well break out into revolution. Republicanism was still an active political force. Any future king would have to be a most exceptional man if the monarchy were to survive; and he could not hope to survive were he not to receive an education of unremitting rigour, rigidly supervised, and kept under constant surveillance. Baron Stockmar, who had already increased Prince Albert's anxiety by warning him that he and the Queen ought to be 'thoroughly permeated' with the truth that their position was a more difficult one than that of any other parents in the kingdom, now told the Queen that the errors in the education of her uncles—who had, in fact, been given a far sounder training than her grandfather, King George III—had 'contributed more than any other circumstance to weaken the respect and influence of royalty in this country'. Both the Queen and Prince Albert were persuaded that this was so, and neither was impressed when Lord Melbourne advised them not to set too much store by education which might 'mould and direct the character' but rarely altered it. They preferred to believe that discipline must continue to be harsh and that the syllabus must remain exacting so that the grand object of the Prince of Wales's education might be fulfilled. This object, declared the Bishop of Oxford, one of those numerous experts consulted by the parents, must be none other than to turn the Prince of Wales into 'the most perfect man'.

When the Prince was two years old the Queen had already made up her mind that before he was six at the latest he 'ought to be given *entirely* over to the Tutors and taken *entirely away* from the women'. And early in 1848 a careful search began for a man who could be entrusted to take over from Lady Lyttelton the duties of creating a Prince 'of calm, profound, comprehensive understanding, with a deep conviction of the indispensable necessity of practical morality to the welfare of the Sovereign and People'.

The choice eventually fell upon Mr Henry Birch, a handsome, thirty-year-old master at Eton where he had formerly been captain of the school. Birch took up his duties, at a salary of £800 a year, in April 1849 and immediately began to regret that he had done so. He found his charge 'extremely disobedient, impertinent to his masters and unwilling to submit to discipline'. It was 'almost impossible to follow out any thoroughly systematic plan of management or thoroughly regular course of study' because 'the Prince of Wales was so different on different days', sometimes cooperative but more often refusing to answer questions to which he knew the answers perfectly well. The Prince was also extremely selfish and unable even 'to play at any game for five minutes, or attempt anything new or difficult without losing his temper'. When he did lose his temper his rage was uncontrollable; and after the fury had subsided he was left far too drained and exhausted to bring his mind to bear on his work. He could not bear to be teased or criticized; and though he flew into a tantrum or sulked whenever he was teased, Birch thought it best, 'notwithstanding his sensitiveness, to laugh at him . . . and to treat him as boys would have treated him in an English public school'. His parents thought so, too; and they caused him anguish by mocking him when he had done something wrong or stupid. 'Poor Prince,' commented Lady Lyttelton one day when he was derided for asking, 'Mama, is not a pink the female of a carnation?' The Queen also considered it essential to put him sharply to silence when, as children will, he made up stories about himself. Charles Greville heard from Lord Melbourne's sister-in-law, Lady Beauvais, that any 'incipient propensity to that sort of romancing which distinguished his [great] uncle, George IV', was instantaneously checked. 'The child told Lady Beauvais that during their cruise he was very nearly thrown overboard, and was proceeding to tell her how, when the Queen overheard him, sent him off with a flea in his ear, and told her it was totally untrue.'

Although he approved of such remonstrances, Mr Birch did not disguise his belief—a belief shared by Prince Albert's friend, Lord Granville—that the policy of keeping the Prince so strictly isolated from other boys was one of the reasons for his tiresome behaviour. It was Birch's 'deliberate opinion' that many of his pupil's 'peculiarities' arose from the effects of this policy, 'from his being continually in the society of older persons, and from his finding himself the centre round which everything seems to move'. Surely it would be better if pupil and tutor were not so constantly in each other's company. Birch recorded:

> I have always found that boys' characters at Eton were formed as much by contact with others as by the precepts of their tutors . . . [The Prince] has no standard by which to measure his own powers. His brother [Prince Alfred] is much too young and too yielding, and nothing that a tutor can say, or even a parent, has such influence as intercourse with sensible boys of the same age, or a little older, unconsciously teaching by example.

When he did take some lessons with Prince Alfred there was 'a marked improvement in his temper, disposition and behaviour'; he was 'far less selfish, far less excitable, and in every way more amiable and teachable'.

There were lessons to be learned every weekday, including Saturday. Holidays, except on family birthdays, were rare; and, when the Prince went away with his parents, the tutors went with them. In August 1849 he accompanied the Queen and Prince Albert on their visit to Ireland and was driven about the streets with them in his sailor suit; but as soon as he got back to Vice-Regal Lodge or aboard the royal yacht, *Fairy*, he had to settle down to his books again. When, two years later, he drove once more in his parents' carriage—this time wearing full Highland dress—to the opening of the Great Exhibition, he knew that the lessons were to begin again on his return to the Palace. And when, some time after this, he went with his parents to Balmoral, he was quickly disabused of the hope that he was to have a short holiday. His tutor thought a little deer-stalking or some other outdoor activity 'such as taking the heights of hills' would not come amiss. But Prince Albert said that 'it must not be supposed that [the visit to Balmoral] was to be taken as a holiday; that the Prince had had mistaken notions about this; but that henceforth work must be done diligently.'

Arithmetic, geography and English the Prince studied with Mr Birch. Other tutors taught him German and French, handwriting, drawing—at which he showed some talent—music and religion. And each tutor was required to send regular reports on his pupil's progress to Prince Albert.

Prince Albert was rarely comforted by what he read, particularly when he was obliged to accept the fact that even at eight years old the Prince was still too backward to begin learning the catechism. It was some comfort that his German was quite good, that by the age of five he could read a German book without much difficulty and carry on a conversation in German without undue hesitation, though this ability seemed to interfere with his mastery of English: despite all the efforts of the actor, George Bartley, who was employed to give him elocution lessons, the Prince never altogether lost his slight German accent and to the end of his life there was a noticeably Germanic guttural burr in his pronunciation of the letter 'r'. His French was not so good as his German, and it was not until later in life that he acquired the accent and vocabulary on which he was to pride himself.

In his anxiety Prince Albert consulted the famous phrenologist, Sir George Combe, who, having examined the boy's cranium, 'pointed out the peculiarities of his temperament and brain'. Sir George subsequently reported:

The feeble quality of the brain will render the Prince highly excitable, and as the excitement will be most strongly experienced in the largest organs, it follows that he will be liable to vehement fits of passion, opposition, self-will and obstinacy, not as voluntary acts, but as mere results of the physiological state of his brain, which he can no more avoid than he can prevent a ringing in his ears . . . The organs of ostentativeness, destructiveness, self-esteem, combativeness and love of approbation are all large. Intellectual organs are only moderately well developed. The result will be strong self-will, at times obstinacy . . . In the Prince self-esteem is so large that he will be unusually sensitive to everything that affects himself . . .

'I wonder whence that Anglo-Saxon brain of his has come,' Prince Albert commented on receiving Sir George Combe's report. 'It must have descended from the Stuarts, for the family has been purely German since their day.' Sir George replied that he suspected that the Prince

had inherited not only the quality of his brain but also its form from King George III [and he emphasized] all that this implied. It will be vain to treat the Prince as a normal child . . . rules and hours of study cannot be safely applied to him. Give him much and frequent repose; solicit but do not *force* him to learn; and when he falls into a fit of obstinacy, this should be viewed as an involuntary action of his organization, to be treated by kind consideration and soft moral remonstrances long and earnestly applied; and, if these fail, let him take his course and have out his fit of ill temper . . . From the size of his moral organs I should not fear his feigning inaptitude in order to escape from study. On the contrary I regard his as a true and loyal nature and anticipate that by a due training . . . he will regard falsehood in any form as utterly unworthy of himself.

To bring out the best in the Prince, Sir George earnestly recommended the employment of a tutor 'thoroughly acquainted with the physiology of the brain'. He had no doubt that a qualified person with the necessary 'large organs of philoprogenitiveness, benevolence and conscientiousness' could be found if diligently sought for. Indeed, he himself was prepared to help in the search and in the training of the person selected.

Prince Albert was not convinced, however, by these arguments and Sir George was left pondering upon 'the manifold evils which the shallow, ignorant and flippant opponents of Phrenology have been the means of inflicting on their country by dissuading and deterring the generation which has been born and grown up to maturity since it was presented to the British public in 1815 from studying it'.

Yet although Prince Albert declined to employ a tutor of the kind suggested by Sir George Combe, he was not entirely satisfied with Mr Birch, who, conscious of the disapproval, offered to resign at once if his employers 'knew of anyone who would be more likely to succeed in the management of so young a child'. Relations between Birch and the parents were further strained by his wish to become ordained. The Queen, who had strongly disapproved of Lady Lyttelton's High Church views, thought that Birch's 'Puseyism' might well render him an unsuitable tutor once he had taken Holy Orders. She agreed to his remaining only on condition that he promise not to be 'aggressive' in his religion, that he attend Presbyterian services when the royal family were in Scotland, and that he not foreswear 'innocent amusements' such as dancing and shooting. Although assured that Birch was 'plain straightforward Church of England', Prince Albert could not agree to his retaining his appointment should he be ordained. It was settled, therefore, that he would not respond to his vocation for the time being. He continued as tutor until January 1852 when, having entered Holy Orders, he resigned.

The Prince of Wales, who in the end had grown attached to Mr Birch, was very upset to see him go. 'It has been a trouble and sorrow to the Prince of Wales who has done no end of touching things since he heard he was to lose him,' wrote Lady Canning, one of the Queen's ladies-in-waiting. '[The Prince] is such an affectionate dear little fellow; his notes and presents which Mr Birch used to find on his pillow were really too moving.'

Birch, too, was sorry to have to say good-bye, for he had grown fond of the boy in return and had at last 'found the key to his heart'. 'The boy is influenced by me just as my Eton pupils used to be,' Birch told Stockmar before his departure, 'and in a way that I dared not expect, and I feel that I am very sincerely attached to him which for some time I could not feel.'

'I saw *numerous* traits of a very amiable and affectionate disposition,' Birch added later. 'He always evinced a most forgiving disposition after I had occasion to complain of him to his parents, or to punish him. He has a very keen perception of right and wrong, a very good memory, very singular powers of observation.' There was every reason to hope that he would eventually turn out a '*good*' and, in Birch's 'humble opinion, a *great* man'.

Birch's successor was Frederick Waymouth Gibbs, a rather staid, un-humorous, unimaginative, fussy and opinionated barrister of twenty-nine who had been a Fellow of Trinity College, Cambridge. His mother being insane and his father bankrupt, he had been brought up with the sons of his mother's friend, Sir James Stephen, Professor of Modern History at Cambridge and grandfather of Virginia Woolf. He was to receive a salary of £1,000 'with any addition to that sum which Baron Stockmar [might] decide to be just and reasonable'.

Gibbs soon learned that his task would not be an easy one. On his arrival the Queen summoned him for an interview at which, so he recorded in his diary,

> she spoke a good deal about the Princes and bade me notice two pecu-liarities in the Prince of Wales. First, at times he hangs his head and looks at his feet, and invariably within a day or two has one of his fits of nervous and unmanageable temper. Secondly, riding hard, or after he has become fatigued, has been invariably followed by outburst of temper.

He had been 'injured by being with the Princess Royal who was very clever and a child far above her age,' the Queen continued. 'She puts him down by a look—or a word—and their natural affection [has been] impaired by this state of things.'

The new tutor's early contacts with the Prince himself, however, were pleasant enough. The day after his predecessor's departure he went for a walk with both the Prince of Wales and Prince Alfred, and the elder boy, now ten years of age, politely apologized for their silence. 'You cannot won-der if we are somewhat dull today,' he said. 'We are sorry Mr Birch has gone. It is very natural, is it not?' Mr Gibbs could not deny that it was, in-deed, very natural. 'The Prince is conscious of owing a great deal to Mr Birch,' he commented, 'and he really loves and respects him.' Gibbs no doubt expected in his self-satisfied way that in time the Prince would develop the same kind of affection and respect for himself. But the Prince never did. On the contrary, he grew to detest him, and was soon as unruly and unpredict-able as he had ever been in the worst days of Mr Birch. In outbursts of un-controlled fury he took up everything at hand and threw it 'with the great-est violence against the wall or window, without thinking the least of the consequence of what he [was] doing; or he [stood] in the corner stamping with his legs and screaming in the most dreadful manner'.

Gibbs discussed his unmanageable pupil with Baron Stockmar, who gloomily agreed that he was 'a very difficult case' and required 'the exercise of intellectual labour and thought'. 'You must do anything you think right,' Stockmar said, 'and you will be supported.'

But Gibbs could do nothing to make his charge more tractable. And his diary entries reveal their shared frustration.

> The P. of W. still in an excited state. In the morning it was difficult to fix his attention . . . In the afternoon he quarrelled with Prince Alfred . . . Began better—we finished the sums left unfinished yesterday —but walking, he was excited and disobedient—trying to make Prince Alfred disobedient also—going where I wished not to go . . . and breaking and plucking the trees in the copse. I played with them but it only partially succeeded. On the Terrace he quarrelled with, and struck, P. Alfred, and I had to hasten home . . . P. of W. very angry with P. Alfred, and pulled his hair, brandishing a paper-knife . . . A very bad day. The P. of W. has been like a person half silly. I could not gain his attention. He was very rude, particularly in the afternoon, throwing stones in my face . . . Afterwards I had to do some arithmetic with the P. of W. Immediately he became passionate, the pencil was flung to the end of the room, the stool was kicked away, and he was hardly able to apply at all. That night he woke twice. Next day he became very passionate because I told him he must not take out a walking stick . . . Later in the day he became violently angry because I wanted some Latin done. He flung things about—made grimaces—called me names, and would not do anything for a long time . . . During his lesson in the morning he was running first in one place, then in another. He made faccs, and spat. Dr Becker complained of his great naughtiness. There was a great deal of bad words.

In the opinion of Dr Becker, Prince Albert's librarian, who taught the Prince German, the principal reason for these fits of violent rage was the excessively demanding nature of his pupil's time-table. The Prince was not obstinately perverse by nature; any child might be expected to react in the same way if his mind and body were overtaxed so continuously. 'To anyone who knows the functions performed by the nerves in the human body,' Becker concluded, 'it is quite superfluous to demonstrate that these outbursts of passion, especially with so tender a child as the Prince of Wales in his moments of greatest mental exhaustion, must be *destructive* to the child.' Becker had tried kindness in such moments, but this had elicited no response; he had tried severity, but this had led to another outburst of violence.

Although he diagnosed the reasons for the Prince's alarming behaviour outspokenly enough, Becker shrank from suggesting a radical cure. He did not really think it *'necessary'* to stop the lessons 'altogether for a sufficiently

long period whenever such a state of weakness' occurred. All that was required was 'to make the instruction interesting and then to afford it in convenient intervals of time . . . After every exertion of *at most* one hour, a
short interruption of, perhaps, a quarter of an hour ought to be made to give
rest to the brain.'

The Prince's other tutors ventured to express similar opinions. The
Revd Gerald Wellesley, for instance, who gave him religious instruction,
told Gibbs that the boy was being overworked. So did Dr Voisin, the French
tutor. 'You will wear him out early,' Dr Voisin said. 'Make him climb trees!
Run! Leap! Row! Ride! . . . In many things savages are much better educated than we are.'

But Prince Albert did not agree. Nor did Stockmar. Nor did the Queen.
'There is much good in him,' she had recorded in her diary on his ninth
birthday during the time of Mr Birch and in one of her rare moments of
hope in a satisfactory future. 'He has such affectionate feelings—great truthfulness and great simplicity of character.' She and Prince Albert had decided
that he 'ought to be accustomed early to work with [them], to have great
confidence shewn him, that he should early be initiated into the affairs of
state.' But now she was not so sure that this was a sensible plan. Bertie's behaviour since the departure of Mr Birch had been so disturbing that there
could be no question of his undergoing any kind of initiation into public
affairs until there had been a marked improvement in his conduct. To bring
about this improvement it would be necessary to 'put down very decidedly'
the Prince's temper. As Prince Albert had decreed, the only satisfactory
methods of overcoming this temper were physical ones, a sound boxing of
the ears or a few sharp raps across the knuckles with a stick. In the meantime
there could be no relaxation in the length and frequency of the Prince's
lessons.

With all this Mr Gibbs professed his wholehearted agreement. So the
chastisements continued, and the pressure of the lessons was not abated. The
lessons began at eight o'clock in the morning and ended at seven o'clock at
night. For six hours every day, including Saturday, he was instructed in the
subjects commonly taught in public schools with such modifications as were
appropriate to the education of an English prince. In addition to the subjects which he had already begun, he was now taught social economy, chemistry 'and its kindred sciences with the Arts dependent upon them', algebra
and geometry with direct reference to 'their applications to Gunnery, Forti-
fications and the Mechanical Arts'. He was required to read the acknowledged masterpieces of English, French and German literature; to write
essays in these three languages on historical and biographical themes; to
learn how to play—though he never did learn how to play—the piano; to
draw maps; to master Latin; to talk to the famous scientists whom his father
asked to come to Windsor especially for this purpose; to attend Michael

Faraday's lectures on metals at the Royal Institution (which he professed to find interesting as they were at least a relief from his usual studies); to grasp the essentials of political economy as expounded by William Ellis (who found him far less responsive than his bright elder sister); in general to store up in his mind a deep fund of 'extensive and accurate knowledge'. Between these intellectual pursuits he was taught riding, gymnastics and dancing, and —under the instruction of a drill sergeant—military exercises. In winter he was taught to skate; in summer to swim and play croquet. He learned about forestry and farming, carpentry and bricklaying. He learned about house-keeping in the children's kitchen in the chalet at Osborne; and at Osborne, too, he learned about gardening and, like his brothers and sisters, he had his own little plot of land and his own initialled tools. He went for walks, and he ran. At the end of each day, when a report upon his progress and con-duct was submitted to his parents, his tutors were instructed to ensure that he was exhausted.

The product of this regimen was not an appealing child. His sense of frustration and inferiority, combined with the strain of exhaustion, led him not only to seek relief in outbursts of furious violence, but also to be aggres-sively rude to those few boys of his own age whom he was ever allowed to meet. The Provost of Eton felt obliged to complain about this to Gibbs; and Gibbs, in turn, spoke to Stockmar, who, characteristically, made gloomy comparisons with George IV and hinted that the streak of madness in the mother's family was manifesting itself again. The Prince of Wales's impulses were far from kindly, Gibbs subsequently reported to the Queen.

They lead him to speak rudely and unamiably to his companions . . . and in consequence his playfulness . . . constantly degenerates into roughness and rudeness . . . The impulse to oppose is very strong . . . The Prince is conscious of not being so amiable as . . . he desires to be, or so forward as is expected for his age . . . In consequence he looks out for reproof and fancies advice even conveys a reproof beyond its mere words.

Although he rarely questioned Prince Albert's rules for the Prince's education—and the Queen, in consequence, considered him a far more satis-factory tutor than Birch—Gibbs did occasionally feel constrained to suggest some modification in their application. But apart from his success in having a few Etonians of impeccable character and family background admitted to the Castle to share one or other of the Prince's organized pursuits, he was unable to shake Prince Albert's confidence in the system so rigidly pre-scribed and practised. On one occasion at least he appealed to the Queen; but although the Queen admitted in confidence to her eldest daughter that 'Papa . . . momentarily and unintentionally [could sometimes be] hasty and harsh', she did not question the necessity for severity with the Prince of Wales.

The Prince responded to this severity with fear as well as violence. One of those few Etonians allowed into Windsor Castle, Charles Wynn-Carrington—who 'always liked the Prince of Wales' and thought that behind the aggression and intolerance lay an 'open generous disposition and the kindest heart imaginable'—was made aware of this fear. 'He was afraid of his father,' Wynn-Carrington wrote; and he did not find it surprising that this was so, for Prince Albert seemed to him 'a proud, shy, stand-offish man, not calculated to make friends easily with children. Individually I was frightened to death of him so much so that on one occasion [when] he suddenly appeared from behind some bushes, I fell off the see-saw from sheer alarm at seeing him, and nearly broke my neck.' Whenever other boys came over to Windsor, Prince Albert never left them alone with his son; and whenever the Prince of Wales went to Eton, as, for instance, to listen to the speeches on the annual celebrations of the Fourth of June, his father went with him. He also went with him to the annual speech days at Harrow. It seemed impossible to escape from his influence. And the Prince was never allowed to forget that he was being constantly and anxiously watched by him; and that by others he was for ever being compared—of course, unfavourably compared—with him. The Queen once informed her son in one of many similar letters:

> *None* of you can *ever* be proud enough of being the *child* of such a Father who has not his *equal* in this world—so great, so good, so faultless. Try . . . to follow in his footsteps and don't be discouraged, for to be *really* in everything like him *none* of you, I am sure, will ever be. Try, therefore, to be like him in *some* points, and you will have *acquired* a great deal.

But to be like his father even in *some* points appeared to the Prince a quite impossible aspiration. He knew that his father read the daily reports of his progress with anxiety and concern. He knew that he studied his essays and exercises with dismay, and that the entries in the Prince's unwillingly kept diary were perused with profound dissatisfaction because they were so carelessly written and so ungrammatical, because the handwriting was not neat enough, because they were full of boring facts and contained no noble reflections or, indeed, any reflections at all. His historical essays were even worse. When writing on modern English history he was fairly reliable, but when he turned to ancient history his compositions were lamentable. One of them, limited to less than seven lines, began in utter confusion: 'The war of Tarrentum, it was between Hannibal the Carthaginian General and the Romans, Hannibal was engaged in a war with it, for some time . . .' The Prince knew only too well, in fact, that he was a failure and a disappointment to both his parents—'poor Bertie!' Sir James Stephen was called in to examine him, and it was found that he could not even spell properly; so he was advised to master the etymologies of all Latin words basic to English and 'scrupulously' to consult a dictionary which ought to form part of the 'furniture' of his desk. But it was no good. His spelling remained bad, and his Latin was worse. He was taken to see the boys of Westminster School perform a Latin play, but he 'understood not a word of it'—*'poor Bertie!'*

Even so, there were occasional days of pleasure. He afterwards remembered how much he had enjoyed going out hunting and deer-stalking, fishing and shooting with his father, though hard as he practised he never learned to shoot very well. He remembered, too, the pride he had felt at being allowed to attend the naval review off Spithead and the funeral of the Duke of Wellington; to stand on the balcony at Buckingham Palace and wave good-bye to the soldiers marching to Portsmouth to fight in the war against Russia; to watch from the deck of the *Fairy*, as the huge fleet sailed for the Baltic; to accompany his mother on an inspection of the new military camp at Aldershot; to stand by her as she distributed medals to returning soldiers at the Horse Guards; and to sit on his pony beside her in Hyde Park while she gave out the first Victoria Crosses. He recalled the delight he had experienced at being taken with his brothers and sisters to the zoo and the pantomime, to Astley's circus, and the opera at Covent Garden; the excitement when Wombwell's menagerie visited Windsor Castle, when General Tom Thumb, the American dwarf from Barnum's 'Greatest Show on Earth', came to Buckingham Palace; and when Albert Smith, who related so vividly his adventures while climbing Mont Blanc, gave a lecture at Osborne. He remembered also the plays which Charles Kean and Samuel Phelps put on at Windsor Castle before presenting them in London at the Princess's Theatre and Sadler's Wells; the performances at Balmoral of the marvellous conjuror, John Henry Anderson, the 'Wizard of the North'—of course, so the Prince confided to one of his father's guests, 'Papa [knew] how all these things [were] done'—and the visits to the waxworks at the Great Exhibition in Hyde Park, particularly the representations of the dreadful Thugs of India—though his enthusiasm for these was rather dampened when Baron Stockmar sternly reminded him that he was 'born in a Christian and enlightened age in which such atrocious acts are not even dreamt of'.

The Prince also recalled with pleasure his first trip across the Channel to spend six days with his great-uncle, King Leopold of the Belgians, at the royal palace of Laeken; the excursions from Cowes in the royal yacht; and the exciting races for the America's Cup. But he longed for independence, to know more of life beyond the walls of Buckingham Palace and the terraces of Windsor, to escape from the suffocating confines of his parents' court. When he was thirteen in August 1855, he went to Paris with them on a state visit to Napoleon III. Lord Clarendon, the Foreign Secretary, who was instructed to keep an eye on him and to tell him how to behave, thought that the Queen's severity was 'very injudicious'. Certainly the boy was constantly asking questions while rarely giving his full attention to the answers. But the Prince's manners and behaviour were perfectly respectable. Lord Clarendon had to admit, though, that there might well be trouble with him later on: he would probably be 'difficult to manage, as he evidently [had] a will of his own and [was] rather positive and opinionated.' In his carriage one day Clarendon had been obliged to contradict something that the Prince had said; but the Prince, quite unabashed, had riposted, 'At all events, that is my opinion.' To this Clarendon had sharply replied, 'Then your Royal Highness's opinion is quite wrong.' The rebuke had seemed to surprise the Prince a good deal.

For his own part, the Prince had never enjoyed himself more than he did in Paris; and he left it with obvious regret, looking intently all around him, the Countess d'Armaille noticed at the Gare de Strasbourg, 'as though anxious to lose nothing' of his last moments there. He had been intoxicated by the excitement of their welcome; the 'roar of cannon, bands and drums and cheers'; his first glimpses of a city he was to grow to love; the pretty, beautifully dressed ladies in the Tuileries. He never forgot the fireworks at the Versailles ball; nor kneeling down in his Highland dress beside his mother to say a prayer at the tomb of Napoleon I while the thunder rolled above them in the stormy sky and the French generals wept; nor how he had hero-worshipped the romantic and mysterious Emperor to whom he had confided one afternoon as they drove round Paris together, 'I should like to be your son.'

He adored the Empress Eugénie, from whom next year he was much excited to receive a lock of her hair entwined with a hair of the Emperor's and a wisp of her baby son's; and he pleaded with her to let him and his sister stay behind for a few days on their own. The Empress replied that she was afraid that the Queen and Prince Albert could not do without them. 'Not do without us!' the Prince protested. 'Don't fancy that, for there are six more of us at home, and they don't want *us*.'

He really felt it to be true. When they got home he was sent away immediately to Osborne with his tutors to make up for the lessons he had missed while he had been in France. 'Poor Bertie' was 'pale and trembling' when his mother and father took leave of him, the Queen recorded in her journal. 'The poor dear child' was 'much affected' at the prospect of this 'first long separation'. But whether the Prince's emotion was due, as the Queen thought, to his sadness at parting from his parents, or, as we may suppose more likely, to his dread of returning to the unremitting grind of his lessons, it was certain that once he had gone the Queen did not much miss him. As she confessed to the Queen of Prussia that autumn, 'Even here [at Balmoral] when Albert is often away all day long, I find no special pleasure in the company of the elder children . . . and only very occasionally do I find the rather intimate intercourse with them either easy or agreeable.' When they were naughty she found them intolerable, and was insistent that they be punished even more severely than their father would have approved. Two years after the state visit to Paris, Prince Albert confided in Lord Clarendon that he regretted this 'aggressive' behaviour of the Queen, that he 'had always been embarrassed by the alarm which he felt lest [her] mind should be excited by any opposition to her will; and that, in regard to the children, the disagreeable office of punishment had always fallen on him'. But Clarendon thought that Prince Albert himself had always been quite as severe with the Prince of Wales as the Queen had asked him to be with the Princess Royal.

2

'A Private Student'

The more I think of it, the more I see the difficulties of the Prince being thrown together with other young men.

After the unsettling excitement of Paris, the Prince felt more frustrated than ever by the restraints imposed upon him in England. He teased and harangued the younger children until the sound of his voice jangled the Queen's nerves unbearably; he exasperated the footmen by jumping out at them and throwing dust on their clean uniforms; he continued to lose his temper and scream at the slightest provocation. An essentially affectionate child, he had no one to lavish his affections on. He could not get close to his father; he strongly felt the disapproval of his mother; he had been parted from his brother Alfred, to whom, so their mother said, his 'devotion was great and very pleasing to see', because it was felt that separation would be good for them both. He felt 'very low' after this parting and was allowed to sit with his mother while she had her dinner though she could do but little to comfort him. He was always well behaved on these occasions, and did his best to talk in a sensible, grown-up way. Indeed, guests at Windsor could scarcely believe what a trial he was to his family. Colonel Henry Ponsonby, who joined the household in 1857 as Prince Albert's equerry, thought the fifteen-year-old Prince of Wales 'very lively and pleasant'. He was taken up to the Prince's room—'such a comfortable room and very full of ship models'—and afterwards wrote to tell his mother, Lady Emily Ponsonby, that the Prince was 'one of the nicest boys' he had ever seen.

A few months later, at the beginning of 1858, the Prince had to go down to Gravesend to say good-bye to his seventeen-year-old sister, Victoria, who was sailing for Potsdam with her husband, Prince Frederick William of Prussia, whom she had married a week before. He loved Victoria, though he knew that she had always been their father's favourite and he had had to suffer constant comparisons with her intelligence, grace and dignity. She was, he reported, 'in a terrible state when she took leave of her beloved Papa'; and the Prince of Wales, taking pity on her sorrow, felt all the more deeply his own, weeping when it was time to kiss her good-bye. She wrote to him regularly thereafter and, though he hated writing letters, he replied to her almost as often.

It was decided that year that the Prince's educational system should be modified. At the beginning of April he was dispatched to White Lodge in Richmond Park where, in the care of Mr Gibbs and the Revd Charles Feral Tarver, his Latin tutor and personal chaplain, he was to be kept 'away from the world' for some months and turned into the 'first gentleman of the country' in respect of 'outward deportment and manners'. To assist them in this task Gibbs and Tarver were to have 'three very distinguished young men of from twenty-three to twenty-six years of age' who were to occupy, in monthly rotation, a kind of equerry's place about the Prince from whose 'more intimate intercourse' the Prince Consort anticipated 'no small benefit to Bertie'. These three men were Major Christopher Teesdale, Major Robert Lindsay (both of whom had won the V.C. in the Crimea) and Lord Valletort, 'a thoroughly good, moral and accomplished' young man who had foregone a public-school education to pass his youth in attendance on his invalid father, the Earl of Mount Edgecumbe.

These three young nonpareils were reminded by the Prince Consort in a lengthy private memorandum that

> a gentleman does not indulge in careless self-indulgent lounging ways, such as lolling in armchairs or on sofas, slouching in his chair, or placing himself in unbecoming attitudes with his hands in his pockets . . . He must borrow nothing from the fashions of the groom or the gamekeeper, and whilst avoiding the frivolity and foolish vanity of dandyism, will take care that his clothes are of the best quality . . . well made and suitable to his rank and position.

The Prince of Wales must always be made to remember that 'the manners and conduct of a gentleman towards others are founded on the basis of kindness, consideration and the absence of selfishness' and must avoid 'anything approaching to a *practical joke*'. 'The most scrupulous civility' should characterize his 'manner and conduct towards others', and he must never indulge in 'satirical or bantering expressions'. He must have 'some knowledge of those studies and pursuits which adorn society' while shunning gossip, cards and billiards. In conversation he must be trained to 'take the lead and should be able to find something to say beyond mere questions as to health and the weather'. He must 'devote some of his leisure time to music, to fine arts, either drawing or looking over drawings, engravings, etc., to hearing poetry, amusing books or good plays read aloud'.

Within three months, however, it became clear that the White Lodge experiment was not proving a success, that the Prince of Wales was bored to death by the 'amusing books' which he was required to read, such as the novels of Walter Scott and the memoirs of Saint-Simon; and that he made very heavy weather of the dinner parties at which it was hoped the conversation of such eminent men as Lord John Russell and Professor Richard Owen, the naturalist, would stir his lazy mind. It was obvious, in fact, that the Prince's educational system, as supervised by Mr Gibbs, could no longer be continued.

'Poor Mr Gibbs certainly failed during the last two years entirely, incredibly, and did Bertie no good,' the Queen wrote to her daughter, Princess Frederick William, in Berlin. He had '*no* influence', Robert Lindsay, gentleman-in-waiting to the Prince of Wales's Household, confirmed to the Prince Consort's private secretary.

> He and the Prince are so much out of sympathy with one another that a wish expressed by Mr Gibbs is sure to meet with opposition on the part of the Prince . . . Mr Gibbs has devoted himself to the boy, but no affection is given him in return, nor do I wonder at it, for they are by nature thoroughly unsuited to one another. I confess I quite understand the Prince's feeling towards Mr Gibbs, for tho' I respect his uprightness and devotion, I could not [myself] give him sympathy, confidence or friendship.

It was decided, therefore, that Mr Gibbs would have to retire, and that Lord Elgin's rather dour and strict but fundamentally good-natured brother, Colonel the Hon. Robert Bruce, would be appointed the Prince's governor, with the Revd Charles Tarver, whom the Prince quite liked, as director of studies. In a letter explaining to the Prince what this would mean to him, his parents made it clear that, although the governor would report on his progress, the reports would not be the kind of communications submitted by Mr Birch: the Prince was now to be responsible directly to his parents and to learn to be responsible for himself. He was to have rooms allotted to his 'sole use in order to give [him] an opportunity of learning how to occupy [himself] unaided by others and to utilize [his] time in the best manner'. Although he was solemnly reminded that life was 'composed of duties, and that in the due, punctual, and cheerful performance of them the true Christian, true soldier and true gentleman [was] recognized', the Prince was touched both by the generally sympathetic tone of the letter and by the relative freedom which it seemed to promise. He showed the letter to Gerald Wellesley, the Dean of Windsor, and burst into 'floods of tears'.

He was already seventeen and his life up to now seemed to him to have been peculiarly uneventful. His few adventures had been very modest: he had been on a pheasant shoot in 1849 when his father had told him and Lord Grey to leave the line and capture a wounded bird, and when—despite Prince Albert's assurances to the Queen that no one would shoot in that direction—Lord Canning had wounded Grey in the head and had himself immediately fainted. The next year the Prince of Wales had been in the Queen's carriage in the Park when a retired lieutenant of the Tenth Hussars had pressed forward through the crowd and hit her as hard as he could over the eye; the colour, the Queen noted, had rushed into 'poor Bertie's' face. There had also been the time when his pony had run away with him, and the Queen had thought it advisable not to tell his father anything about it for fear of upsetting him. But nothing else very dramatic had ever happened to him.

Nor had his occasional holidays been particularly amusing. In 1856, travelling incognito as Lord Renfrew, he had gone on a walking tour in Dorset with the uncongenial Mr Gibbs and another man, Colonel Cavendish, a groom-in-waiting to Prince Albert, even older than Gibbs. The next year there had been another walking tour, this time in the Lake District and with four carefully selected young companions and the Revd Charles Tarver. But although he had quite enjoyed himself from time to time, particularly when he and one of the other boys had chased a flock of sheep into Lake Winder-mere, the tour was rather blighted from the outset by his being required to write an essay entitled 'Friends and Flatterers'. Also in 1857, he had been sent to the Continent, to Germany, Switzerland and France, in the company of his father's secretary, Major-General Charles Grey, Colonel Henry Ponsonby, Gibbs, Tarver and a doctor. But this tour had been specifically described as being 'for the purposes of study', and he had had to keep a diary which had been sent home in instalments to his father, who objected to his setting down the 'mere bare facts' instead of giving his impressions and opinions. The Prince had also been asked to contribute to a notebook entitled 'Wit and Whoppers' in which were recorded, amongst other things, the atrocious puns concocted by his companions on their travels; and this, too, had to be shown to his father, who could have derived as little satisfaction from its perusal as from the Prince's diary.

The Prince was considered likeable enough by his fellow-tourists. Even the aged and discriminating Prince Metternich, with whom the party dined in his castle at Niederwald, found him 'pleasant to everyone'. The Prince, in turn, described Metternich in his journal as 'a very nice old gentleman and very like the late Duke of Wellington'. But his companions noted that the Prince of Wales seemed rather uneasy, if not bored by their host's conversation and recollections; and Metternich was forced to conclude that there was after all about the young man an *air embarrassé et très triste*.

For the Prince of Wales the highlight of the tour was an evening at Königswinter where he got a little drunk and kissed a pretty girl. The Chancellor of the Exchequer's sixteen-year-old son, William Henry Gladstone, who was a member of the party, wrote home to describe the incident which his father categorized as a 'little squalid debauch'. It confirmed the

Chancellor in his belief 'that the Prince of Wales has not been educated up to his position. This sort of unworthy little indulgence is the compensation. Kept in childhood beyond his time, he is allowed to make that childhood what it should never be in a prince, or anyone else, namely wanton.'

But now, so the Prince happily supposed when he heard that Colonel Bruce was to be his governor, he was not 'to be kept in childhood' any longer. He gathered from his parents' letter which had moved him to such floods of tears that he was going to have much more independence, and much more money. The year before he had been given an annual allowance of £100 and granted permission to choose his own clothes, payment for which did not have to come out of the allowance. Yet while he had been assured that his parents did not wish to control his tastes and fancies, he had at the same time been warned that they did expect him never to wear anything 'extravagant or slang' or to identify himself with the *'foolish and worthless* persons' who dressed 'loudly', because this would 'prove a want of self-respect and be an offence against decency, leading—as it has often done in others—to an indifference to what is morally wrong'. His new allowance was to be £500, and he gathered that he would be able to exercise far greater freedom of choice in the manner of his spending it. Also, he was to be allowed to achieve a long-felt ambition and join the army.

For as long as he could remember he had wanted to do this, and had been encouraged in his ambition by his mother's cousin, the Commander-in-Chief of the army, the Duke of Cambridge, of whom he had always been fond and who, in turn, considered his nephew 'really a charming and unaffected lad'. When the Prince had been given his first Windsor uniform he had blushed with pleasure. And he had shown equal pleasure when the former French King, Louis Philippe, after a visit to Windsor, had given him a toy gun as a replacement for one he had told the King he had lost. It had been noticed with what pride and awe he had looked upon the regiments marching past at Aldershot after the Crimean War and with what rapt attention he had listened to young officers describing their exploits at the front. His admiration was boundless for such military monarchs as the King of Sardinia, that 'great, strong, burly, athletic man', who had shown him a sword that could slice off an ox's head at a blow, the only Knight of the Garter that the Duchess of Sutherland had ever seen 'who looked as if he would have the best of it with the dragon'.

The Prince had told his mother of his military ambitions on a walk with her soon after his fifteenth birthday. He had been 'very sensible and amiable on that occasion', although she had had to tell him that, as heir to the throne, he could never serve in the army, though he 'might learn in it'. He had not minded that so much at the time, but he was now distressed to discover that he was not even to be allowed to learn in it as others did. He was to be gazetted a lieutenant-colonel without taking any of the usual examinations, which it was feared he might not pass. At the same time he found that the freedom to which he had so eagerly been looking forward under his new governor was to be severely curtailed. He was not even to be permitted to leave the house without seeking the approval of Colonel Bruce, who was reminded that in the execution of his 'momentous trust' he was strictly to 'regulate all the Prince's movements, the distribution and employ-ment of his time, and the occupation and details of his daily life'. Bruce was furthermore to instil into his charge 'habits of reflection and self-denial, the strictest truthfulness and honour, above all the conscientious discharge of his duty towards God and man'.

The truth was that his parents had no more confidence in the Prince's ability to regulate his own life properly than they had in the likelihood of his passing the army examination. They both continued to criticize him severely, to compare him unfavourably with his brothers and sisters, and to dread the thought of what might happen to the monarchy if he were to succeed to the throne in his present lamentable state of development.

'Bertie continues such an anxiety,' the Queen wrote to her eldest daugh-ter in Germany in April 1859.

> I tremble at the thought of only three years and a half before us—
> when he will be of age and we can't hold him except by moral power!
> I try to shut my eyes to that terrible moment! He is improving very
> decidedly—but Oh! it is the improvement of such a poor or still more
> idle intellect. Oh! dear, what would happen if I were to die next winter.
> It is too awful a contemplation. His journal is worse a great deal than
> Affie's [Prince Alfred's] letters. And all from laziness! Still we must
> hope for improvement in essentials; but the greatest improvement I fear,
> will never make him fit for his position. His only safety—and the coun-
> try's—is his implicit reliance in everything, on dearest Papa, that perfec-
> tion of human beings!

'I feel very sad about him,' she told her daughter on another occasion, 'he is so idle and so weak. God grant that he may take things more to heart and be more serious for the future.' He was such 'a very dull companion' compared with his brothers, who were 'all so amusing and communicative'. 'When I see [Affie] and Arthur and look at ... ! (You know what I mean!) I am in utter despair! The systematic idleness, laziness—disregard of every-thing is enough to break one's heart, and fills me with indignation.' Even his physique depressed her. She had thought him 'growing so handsome' when he had returned from his continental tour; but now, in reply to his sister's commendation of his good looks, she complained of his small head, his big Coburg nose, his protuberant Hanoverian eyes, his shortness, his receding chin, his tendency to fat, 'the effeminate and girlish' way he wore his hair.

'His nose and mouth are too enormous,' she wrote when he was eighteen, and 'he pastes his hair down to his head and wears his clothes frightfully . . . That coiffure is really too hideous with his small head and enormous features.' As for his voice, it sometimes made her 'so nervous' she 'could hardly bear it'.

When he was created a Knight of the Garter in November 1858 she noticed how knock-kneed his legs appeared in court dress. Later she commented disapprovingly upon his 'pallor, dull, heavy, blasé look'. His heart was warm and affectionate, she had to admit; but 'O, dear!'

Part of the trouble was that she considered him to be a 'caricature' of herself; she saw her own failings magnified in him. So, in fact, had Baron Stockmar, who confided in Gibbs that the boy was 'an exaggerated copy of his mother'. But whereas *she* had tried to improve herself, *he* appeared incapable of the effort. 'It is such a difficult age,' the Queen lamented. 'I *do* pray God to protect, help and guide him.' His father had had many evening discussions with him, as he had with his other children, but he had not appeared to profit very much even from these. 'Oh! Bertie alas! alas!' It was just 'too sad a subject to enter on'.

The Prince Consort expressed quite as deep a concern, particularly after receiving far from encouraging reports from Colonel Bruce, who had to admit that, while his charge could undoubtedly be charming, he was still far too prone to outbursts of temper, to egotism and to the adoption of domineering attitudes. He exaggerated the importance of etiquette and dress; had little or no respect for learning; possessed small powers of reflection and was 'prone to listlessness and frivolous disputes'. After a time Bruce noticed an improvement in his behaviour: the boy undoubtedly had 'a fund of natural good sense and feeling', yet with this went a 'considerable share of wilfulness and constitutional irritability'; and while he seemed 'really anxious to improve himself', the progress was 'but slow and uncertain'.

In November 1858, when writing to his eldest daughter, to whom the Prince of Wales was to be allowed to make a short visit, the Prince Consort asked her urgently not to 'miss any opportunity of urging him to hard work'; their 'united efforts must be directed to this end'. She would find her brother 'grown-up and improved', but 'unfortunately he [took] no interest in anything but clothes, and again clothes. Even when out shooting he [was] more occupied with his trousers than with the game!' It was particularly important that he should have 'mental occupation' while he was in Berlin. The Prince Consort had already urged Bruce to ensure that the boy was kept fully occupied for several hours a day with 'serious study'; and he now urged his daughter to try to arrange this, to suggest, perhaps, that he went to some lectures.

The Prince did not go to any lectures, preferring dinners and balls. But he did sit patiently while his sister, in obedience to her father's injunction, read aloud to him from improving books; and his visit was an undoubted success. The Germans found him charming and tactful, most *bezaubernd;* and he and his brother-in-law, who was ten years older than himself, got on together extremely well. Even the Prince Consort had to agree that Bertie had shown a 'remarkable social talent', and that 'his manners [had] improved very much'. He was certainly

> lively, quick and sharp when his mind [was] set on anything, which [was] seldom . . . But usually his intellect [was] of no more use than a pistol packed in the bottom of a trunk if one were attacked in the robber-infested Apennines . . . You would hardly believe it, but whilst he behaved so well and showed such tact under the restraint imposed by society, he tormented his new valet more than ever in every possible way, pouring wax on his livery, throwing water on his linen, rapping him on the nose, tearing his ties, and other *gentilesses.*

The Queen was equally exasperated. 'Poor Bertie! He vexes us much,' she had written to her daughter before the visit. 'There is not a particle of reflection, or even attention to anything but dress! Not the slightest interest to learn, on the contrary, *il se bouche les oreilles,* the moment anything of interest is being talked of.' Now that he had arrived home he spoke endlessly about his visit, but it was all about parties and theatres and 'what people said etc. Of the finer works of art etc., he [said] nothing, unless asked.'

To encourage his appreciation of art and to acquire 'knowledge and information', the Prince was sent to Rome immediately on his return from Berlin. Colonel Bruce was once more in charge of the party and was provided by the Prince Consort with a detailed itinerary together with the most exact instructions as to the Prince's behaviour and course of study. At the same time Bruce was instructed by the Queen to be present whenever the Prince talked to any 'foreigner or stranger'. It was 'indispensable that His Royal Highness should receive no foreigner or stranger alone, so that no report of pretended conversations with such persons could be circulated without immediate refutation.'

Colonel Bruce's duties were to be made less onerous by the presence in the party of his wife as well as Mr and Mrs Tarver, an equerry and a doctor; and in Rome he was also to be provided with the services of an Italian tutor, of Joseph Barclay Pentland as archaeological guide, and, as artistic adviser, John Gibson, the sculptor, who had lived in the city for several years and whose statue of Queen Victoria had recently been completed for the Palace of Westminster.

The travellers sailed from Dover to Ostend on 10 January 1859 and, after a visit to King Leopold at Laeken, made a sightseeing tour of various German cities before crossing the Brenner Pass on their way to Verona and thence to Rome where, on 4 February, their luggage was unpacked in the Hôtel d'Angleterre. Here, early every morning, the Prince was set to work at his lessons. Before breakfast, so Bruce reported to his father, 'he learns by heart and prepares for his Italian master who comes from 10 to 11 a.m. He reads with Mr Tarver from eleven to twelve, and translates French from 5 to 6 p.m., and has the next hour in the evening for private reading or music. He has a piano in his room.' The afternoons were spent inspecting ancient remains and the contents of art galleries, none of which the Prince appeared to find as intriguing as the portraits of a lovely Italian woman in John Gibson's studio. Sometimes in the evening he was taken to the opera; often he was required to give dinner parties at which Odo Russell, the diplomat, Frederic Leighton, the artist, the Duke of St Albans, Robert Browning, Lord Stratford de Redcliffe, the French writer Jean Jacques Ampère, and the American historian J.L. Motley were all occasional guests. Once he was allowed to watch the spring carnival and to join in the confetti-throwing in the Corso.

Within a week of his arrival, the Prince was taken for an audience with the Pope by Colonel Bruce, who, remembering the Queen's earnest injunction, sought and obtained permission to be present. The Pope spoke in French which the Prince appeared to understand quite well; and the audience progressed smoothly enough, despite Bruce's nervous coughs, until His Holiness raised the delicate subject of the Roman Catholic hierarchy in England, which so alarmed Bruce that, in defiance of curial protocol, he hastily removed his charge from the papal presence and left the Vatican without calling upon the Secretary of State, Cardinal Antonelli, as customary etiquette required.

The English travellers had already given offence to the Pope's enemies in the north, to King Victor Emmanuel, and his minister, Count Cavour, by declining to visit them in Turin lest the Prince became involved in Italian politics or was corrupted by the vulgar King, who had behaved badly enough at Windsor and could be expected to be even more uncouth in his own palace. Undeterred by this rebuff, however, the King offered to confer upon the Prince the Order of the Annunciation; and this, it was decided after some hesitation, the Prince might accept, particularly as the investiture was to be performed by Massimo Taparelli, Marchese d'Azeglio, the much respected statesman and author who had once been Victor Emmanuel's Prime Minister.

The Prince's gratification at receiving so imposing an order from 'so distinguished a personage' was expressed in an unusually long entry in his diary. This, for the most part, unfortunately continued to distress his father, who, reading the extracts regularly posted home to him, noted with regret that there was as little improvement in the style of the jejune entries as evidence of a mature mind at work in their composition. Nor was the Prince

Consort comforted by the reports he received from Colonel Bruce, who was unable to record any improvement in the Prince's 'learning and mental qualities' and had cause to complain of his continued outbursts of temper. 'His thoughts are centred on matters of ceremony, on physical qualities, manners, social standing, and dress,' Bruce wrote. 'And these are the distinctions which command his esteem.'

Other reports were more favourable. Robert Browning, who had been told by Bruce to 'eschew compliments and keep to Italian politics', found the Prince 'a gentle refined boy' who listened politely even if he did not say much. And J.L. Motley was much taken with him. 'His smile is very ready and genuine,' Motley wrote, 'his manners are extremely good . . . His eyes are bluish-grey, rather large and very frank in expression . . . I have not had much to do with royal personages, but of those I have known I know none whose address is more winning, and with whom one feels more at one's ease.'

'Nobody could have nicer and better manners,' wrote Edward Lear, to whose lodgings the Prince was taken by Colonel Bruce.

I was afraid of telling or shewing him too much, but I soon found he was interested in what he saw, both by his attention and by his intelligent few remarks. Yet I shewed him the Greek pictures, and all the Palestine oils, and the whole of the sketches, and when I said,—'please tell me to stop, Sir, if you are tired by so many'—he said—'O *dear no!*' in the naturalest way.

Indeed, it was generally admitted that the Prince was an attractive boy. Disraeli, who had sat next to him at dinner the evening before he went to see his sister in Berlin, found him 'intelligent, informed and with a singularly sweet manner'. And even his father had to admit that he showed quite a 'turn' for social functions. Yet the Prince Consort could not find much else to be said in his favour. Certainly he had displayed markedly little enthusiasm for the wonders of Rome. And when his intended tour of northern Italy was cut short by the outbreak of war, he seemed happy enough to sail to Gibraltar, where there was 'plenty of larking', and to travel from there to Lisbon to see his cousin, King Pedro V, son of the late Queen Maria da Gloria, who had married Prince Ferdinand of Saxe-Coburg. It had also to be regretted that the journal entries he sent home to his father from Italy were as flat, brief and unilluminating as all the others he had written. His father begged him to write in a less stilted, more reflective, manner; but the reply was not very encouraging: 'I am sorry you were not pleased with my Journal as I took pains with it, but I see the justice of your remarks and will try to profit by them.'

Having failed to derive much profit from Rome, he was now sent up to Edinburgh for three months' intensive work before embarking on the next stage of his education, a period of study first at Oxford, then at Cambridge. He arrived at the Palace of Holyroodhouse in June 1858 with Colonel Bruce and the Revd Charles Tarver, and was required to settle down immediately to a course of lectures on all manner of subjects from chemistry to Roman history. He was allowed little time off from his work, and then not to go shooting with the Duke of Atholl as he wanted, but to make excursions to admire the scenic beauty of the Trossachs and the Scottish lakes, and to give dinners to the local worthies and his various instructors. His time in Edinburgh over, he went up to Oxford in October 1858. He was still not yet eighteen.

The Prince, who would rather have gone straight into the army than to Oxford, had hoped that his father would at least allow him to live in a college. But the Prince Consort had been adamant that he must live in a private house where his activities could continue to be supervised by Robert Bruce, now a major-general, and Major Teesdale. Ideally the Prince Consort would have liked his son not to be attached to any particular college at all. He had only consented to his being admitted to Christ Church when informed by the Vice-Chancellor that such an arrangement was essential, and then on the strict understanding that General Bruce was 'entirely master of the choice of society which he might encounter'. 'The more I think of it,' the Prince Consort wrote to the Dean of Christ Church, 'the more I see the difficulties of the Prince being thrown together with other young men and having to make his selection of acquaintances when so thrown together with them.'

And so the Prince moved into Frewin Hall, a gloomy house off Corn-market Street; and there he and six Christ Church undergraduates, selected as his companions, listened to lectures specially composed for his benefit. In the dining-room he attended lessons in English history given by the Regius Professor of Modern History, Goldwin Smith, who was more interested in academic reform than in teaching and seems to have directed the attention of his royal pupil almost exclusively to the tedious pages of W.E. Flaherty's *Annals of England*. The Prince, polite but bored, learned little, and Smith felt driven to suggest that he might well have acquired more knowledge of history from reading the novels of Walter Scott.

Occasionally the Prince could be glimpsed in the town, a slight, boyish figure with curly hair and a fresh complexion, wearing the gold-tasselled mortar-board with which all undergraduates of noble birth were then privileged to adorn themselves, walking to a lecture in the Divinity Schools, a service in the Cathedral, or a debate—the quality of which he usually condemned unreservedly—in the Union where, upon his arrival, the assembled undergraduates would immediately rise to their feet. Sometimes he was allowed out hunting or to play racquets or tennis, at which he was a 'poor hand'. Sometimes he was allowed to attend dinners with such respectable people as Lord and Lady Harcourt at Nuneham Courtenay, or the Bishop of Oxford at Cuddesdon. Often he was obliged to give dinners himself to various senior members of the University interspersed with one or two undergraduates, all of whose names were suggested to him by General Bruce in consultation with the Vice-Chancellor and the Dean of Christ Church. He succeeded in making friends with two extravagant, amusing members of the Bullingdon Club, whose company he found congenial: Sir Frederick Johnstone, already a notorious philanderer, and Henry Chaplin, a clergyman's son. Chaplin, an exceptionally good-looking young man, had been brought up after his father's death at Blankney Hall in Cambridgeshire by a rich uncle who had made him his heir, sent him to Harrow, then to Christ Church, and enabled him to keep four hunters. But most of the Prince's time was allotted to study. 'The only use of Oxford is that it is a place for *study*, a refuge from the world and its claims,' General Bruce was reminded by the Prince Consort, who, possessed by a terrible anxiety that 'time was being wasted in pleasure', was—after restless nights of worry—a frequent visitor to Frewin Hall where he complained that recreations, especially hunting, were encroaching too much upon the Prince's intellectual pursuits.

'Bertie's propensity is indescribable laziness,' the Prince Consort wrote to his daughter in Germany. 'I never in my life met such a thorough and cunning lazybones . . . It does grieve me when it is my own son, and when one considers that he might be called upon at any moment to take over the reins of government in a country where the sun never sets.'

As well as being more interested in clothes than in government, the Prince far preferred 'good food' to 'mental effort'. There had been trouble over this particular propensity already. On his fifteenth birthday he had been given permission to choose his own food 'in accordance with what the physicians say is good for you'. But the experiment had not been a success. Eighteen months later, strict diet sheets had been prepared for him, authorizing three meals a day—a light breakfast of bread and butter, tea, coffee or cocoa and an egg; a luncheon of meat and vegetables with seltzer water to drink and preferably no pudding; a rather more substantial dinner, but still as light as possible. Claret was to be mixed with seltzer water in hot weather, and sherry with tap water in cold. There was to be no coffee after dinner, but at half past nine a cup of tea might be taken or a glass of seltzer water. It was not practicable to keep to this diet at Frewin Hall, but he was urged to be much more moderate. He was already too fat, and if he were not careful his excellent chef would make him fatter. And as well as eating too much he was dressing far too sloppily. He must give up wearing slippers and '*loose long jackets*' which were 'so slang'. He was also smoking too much, though his parents did not know this, tobacco being strictly prohibited by General Bruce.

Having so much to condemn and criticize, the Queen and Prince Consort were all the more surprised to learn that their son had done quite well in the first of the examinations which he was required to undergo at the end of each term. The Dean, who thought the Prince 'the nicest fellow possible, so simple, naïf, ingenuous and modest', was 'quite satisfied' with the results, Princess Frederick William was informed. And her father was thankful to be able to assure her that Bertie, 'a very good-natured' boy at heart, had at least done what he had to do 'very well'.

The Prince Consort received further favourable reports about his son from Germany, where he was sent for part of his Easter holidays in 1860 and where the ageing Baron Stockmar was much impressed by the great improvement he detected in him. 'That you see so many signs of improvement in the young gentleman is a great joy to us,' his father replied to Stockmar's letter of commendation. 'For parents who watch their son with anxiety, and set their hopes for him high, are in some measure incapable of forming a clear estimate, and are apt at the same time to be impatient if their wishes are not fulfilled.'

In the summer of that year the Prince of Wales was sent out to represent his parents in Canada and on that occasion they acknowledged the compliments paid to him with less grudging satisfaction. It was a long and demanding journey. He left Plymouth in the battleship *Nero* on 10 July 1860 with a large suite including the Duke of Newcastle, Secretary of State for the Colonies, and General Bruce; and a fortnight later, the first heir-apparent to the British throne ever to cross the Atlantic, he landed in Newfoundland, wearing his colonel's uniform with the ribbon of the Order of the Garter. From St John's—where he 'acquitted himself admirably,' so Bruce reported, 'and seemed pleased with everything, including himself'—he travelled to Halifax, then to Quebec, then up the St Lawrence in a steamer to Montreal to drive the last rivet into the new Victoria railway bridge and to open the Industrial Exhibition. From Montreal he went on to Ottawa, where he laid the cornerstone of the Federal Parliament building and rode a timber shoot down the Ottawa River; then on, past Kingston, to Toronto and across Lake Ontario to the Niagara Falls, where he saw Charles Blondin, the French acrobat, walk across the Falls on a tightrope, pushing a man in front of him in a wheelbarrow. Blondin offered to put the Prince into the wheelbarrow for the return journey across the tightrope to the United States. The Prince accepted the offer, but was naturally prevented from going. So Blondin went back by himself, this time on stilts, leaving the Prince to travel on to Hamilton, where he opened the annual Agricultural Exhibition.

Almost everywhere he went the Prince was greeted with the most enthusiastic welcome from enormous crowds. He received countless addresses, inspected parade after parade of volunteers, made numerous speeches written out for him by the Duke of Newcastle, held levee after levee, shook countless people by the hand, went from one public engagement to another, waved to a cheering crowd of 50,000 people at Toronto, acknowledged the acclamations of another vast crowd at Montreal, attended lengthy banquets and night-long balls, dancing tirelessly, cheerfully humming his favourite tunes; and at one particular ball, held in a specially constructed ballroom at the foot of Mont Royal, where champagne as well as claret gushed from the fountains and newly transplanted trees surrounded an artificial lake, he never sat out once until five o'clock in the morning. The newspapers were full of talk about him; his features appeared in advertisements for cider and tins of pork and beans; his name was used to sell all manner of goods from boots to umbrellas; the Prince of Wales's feathers sprouted everywhere.

He behaved himself admirably. To be sure, at Montreal he blushed deeply and looked rather annoyed as his fellow guests crowded round him, staring. But afterwards, he 'became all gaiety and animation,' the *New York Herald* reported. He entered into the spirit of the occasion 'with all the zest and lightheartedness of an ardent temperament, and with a spirit truly democratic'. So it was at Hamilton, where the Prince had never 'seemed more manly or in better spirits. He talked away to his partner . . . He whispered soft nothings to the ladies as he passed them in the dance, directed them now to go right, and shook his finger at those who missed the figures . . . in short he was the life of the party.'

There was but one serious misfortune: in a speech delivered at the French University of Laval, the Prince gave offence to the Roman Catholic members of his audience by addressing their bishops as 'Gentlemen' instead of 'My Lords', while the Duke of Newcastle offended the violently antipapist Protestant Orangemen by the placatory tone of his published explanation. This explanation led to unpleasant demonstrations by Orangemen shouting slogans and waving placards on the quay at Kingston. The Duke of Newcastle having insisted that the Prince should not go ashore, their steamer departed to hisses and shouts of derision and to the sound of the Orangemen's bands playing their provocative tunes. In Toronto arches bearing Protestant slogans and colours and portraits of King William III were erected across the route which the Prince was to take to Government House. The Duke of Newcastle obtained an undertaking from the Mayor that all these arches would be removed; but, finding that one of them had been left standing, he sent for the Mayor to come to him at Government House, upbraided him in the strongest terms and told him that his invitation to the Prince's levee would be cancelled. The Mayor, thoroughly disgruntled by this treatment and protesting that he had done all he could to get the offending arch taken down, at first refused to apologize, but later relented and was invited to attend a subsequent levee with his Corporation. At this levee he declined to shake hands with the Duke of Newcastle; but when the Prince told him that all was forgiven and that the Queen would be assured of his loyalty and sincerity, the Mayor broke down and could scarcely get through his reply.

On 20 September, on the understanding that he was to stay in hotels rather than in houses and to travel in the character of a private student intent upon the private observation of American life, the Prince was permitted to enter the United States. Not being a party to his parents' conditions, the Americans could hardly be expected to treat him as a private person. Special trains were placed at his disposal, and crowds gathered wherever he stopped on his way across the country—at Detroit and Chicago, at Cincinnati, Pittsburgh, Harrisburg and Baltimore. He was required to shake hundreds of hands and to smile at thousands of people. There were a few insulting remarks from Americans of Irish descent; there were one or two newspaper editorials which advised their readers not to behave like flunkeys in welcoming royalty; there were occasional disparaging remarks about his diminutive size: one writer in the *New York Daily Tribune* rudely comparing him to 'a dwarf at a country fair', another writing of his having shaken 'some of the gigantic hand' of Chicago's Mayor 'Long John' Wentworth and of his having addressed a few complimentary remarks to the Mayor's 'lower waistcoat button'. There was a nasty episode at Richmond, Virginia, which was included in the itinerary when Newcastle gave way to demands that the Prince should visit at least one of the Southern states to see for himself how humanely Negro slaves were treated. During this visit he was jeered and jostled for his supposed preference for the ways of the Yankee North. But, in general—despite the bustle of an electoral campaign which was to result in the return of Abraham Lincoln as President—the 'whole land', as the actress Fanny Kemble said, 'was alive with excitement and interest' in the progress of the Prince. In Washington he was met by the Secretary of State, General Cass, and taken to the White House to see President James Buchanan, to whom he gave portraits of his parents painted by Winterhalter. The President accepted them enthusiastically, but his niece, Harriet Lane, who acted as his hostess, took the portraits to be their personal property and was most reluctant when later she had to hand them over to President Lincoln. The Prince was introduced to members of the Cabinet and was the guest of honour at a luncheon at the Capitol; he was taken up the Potomac to see George Washington's house and grave at Mount Vernon, where he planted a chestnut sapling. At Philadelphia, which he thought the 'prettiest town' he had seen in America, he went to the opera—where the audience stood up to sing 'God Save the Queen'—and he visited the big, modern penitentiary, where he met a former judge, Vandersmith, who was serving a sentence for forgery. He asked him if he would like to talk. 'Talk away, Prince,' Vandersmith replied breezily. 'There's time enough. I'm here for twenty years!' At St Louis, closely followed by a wagon advertising a local clothing store, he had visited the Great Fair, where he was given a meal in a wooden shed and, although he could not overcome his disgust at the sight of his hosts ejecting streams of tobacco-coloured saliva into repulsive-looking spittoons, he was apparently less shocked than the Duke of Newcastle by the table manners of the St Louis citizens who, like 'ravenous animals', set upon the sides of beef and buffalo tongue with pocket knives.

In New York, where he stayed in a suite at the Fifth Avenue Hotel—which, he said, was far more comfortable than any of his rooms at home—he was welcomed by a cheering, flag-waving crowd which, he was told, numbered 300,000. He also attended a ball in the old Academy of Music, where the floor gave way beneath the weight of 5,000 guests; and went to a breakfast given by the Mayor, who invited also the heads of twenty families, one of whom described his reception as 'truly enthusiastic and genuine'. He was introduced to the Commander-in-Chief, General Winfield Scott, hero of the Mexican campaign of 1847, who took him to West Point to inspect a parade of cadets, and in Boston he met Longfellow, Emerson and Oliver Wendell Holmes. From Boston he went to Bunker Hill to survey the site of the first important engagement of the War of Independence; and to Harvard to see the university. Finally, the next week, on 20 October, he stepped once more aboard the *Nero* at Portland, Maine.

Apart from a quiet expression of regret that he was expected to dance all the time with middle-aged ladies instead of young girls, a muttered protest about being hurried about from one place to the next was his only complaint during the whole of this American tour. He had found some of the long railroad journeys exceedingly tedious, and at both New York and Chicago, exhausted by the rush and commotion, he had had to go to bed with a fearful headache. Still, he afterwards agreed that he had enjoyed himself enormously; and the Americans had clearly enjoyed him. General Winfield Scott described him as 'enchanting'; and the roar of cheering voices that greeted him as he drove down Broadway in a barouche with the Mayor, Fernando Wood, persuaded his suite that most Americans were prepared to agree.

General Bruce told Sir Charles Phipps, Keeper of the Queen's Privy Purse, that it was quite impossible to exaggerate the enthusiasm of the Prince's reception in New York; he despaired of its 'ever being understood in England'. He went on:

> This is the culminating point of our expedition and . . . with the exception of the Orange difficulty, the affair has been one continual triumph. No doubt the primary cause has been the veneration in which the Queen is held . . . but it is also true that, finding that sentiment in operation, the Prince of Wales has so comported himself as to turn it to the fullest account and to gain for himself no small share of interest and

attraction. He has undergone no slight trial, and his patience, temper and good breeding have been severely taxed. There is no doubt that he has created everywhere a most favourable impression.

His mother was delighted with these reports and, for once, gave him credit unreservedly. 'He was immensely popular everywhere,' she told Princess Frederick William as the Prince was on his way home through stormy seas, 'and he really deserves the highest praise, which should be given him all the more as he was never spared any reproof.' The Prince Consort, too, was prepared to recognize that much of the credit for the resounding success of what King Leopold called this 'tremendous tour' must rest with his son, though he had been more than usually pained by the letters addressed to him from North America which—containing such passages as 'St John's is a very picturesque seaport town, and its cod fisheries are its staple produce'—might well have been copied out of some peculiarly boring guidebook. The Prince Consort was also sorry to note that Bruce's praise was tempered by criticism of the Prince's poor showing in conversation, his 'growing sense of his own importance' which was 'stimulating a longing for independence of control'. But these reservations were exceptional. President Buchanan reported:

In our domestic circle he won all hearts. His free and ingenuous intercourse with myself evinced both a kind heart and a good understanding . . . He has passed through a trying ordeal for a person of his years, and his conduct throughout has been such as becomes his age and station. Dignified, frank and affable, he has conciliated, wherever he has been, the kindness and respect of a sensitive and discriminating people.

Lord Lyons, the British Minister in Washington, praised his 'patience and good humour . . . his judgement . . . and tact'. Sir John Rose, the Canadian Minister, spoke warmly of his 'kind and gentle demeanour'. All in all, the Prince Consort was driven, albeit ironically, to conclude, his son had been 'generally pronounced "the most perfect production of nature" '.

The young hero arrived home and was welcomed at Windsor with warm congratulations. Although he was 'a little yellow and sallow' and his hair looked so fair when he stood next to Affie (who was 'very dark and very handsome'), the Queen thought that he looked well, had grown a little taller and was 'decidedly improved'. Yet she felt constrained to add, with more than a hint of disapproval, that he had become 'extremely talkative'. He had also taken, she later noticed, to lounging about with a cigar stuck in his mouth. There were soon to be complaints far more severe than these.

3

The Suitor

I never can or shall look at him without a shudder.

After the excitement of the American tour, the Prince found it more difficult than ever to settle down to study. He renewed persistently his pleas to be allowed to join the army, to go on a military course to Aldershot. But General Bruce warned his parents of the dangers of such a plan, of 'the temptation and unprofitable companionship of military life'. He was still too immature to resist temptation. He had been almost seventeen before he had made enquiries about the meaning of certain words and had revealed his ignorance about the facts of life which—no one having spoken to him of such matters before—one of his tutors had discreetly explained in a lecture on the 'purpose and the abuse of the union of the sexes'. The Prince had 'never experienced to their full extent those checks and restraints, and those practical lessons in what is due to others, and ourselves, which belong to the ordinary social intercourse of equals'. He was still inclined to be intolerant, to form 'hasty and mistaken judgements'; while his love of excitement carried him 'almost unconsciously into the company of the idle and the frivolous'. It would be far better, Bruce concluded, if he returned to university.

So it was decided that the Prince's initiation into military life would be postponed and that, having completed his courses at Oxford, he should go to Cambridge, where he was to be entered on the books of Trinity College. He was not, however, to be allowed any more intimate acquaintance with undergraduate life there than he had been permitted at Frewin Hall. A set of rooms at Trinity was to be allocated to him for his occasional use, but he was never to be allowed to sleep there or to join in any of the social activities of the College without supervision. Much against his wishes, he was to be installed, with General and Mrs Bruce and various other custodians and attendants, in a big country house, Madingley Hall, four miles outside Cambridge. There were, he was assured, 'capital stables' there, and he would be able to ride or drive in his phaeton to the university every morning.

On the last day of 1860 the Prince Consort went over to inspect Madingley Hall and, as General Bruce informed the owner, Lady King, 'his Royal Highness, on the whole, was much pleased with the place', though it was considered that she had not cleared enough space in the library for the Prince's books and that a larger fireplace would have to be installed in the drawing-room. Money would also have to be spent on the stables; but, on the whole, the £1,200 asked for a year's tenancy was considered 'a fair demand'.

The Prince of Wales arrived at Madingley Hall on 18 January 1861, and the next morning presented himself at Trinity College, where he was formally welcomed to Cambridge by the Vice-Chancellor and by other senior members of the University, as well as by the Mayor and representatives of the town. He was then escorted to Magdalene College, where the Registrar made a short speech and he was handed a copy of the University statutes. The Registrar, Joseph Romilly, thought that the Prince behaved well, 'graciously' acknowledging the complimentary remarks that were addressed to him, though making no reply, and penning 'a good, clear signature' in the admission book. One of Romilly's more critical colleagues, however, dismissed the Prince slightingly as 'an effeminate youth with no colour in his cheeks'.

The Prince admitted afterwards to having felt rather nervous and apprehensive that first day. Despite the unwelcome restrictions imposed upon him, however, he settled down after a few weeks and even began to enjoy himself. His American tour had increased his self-confidence and he made friends much more easily, growing especially attached to Charles Wynn-Carrington, whom he had met briefly in his Eton days and who was now a fellow-undergraduate at Trinity.

The Prince became a familiar figure in the streets of the town, where he was pointed out as 'one of the principal sights'. He was often cheered by the crowd when he went to watch a game of football or a review of the University Corps on Parker's Piece.

A.J. Munby, the poet, who had himself been an undergraduate at Trinity some years before, went to dine in the College Hall one evening in May 1861 when, while waiting for grace to be said, he suddenly realized that the 'manly sunburnt face of the youth in [a nobleman's full dress gown of] purple and gold' standing next to him belonged to the Prince of Wales. Munby, an ardent royalist, recorded in his diary:

> He stands apparently about five feet seven, is manly and well made; and his frank intelligent face (with a good deal of fun and animal vigour in it too) has a pure rich sunbrown tint, which his soft gold hair and large blue eyes make all the more artistic. The full underlip, receding chin and prominent eyes are Brunswick all over. His hands, I observed, are square and strong, and neither white nor delicate; but suggestive of

healthy outdoor use . . . He spoke to the dons he knew and shook hands; and was treated with respect, but no ceremonial whatever . . . Presently the Master [William Whewell] came up, his bearish old face warped into a courtly grin; and shook hands with the Prince, and led him to his own right hand.

The Prince's neighbours at dinner usually found him a pleasant companion, though his conversation, in the opinion of one of them, was limited to 'subjects of amusement' and he was prone to ask rather thoughtless questions—as, for instance, of the Master of St John's, a learned mathematician whose friends doubted that he had ever so much as been astride a horse, if he was fond of hunting. 'The Prince talks agreeably,' the Vice-Chancellor told Romilly, the Registrar, who suspected that by this was meant 'he listens agreeably'. And Romilly himself, having been to dinner at Madingley Hall, could afterwards think of no more than one small scrap of conversation worth recording in his journal: 'I ventured to talk to the Prince about his gigantic black Newfoundland dog [Cabot] (which he brought from Canada), saying that I had heard of his upsetting a railway porter. The Prince said that he was, indeed, most powerful: this grand dog on first landing was bitten by another dog, but he "killed his assailant off hand".'

But if the Prince was not a gifted conversationalist, his various tutors found him well-mannered and attentive. Charles Kingsley, the newly appointed Regius Professor of Modern History, gave him lectures in company with eleven other undergraduates at the Kingsleys' house in Fitzwilliam Street and once a week went over the work with him on his own. The professor, 'the ugliest man' Romilly had ever seen in his life, seemed 'rather nervous and uncomfortable at having to see the Prince by himself'. He had already confessed to a friend that he had been reduced to 'fear and trembling' by a letter from the Prince Consort which stated the exact way in which the Prince of Wales was to be taught and the period of history which was to be covered, 'a totally different period' from that which Kingsley had intended to deal with in his lectures. But after some experience of teaching the Prince, Kingsley told Romilly that he was 'much pleased with his attention to his lectures' and that he asked 'very intelligent questions'. 'The Prince is very interesting, putting me in mind of his mother in voice, manner, face and everything,' Kingsley later decided. 'I had him in private today, and we had a very interesting talk on politics, old and new, a free press, and so forth. I confess I tremble at my responsibility: but I have made up my mind to speak plain truth as far as I know it.'

Other tutors, while acknowledging that their pupil was amiable, that he was, in Kingsley's phrase, a 'jolly boy', had to admit, however, that he would never make a scholar; and certainly his mind turned constantly from his studies to the army. The dinner parties he gave at Madingley Hall—at which the frivolous Duke of St Albans and Lord Pollington, both undergraduates at Trinity, were amongst the very few guests prepared to have with him the sort of gossipy conversation he most enjoyed—seemed to the Prince very boring affairs compared to what he supposed to be the merry dinners in a Guards officers' mess.

At length, in the middle of March 1861, when his son was nineteen, the Prince Consort decided, on one of those regular visits he made to Madingley Hall to ensure that his rules and memoranda were being observed, that his son might profit after all from a break in his studies. General Bruce had changed his mind about the possible effects of the army on the Prince's character and had now decided that he might well find camp life 'a good field for social instruction'. It was accordingly settled that during the summer vacation he should spend ten weeks attached to the Grenadier Guards at the Curragh military camp near Dublin.

The Prince's excitement at the prospect of this escape into military life was somewhat dampened when he learned of the severe restrictions which were to be imposed upon him in Ireland. For, from a memorandum which was drawn up with meticulous care by his father—and which the Prince of Wales, the Duke of Cambridge, as commander-in-chief, and General Sir George Brown, as general officer commanding in Ireland, were all required to sign—he learned that, while he was to wear the uniform of a staff colonel, he was to undergo a most exacting training in the duties of every rank from ensign upwards. As soon as he had thoroughly mastered the duties of one grade he was to proceed to master those of the next, until by the end of the ten weeks' course he might, 'with some exertion, arrive . . . at the command of a Battalion . . . and [be rendered competent] to manoeuvre a Brigade in the Field'.

While undergoing this rigorous cramming course, the Prince was also to acquire the social graces of an officer and a gentleman. He would dine twice a week in the Grenadier Guards' mess; once a week in the messes of other regiments; twice a week he would give a dinner party himself to senior officers; and on the two remaining evenings he would dine quietly in his own quarters—which were to be close to General Brown's—and afterwards devote himself to reading and writing. It was considered indispensably necessary that his relations with other officers would have to be placed on 'a becoming and satisfactory footing, having regard to his position both as a Prince of the Blood and Heir to the throne, as well as a Field Officer in the Army'.

It was naturally all too much for him. The most dedicated and proficient recruit would have found it extremely difficult to keep pace with the Prince Consort's programme of training; the Prince of Wales found it impossible. After seven weeks' training, the commanding officer of the battalion to which he was attached considered him totally inadequate to perform the duties of the rank to which his father had decided he ought by then to have risen. And during the visit that his parents and his 'Uncle George', the Duke of Cambridge, made to the camp on 23 August he was humiliated by having to perform, while wearing his colonel's uniform, the duties of a subaltern. He begged to be allowed to command, if not a battalion, at least a company; but his commanding officer would not hear of it. 'You are imperfect in your drill, Sir. Your word of command is indistinct. I will *not* try to make the Duke of Cambridge think that you are more advanced than you are.'

In fact, the Duke of Cambridge had already decided that the Prince was not likely to make a very good soldier; he had neither the will nor the energy. The Prince Consort was compelled to agree. After witnessing the review on the Curragh, he confessed to his host, the Lord-Lieutenant, that the Prince was not taking his duties seriously enough—not that many young gentlemen did, he added, lamenting the 'idle tendencies of English youth' and the disinclination of English army officers to discuss their profession on the grounds that it was 'talking shop'. The Queen was almost equally discouraged. All she could find to record of Bertie's part in the review was that when he marched past he did not look 'so very small'.

For the Prince, however, his time on the Curragh had its compensations. He had been allowed to have with him there Frederick Stanley, the Earl of Derby's second son, one of those Etonians whom the headmaster had selected as a suitable companion for his walking tour in the Lake District. There were also other convivial young Guards officers at the camp; and one evening, after a noisy and rather drunken party in the mess, some of these persuaded a young actress to creep into his quarters and wait for him in his bed. This was Nellie Clifden, a vivacious, cheerfully promiscuous and amusing girl who was also unfortunately most indiscreet. The Prince was much taken with her. On his return to England, he continued seeing her when he could, evidently sharing her favours with Charles Wynn-Carrington; and, on one occasion at least, she seems to have gone down to Windsor. Delighting in her company, and in the pleasures of her body, the Prince felt more than ever disinclined to concentrate upon a subject to which his parents had urged him to lend his mind—his marriage.

The subject had first been broached soon after the Prince's return from America when the difficulty that had faced King George III in similar circumstances now faced the Queen and the Prince Consort: a Protestant being required by law, and a princess by custom, there were extremely few young ladies available and, of those, even fewer who were in the least good looking and whose character would not, as the Queen put it, 'knock under' when subjected to the strain of having Bertie for a husband. Moreover, like George III's heir, the Prince of Wales did not want to marry a princess anyway, not

—as his parents had reason to be thankful—because he was secretly married already, which had been the case with his unfortunate predecessor, but because he was vociferously determined to marry only for love. When the Queen wrote to him about his duty to get married to a suitable bride, he replied to her, so she complained to Bruce, 'in a confused way'. His sister, now Crown Princess of Prussia, when asked to help in the search for a suitable bride, thought that his problem might be solved when she produced photographs of Princess Elizabeth of Wied; but the Prince professed himself unmoved by the pictures of this nineteen-year-old girl and declined to give them a second glance. Persuaded that their son's mind was quite made up on the subject of Princess Elizabeth, the parents began to reconsider other possible girls who could fulfil the Queen's requirements of 'good looks, health, education, character, intellect and good disposition'. There was Princess Anna of Hesse, of whom the Crown Princess gave 'a very favourable report'; there was Princess Marie of Hohenzollern-Sigmaringen, who was certainly *quite lovely*—but she was a Roman Catholic. There was Princess Marie of Altenburg, but she was 'shockingly dressed and always with her most disagreeable mother'. There was Princess Alexandrine of Prussia, but she was '*not* clever or pretty'. There was the nice little Princess of Sweden, but she was 'much too young'. And there were the Weimar girls, who were also nice, 'but delicate and not pretty'. Indeed, the more the Queen and the Prince Consort thought about the problem, the more their minds kept returning to another young girl, Princess Alexandra of Schleswig-Holstein-Sonderburg-Glucksburg, whom they had at first firmly rejected.

She was the daughter of Prince Christian of Denmark, a distant relative of the drunken, divorced King Frederick VII and recognized as his heir. Her mother was Princess Louise, daughter of the Landgrave William of Hesse-Cassel. There were thus two strong objections to this match which the Queen and Prince Consort had initially dismissed out of hand. In the first place, they much disapproved of the Hesse-Cassel family, whose castle at Rumpenheim near Frankfurt was said to be the scene of the wildest and most indecorous parties; and in the second place they were most reluctant to become entangled in the complicated question of the Duchies of Schleswig and Holstein, which had been ruled for years by the Kings of Denmark but which the Germans considered they had a good right to annex.

As opposed to these objections, however, Princess Alexandra herself was wholly unexceptionable. Indeed, the reports of her from Copenhagen were enthusiastic. She was only just seventeen and still at school; but, though so young, she displayed a remarkable grace of movement and manner. And when the Queen saw the photographs sent to her by Walburga Paget, the German wife of the British Minister in Copenhagen, who had once been Crown Princess Frederick's lady-in-waiting, she had to admit that Alexandra was, indeed, *unverschämt hübsch*, 'outrageously beautiful'. The Princess was not in the least intellectual and had rather a quick temper, but few other faults could be found in her. If she occasionally displayed a lamentable ignorance, she was never tactless; and if she was sometimes a little stubborn, she was never unkind. When sending her parents another photograph of 'Prince Christian's lovely daughter', the Crown Princess wrote, 'I have seen several people who have seen her of late—and who give such accounts of her beauty, her charm, her amiability, her frank natural manner and many excellent qualities. I thought it right to tell you all this in Bertie's interest, though I as a Prussian cannot wish Bertie should ever marry her . . . She is a good deal taller than I am,' the Crown Princess added later, 'has a lovely figure but very thin, a complexion as beautiful as possible. Very fine white regular teeth and very fine large [deep blue] eyes . . . She is as simple and natural and unaffected as possible—and seems exceedingly well brought up.' The only physical blemish was a slight scar on her neck which might, the Crown Princess thought, have been the result of an attack of scrofula; but this, the Queen was subsequently assured, was not the cause of the mark which, in any case, could be concealed—as Princess Alexandra later did conceal it, thus setting a long-lasting fashion—by wearing a jewelled 'dog-collar'.

The Queen was rather sceptical of her daughter's lavish praise of the girl, since the Crown Princess was 'perhaps a little inclined to be carried away' when she liked someone. But the Crown Prince agreed with everything his wife said. So the Queen allowed herself to be convinced that Princess Alexandra must 'be charming in every sense of the word'. She seemed all the more desirable because not only was the Russian court also interested in her as a bride for the Tsar Alexander's heir, but so was the Queen of Holland on behalf of the Prince of Orange. Evidently she was a 'pearl not to be lost'.

'We dare not let her slip away,' the Prince Consort wrote to his daughter. 'If the match were more or less your work . . . it would open the way to friendly relations between you and the Danes which might later be a blessing and of use to Germany.' At the same time the Prince Consort informed his son that, if Princess Alexandra appealed to him, the marriage would be considered more important than either the Schleswig-Holstein question or his parents' disapproval of the Hesse-Cassel family. So eager for the match did the Prince Consort become, in fact, that when he heard that his brother, Ernest, Duke of Coburg, was raising objections to it on the grounds that it would not be in the best interests of Germany, he wrote him a furious letter: 'What has that got to do with you? . . . Vicky has racked her brains to help us to find someone, but in vain . . . We have no choice.' To his son, the Prince Consort wrote, 'It would be a thousand pities if you were to lose her.'

So, in September, without marked enthusiasm, the Prince of Wales embarked for the Continent with General Bruce to see the girl whom his sister, having contrived a meeting with her at Strelitz, now described as 'the most fascinating creature in the world'. It was given out that the purpose of his visit was to continue his military studies by accompanying his brother-in-law, the Crown Prince, to the autumn manoeuvres of the Prussian army. But the German newspapers hinted that there might be other reasons for the Prince's journey, particularly as, in the same week, Princess Alexandra left Copenhagen for her grandfather's castle at Rumpenheim which was not far from the area selected for the forthcoming army manoeuvres. The Prince carried with him detailed instructions from his father as to how he must behave if his Uncle Ernest endeavoured to interfere with the proposed arrangements. He was warned:

> Your Uncle Ernest . . . is going to the Rhine, and will try his hand at this work. Your best defence will be . . . not to enter upon the subject, should he broach it. Saying nothing is not difficult . . . Should you be told that it is known that you will meet Princess A., your answer should be that you will be very glad to have an opportunity of seeing a young lady of whom you have heard so much good.

'I am afraid that I shall have many difficulties,' the Prince rather mournfully acknowledged. 'But I feel sure that the best plan is not to be too precipitate. The newspapers I see have taken it up, and say that, if I marry a Danish princess, there will be immediate rupture between the British and Prussian courts.' Anyway, he would keep his father's letter in his pocket; and if there was trouble with Duke Ernest or anyone else he would talk to no one but General Bruce or the Crown Prince Frederick.

Duke Ernest's threats to prevent it having come to nothing, the meeting between the Prince and Alexandra took place at Speyer on 24 September. The place chosen for the meeting was the cathedral, and here Princess Alexandra with her parents and the Crown Princess all assembled during the morning of that day. The Prince and Bruce were travelling incognito but they were immediately recognized by the Bishop, who insisted upon conducting them around the cathedral, so that it was some time before the necessary introductions could take place. Having effected them before the altar, the Crown Princess took the Bishop away, ostensibly to look at the cathedral frescoes 'but in reality', as she reported to her parents, 'to watch the course' of her brother's conversation with Princess Alexandra.

The Crown Princess 'felt very nervous the whole time', she admitted; and her nervousness increased when she saw that her brother had evidently begun the conversation rather awkwardly.

> At first, I think, he was disappointed about her beauty and did not think her as pretty as he expected, but as . . . her beauty consists more

in the sweetness of expression, grace of manner and extreme refinement of appearance, she grows upon one the more one sees her; and in a quarter of an hour he thought her lovely . . . He said that he had never seen a young lady who pleased him so much . . . [though] her nose was too long and her forehead too low. She talked to him at first, in her simple and unaffected way [speaking English fluently, though with a strong Danish accent]. She was not shy. I never saw a girl of sixteen so forward for her age; her manners are more like twenty-four . . . I see that [she] has made an impression on [him] though in his own funny and undemonstrative way.

The Prince's personal report was as flat and unrevealing as his parents had come to expect:

We met Prince and Princess Christian, and the young lady of whom I had heard so much; and I can now candidly say that I thought her charming and very pretty. I must ask you to wait till I see you, and then I will give you my impressions about her. Princess Christian seems a very nice person, but is, unfortunately, very deaf. The Prince is a most gentlemanlike agreeable person. After having thoroughly seen over the cathedral we lunched at the hotel and then proceeded here [Heidelberg] . . . The Prince and Princess accompanied us and are living at the same hotel.

The Prince of Wales was little more forthcoming when he arrived home and reported in person to his parents at Balmoral. The Queen gathered that he was 'decidedly pleased with Pcss. Alix' and thought her face and figure pretty. But he 'seemed nervous about deciding anything yet'. 'A sudden fear of marriage, and, above all, of having children which for so young a man [was] so strange a fear [seemed] to have got hold of him.' And 'as for being in love,' she added in a letter to her daughter, 'I don't think he can be, or that he is capable of enthusiasm about anything in the world . . . Poor boy—he does mean well—but he is so different to darling Affie!' The Crown Princess had rallied to the Prince of Wales's defence when their mother had been particularly critical of him before the meeting with Princess Alexandra. She had been brave enough to write then:

Only one thing pains me, and that is the relation between you and Bertie! . . . His heart is very capable of affection, of warmth of feeling and I am sure that it will come out with time and by degrees. He loves his home and feels happy there and those feelings must be nurtured . . . I admire dear Papa's patience and kindness and gentleness to him so much that I can only hope and pray that there may never be an estrangement between him and you.

But now she felt compelled to agree with what her mother had said about
his being incapable of true affection:

> What you say about Bertie is true . . . His head will not allow of
> feelings so warm and deep, or of an imagination which would kindle
> these feelings which would last for a long time! I own it gives me a
> feeling of great sadness when I think of that sweet lovely flower [Prin-
> cess Alexandra]—young and beautiful—that even makes my heart beat
> when I look at her—which would make most men fire and flames—not
> even producing an impression enough to last from Baden to England . . .
> Bertie may look far before he finds another like her. If she fails to kindle
> a flame—none will ever succeed in doing so. Still there is this to be said
> for him—he is young [for] his age . . . I love him with all my heart and
> soul but I do not envy his future wife.

The Prince Consort considered the whole situation thoroughly unsatisfactory; and, as was his habit on such occasions, he decided to put the whole
problem down on paper in an effort to bring some clarity into his son's mind
which, at the moment, appeared to be 'a little confused'. He reminded his
son of the trouble and inconvenience his family had been put to on his behalf, of the great difficulty there had been in procuring an interview with
Princess Alexandra 'without causing political alarm in Germany and more or
less compromising the parties concerned'. He thought it 'quite reasonable
and proper' that, although he had given a most favourable report of his
feelings towards the Princess, the Prince still refused to commit himself or
go further in the matter without due reflection. Indeed, it would have been
imprudent of him to have done so unless he had actually fallen in love,
'which, after this apparent hesitation, [could] hardly be supposed to be the
case'. But the Prince must clearly understand that if the Princess and her
parents were to be invited to England before he made up his mind, he must
'*thoroughly understand*' that this would be in order that he might propose
to the young lady if she pleased him on further acquaintance as much as she
did at first; and if she did not please him he must say at once that the matter
was at an end so as to avert further mischief, though a great deal of mischief
had been done already. Any delay would be 'most ungentlemanlike and insulting to the lady and her parents and would bring public disgrace' upon
both the Prince and his parents.

The Prince assured his father that he understood the position perfectly
well, and agreed to do as he suggested. But he remained as unenthusiastic
as ever; and the Prince Consort was quite baffled by the 'unsolved riddle' of
his son's reluctance to marry since his time on the Curragh, having earlier
expressed a 'desire to contract an early marriage' as soon as he was of age.
The next month, however, the Prince Consort did solve the riddle at last;

and he sat down to write to his son 'with a heavy heart upon a subject which [had] caused him the greatest pain' he had ever felt in his life.

The Prince Consort was already ill when he wrote the letter. Suffering from neuralgia and toothache, insomnia and fits of shivering, he had been brought to a pitiable state by overwork and worry. It was not only that he was concerned about the Prince's strange reluctance to marry; he was concerned, too, about the Queen, who had abandoned herself to grief upon her mother's recent death with an alarming intensity, bewailing the 'DREADFUL, DREADFUL . . . terrible calamity', giving away to 'fearful and unbearable . . . outbursts of grief', eating her meals alone, sitting by herself in her mother's 'dear room' at Frogmore, accusing the Prince of Wales of being heartless and selfish for not fully sympathizing with her sorrow and for writing to her on paper with insufficiently thick black borders. The Duchess of Kent's death had been followed by that of the Prince Consort's cousin, the young King Pedro V, a victim of a typhoid epidemic in Portugal. The Prince Consort had been extremely fond of this young man whom he had 'loved like a son'; and, 'shocked and startled' by his death, he had felt overwhelmed by a growing lassitude and sense of desolation. Then came the blow which, so the Queen afterwards decided, proved too much to bear—the story of the Prince of Wales's seduction by Nellie Clifden.

The Prince's liaison with this young woman—long discussed in London where Nellie was known as 'the Princess of Wales'—first reached Windsor in a letter from Baron Stockmar, who wondered if the rumours circulating on the Continent would endanger the Prince's marriage to Princess Alexandra. These rumours were elaborated by that 'arch gossip of all gossips', Lord Torrington, who had recently come into waiting. Although Torrington's stories were notoriously unreliable, 'a searching enquiry' had revealed the truth of this one. The Prince Consort was forced to recognize that there could be no doubt of the appalling fact that the Prince of Wales had had sexual experience with a woman who was a known *habituée* of the most vulgar dance halls in London. Sparing her the 'disgusting details', the Prince Consort broke the news to the Queen, then wrote an enormously long and anguished letter to his son in which he elaborated the likely consequences of his terrible sin, the possibility that the woman might have a child by him or get hold of a child and pretend that it was his.

If you were to try and deny it, she can drag you into a Court of Law to force you to own it and there with you (the Prince of Wales) in the witness box, she will be able to give before a greedy Multitude disgusting details of your profligacy for the sake of convincing the Jury; yourself cross-examined by a railing indecent attorney and hooted and yelled

at by a Lawless Mob!! Oh, horrible prospect, which this person has in
her power, any day to realize! and to break your poor parents' hearts!

He was too heartbroken to see his son at present, he went on; but he
assured him that he would do his best to protect him from the full consequences of his 'evil deed'. The Prince must, therefore, confess everything,
'even the most trifling circumstance', to General Bruce, who would act as the
channel of further communication between them.

The Prince did confess everything in the most abjectly apologetic and
contrite manner. He declined to name the officers responsible for his degra-
dation; and his father accepted his refusal as right and proper, telling him
that it would have been cowardly for him to have done so. But everything
else was admitted and regretted: he had yielded to temptation, having tried
to resist it. The affair, so far as he was concerned, was now at an end.

The Prince Consort was thankful to recognize that the letter displayed
a sincere repentance, and he was prepared to forgive his son for 'the terrible
pain' which he had caused his parents. But forgiveness could not restore him
to the state of innocence and purity which he had lost for ever, and the
Prince must hide himself from the sight of God. An early marriage was now
essential. Without that he would be lost; and he '*must* not, [he] *dare* not be
lost. The consequences for this country and for the world would be too
dreadful!'

Two days after writing this letter of forgiveness and exhortation, the
Prince Consort went to Sandhurst to inspect the buildings for the new Staff
College and the Royal Military Academy. It was a cold wet day and he
returned to Windsor tired out and racked by rheumatic pains. The next day
he caught a cold and this, combined with his continuing anxiety over his
son, aggravated his insomnia. 'Albert has such nights since that great worry,'
the Queen wrote anxiously. 'It makes him weak and tired.'

Ill as he was, however, he felt he must go up to Madingley Hall to talk
to his son, to try to make him understand the disgrace he had brought upon
himself and his family, and the urgent need to get married. He left on 25
November, feeling 'greatly out of sorts', having scarcely closed his eyes at
night for the last fortnight. It was another cold, wet day; but he went out
for a long walk with his son, who lost the way in his unhappiness and embarrassment so that when they arrived back at the Hall the Prince Consort,
though comforted and consoled by their conversation, was utterly exhausted. 'I am at a very low ebb,' he told his daughter, the Crown Princess,
a few days later. 'Much worry and great sorrow (about which I beg you
not to ask questions) have robbed me of sleep during the past fortnight. In
this shattered state I had a very heavy catarrh and for the past four days
am suffering from headache and pains in my limbs which may develop into
rheumatism.' In fact, they were developing into a complaint far more serious.

By the beginning of the next month the Prince Consort was dying of typhoid fever.

The Queen had no doubt that Bertie was to blame, and she did not want to have him in the Castle. Her 'dearest Albert' grew weaker and weaker, shivering and sleepless, listless and resigned to death, his mind wandering from time to time, asking repeatedly for General Bruce. His doctor considered him '*very ill*' and reported that it was 'impossible not to be very anxious'. Yet the Queen refused to send for the Prince of Wales, who was taking examinations at Cambridge, and it was without her knowledge that Princess Alice summoned him by telegram. But the telegram was so worded that he still had no idea of the gravity of his father's condition, particularly as a letter he had just had from Princess Alice had informed him that his father continued to improve. He kept a dinner engagement, caught the last train and arrived at three o'clock on the morning of 14 December, talking cheerfully.

Later that day he went into his father's room. The dying man smiled at him but did not seem to recognize him and could not speak. Watching over the bed, Princess Alice whispered calmly to General Bruce's sister, Lady Augusta, 'This is the death rattle'; and then went out to fetch her mother. The Queen hurried into the room, and knelt down beside the bed. The Prince of Wales and the other children knelt down too.

> I bent over him and said to him, 'Es ist Kleines Fräuchen' (it is your little wife) and he bowed his head; I asked him if he would give me 'ein Kuss' (a kiss) and he did so. He seemed half dozing, quite quiet . . . I left the room for a moment and sat down on the floor in utter despair. Attempts at consolation from others only made me worse . . . Alice told me to come in . . . and I took his dear left hand which was already cold, tho' the breathing was quite gentle and I knelt down by him . . . Alice was on the other side, Bertie and Lenchen [Helena] . . . kneeling at the foot of the bed . . . Two or three long but perfectly gentle breaths were drawn, the hand clasping mine, & (Oh! it turns me sick to write it) *all, all*, was over . . . I stood up, kissed his dear heavenly forehead and called out in a bitter and agonizing cry, 'Oh! My dear Darling!' and then dropped on my knees in mute, distracted despair, unable to utter a word or shed a tear.

She was led out of the room and lay down on a sofa in the Red Room. Princess Alice knelt down beside her, putting her arms round her. Princess Helena stood behind the sofa 'sobbing violently'. The Prince of Wales was at the foot of the sofa 'deeply affected', so Major Howard Elphinstone, Prince Arthur's governor, thought, 'but quiet'.

'Indeed, Mama, I will be all I can to you,' he had said to her.

'I am sure, my dear boy, you will,' she had replied and kissed him time and again.

But she could not forgive him. She told the Crown Princess a fortnight later:

> I never can or shall look at him without a shudder, as you may imagine. [He] does not know that I know all—Beloved Papa told him that I could not be told all the disgusting details . . . Tell him [the Crown Prince, who had made an appeal to the Queen on his brother-in-law's behalf] that I try to employ him, but I am not hopeful. I believe firmly in all Papa foresaw. I am very fond of Lord Granville [Lord President of the Council] and Lord Clarendon [the former Foreign Secretary], but I should not like them to be his Moral Guides; for dearest Papa said to me that neither of them would understand what we felt about Bertie's 'fall'. Lord Russell [Clarendon's successor as Foreign Secretary], Sir G[eorge] Lewis [Secretary of War], Mr Gladstone [Chancellor of the Exchequer], the Duke of Argyll and Sir G[eorge] Grey [Home Secretary] might. Hardly any of the others.

The Prince Consort's friend, Colonel Francis Seymour, encouraged the Queen to believe that the Prince of Wales's 'fall' was, in reality, no more than 'a youthful error that very few young men escape', that it was 'almost impossible' to hope that the Prince would be one of them, and that the father's 'extraordinary pureness of mind' had led him to exaggerate the seriousness of what most other men would consider a venial fault. But the Queen would not be persuaded, and when the Crown Princess urged her not to be so hard upon the boy, she replied:

> All you say about poor Bertie is right and affectionate in you; but if you had seen what I saw, if you had seen Fritz [your husband] struck down, day by day get worse and finally die, I doubt if you could bear the sight of the one who was the cause; or if you would not feel as I do, a shudder. Still more, if you saw what little deep feeling about anything there is . . . I feel daily, hourly, something which is too dreadful to describe. Pity him, I do . . . But more you cannot ask. This dreadful, dreadful cross kills me!

The Prince did what he could to heal the breach, writing letters for his mother, doing what little he could to comfort her, letting her know that he shared her grief for the loss of 'one of the best and kindest of fathers'. But it was all to no avail. And relations between mother and son became so bad that the Prime Minister, Lord Palmerston, came to see the Queen to tell her that the country was 'fearful [they] were not on good terms'. The Prince was so much away from home there was talk of a serious estrangement. The Queen protested that this was not so and the Prince was 'a very good and dutiful son'. Certainly he was much away from home, but this was 'unavoidable, as Bertie's living in the house, doing nothing, was not a good thing'.

In writing to her daughter, the Queen was more open. Contact with her son was 'more than ever unbearable' to her, she admitted. She had decided it would be best if he left the country again for a time. His father had planned that his education ought to be completed by a tour of Palestine and the Near East, and now was a suitable time for him to embark upon it. 'Many wished to shake my resolution and to keep him here,' she wrote, but she would not change her mind. And on 11 January 1862 she reported, 'Bertie's journey is all settled.'

The next month, accompanied as usual by General Bruce, he set out for Venice by way of Vienna. The 'poor Boy' was 'low and upset' when he wished his mother good-bye. So was she; and he returned for a moment after he had left her room, close to tears. He had felt his father's death far more deeply than she had supposed, and was distressed to leave her, knowing that in her misery she had almost grown to hate him. Still, he was thankful to get away; time might heal the wound.

4

The Bridegroom

Alix looked so sweet and lovely . . . and Bertie so brightened up.

The Prince embarked upon his tour looking 'very gloomy'. He had been instructed by his mother to travel in 'the very strictest incognito', to visit sovereigns in 'strict privacy', to accept no invitations which did not accord with his 'present very deep mourning', and then only from persons of 'royal or high official or personal rank or [of] superior character and attainments'. At the same time Bruce had been told to bring his charge's mind constantly to bear upon the path of duty which had been marked out for him by his father.

In Vienna the Emperor Franz Joseph, who was with difficulty dissuaded from holding a military parade and state dinner, visited the Prince in his hotel and conducted him round the city. In Venice he was entertained by the Empress Elizabeth of Austria; and in Trieste by the Archduke Maximilian, the Emperor's brother. At Trieste he went aboard the royal yacht, *Osborne*, which had been sent out to meet him there, seeming quite as despondent as he had been on leaving England. But as he sailed down the Dalmatian coast, calling in at Corfu and Albania, he began, for the first time since his father's death, to display some of his former cheerful spirits. He wrote home to Charles Wynn-Carrington, thanking him for news of Nellie Clifden, whom he 'had not heard about for a long time', trusting that he would '*occasionally* look at a book', and telling him of the charms of Vienna, a city 'especially well adapted to a gay fellow like you'.

On 1 March the *Osborne* docked at Alexandria where Canon Arthur Penrhyn Stanley, Regius Professor of Ecclesiastical History at Oxford—an indefatigable sightseer and an expert on the Holy Land, about which he had written a book—joined the party as the Prince's chaplain and guide. Canon Stanley had not in the least wanted to leave Oxford for such a purpose, and the more he saw of the Prince the more he regretted having given way to the Queen's pressing request that he should do so. The young man appeared not only to be exasperatingly conscious of his own importance but not in the least interested in sightseeing, admitting to the Canon that he would much rather go out shooting crocodiles than be taken round a lot of 'tumble-down' old temples. After a fortnight, however, Stanley began to change his mind. Admittedly the boy was on occasions rather frivolous, insisting, for example, on riding a donkey through the streets of Cairo to the horror of an elderly pasha who had been deputized to look after him; seeming more anxious to climb to the top of the Great Pyramid than in learning about its history; and affecting to find in the features of the relief of Queen Cleopatra in the temple of Dendera an uncanny resemblance to those of Samuel Wilberforce, the eloquent, diplomatic Bishop of Oxford. Yet there was more in the Prince than he had at first thought, decided Stanley, who was particularly gratified by the obliging manner in which the young man agreed to give up shooting on Sundays; and towards the end of March this more favourable opinion was confirmed when news arrived in Egypt that the Canon's mother had died during their absence from England and the Prince's sympathy was touchingly sincere. 'It is impossible not to like him,' Stanley concluded; 'and to be constantly with him brings out his astonishing memory of names and persons.'

From Cairo, where they stayed in a splendid palace provided for them by the Viceroy of Egypt, Said Pasha—whose hospitality, the Prince reckoned, cost him £8,000—the party steamed up the Nile to Karnak, then back to Cairo where they embarked on the *Osborne* for Jaffa. From Jaffa, escorted by a troop of Turkish cavalry and attended by a caravan of fifty servants, they rode down to Jerusalem, Bethlehem, Jericho and Hebron. Here, on being asked by the local governor not to enter the mosque for fear of provoking an outbreak of Muslim fanaticism, General Bruce loftily informed the Governor-General of Palestine that the Prince of Wales's 'extreme displeasure' would be aroused were he to be denied entrance to a building beneath which Abraham, Isaac and Jacob were supposed to be buried—even though it had been sealed to Christian travellers since before the Third Crusade almost seven centuries ago. The local governor being overborne by Bruce's domineering manner, a regiment of cavalry was detailed to stand by while the Christians entered the mosque. 'Well, you see,' the Prince commented to Stanley, 'exalted rank has some advantages, after all.' 'Yes, Sir,' the Canon replied gravely, 'and I hope that you will always make good use of them.'

After spending Good Friday at Nazareth and Easter Sunday at Tiberias on the shore of the Sea of Galilee, the Prince arrived, towards the end of April, at Damascus. Here, on entering the bazaar, he was watched in resentful silence by Muslim traders who remained seated as he passed, despite the attempts by some members of his party to make them pay 'more proper respect'. At Damascus was the former Lady Ellenborough, the notorious, old but still beautiful adventuress, who, having been divorced by Ellenborough

for her adultery with Felix von Schwarzenberg, was now married to a Bed-
ouin sheikh. More intrigued by this exotic old lady than by many of the
other sights he had seen, the Prince, to Canon Stanley's distress, was also
more happy with his guns than his guide-books. As well as gazelles and
hares, he shot vultures and larks, partridges, quails, geese, crows, owls and
even lizards when nothing more suitable came within his sights. With
markedly less enthusiasm he collected flowers and the leaves of strange trees
and plants, which he pressed in a book for his sister Victoria.

On 6 May he rode into Beirut and from there sailed in the *Osborne* for
Tyre and Sidon, Tripoli and Rhodes, Patmos and Smyrna. Anchoring off
the Dardanelles where the British Ambassador came aboard with various
Turkish officials, he arrived at Constantinople on 20 May; and, after a long
and rather awkward audience with the Sultan—whom the British Ambassador thought that he nevertheless handled with precocious tact—he had a
pleasant week's stay at the British Embassy before departing for Athens.

His stay in Greece being cut short by the threat of riots against the
unpopular King Otto, the Prince sailed for home on the last day of May.
He stepped ashore on his way at various Ionian islands, and arrived at
Marseilles on 10 June. Four days later, having bought some presents in Paris
and visited the Emperor at Fontainebleau, he was home again with his
mother at Windsor after an absence of just over four months. He looked
well and sunburned and had begun to grow the beard that he never afterwards shaved.

When in Constantinople he had received a letter from his mother and,
so General Bruce reported, he 'was actually beaming with pleasure' as he
read it. 'He felt that he had really deserved the genuine outpouring of a
mother's tenderness and affection.' It was, Bruce commented, 'a hopeful
feature in his character that he [had] a strong love of approbation'. Bruce
himself had also heard from the Queen, but his letter had been less encouraging. In it the Queen had urged him to warn the Prince against indulging in
her presence in any 'worldly, frivolous, gossiping kind of conversation'; he
must remember that he would be returning to a house of mourning where
cureless melancholy reigned.

The Prince was profoundly relieved when his mother, who appeared
to have overcome those feelings of resentment and dislike which had so
distressed him at the time of his father's death, seemed actually glad to have
him home again. She confessed that she was at first 'much upset at seeing
him' because 'his beloved father was not there to welcome him back'. But
he was so much improved, looking 'so bright and healthy'. He was 'most
affectionate and the tears came into his eyes' when he saw her. His time away
had 'done him so much good', she continued a few days later; and he went
on 'being as good, amiable and sensible' as anyone could have wished. Im-

proved 'in every respect', he was 'so kind and nice to the younger children, more serious in his ways and views'. She was especially pleased to note that he was 'very distressed about General Bruce', who, having contracted a fever in the marshes of the Upper Jordan, had died soon after his return to England in his sister's rooms in St James's Palace.

Bruce's death was, indeed, a 'terrible blow' to him, he confessed to his doctor, Henry Acland. It was really 'too sad to think his end was caused by catching a fever, on a tour which [they had] all so thoroughly enjoyed'. He had lost, in him, 'a most useful and valuable friend'. But he was somewhat comforted to know that Bruce was to be replaced by General William Knollys, a fatherly figure whom he liked 'very much' and was ultimately to consider one of his 'most intimate friends'. His mother told him that General Knollys would 'naturally be a species of Mentor, for no young Prince can be without a person of experience and of a certain age who would keep him from doing what was hurtful to him, or unfit for his position, and who would be responsible to me to a great extent for what took place.' Knollys, however, was not to be the Prince's governor but comptroller and treasurer, a title that seemed to promise a degree of independence greater than any he had previously known.

The Prince was now nearly twenty-one and his mother was anxious that there should be no further delay in his marriage. He, too, she was thankful to say, seemed 'most anxious' to make his formal proposal to Princess Alexandra, for whom he had bought a 'number of pretty things' on his travels. But he was 'furious' to hear that his Uncle Ernest was still determined to prevent the marriage. Not content with spreading stories that 'Princess Christian had had illegitimate children and Princess Alix had had flirtations with young officers', he had written to Princess Christian to tell her what had happened on the Curragh and to warn her what an unfortunate choice as a husband for her daughter the Prince would be. The Prince had already been reminded of that embarrassing affair when the Queen had informed him that she was going to tell General Knollys all about it. He had almost lost his temper then, but had written the next day to apologize, saying that on reflection he thought it would certainly be better if Knollys were told, but at the same time hoping that this would be the last conversation he would have with her on this 'painful subject'.

He agreed immediately, however, that it would be wise to let Princess Christian know the full story now that she had heard some no doubt maliciously exaggerated version of it from the Duke of Coburg. So the Queen told her daughter in Germany that 'it would be well' if Walburga Paget could let Princess Christian know the truth. 'Quite in ignorance of the character of Bertie the mother must not be,' the Queen wrote, 'for were the poor girl to be very unhappy I could not answer for it before God had she been entrapped into it.' Princess Christian must therefore be told 'that *wicked wretches* had led our poor innocent Boy into a scrape' which had caused his parents the 'deepest pain'; but that both of them had forgiven him 'this (*one*) *sad mistake*'; that the Queen was very confident he would make 'a steady Husband'; and that she 'looked to his wife as being HIS SALVATION'.

All this was accordingly passed on to Princess Christian, who was further assured, without too strict a regard for accuracy, that the Prince was 'very domestic and longed to be at home'.

Princess Christian had, in fact, already been told of the Prince's affair by her cousin, the Duke of Cambridge. She had also been informed that the Queen and her son were on extremely bad terms; and this news so distressed her that she burst into tears, feeling sure that the dislike of the son would be extended to include the proposed daughter-in-law. Arrangements for the marriage nevertheless went ahead, and the Queen used a proposed visit to the places where her husband had lived as a child in Coburg as an excuse to meet Princess Alexandra and her parents at King Leopold's palace at Laeken.

The Queen was immediately taken with the Princess, who was as lovely as she had been said to be, with 'such a beautiful refined profile and quiet ladylike manner'. Her parents seemed perfectly happy to accept the Prince of Wales as their son-in-law should he care to propose to Alexandra, who, in turn, was reported to be 'very much taken' with him. And the Queen, though she found the parents not nearly so '*sympathique*' as the daughter, left for Coburg in the contented knowledge that all should now go well.

A few days later the Queen heard from her son that the 'all-important event' had taken place. He had seen Princess Alexandra at Ostend and afterwards at Brussels, where she and her parents had had luncheon together in the hotel where they were all staying. After the meal he had asked Prince Christian to come to his room and had there told him how he loved his daughter and wanted to marry her. 'I don't think I ever saw anybody so much pleased as he was,' the Prince continued. 'We then went driving. . . . On our return I saw Princess Christian and told her the same as I had told her husband. She said she was sure I should be kind to her [daughter] and . . . we then arranged that I should propose to her.'

The next day they all went over to Laeken, where King Leopold suggested a walk in the garden. The Prince and Princess Alexandra walked one or two paces behind the others, exchanging 'a few commonplace remarks' until the Prince asked her how she liked England, and 'if she would one day come over [there] and how long she would remain. She said she hoped some time'.

'I said that I hoped she would remain always there, and then offered her my hand and my heart,' the Prince wrote.

She immediately said *yes*. But I told her not to answer too quickly but to consider over it. She said she had long ago. I then asked her if she liked me. She said *yes*. I then kissed her hand and she kissed me. We then talked for some time and I said I was sure you would love her as your own daughter and make her happy in the new home, though she would find it very sad after the terrible loss we had sustained. I told her how *very* sorry I was that she could never know dear Papa. She said she regretted it deeply and hoped he would have approved of my choice. I told her that it had always been his greatest wish; I only feared I was not worthy of her . . . I cannot tell you with what feelings my head is filled, and how happy I feel . . . You must excuse this hurried account as . . . I really don't know whether I am on my head or my heels . . .

The more he saw of her the more pleased the Prince was with his choice. General Knollys assured Queen Victoria that it 'was a happy sight to witness the happiness of the young couple in the society of each other'. Knollys sincerely believed that the Prince of Wales was 'as much attached to the Princess Alexandra as Her Royal Highness [was] to him.'

'I indeed now know what it is to be really happy,' the Prince himself assured Dr Acland, 'though I daresay I have never done anything to deserve it.' He told Mrs Bruce that he really felt 'a new interest in everything' now that he had found 'somebody to live for'. And to his mother he wrote, 'I frankly avow that I did not think it possible to love a person as I do her. She is so kind and good, and I feel sure will make my life a happy one. I only trust that God will give me strength to do the same for her.'

The Queen hoped so too, but rather doubted it. 'May he be only worthy of such a jewel!' she commented. 'There is the rub!' Even though they were now engaged there must be no question of their being left alone together, except 'in a room next to the Princess's mother's with the door open, for a short while'. The Queen's main worry for the moment, however, was that the Prince would be persuaded to adopt an anti-German position on the Schleswig-Holstein question; and she insisted that, before the marriage took place, Princess Alexandra must come over to England by herself so that the Queen might be given an opportunity to give her due warning not to 'use her influence to make the Prince a partisan . . . in the political questions now unhappily in dispute [which] would be to irritate all the Queen's German connections and to create family feuds—destructive of all family comfort and happiness'.

The Princess was naturally reluctant to come. She did not want it to appear that she had been summoned to England 'on approval'; and, apart from that, she was 'terribly frightened' at the prospect of being left alone with the Queen for so long. Both the Prince of Wales and the King of the

Belgians tried rather diffidently and wholly unsuccessfully to persuade the Queen not to subject Alexandra to such embarrassment. The Queen, however, was adamant: trouble enough had already been caused in Germany, where old Baron Stockmar's 'rage and fury knew no bounds'. The Princess *must* come. While she was here, the Prince could go on a cruise aboard the royal yacht in the Mediterranean. General Knollys could go with him. So, too, could the Crown Prince and Princess of Prussia, who would find this an excellent excuse for leaving Berlin where their known promotion of the Danish marriage, as well as their disapproval of Bismarck's recently declared preference of 'blood and iron' to 'parliamentary resolutions', had rendered advisable a temporary withdrawal from court. At the beginning of October, therefore, the Prince was dispatched abroad once again. He went to Dresden where the King of Saxony placed him in the care of Count Vitzthum, the Saxon Minister at St James's, who happened to be on leave of absence. Vitzthum found him 'gay, extremely amiable, well informed . . . simple and unaffected'. Vitzthum later told Disraeli that after he and the Prince

> had examined the museums, galleries, etc., the Prince said to him: 'Don't you think now we might have a little shopping?' Agreed: and they went to a great jeweller's, and the Prince bought some bracelets for his future bride; and to some porcelain shops, where he purchased many objects for his brothers and sisters; but he never asked the price of anything, which quite delighted the Saxons, who look upon that as quite *grand seigneur*.

Leaving Dresden, and having toured South Germany and Switzerland, he embarked at Marseilles for his first visit to the Riviera. Then, after spending a few days at Hyères, he sailed down to Palermo, across to Tunis, where he inspected the ruins of Carthage and visited the Bey at his castle of Al-Bar, and on to Malta before landing at Naples, from which Garibaldi had recently driven the Bourbon King of the Two Sicilies. General Alfonso La Marmora, representative of Victor Emmanuel, now King of the new united Italy, provided the English travellers with an escort of *bersaglieri* for the inevitable ascent of Mount Vesuvius and afterwards came aboard the *Osborne* for dinner. Three evenings later, on 9 November 1862, while the British ships in the Bay fired rockets and showed blue lights, the Prince quietly celebrated his twenty-first birthday, regretting 'very much not being at home'.

Meanwhile, Princess Alexandra was listening to the Queen's lectures with tactful acquiescence. She concealed the resentment which she subsequently admitted to have felt that her father, who had brought her over to England, had—for want of any invitation to stay at Osborne—been obliged to put up at a hotel; and that her mother, from whom she had never been parted before, had not been asked to come to England at all. She was polite, charming, understanding, affectionate; and the Queen was more delighted with her than ever, particularly when, after listening to many stories about the Prince Consort, the Princess burst into tears at an account of his death.

'How beloved Albert would have loved her!' the Queen wrote. She certainly adored her now herself. 'I can't say how I and we all love her!' she told the Crown Princess. 'She is so good, so simple, unaffected, frank, bright and cheerful, yet so quiet and gentle that her [companionship] soothes me. Then *how* lovely! . . . *She is one* of those sweet creatures who seem to come from the skies to help and bless poor mortals and lighten for a time their path . . . She is so pretty to live with.'

There was no doubt, the Queen thought, that—provided she did not 'knock under'—she would make a perfect wife for the Prince of Wales who was given permission to meet her at Calais and to accompany her and her father as far as Harburg-on-Elbe on their way home to Copenhagen. The Prince was, however, on no account to cross the Danish frontier. As the Queen's acting secretary, General Grey, explained to Augustus Paget, the British Minister in Copenhagen, it was not only the political question 'and the storm that would be raised among her German connections were any extra civility to be shown towards Denmark' which weighed on the Queen's mind, but the fear—Grey felt he 'might almost say horror'—the Queen had of the Princess's mother's family. 'The Queen's own expression is, "The Prince of Wales is so weak that he would be sure to get entangled with Princess [Christian's] relations," ' Grey continued, ' "and it would be *too horrid* if he should become one of *that* family." These are reasons which cannot be stated; but I cannot tell you how firmly rooted they are in the Queen's mind.'

The Prince obeyed his mother's instructions without complaint and arrived home on 3 December, looking 'extremely well'. He was also, the Queen decided—as so often she did when she had not seen her son for some time—'really very much improved'. It was 'such a blessing to hear him talk so openly, and sensibly, and nicely . . . I feel God has been listening to our prayers.'

The engagement, which had been publicly announced on 16 September, had been widely welcomed in England, where public opinion was wholeheartedly on the side of Denmark in her quarrel with Prussia, and where newspaper readers were constantly assured that Princess Alexandra was the very ideal of youth and beauty. 'It is impossible to exaggerate how pleased every one in all classes here is with the good news,' Lord Granville assured the Prince of Wales. 'All accounts agree as to the beauty, the excellence and charm of the person whom your Royal Highness has secured.'

Indeed the *Morning Post* reported that the people were almost as excited as was the Prince himself at the prospect of welcoming Princess Alexandra to England. A.J. Munby recorded in his diary on 3 March:

> The preparations for celebrating the Princess's arrival go on at a wondrous rate. Every house has its balcony of red baize seats; wedding favours fill the shops, and flags of all sizes; often the banners are already waving, and the devices for illumination fixed. In Pall Mall this evening rows of workmen were supping on the pavement ready to begin again by gaslight, with their work. The town seems as full as in the height of the season: one may say that the carpenters and gasfitters are all working day and night, while the rest of the population spend their time in watching them.

Princess Alexandra arrived at Gravesend aboard the *Victoria and Albert* on the morning of 7 March. 'A deafening cheer' went up from the crowds along the banks of the river, and from scores of craft bobbing about in the water, as the Prince eagerly hurried up the gangway to kiss the Princess affectionately. He introduced her to various members of his household, then led her to the railway station where a train was waiting to take them to Southwark.

Huge crowds of people, wearing wedding favours and waving Danish flags, had gathered at Southwark and all along the lavishly decorated carriage route over London Bridge, across the City, and down the Strand through Pall Mall, St James's Street, Piccadilly and Hyde Park to Paddington Station, where another train waited to take them on to Slough. So many people, in fact, were crammed between the triumphal arches and the streaming banners that the police lost control of them in the City, and the Life Guards who had escorted the carriages from Southwark had to clear the way with drawn sabres.

At about a quarter to three A. J. Munby, who had with great difficulty gained a place of vantage in King William Street, heard the bands approaching and 'the sound of deep hurrahs' coming nearer and nearer.

> The great crowd surged to and fro with intense expectation. The glowing banners of the City procession reappeared and passed; and the countless carriages full of blue robes and scarlet robes and Lord Lieutenants' uniforms; and the Volunteer bands and the escort of the Blues; and the first three royal carriages whose occupants . . . were heartily cheered. But when the last open carriage came in sight, the populace, who had been rapidly warming to tinder point, caught fire all at once. 'Hats off!' shouted the men; 'Here she is' cried the women; and all those thousands of souls rose at her, as it were, in one blaze of triumphant

irrepressible enthusiasm; surging round the carriage, waving hats and kerchiefs, leaping up here and there and again to catch sight of her, and crying Hurrah . . . She meanwhile, a fair haired graceful girl, in a white bonnet and blush roses, sat by her mother, with 'Bertie' and her father opposite, smiling sweetly and bowing on all sides; astounded—as she well might be—but self possessed; until the crowd parted at length.

Throughout the tedious four-hour-long journey the Princess remained calm and composed, acknowledging the cheers with smiles and nods, waving her gloved hands, 'bowing so prettily, so gracefully, right and left incessantly'. All the way from Slough to Windsor the Princess retained this remarkable composure, smiling at the cheering Eton boys as though refreshed rather than exhausted by the excitement and strain of the day.

There was further strain to endure at Windsor, where her carriage arrived in darkness and torrential rain; for although the Queen greeted her kindly, it was clear that the sad memories aroused by thoughts of the ceremony that was to take place in St George's Chapel on 10 March were to cast their gloom over what she professed to be 'the only ray of happiness in her life since her husband's death'. She was too 'desolate' to come down to dinner, which she had served to her and a lady-in-waiting in a different room; and was 'much moved' when, to show her sympathy with the Queen's distress, 'Alix knocked at the door, peeped in and came and knelt before [her] with that sweet, loving expression which spoke volumes'. The Queen kissed her 'again and again'.

Princess Alexandra was 'much moved' herself, so the Queen recorded, when, the day before the wedding, she took the bride and bridegroom to the mausoleum at Frogmore where Prince Albert was buried: 'I opened the shrine and took them in . . . I said, "*He* gives you his blessing!" and joined Alix's and Bertie's hands, taking them both in my arms. It was a very touching moment and we all felt it.'

The Queen, 'very low and depressed', according to Lady Augusta Bruce, remained preoccupied with thoughts of her husband even on the day of the wedding. She had decided that she could not bring herself to take part in the procession to the chapel, nor to discard her mourning for the day. She would continue to wear the black streamers of widowhood and her black widow's cap with a long white veil. She would put on the badge of the Order of the Garter that her 'beloved one had worn' and a miniature of his noble features. She would proceed to the chapel from the deanery by a specially constructed covered way and enter directly into the high oak closet on the north side of the altar which Henry VIII had built so that Catherine of Aragon could watch the ceremonies of the Order of the Garter. She would have herself photographed, sitting down in front of the bridal pair, looking at neither of them but gazing instead at a marble bust of the Prince Consort.

Princess Alexandra, in happy contrast, looked radiant, 'regular nailing', in the opinion of an Eton boy. 'She was a little pale but her eyes weren't red.' Her white dress was trimmed with Honiton lace and garlanded with orange blossom; and, as she prepared to enter the chapel, its enormously long silver train was held up by eight English bridesmaids, 'eight as ugly girls,' so Lady Geraldine Somerset thought, 'as you could wish to see'. The Princess had cried earlier when she said good-bye to her mother, but now she appeared as content as she was assured and beautiful.

The bridegroom seemed less assured but 'very like a gentleman', in Lord Clarendon's opinion, 'and more *considerable* than he [was] wont to do'. Disraeli felt sure that he had grown since he had last seen him two years before. 'Sir Henry Holland says that he is five foot eight inches high, but, then, Sir Henry is not only a physician but a courtier,' Disraeli told his friend, Mrs Brydges Willyams. 'However, the Prince certainly looks taller than I ever expected he would turn out to be.' He was, in fact, as A.J. Munby had estimated, five foot seven inches, though he appeared taller because of the high heels he had fixed to his size eight boots.

He was wearing a uniform expertly made for him by Henry Poole of Savile Row and the insignia of a general, a rank to which he had been promoted on his twenty-first birthday. The cloak of the Order of the Garter hung from his shoulders and its gold collar round his neck. As he waited at the altar with his brother-in-law, the Crown Prince of Prussia, on one side and his uncle, the somewhat mollified Duke of Coburg, on the other, he was seen to cast a series of nervous glances at the gallery where his mother sat with her ladies. She was 'agitated and restless', Lady Augusta recorded, moving her chair, putting back her long streamers, asking questions of the Duchess of Sutherland. Her expression was 'profoundly melancholy'. When the organ played the first anthem and Jenny Lind sang in the chorale which had been composed by Prince Albert, Charles Kingsley, one of the Queen's Chaplains in Ordinary, who was 'exactly opposite to her the *whole* time', saw her throw back her head and look 'up and away with a most painful' expression on her face. Norman McLeod, a Dean of the Chapel Royal, who was standing next to Kingsley, touched him on the arm, and, with tears in his eyes, whispered in his 'broad Scotch', 'See, she is worshipping him in spirit!'

McLeod drew Kingsley's attention also to the bridegroom's sisters, for 'the blessed creatures' were all crying. As Kingsley's daughter, Rose, reported on her parents' evidence, the Princess Royal had burst out crying 'as soon as the Prince of Wales came up to the Altar'. And this 'set Princess Alice (who looked quite beautiful) and all her sisters off crying and blubbering too: but it was only from affection and they soon recovered themselves'.

The bride, on the other hand, was still quite controlled and '*perfectly lovely*', walking demurely down the chapel on her father's arm, casting her eyes down shyly when—twenty minutes late—she reached the altar, but raising them from time to time to look at the Archbishop of Canterbury and the Bishops of London, Oxford, Winchester and Chester, who were assisting him in the service. Mrs Kingsley thought it rather absurd that the Archbishop considered it necessary to repeat the bride's names in groups, as though the Prince had 'not known the Princess long enough to say all her six names off at a breath'. Other guests were rather shocked by the way the Knights of the Garter hurried down the aisle in a kind of gaggle instead of proceeding decorously two by two. There was only one really embarrassing moment, however; and that was when the bridegroom's four-year-old nephew, the future Kaiser Wilhelm II, who was wearing Highland dress, decided to enliven the proceedings by trying to throw the cairngorm from the head of his dirk across the choir. He had already caused great consternation by hurling his aunt's muff out of the carriage window and by addressing the Queen familiarly as 'Duck'. He now created further disturbance by turning on his uncles, Prince Alfred and Prince Leopold, who tried to restrain his bad behaviour in the chapel, and by biting them both as hard as he could on their legs.

Yet everyone agreed that, although the nine hundred guests were excessively cramped and the ceremonial might have been better rehearsed, the wedding was a great success. William Powell Frith, who had been asked to paint the scene, found the colour of the uniforms, the glitter of the diamonds, the mediaeval costumes of the heralds and the Yeomen of the Guard an inspiration. The Bishop of Oxford professed that he had never seen a more moving sight. And Disraeli, who had been seated immediately opposite Gladstone and had been further discomfited by having received a frigid glance from the Queen for raising his eye-glass in the direction of her closet, thought it 'a fine affair, a thing to remember, a perfect pageant', the only pageant, in fact, which had not disappointed him—'the beautiful chapel, the glittering dresses, the various processions . . . the heralds, the announcing trumpets, the suspense before the procession appeared, the magnificent music . . .'

After the ceremony a luncheon was held for the royal guests, but the Queen did not attend it, preferring still to eat alone. Afterwards, at about four o'clock, from a window in the Grand Corridor, she watched the bridal carriage set off for Windsor Station. Disraeli told Mrs Willyams that the Queen had been

very anxious that an old shoe should be thrown at the royal pair on their departure, and the Lord Chamberlain showed me in confidence the weapon with which he had furnished himself. He took out of his pocket a beautiful white satin slipper which had been given him, for the occasion, by the Duchess of Brabant. Alas! When the hour arrived, his courage failed him, and he hustled the fairy slipper into the carriage. This is a genuine anecdote which you will not find in the *Illustrated News*.

The carriage halted for a moment below the Queen's window. The Prince of Wales stood up, and both he and his bride looked up at her 'lovingly'. She hoped that perhaps all would now go well with Bertie though she felt compelled to confess to King Leopold that she had of late found her son 'a very unpleasant element in the house' and was 'very *anxious* for the result of the marriage'. When the bride and bridegroom and the guests had all gone she walked down the path to the mausoleum at Frogmore, to pray alone, 'by that blessed resting-place', and felt 'soothed and calmed'.

The drive of the bridal carriage through streets thronged with Eton boys was, in contrast, far from calm. One of these excited boys, Lord Randolph Churchill, told his father:

Nothing stood before us. The policemen charged in a body, but they were knocked down. There was a chain put across the road, but we broke that; several old *genteel* ladies tried to stop me, but I snapped my fingers in their face and cried, "Hurrah!" and "What larks!" I frightened some of them horribly. There was a wooden palisade put up at the station but we broke it down . . . I got right down to the door of the carriage where the Prince of Wales was, wildly shouting, "Hurrah!" He bowed to me, I am perfectly certain; but I shrieked louder.

Lord Randolph was sure that if the Princess had not possessed 'very strong nerves she would have been frightened'. But, as when the crowds had got out of hand during her drive through the City three days before, 'all she did was to smile blandly'.

She continued to smile during the week's honeymoon at Osborne. 'It does one good to see people so thoroughly happy as this dear young couple are,' the Crown Princess reported to the Queen. 'Darling Alix looks charming and lovely and they both seem so comfortable and at home together. Love has certainly shed its sunshine on these two dear young hearts and lends its unmistakable brightness to both their countenances . . . As for Bertie he looks blissful. I never saw such a change, his whole face looks beaming and radiant.'

On their return to Windsor the Queen was equally pleased with the look of them both. 'Alix looked so sweet and lovely at luncheon,' she recorded the day they arrived back in the castle, 'and Bertie so brightened up.' Two days later, as bright as ever, he left Windsor for Buckingham Palace where he and his bride were to stay until their own London house was ready for them.

5
Marlborough House and Sandringham

I fear the Queen is not disposed to let him interfere in public.

The Prince's London home, Marlborough House in Pall Mall, had been built by Christopher Wren for the first Duke of Marlborough in 1709–10. Reverting to the Crown on the expiry of the lease in 1817 it had been allotted to Princess Charlotte and Prince Leopold. On Princess Charlotte's death, Prince Leopold, who had continued to live there, had angered King George IV by entering into negotiations for the sale of the lease to Queen Caroline. This had fortunately been prevented and the house had eventually been handed over to Queen Adelaide, who had lived there until her death in 1849. The next year Queen Victoria had asked for an Act of Parliament to be passed assigning the house for the use of the Prince of Wales on his nineteenth birthday; and since then the government had spent £60,000 on modernization and additions which had been carried out under the direction of Sir James Pennethorne.

The Prince had also acquired a country house, and this had been bought for him with his own money. Thanks to his father, who had administered the estates of the Duchy of Cornwall with characteristic efficiency, there was plenty of money available. At the time of his birth the income from the Duchy's properties in Cornwall and in London, which traditionally belonged to the heir apparent when he came of age, was no more than £16,000 a year. But by 1860 this had been increased to almost £60,000 a year; and, the income being allowed to accumulate, the Prince had come into a capital sum of about £600,000, 'a very large capital', as the Keeper of the Queen's Privy Purse, Sir Charles Phipps, reminded General Knollys when pressing for a larger contribution towards the cost of the building of the mausoleum at Frogmore than the Prince, who had not been much consulted about it, at first felt disposed to pay. So, after £100,000 had been spent on furniture for Marlborough House, on jewellery and carriages, and £10,000 had been contributed to the mausoleum, there had still been more than enough for the purchase of an estate in the country; £220,000 had therefore been offered for an estate at Sandringham in Norfolk owned by the Hon. Charles Spencer Cowper, Lord Palmerston's stepson who had gone to live abroad after marrying his mistress, Lady Harriet d'Orsay, and was only too pleased to accept so generous a sum for his English property. The house at Sandringham was rather small and much neglected; but there were over 7,000 acres of land abounding in all sorts of game and bringing in rents worth about £6,000 a year. And this, added to the interest on his remaining £270,000 invested capital, brought the Prince's annual income to about £65,000 a year.

Ample as this sum appeared to several advanced Liberal members of the House of Commons, it was paltry compared to the £125,000 a year which, in addition to the revenues of the Duchy of Cornwall, had been granted to King George III's heir on his marriage to Queen Caroline, and even more paltry in comparison with the fortunes owned by various leading figures in the society over which the Prince was now required to preside. So Parliament agreed to provide another £40,000 for the Prince and £10,000 as 'pin money' for the Princess, who was at the same time promised £30,000 a year in the event of her widowhood. But even so, the Prince's income was much less than half that enjoyed by the Marquess of Westminster. And there were several other landowners, including the Dukes of Sutherland, Buccleuch, Devonshire and Northumberland, and the Marquess of Bute and the Earl of Derby, who received rents from their estates far in excess of the whole of the Prince's income. There were still others who, with landed estates far more profitable than Sandringham, augmented their great fortunes by marrying the daughters of multi-millionaires.

The Princess of Wales had no money of her own at all. Indeed, when her father heard that she was to receive £10,000 a year from the English government, he could not refrain from remarking that it was five times as much as he had himself. But although the Prince had married a Princess without any money, and although Lord Palmerston, the Prime Minister, was not alone in thinking that his income, even when increased by Parliament, was wholly inadequate to his needs, he was able, by spending some £20,000 of capital a year, to live more or less as comfortably as he wished for the time being. He was also able to turn Sandringham into a model country estate, building new roads, planting trees, redesigning the garden with the help of the head gardener from Balmoral, establishing working-men's clubs, schools and a hospital, improving the farms and cottages, extending the sporting facilities, buying an additional 4,000 acres and completely reconstructing the house.

The Prince and Princess went to stay at Sandringham together for the first time the week after their return from honeymoon, on 28 March 1864. They were both completely happy there, as Disraeli discovered when invited to dinner at Windsor the next month. Disraeli wrote of that occasion:

The Prince proposed that he should present me to Her Royal Highness and I went up accordingly. I had therefore, at last, a good opportunity of forming an opinion of her appearance, which was highly favourable. Her face was delicate and refined; her features regular; her brow well moulded; her mouth beautiful; her hair good and her ears small. She was very thin. She had the accomplishment of being gracious without smiling. She had repose. She spoke English, but not with the fluency I had expected, and I don't think she always comprehended what was said. The Prince hovered about her.

The Princess told Disraeli that they were 'delighted with their London residence' and that when they awoke in the morning they looked out into the garden together and listened to the birds singing. They spoke of nightingales, and Disraeli asked the Princess if she knew what they fed upon:

She addressed the question to the Prince, which he could not answer. I told them—upon glow worms; exactly the food which nightingales should require. The Prince was interested by this and exclaimed: 'Is that a fact, or is it a myth?'

'Quite a fact, Sir; for my woodman is my authority, for we have a great many nightingales at Hughenden, and a great many glow worms'.

'We have got one nightingale at Sandringham,' said the Prince, smiling.

Both he and the Princess were as pleased with Sandringham as they were with Marlborough House. The Prince was delighted to have a place of his own where he could do as he liked, the Princess as charmed with the room which had been specially decorated for her as a private sitting-room as with the flat surrounding countryside that reminded her of Denmark. Not all their attendants were so taken with Sandringham, however. The Princess's lady-of-the-bedchamber, Lady Macclesfield, lamented the fact that there were

no fine trees, no water, no hills, in fact no attraction of any sort. There are numerous coverts but no fine woods, large enclosed turnip fields, with an occasional haystack to break the line of the horizon. It would be difficult to find a more ugly or desolate-looking place . . . The wind blows keen up from the Wash and the spring is said to be unendurable in that part of Norfolk. It is of course a wretched hunting country and it is dangerous riding as the banks are honeycombed with rabbit-holes. As there was all England to choose from I do wish they had had a finer house in a more picturesque and cheerful situation.

But even though the countryside was rather bleak and the alterations to the house had not yet been finished, most of the Prince's first guests enjoyed themselves. Lord Granville sent 'great reports' to the Queen; and Canon Stanley, who was also there, had a very pleasant time and was deeply touched when the Princess, 'so winning and so graceful, and yet so fresh and free and full of life', brought her new English prayer-book to the drawing-room on Easter Saturday evening and asked him to explain the English Communion Service to her.

Alterations to the house continued intermittently for months. A billiard room was built, the conservatory was converted into a bowling alley, and then, in 1870, the house was entirely reconstructed at enormous expense in an Elizabethan style by A.J. Humbert, an undistinguished architect who had helped to design the mausoleum at Frogmore. Filled with contemporary furniture and pictures, with trophies and mementoes brought back by the Prince from his travels, with paintings of Danish castles and Highland cattle, with weapons and armour, palms and statuary, display cabinets full of china, masses of photographs on tables, and with all manner of ornaments including models of the owners' animals and a big stuffed baboon with paws outstretched for visitors' cards beside the front door, it was as cluttered as any house of its period. The main rooms were large and light with tall bay windows; but some of the upstairs rooms were extraordinarily poky, though for a Victorian house unusually well supplied with bathrooms.

Guests arrived by special train at Wolferton. They were met at the station and driven through the immense wrought and cast iron gates, designed by Thomas Jeckell, which were a wedding present from the gentry of Norfolk. On either side of the drive they could usually see an assortment of the Princess's innumerable dogs—pugs and spaniels, beagles and borzois, basset hounds, chows and terriers, Eskimo sledge-dogs and French bull-dogs —or a number of curiously unconcerned rabbits. They entered the hall, known as the saloon, which was also the living quarters of a white cockatoo, to be met there by their host. And, once settled in, they were almost certain to enjoy themselves, provided they were not the victim of one of those dreadful practical jokes which were enjoyed by host and hostess alike but which were fortunately not often as heartless as that played upon a young midshipman who, on accepting a mince pie at tea-time, found it full of mustard.

Disraeli certainly enjoyed himself. He thought Sandringham 'both wild and stately' and fancied himself paying a visit to one of 'the Dukes and Princes of the Baltic: a vigorous marine air, stunted fir forests . . . the roads and all the appurtenances on a great scale, and the splendour of Scandinavian sunsets'. The host was 'very gracious and agreeable'; the hostess charming.

The Gladstones were equally taken with both of them; and after one of their visits, Gladstone told his secretary, Edward Hamilton, that they had 'enjoyed themselves greatly, that nothing could have exceeded the kindness of their Royal Highnesses as host and hostess'. Mrs Gladstone wrote warmly of their 'wish to make their guests happy' and the welcome 'absence of much form or ceremony'. As she was undressing on the last night of one of her visits, the Princess put her head round the bedroom door 'offering in fun to help [her] and in the end tucking [her] up in bed'.

After a subsequent visit Mr Gladstone wrote of his reception being 'kinder if possible even than heretofore', and of the Prince's 'pleasant manners': he was 'far lighter in hand' than his brother, Prince Alfred. Most people, indeed, were rather dismayed when Prince Alfred was one of the party, particularly when there was music in the evening as there often was. One evening the Prince of Wales and his former French tutor, Brasseur, were playing whist against Gladstone and the Queen's private secretary, Henry Ponsonby. Gladstone, reluctant to gamble, had asked the Prince, 'For love, Sir?' The Prince had complaisantly replied, 'Well, shillings and half-a-crown on the rubber'; and, Gladstone having submitted to this, all had gone well until Prince Alfred started accompanying the pianist on the fiddle. 'Anything more execrable I never heard,' Ponsonby complained. 'They did not keep time. They or perhaps the fiddle was out of tune and the noise abominable. Even Wales once or twice broke out, "I don't think you're quite right." This for an hour. I quite agreed with Gladstone that it was a relief when we got away from that appalling din.'

Throughout their married life the Prince and Princess made a practice of coming to Sandringham for his birthday in November, for his wife's birthday on 1 December and for the Christmas holidays. And on almost every occasion there was a large house party composed of guests from the most varied backgrounds, all of whom, on departure, were placed on a weighing-machine by the Prince, who recorded the readings in a note-book. One Christmas the Bishop of Peterborough arrived just as all the other guests were having tea in the entrance hall and he found the company 'pleasant and civil' but 'a curious mixture': 'two Jews, Sir Anthony de Rothschild and his daughter; an ex-Jew, Disraeli; a Roman Catholic, Colonel Higgins; an Italian duchess who is an Englishwoman, and her daughter, brought up a Roman Catholic and now turning Protestant; a set of young Lords and a bishop'.

The Prince's most intimate friends were either rich or aristocratic and usually both. Out of a sense of duty he often asked to Sandringham his fellow East Anglian landowners, the Earl of Leicester of Holkham Hall, Lord Hastings of Melton Constable, Sir Somerville Gurney of North Runcton Hall and Sir William ffolkes of Congham Lodge. But although he frequently went to stay with them in turn, he became a close friend of none of them. He preferred the company of other rich men who were more original, more amusing and, usually, more raffish.

Still one of his favourite companions was Henry Chaplin, his friend from Oxford days who, after a year at Christ Church, had decided that he had had enough of university life and had gone on an expedition to the Rocky Mountains of Canada where, encountering Blackfoot Indians on the warpath, he had prudently turned back to enjoy the more familiar excitements of the Burton hunt and the pleasures of life at Blankney Hall. Amusing, gregarious, extravagant and rumbustious, he was the subject of numerous scandalous stories set in the Midlands and in many of these stories the Prince of Wales appeared as a subsidiary character. It was, for instance, related how, returning together to Blankney after a drunken night with some local squire, Chaplin had driven his four-in-hand full tilt into the closed iron gates at the end of his drive, killing the two leading horses outright; and how, coming across a fat old peasant woman in a lane on his estate one day, he and the Prince had pulled her skirt over her head and stuck a £5 note in her bloomers. Soon after the Prince's marriage, Chaplin became engaged to the Marquess of Anglesey's only daughter, who, within a few days of the date fixed for the wedding, eloped with the Marquess of Hastings. Eventually Chaplin married Lady Florence Sutherland-Leveson-Gower, elder daughter of the Duke of Sutherland.

The Duke himself was also a close friend of the Prince. Thirteen years the Prince's senior, the Duke was a man of liberal views and eccentric tastes whose great delight was to drive the steam engines on the Highland Railway, and to assist the men of the Metropolitan Fire Brigade in the exercise of their hazardous duties. More than once the Prince, given notice of a fire by the Brigade's organizer, Captain Eyre Shaw, accompanied the Duke on these unconventional escapades; and frequently he went to stay with him at Trentham in Staffordshire, at Stafford House in London and at Dunrobin Castle in Sutherland where he enjoyed to the full the hospitality of a host who, as the owner of 1,358,000 acres—the biggest landed estate in the country—was well able to afford to entertain him in the grandest style.

The Duke had been Member of Parliament for Sutherland until his father's death in 1861; but he took little interest in politics, unlike many others of the Prince's rich friends who combined public duty with private pleasure. Lord Cadogan, for example, was one of those Etonians who had been allowed to visit the Prince at Windsor when they were boys and who had accompanied him on his holiday in the Lake District; he accepted office under Disraeli, later joined the Cabinet as Lord-Lieutenant of Ireland and became the first mayor of Chelsea where, as lord of the manor, he owned an extremely valuable estate. Charles Wynn-Carrington, who succeeded his father as third Baron Carrington in 1868, became Governor of New South Wales and was later given a seat in the Cabinet. Lord Hartington, afterwards eighth Duke of Devonshire, another intimate friend, also distinguished himself in public life as well as in the world of sport, occupying important positions in various governments while remaining, as Lord Rosebery said, 'the most magnificent of hosts'. Such, too, was the case with Lord Spencer, the Prince's Groom of the Stole, who became Lord-Lieutenant of Ireland, Lord President of the Council and subsequently First Lord of the Admiralty. Even Henry Chaplin, who was a Member of Parliament for thirty-eight years, joined the Cabinet as President of the Board of Agriculture.

Yet much as he relished the company of rich sportsmen whose political ambitions he encouraged, the Prince never neglected those more staid friends and mentors who had claims upon his regard. Indeed, he prided himself, with justification, upon his loyalty, as he did upon his readiness to forgive those who had offended him or ruffled his quick temper. 'I may and have many faults,' he once wrote. 'No one is more alive to them than I am; but I have held one great principle in life from which I will never waver, and that is loyalty to one's friends, and defending them if possible when they get into trouble.' Neither Dean Stanley nor Dean Wellesley nor Canon Kingsley had need of his defence, but they all had cause to appreciate his continuing friendship throughout their lives. They were made to feel as welcome at his table as those aristocrats and actors, politicians and bankers, sportsmen and diplomatists, Scottish financiers, Frenchmen and Germans, Americans and Jews whom he was known to find so stimulating. They could expect to meet such wits and anecdotists as Lord Houghton, the charming dilettante and poet, friend of Carlyle and champion of Swinburne; Ralph Bernal Osborne, the brilliant orator who changed his constituency so often in his parliamentary career that his friend, Disraeli, claimed that he could never remember what place he represented; Dr Frederic Hervey Foster Quin, the eccentric homeopath, friend of Dickens and Thackeray and follower of the fashions set by Count d'Orsay, who, after going to Italy as travelling physician to the Duchess of Devonshire, had become the doctor of Prince Leopold and the Duchess of Cambridge; and Lord Granville, whose *bons mots* the Prince admitted he tried to palm off as his own.

Many of the Prince's friendships much distressed the Queen, who was equally disturbed by the Prince's intimacy with such fast women as Lady Filmer and the Duchess of Manchester, a witty, beautiful German-born woman who enjoyed the attention of numerous distinguished admirers while her husband was alive and, when he was dead, married the most ardent and constant of her lovers, the Duke of Devonshire. The Queen did all she could to prevent her son and daughter-in-law entertaining, or being entertained by, these people and others like them. The Duchess of Manchester '*is not a fit companion for you*', she warned Princess Alexandra. The Duchess of Sutherland was 'a foolish, injudicious little woman' whose husband did 'not live as a *Duke* ought'. Yet the Prince—making excuses for the Duchess of Manchester and protesting that, 'despite certain eccentricities and, formerly, faults', the Duke of Sutherland was 'a clever and most straightforward man' —continued to ask them both to Marlborough House and Sandringham and to accept invitations to Kimbolton, to Trentham and to Stafford House, the Sutherlands' London house, where, at a masked ball, he much amused Disraeli by walking up to the Duchess and addressing her, 'How do you do, Mrs Sankey? How is Mr Moody?'

Nor could the Queen dampen her son's whole-hearted enthusiasms for the club life of London. His membership of White's and the Turf Club was not entirely exceptional; his recurrent visits to the Cosmopolitan Club might be excused on the grounds that he met many of the distinguished foreign visitors who were so often entertained there. But his patronage of the Garrick Club and, even worse, of the Savage Club was, the Queen considered, scarcely compatible with his position.

'Bertie is not improved since I last saw him,' the Queen complained to the Crown Princess a fortnight after he had moved into Marlborough House, 'and his ways and manners are very unpleasant. Poor dear Alix! I feel so for her.' A few weeks later she renewed her strictures:

> Bertie and Alix left Frogmore today, both looking as ill as possible. We are all seriously alarmed about her. For although Bertie says he is so anxious to take care of her, he goes on going out every night till she will become a Skeleton . . . Oh, how different poor foolish Bertie is to adored Papa, whose gentle, loving, wise motherly care of me, when he was not twenty-one, exceeded everything!

What on earth, wondered the Queen, would become of the poor country when she died? She foresaw, if Bertie succeeded, 'nothing but misery, and he would do anything he was asked and spend his life in one whirl of amusements', as he did now. It made her 'very sad and anxious'.

He and the Princess really 'should not go out to dinners and parties' so much during the London season, she told Lord Granville. They ought to restrict themselves to occasional evening visits to senior members of the Cabinet such as the Prime Minister, the Lord President of the Council and 'possibly Lord Derby', and to such respectable houses as Apsley House, Grosvenor House and Spencer House, but 'not to *all* these the *same* year'.

She said as much to the Prince himself in a letter to General Knollys which she asked to be brought to her son's attention. Society had become 'so lax and so bad' that the Prince and Princess of Wales had a duty to deny themselves amusement in order to keep up 'that tone . . . which *used* to be the pride of England'. They must show their disapproval of its looser members by 'not asking them to dinner, nor down to Sandringham—and, above all, not going to their houses'.

To associate the Crown with such frivolous and worthless people was both disgraceful and dangerous, for not only was 'every sort of vice' tolerated in the aristocracy 'whereas the poorer and working classes, who [had] far less education and [were] much more exposed, [were] abused for the tenth part less evil than their betters commit without the slightest blame', but also 'in the twinkling of an eye, the highest may find themselves at the feet of the poorest and lowest'.

The Prince, too, was concerned about this and—worried, also, by the bomb outrages committed by Irish revolutionaries in England—he wrote to the Queen to advise her to urge the government to 'use the high hand, be firm and deal with these rebels' most summarily. 'If they do not,' he went on, 'the lower classes who already have a much greater power than they, I think, have any idea of, will be very difficult to manage; and then it will cause bloodshed.'

The Queen, however, saw the danger in a different light: the rebels were just a few ruffians; the country as a whole 'never was so *loyal* or *so devoted to their Sovereign as now*'. But there certainly was a danger, a *'great danger'*, and one which it was the duty of all to try to avert. As the Queen informed her son:

> This danger lies *not* in the *power given to the lower orders, who* are daily becoming more well-informed and more intelligent, and who will *deservedly* work themselves up to the top by their own merits, labour and good conduct, but in the conduct of the *Higher* Classes and of the *Aristocracy*.
>
> Many, many with whom I have conversed, tell me that at no time for the last sixty or seventy years was frivolity, the love of pleasure, self-indulgence, and idleness (producing ignorance) carried to such excess as now in the Higher Classes, and that it resembles the time before the first French Revolution; and I must—alas!—admit that this *is true*. Believe me! It is *most alarming*, although you do not observe it, nor will you *hear* it; but those who do not live *in* the gay circle of fashion, and who view it calmly, are greatly, seriously alarmed. And in THIS lies the REAL danger.

The Prince took leave to disagree. He granted the truth of what his mother said about the 'really hardworking labouring classes'; but there were many 'toughs' outside these classes, and they were getting 'a greater power . . . to a much greater extent than people [were] aware of'. As for the aristocracy, he thought it 'hard to say that all' were as given over to 'amusement and self indulgence' as she had suggested. He continued:

> In every country a great proportion of the aristocracy will be idle and fond of amusement, and have always been so; but I think that in no country more than ours do the Higher Classes occupy themselves, which is certainly not the case in other countries. We have always been

an Aristocratic Country, and I hope we shall always remain so, as they are the mainstay of this Country, unless we become so Americanized that they are swept away.

Although he insisted that in no country did the higher classes occupy themselves more than they did in England, the Prince himself found very little useful work to do. When the Prince Consort was alive the Queen had dreaded the thought that her son might usurp the place which she considered her husband ought to fill; and the government had had to appeal to Stockmar to dissuade her from insisting that a bill should be introduced into Parliament giving Prince Albert legal precedence over the Prince of Wales. After her husband's death she was even more determined to exclude her son from any position of authority. She reluctantly admitted on occasions that he ought to become 'more and more acquainted with affairs and the way in which they [were] conducted'; yet she shrank from actually bringing him closer to matters which she wanted to deal with entirely by herself. 'No human power,' she assured her uncle, King Leopold, 'will make me swerve from what *he* decided and wished . . . I apply this particularly as regards our children—Bertie, etc.—for whose future he had traced everything so carefully. I am *also determined* that *no one* person, may he be ever so good, ever so devoted . . . is to lead or guide or dictate to me.' As she recorded in her diary, she could 'hardly bear the thought of anyone helping [her] or standing where [her] dearest had always stood'.

As the months went by the Queen continued to remark from time to time that the Prince ought to 'prepare himself more and more for that position' which she could not help thinking he might not be as far removed from 'as many wished to think'. But at the same time she continued to rebuff all attempts to gain for the Prince that experience which she agreed to be essential, preferring to call upon the younger children, especially the rather sickly Prince Leopold, when she needed any help with her paper work, and treating with scorn any suggestion that, in view of the seclusion in which she had chosen to live since the first day of her widowhood, she might consider abdicating in favour of her eldest son. When Lord Clarendon was heard to remark that even the Prince Consort would have found for his son, now that he was of age, some sort of regular work which would keep him out of harm's way, the Queen let it be known that she was much offended. As Prince Arthur's tutor, Major Elphinstone, observed, 'I fear the Queen is not disposed to let him interfere in public.'

She categorically informed Lord Granville that the Prince should '*upon no account* be put at the head of any of those Societies or Commissions, or preside at any of those scientific proceedings in which his beloved Father took so prominent a part'. And when the Prince was offered the post of President of the Society of Arts, she vetoed the proposal on the grounds that he was too young and inexperienced. Nor would she hear of his being allowed to represent her in public. She was 'very much opposed' to the system of putting the Prince of Wales forward as the representative of the sovereign. She told the Home Secretary:

Properly speaking, no one can represent the Sovereign but Her, or Her Consort. There are certain duties and forms which . . . as the Queen is unable to perform them she can and does depute someone else to perform . . . but her Majesty thinks it would be most undesirable to constitute the Heir to the Crown a general representative of Herself, and particularly to bring Him forward too frequently before the people. This would necessarily place the Prince of Wales in a position of competing as it were, for popularity with the Queen. Nothing . . . should be more carefully avoided.

On the grounds that he was not as discreet as he ought to have been, the Queen also refused to allow the Prince to receive copies of the Foreign Office dispatches which were sent to her and to members of the Cabinet. He must be content with 'a précis made of such dispatches' as she thought it proper for the Prince to see. He protested; and the Foreign Secretary, Lord Russell, supported his protest; but the Queen was adamant, and the Prince had to glean what information he could from unofficial correspondence, newspapers and conversations with ministers and diplomats. Year after year passed; the position was still the same; and the Prince felt obliged to complain to his mother that he was less trusted with official information than were the private secretaries of government ministers. He was not even allowed to know what went on in the Cabinet, and was driven to writing rather apologetic letters to friendly ministers for any information they might feel able to give him. 'Would you consider it very indiscreet if I asked you to let me know what steps the government are going to take since the meeting of the Cabinet,' he wrote in one characteristic letter dated 12 March 1873 to his friend Lord Hartington, at that time Chief Secretary for Ireland in Gladstone's Cabinet.

The Prime Minister was sympathetic and asked the Queen if he might be allowed to know 'anything of importance' that took place in the Cabinet. But no, the Queen decided, he was no less imprudent in his conversation than he had ever been. It would be 'quite irregular and improper' for him to have copies of Cabinet reports, which were, by precedent, for her eyes alone.

The Queen's determination not to let the Prince have access to confidential papers had been reinforced at the outset of the dispute by his attitude towards the invasion of Denmark by German armies intent on wresting from King Christian IX the Duchies of Schleswig and Holstein. The Prince's sympathies were naturally with his father-in-law and he made no secret of them.

They were shared by the British people. But the Queen warmly, not to say heatedly, supported the claims of Duke Frederick of Schleswig-Holstein-Sonderburg-Augustenburg; and she strongly criticized her son for his out-spoken comments, his refusal to recognize that there were faults on both sides, his unconcealed championship of the Danes and his denigration of the government's refusal to help them. 'This horrible war will be a stain for ever on Prussian history,' the Prince wrote to Mrs Bruce after listening very attentively, 'with his hat on all the while', to a declaration of the govern-ment's neutrality in the House of Lords, 'and I think it is *very* wrong of our government not to have interfered before now. As to Lord Russell's ever-lasting Notes, nobody cares two-pence about them on the Continent, and the Foreign Ministers to whom they are addressed probably only light their cigars with them.' The British would have 'cut a much better figure in Europe' if instead of sending notes, they had sent their fleet to the Baltic; and then 'all this bloodshed might possibly have been avoided'.

'This dreadful war in Denmark causes both the Princess and myself great anxiety,' he told Lord Spencer, 'and the conduct of the Prussians and the Austrians is really quite scandalous.' Such remarks were not only ad-dressed to his friends. The Prussian Ambassador, the disagreeable Count Bernstorff, one of the very few foreign diplomats in London whom the Prince did not like, felt constrained to register a formal complaint about the Prince's behaviour, which was matched by that of the Princess, who pointedly refused to speak to Bernstorff after she had observed him declining to raise his glass in a toast to the King of Denmark. Even the French Ambassador, Prince de la Tour d'Auvergne, whom the Prince *did* like, disapprovingly reported to Paris that he had been taxed by him at Marlborough House and bluntly asked in a most undiplomatic manner whether or not there was any truth in the reports that the Emperor Napoleon intended to try to bring about a settlement not entirely in Denmark's favour.

But the Prince refused to be silenced. Nothing that either the Queen or the King of the Belgians could do prevented him from speaking his mind. So strongly did he feel, in fact, that he even discussed what he considered to be the pusillanimous policies of the government with leading members of the opposition after his offer to act as an intermediary between London and Copenhagen had been treated—as the Queen instructed that it should be treated—'*with extreme caution*'.

In the Queen's opinion, the Prince's irresponsibility had been only too amply demonstrated that same spring when the Italian revolutionary, Gen-eral Giuseppe Garibaldi, who had fallen out with the Italian government, came to London with the publicly declared intention of 'obtaining the benefit of medical advice and paying a debt of gratitude to the English people', but with the privately expressed purpose of securing English help for Denmark. Lord Palmerston had made it clear to Garibaldi's sponsors that the visit must be a private one and that the General should be discouraged from accepting invitations to public entertainments at which he might be induced to make compromising speeches. But it had not been possible to prevent Garibaldi's being accorded 'such demonstrations of affection and respect as are seldom seen in England'. Nor had it proved possible to prevent his referring more than once in a speech delivered to a huge and enthusiastic audience in the Crystal Palace to the plight of 'poor little Denmark'.

This speech, like Garibaldi's every public appearance in England, was greeted with tumultuous cheers. As the Countess Martinengo Cesaresco commented, 'No sovereign from overseas was ever received by the English people as they received the Italian hero.' It was estimated that over half a million people turned out in the streets to welcome him; and *The Times* found it 'almost impossible to describe' their enthusiasm. The courtyard of Stafford House, the Duke of Sutherland's house where he stayed, was continually thronged with people hoping to catch a glimpse of him; and the Duke's servants found a ready market for bottles of soapsuds from his washbasin. Special performances of a Garibaldi musical play were given; Garibaldi biscuits became more popular than ever; and 'Garibaldies, in the science of millinery the feminine for the Garibaldi shirt', became the height of fashion.

The Queen, who had taken the precaution of leaving for Balmoral a few days before the General was shown over the royal farms at Windsor, was appalled by the people's behaviour and felt 'half-ashamed of being the head of a nation capable of such follies'. She wrote crossly to Lord Russell:

> The Queen much regrets the extravagant excitement respecting Garibaldi which shows little dignity and discrimination in the nation, and it is not very flattering to others who are received. The Queen fears that the Government may find Garibaldi's views and connections no little cause of inconvenience with foreign governments hereafter, and trusts they will be cautious in what they do for him in their official capacity. Brave and honest though he is, he has ever been a revolutionist leader.

The Queen was, therefore, '*very* much shocked' to learn that, without her knowledge or permission, the Prince of Wales had been guilty of the 'incredible folly and imprudence' of going to Stafford House to call upon Garibaldi. She curtly told General Knollys that she held him responsible and that she must in future '*insist* that no step of the *slightest political importance*' was ever taken without her being consulted.

She was not in the least mollified by her son's explanation that he had gone to Stafford House '*quite privately*' and that he had been 'much pleased' with Garibaldi. The Prince went on conversationally:

He is not tall, but such a dignified and noble appearance, and such a quiet and gentle way of speaking—especially never of himself—that nobody could fail to be attracted by him ... He asked a great deal about you, and ... referred to Denmark and said how much he felt for all the brave soldiers who had perished in the war. Though, of course, it would have been very different for you to have seen him, still I think you would have been pleased with him as he is *uncharlatanlike* ... and though his undertakings have been certainly revolutionary, still, he is a patriot, and did not seek for his own aggrandisement.

There were others, apart from the Queen, who considered the Prince had behaved unwisely. 'What do you think of the Prince of Wales and Garibaldi?' Disraeli asked his friend, Lady Dorothy Nevill. 'For a quasi-crowned head to call on a subject is strange, and that subject is a rebel!' But the Prince himself was unrepentant. His visit had been 'hailed with joy throughout the country', he informed his mother. He declined to admit that he had been wrong to make it; he had always believed in the unity of Italy, which was, after all, the 'avowed policy of the present Government'; and, as for Knollys, the Prince added, 'he is not, and cannot be, responsible for my actions. I have now been of age for some time and am *alone* responsible, and am only too happy to bear *any* blame on my shoulders.'

There was more blame soon to come.

6

A Troubled Family

She comes completely from the enemy's camp in every way—
Stockmar was right.

The Christmas of 1863 was unusually cold, and on the following
Twelfth Day the lake at Frogmore was still frozen hard. During the afternoon a band came down to play by a charcoal fire on the frosty grass by
the water's edge while children slid about on the ice and skaters played ice
hockey. The Princess of Wales loved skating, but since she was seven
months pregnant she thought it advisable merely to watch others, though she
presided energetically over a children's party that evening. The next day
she again went out to watch the skating, disregarding twinges of pain in her
womb. Lady Macclesfield warned against it, but the Princess made light of
her fears and had herself pushed out onto the ice at Virginia Water in a
sledge-chair. Returning to Frogmore at dusk she realized that the birth was
imminent; and, just before nine o'clock, the child was delivered onto a
flannel petticoat belonging to Lady Macclesfield, who, in the absence of
medical attendants other than the hastily summoned local doctor, had acted
as nurse—an office which, as the mother of thirteen children, she was able to
perform with reassuring confidence. She allowed Lord Granville—Lord
President of the Council and the only minister readily available—to see the
baby so that he could give official assurance of the birth of a future heir to
the throne. She then ushered him out of the room and asked the Prince,
who had been present at the birth, to leave as well so that the mother could
go to sleep in peace. A few minutes later she looked round the door to make
sure that all was well. She found that the Prince had slipped back into the
room and was holding his wife in his arms. They were both in tears.

The next day the Princess was as happy as ever; and when no less than
six famous doctors came into her room, and approached her bed importantly
to hold a consultation over her, she burst out laughing. Yet she could not
treat so lightheartedly the advent, on the same day, of her mother-in-law.
For some time now she had been aware that the Queen, though still extremely fond of her, had been increasingly critical of her behaviour, that

she strongly disapproved of the way she and the Prince had spent so much time gadding about when they should have been quietly awaiting the birth of a baby who might have been expected to enter the world weighing more than a puny three and three-quarter pounds and—'poor little boy'—having some proper clothes to wear instead of being 'just wrapped in cotton wool'.

The Queen's letters to the Crown Princess had of late been full of complaints about her daughter-in-law's lack of intellectual attainments and her son's thoughtlessness. 'She never reads,' the Queen lamented, 'and I fear Bertie and she will soon be nothing but two puppets running about for show all day and night . . . I fear the learning has been much neglected and she cannot either write or I fear speak French well.' Nor did she write English well, though she seemed to spend half her time writing letters. Even worse than this, she was deaf and everyone noticed it, which was a 'sad misfortune'.

Then there was Prince Alfred's unfortunate passion for going to Marlborough House. He was only nineteen and 'far too *épris* of Alix to be allowed too much there without possibly ruining the happiness of all three'. It was 'like playing with fire', for Affie did not have the 'strength of mind or rather of principle and character to resist the temptation'.

Nor did Bertie have the strength of character to resist rushing about with Alix from one entertainment to the next. He had even wanted to interrupt their autumn visit to Abergeldie, the castle near Balmoral which was lent him by the Queen, for a mad dash over to Rumpenheim for a week. She had had to refuse this, of course, since 'really they ought to be quiet and that Rumpenheim party' was 'very mischievous' for her 'poor weak boy's head'.

Now that the baby was born, there was further trouble over his name. The grandmother insisted that there could be no question of his not being called Albert, with Victor as a second name; and she told her youngest daughter, the six-year-old Princess Beatrice, who in turn told Lady Macclesfield, that this had been decided. When the news reached the father, he was much put out. 'I felt rather annoyed,' he complained to the Queen, 'when . . . told . . . that you had settled what our little boy was to be called before I had spoken to you about it.' Nor did the Prince altogether approve of the Queen's suggestion that all his descendants must bear the names of either Albert or Victoria, generation after generation for ever, and that when he himself succeeded to the throne he should be known as King Albert Edward. He reluctantly agreed that there was 'no absolute reason why it should not be so', but felt constrained to point out that no English sovereign had borne a double name in the past.

In the end, however, the Queen had her way and the baby's first two names were Albert Victor, with Christian added in compliment to his maternal grandfather and Edward after his other grandfather, the Duke of Kent. His parents thereafter knew him as Eddy, though the Queen did not. And as if distressed by the disagreements which his christening provoked, the baby 'roared all through the ceremony'; while the mother, so the Queen noted, 'looked very ill, thin and unhappy' and was 'sadly gone off'.

The Princess's 'altered appearance' was the 'observation of everyone', the Queen later informed the King of the Belgians. She was 'quite worn out by the *most* unhealthy life they lead'. The Queen wanted King Leopold to speak to his great-nephew about it. 'You must not mince the matter but speak strongly and frighten Bertie [who must also be made to] understand what a strong right I have to *interfere* in the management of the child or children, and that he should never do anything about the child without consulting me.'

Exasperated as she was about the behaviour of the young parents in England, she was even more exasperated when they insisted on visiting Denmark to see Princess Alexandra's family. She had 'not felt it safe' to tell the Prince of the Cabinet's decision that nothing could be done to help the Danes, who had to give up Schleswig and Holstein to Prussia and Austria; and, now that the war was over, she was 'extremely reluctant' to allow him and the Princess to visit Copenhagen where their reception was likely to give great offence to the Germans. Eventually she gave way to their insistent entreaties, but on three conditions: they must visit Germany as well as Denmark; they must travel in the strictest incognito; and the baby must be sent home after three weeks with Lord and Lady Spencer, who, with Sir William Knollys and two doctors, were to accompany them.

Agreeing to these conditions, the second two of which were to be broken, the Prince and Princess set sail from Dundee aboard the *Osborne* on 3 September 1864, docking at Elsinore four days later. They were given just such a tumultuous welcome in Copenhagen as the Queen had feared. But although the Princess was happy as always to be with her family once again, the Prince was bored with the humdrum routine of the Castle of Fredensborg where the meals were uninspired, the evenings were spent playing tiresome card games like loo, and the only member of his wife's family whom he found remotely entertaining was the Crown Prince Frederick. His other brother-in-law, Princess Alexandra's younger and favourite brother, William, had been elected King of Greece; her eldest sister, Dagmar, was completely preoccupied with the forthcoming visit to Copenhagen of Tsar Alexander II's heir, to whom she was to become engaged; and the two younger children, Thyra and Waldemar, were in the schoolroom.

So the Prince was thankful when Grand Duke Nicholas arrived and he could escape with his wife from the dreary castle and, as had been arranged in England, pay a visit to King Charles XV of Sweden, grandson of Napoleon I's marshal, Bernadotte, and a far more lively man than King Christian IX of Denmark. But what had not been arranged in England was that the Prince and Princess should stay in the royal palace at Stockholm rather than at a hotel or the British Legation; that they should attend a public reception; and that there should be an elk hunt, full details of which, and of the Prince of Wales's presence and deportment, were reported in newspapers all over Europe.

Extremely angry with the Prince for having so flagrantly broken her rule about his incognito and for having failed to send the baby home despite repeated requests that he should do so, the Queen wrote a letter sternly reproaching him for past faults and warning him that he and Princess Alexandra must on no account stay with the Emperor and Empress on their way home through France, 'the style of going on [at Compiègne and Fontainebleau] being quite unfit for a young and reputable Prince and Princess'.

The Prince replied that he had stayed at the royal palace in Stockholm only because Swedish hotels were dingy, the Legation was cramped and he had 'no intention of letting Alix be uncomfortably lodged' if he could help it. Besides, as he had said before, 'the King was immensely gratified' by their visit and 'what would have been the good of annoying him by not going to the Palace?' He had not sent the baby home before because the doctors had advised against it and Alix was naturally upset at having to part with 'her little treasure' for the first time. As General Knollys had already suggested, 'the Queen's kind consideration will perhaps make a little allowance for a young mother wishing to delay the first separation from her child as long as she could and hardly ever weighing the consequences likely to follow an infringement of the terms. You may be sure,' the Prince concluded, 'that I shall try to meet your wishes as much as possible, but . . . if I am not allowed to use my own discretion we had better give up travelling altogether.'

More angry than ever on receipt of this letter, the Queen dispatched a telegram ordering them to cancel altogether their journey through France: they were to come home instead through Belgium, where the Prince would be able to have the benefit of the wise counsels of the King of the Belgians, who, now ailing and nearly seventy-four, would not be spared much longer to give them. First of all, though, they would be required to visit the Prince's German relations to show that he was not only the son-in-law of the King of Denmark, as the Queen put it to Lord Russell, but the child of his parents.

The Prince and Princess went to Germany as instructed, first visiting the King of Hanover, then going on to Darmstadt to see the Prince's sister Alice, now married to Prince Louis of Hesse, and afterwards staying at Cologne with the Crown Prince and Princess of Prussia. But it was not an agreeable time. 'I can assure you,' the Prince told Lord Spencer, 'it was not pleasant to see [the Crown Prince] and his A.D.C. always in Prussian uniform flaunting before our eyes a most objectionable ribbon which he received for his *deeds of valour???* against the unhappy Danes.' For once he was not at ease with his sister either; and she, in turn, wrote home to their mother making unaccustomed complaints about him, particularly about his new and irritating habit of never answering letters. The trouble was, the Queen replied, that Bertie was becoming 'quite unmanageable'. He was entirely in the hands 'of that most mischievous Queen of Denmark'. As for Alix, kind as she was, she had not proved 'worth the price we have had to pay for her in having such a family connection'.

When the unruly children arrived home and went to stay at Osborne, however, all was for the moment forgiven. While they were away the Queen had spoken to her Household about the trouble she was having with her son; and Sir Charles Phipps, Keeper of the Privy Purse, had advised that it was 'of the highest importance that her Majesty's authority should be distinctly defined and constantly supported and maintained by the Government . . . but the Government should lay it down, so that control should not constantly be associated in the Prince of Wales's mind with [the Queen's] authority for which he should feel nothing but confiding affection.'

Affection certainly warmed the atmosphere at Osborne that November. The visit was 'most satisfactory', the Queen thought; and Alix was, after all, 'a dear, excellent right-minded soul' whom one could not help but 'dearly love and respect'. Her lot was 'not an easy one'; she was 'very fond of Bertie, though not blind'.

Indeed, the Queen usually did feel that she loved and respected her daughter-in-law when they were together, for she readily succumbed to her charm; yet no sooner had they parted than reservations once again overcast her regard for her. Fond of her as she was, she could never 'get more intimate' with her; 'she comes completely from the enemy's camp in every way—Stockmar was right'. The Queen could not depend on her to take the place of her own daughters when they got married: Alix never stayed with her for long enough; besides, she knew 'none of [the Queen's] intimate affairs'.

The Queen's reservations about the Princess of Wales grew appreciably more pronounced when the time came for her third daughter, the nineteen-year-old Princess Helena, to get married. The Queen had hoped to be able to keep Princess Helena at home, and had looked for a husband prepared to settle in England. But it was proving difficult to find a suitable prince willing to do so. Eventually the Queen had agreed to Helena's becoming engaged to Prince Christian of Schleswig-Holstein-Sonderburg-Augustenburg, the Duke of Augustenburg's younger brother, though it was not considered a very good match for her, the intended bridegroom being fifteen years older than she was and neither rich nor clever. He was also extremely boring and very plain, his features being further marred in later years by a shooting accident which deprived him of an eye. This loss he remedied by assembling a collection of glass replacements which were occasionally shown to his dinner-table guests, whose attention was particularly drawn to one of them—a realistically blood-shot specimen—for wearing when he had a cold.

The Queen was aware of Prince Christian's failings; but she also recognized that, while Helena was certainly much more alert and intelligent than he was, she was not at all charming herself and might well find it difficult to make a better marriage. The Prince and Princess of Wales, on the other hand, were uncompromisingly opposed to Helena's marriage with a man whose family had sided with Denmark's enemies in the recent war. 'What do you say to this charming marriage of Helena?' Princess Alexandra asked Lady Macclesfield. 'I cannot say how painful and dreadful it will be to me.' But the Queen was determined to stand firm. 'I will not allow [any argument],' she told King Leopold. 'I had much to go through with *his* marriage which was disliked by *all* our family.'

Although he behaved tactfully at Balmoral where he first saw the Queen after the engagement had been announced, the Prince of Wales subsequently made it clear that he was not prepared to withdraw his objections to the marriage: if it took place he would not attend the ceremony. On their mother's behalf, Princess Alice pleaded with him to be more reasonable. So did the Crown Princess. So, too, did Prince Alfred. 'The engagement has taken place and we must put a good face on it,' Prince Alfred advised his brother. 'Of course, the relationship is painful to you but you must try to accept him for what he is worth personally, and don't look at him with a prejudiced eye for he is really a very good fellow though not handsome.'

Eventually the Prince of Wales gave way; but his wife stubbornly declined to accept a marriage which she held to be a betrayal of her family, as well as an indication of the Queen's changed attitude to herself. 'Bertie is most affectionate and kind,' the Queen told the Crown Princess in December, 'but Alix is by no means what she ought to be . . . I cannot tell you what I have suffered . . . It will be long, if ever, before she regains my confidence.' And while still complaining about her daughter-in-law's misconduct over this matter, she was given further offence by her thoughtlessness in other ways.

The Princess's second child, Prince George, had been born six months before, a month earlier than the Queen had been led to expect, an accident which the Queen believed to have been deliberate, supposing that she had been misinformed so that she could not fulfil her intention to be present— as she always deemed it her duty to be present—at the birth of a new grandchild. Then to exacerbate the Queen's displeasure, as soon as the Princess had recovered from her confinement, she resumed her constant 'going out in society'. Within a few weeks she was down at Cowes racing in the Prince's new cutter, *Dagmar;* then she went off with him to that dreadful castle at Rumpenheim; and on her way home she insulted the Queen of

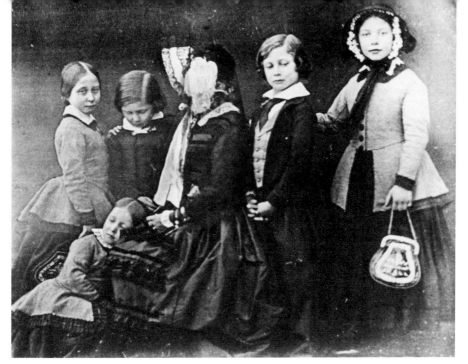

Queen Victoria with her five elder children about 1850. Left to right: Princess Alice, Princess Helena, Prince Alfred, the Queen, the Prince of Wales, the Princess Royal.

The Prince of Wales (right) at twelve with his brother Prince Alfred and his tutor, F. W. Gibbs.

The Prince of Wales in June 1857.

A family group in June 1859, when the Prince of Wales was seventeen and about to go up to Oxford. Left to right: the Count of Flanders, the Prince Consort, Princess Alice, the Duke of Oporto, the Prince of Wales, Queen Victoria, King Leopold I of the Belgians.

The Prince of Wales and the Danish Royal Family in September 1862. Left to right: Prince Christian, Princess Christian, the Duke of Brabant, the Duchess of Brabant, Princess Dagmar, Princess Alexandra, the Prince of Wales.

The Prince of Wales in September 1862, shortly before his twenty-first birthday.

The Prince and Princess of Wales in 1863, the year of their marriage.

Sandringham, house and garden from the west, in 1871.

*The Prince and Princess after the
Princess's illness in August 1867.*

The Princess of Wales's boudoir at Sandringham as it was furnished in 1889.

The Prince of Wales in November 1871, on his thirtieth birthday.

The Princess of Wales aboard the royal yacht in the summer of 1881.

The Prince of Wales's study at Marlborough House.

*The Prince of Wales
in middle age.*

*The Princess of Wales
with Prince Albert Victor (Eddy)
in the mid-1880s.*

*A family group in 1883. Left
to right: Princess Victoria,
Prince George, the Princess
of Wales, Princess Louise,
Prince Albert Victor (Eddy),
Princess Maud.*

Lord Charles Beresford
in 1885, aged thirty-nine.

A family group at Balmoral in 1887.
Queen Victoria with (left to right)
Prince Albert Victor (Eddy),
Princess Alix of Hesse, Princess
Beatrice (Princess Henry of
Battenberg), Princess Irene of Hesse.

Lillie Langtry.

General Sir William Knollys.

Prussia, who had gone to Coblenz to see her, by refusing to get out of the train and leaving her husband to make some sort of apology. As well as being indiscreet and obstinate, she was becoming 'haughty and frivolous', lacking in 'softness and warmth'. 'Alix and I never will or can be intimate,' the Queen complained; 'she shows me no confidence whatsoever especially about the children.'

The Crown Princess responded by assuring her mother that 'Alix [had] the greatest wish to be now and then alone with you. She says she is not amusing, she knows, and she fears she bores you, but she loves you so much, and it seems to be a little ambition of hers to be allowed to be close with you sometimes. It was Bertie who told me this and it quite touched me.'

A few days after this letter was written Princess Alexandra and the two 'tiny little boys' arrived at Windsor; and, as always once the women were alone together, past differences were forgotten and the relationship between them was perfectly relaxed. 'Nothing could be nicer or dearer than she is,' the Queen reported. 'It is quite charming to see her and hear her . . . I do love her dearly . . . She is dear and good and gentle, but looking very thin and pale.'

She was already pregnant again; and, to her great disappointment, had not been able to go to St Petersburg to attend the wedding of her sister Dagmar, who was to marry the Grand Duke Alexander at the Winter Palace on 9 November 1866, the Prince of Wales's twenty-fifth birthday. The Prince had gone without her, 'only too happy to be the means in any way of promoting the *Entente Cordiale* between Russia and our own country,' as he assured the Prime Minister, Lord Derby; and, as he afterwards told his mother, who had thought it sufficient for him to be represented 'by one of his gentlemen', not only wanting to be present personally at his sister-in-law's wedding but also in the expectation that 'it would interest [him] beyond anything to see Russia'. He was not disappointed. Indeed, he enjoyed himself enormously, being splendidly entertained in Moscow as well as St Petersburg, where he was provided with apartments in the Hermitage. He attended banquets, fêtes and military parades, going on a wolf hunt at Gatchina and to a ball at the British Embassy where the Imperial family watched him dancing in his Highland dress.

The British government had feared that he would give the Tsar a wrong impression of the British attitude to Turkey by voicing those 'strong anti-Turkish opinions' which he had openly entertained ever since his brother-in-law, the King of Greece, had discovered what a tiresome neighbour the Sultan could be. And, gratified that he had not, the government granted £1,000 towards his expenses, though it had to be admitted that, while he may well have carried home with him 'the goodwill and affection of every one with whom he had been thrown in contact'—as his equerry,

Major Teesdale, assured the Queen—the visit had not really done much to ensure that the improved relations between Russia and England would be permanent.

On his return home, the Prince found that his wife was not at all well. She had a slight fever and was suffering from pains in her limbs. He did not take her complaints too seriously, however, and he left her at Marlborough House to go to a steeplechase and a dinner at Windsor. The Princess grew worse, and a telegram was dispatched to the Prince to call him home. He did not return. Two further telegrams were dispatched, but it was not until noon the next day that he arrived back in London. By then it was clear that the Princess was seriously ill with rheumatic fever. She had dreadful pains in her leg and hip which, on 20 February, were greatly aggravated by the pangs she suffered in giving birth to her third child, a daughter, without the anodyne of chloroform, her doctors believing that in her already weak condition it would be dangerous to administer it.

For days she lingered 'in a most pitiable state', according to the Queen, who often came up from Windsor to see her, while the doctors' bulletins continued—in the usual manner of such announcements—to be blandly reassuring. The Prince of Wales appeared to share the doctors' unconcern. His wife could not eat because her mouth was so painfully inflamed, she could not sleep without heavy doses of drugs, and she turned almost pleadingly for comfort to Lady Macclesfield, 'dearest old Mac', who wept herself to hear her crying so piteously from the dreadful pain in her knee. Yet the Prince, 'childish as ever', did not seem to 'see anything serious about it'. Most nights he went out as though his wife's complaint were nothing more serious than a slight chill. He had his desk brought into her room so that he could be with her while he wrote his letters, but he would soon grow bored and restless and, evidently irritated by the fussing anxiety of Lady Macclesfield and the mournful face of Sir William Knollys, he would march out of the house to a club or a more congenial sitting-room. Even when he told his wife he would be back at a certain time, it was frequently much later. 'The Princess had another bad night,' Lady Macclesfield reported one day, '*chiefly* owing to the Prince promising to come in at 1 a.m. and keeping her in a perpetual fret, refusing to take her opiate for fear she should be asleep when he came! And he never came till 3 a.m.! The Duke of Cambridge is quite *furious* at his indifference to her and his devotion to his own amusements.' Lady Macclesfield was equally furious when the Prince, who had been warned to break the news of his wife's grandmother's death very gently to her, chose to do so one evening after the Princess had had an exceptionally trying and painful day. Hearing the Princess sobbing helplessly,

Lady Macclesfield sharply observed, 'He really is a *child* about such things and will not listen to advice.'

When the Princess slowly began to improve in the late spring, her husband's neglect became even more insensitive and obvious. Already there had been rumours that the Prince had been unduly attentive to various pretty young Russian women in St Petersburg and Moscow. Now, after a visit paid by the Prince to France, where he had attended the opening of the Paris Exhibition, Sir William Knollys received 'very unsatisfactory' accounts of his conduct, his going to 'supper after opera with some of the female Paris notorieties, etc. etc.' The next month at Ascot—where he received 'a very flat reception as the Princess was not there but suffering at home'—he invited to luncheon various other 'fashionable female celebrities'. There were reports, too, that he had been seen 'spooning with Lady Filmer', and riding about in a public cab on his way to supper with young actresses. And one day in August Sir William Knollys was 'greatly concerned' by a conversation with one of Princess Alexandra's doctors who 'spoke out very forcibly' and, Knollys feared, 'truly, on the tone people in his own class of society now used with respect to the Prince, and on his neglect of the Princess, and how one exaggeration led to another'.

Although the Princess always preferred to ignore what accounts she ever heard of her husband's peccadilloes, it was much more difficult to overlook his thoughtless neglect of her when she had been so ill. It was all very well for Lady Macclesfield to lament his immaturity—he certainly was immature—but his inconsiderate disregard of her need for his comfort and sympathy had been publicly flaunted and that was a wound that she could not find it easy to forget.

On the day of her marriage she had gaily remarked to the Crown Princess of Prussia, 'You may think that I like marrying Bertie for his position; but if he were a cowboy I would love him just the same and would marry no one else.' More recently she had confessed to her other, favourite sister-in-law, the eighteen-year-old Princess Louise, that the six weeks her '*beloved one*' had spent in Russia the year before had seemed to her an endless time. But there were, in the immediate future, to be few other such remarks as these.

On 2 July the Queen called at Marlborough House and found the Princess sitting in a wheel chair. She described her as 'looking very lovely' but '*altered*'. As well as being changed in character, she was also permanently impaired physically. Her leg was so stiff that she ever afterwards walked with a limp—the 'Alexandra limp' which some ladies thought so fetching that they adopted it themselves. She was also much more deaf, the otosclerosis which she had inherited from her mother being liable to be accentuated by both serious illness and by pregnancy. For the moment the

Princess's deafness was not a serious liability; but, as the years went by, it grew increasingly worse until her whole social life was moulded by it.

By the middle of August, however, the Princess was sufficiently recovered to leave England to undergo a cure in the baths at Wiesbaden. Her two little boys went with her; so did the new baby, Princess Louise; so did her husband, two doctors, and a household including twenty-five servants. The trip was not a success. On the way the Princess horrified Sir William Knollys by insisting on listening to the songs the sailors sang aboard the royal yacht, *Osborne*, of which one in particular was 'a very objectionable one to be sung before modest women'. Knollys tried to stop the sailors singing. It was a Sunday, he protested, and the singing would 'scandalise Protestant Dordrecht' where the yacht was anchored. 'I was, however, overruled,' Knollys recorded. 'I consoled myself in trusting that the Princess only half-heard the song and only half-understood its meaning, but the Princess seemed seriously annoyed with me for trying to get her away before this objectionable song was sung.'

She was even more annoyed when her chair was wheeled off the *Osborne* and carried aboard a river steamer which, to her utter indignation, was flying the Prussian flag at the stern. She demanded that it be taken down; and it was pointed out to her in vain that it was the universal custom to fly such a flag in those waters, that the Union Jack was flying at the mizzen and the Danish flag at the fore.

It was possible to make light of this particular display of the Princess's obsessional abhorrence of all things Prussian; but when the party arrived at the house which had been rented for them at Wiesbaden and their behaviour was open to public inspection it was more difficult to conceal the Princess's embarrassing sentiments. For at Wiesbaden a telegram arrived from the King of Prussia offering to call upon the Princess at a time convenient to her that evening or the next day. The Prince of Wales being away at the time, the telegram was handed to her by an apprehensive Sir William Knollys. He had already had a foretaste of the troubles to come at the Castle of Rumpenheim where he had found 'a most rabid anti-Prussian feeling, where everyone seemed to have been bit by some Prussian mad dog, and the slightest allusion set the whole party— . . . thirty-six at dinner—into agitation'. The Princess glanced at the telegram and dictated so rude a reply that Knollys declined to write it down.

On his return to Wiesbaden the Prince of Wales failed to persuade his wife to see the King; so he sent a telegram regretting that she was not yet well enough to receive visitors but that he himself would pay his Majesty a visit at any time convenient to him. This excuse having been provided for her, the Princess then insisted on demonstrating that she was not really as ill as all that by travelling to Rumpenheim for her grandfather's funeral.

Deeply resentful of the insult offered to her husband, Queen Augusta complained to Queen Victoria, whose doubts as to the propriety of her daughter-in-law's conduct in Germany—not to mention her son's—were only too amply confirmed. She was already annoyed with the Prince of Wales for having disobeyed her instructions by attending the races at Baden, a most notorious town, a 'little Paris', whose society was such—so she had been informed by the Queen of Prussia—that 'no one [could] mix in it without loss of character'. Yet not only had the Prince gone there and spent a great deal of money on betting and jewellery, he had protested against its being considered necessary to give him such advice on the subject at his age: one might imagine that he were 'ten or twelve years old, and not nearly twenty-six'. The Prince's protest had been followed by a letter of apology and explanation from Sir William Knollys; he lamented the failure of his efforts to prevent the Prince's going to the races, but thought he owed it to himself to add that 'in no points [would] his Royal Highness brook Sir William's interference less than in any matter connected with his plans and intentions'.

Now there was all this trouble over Princess Alexandra and the Prussians. The Prince wrote in attempted exculpation of his wife's conduct:

> I myself should have been glad if she had seen the King, but a lady may have feelings which she cannot *repress*, while a man *must* overcome them. If Coburg had been taken away as [other territories have been by the Prussians] I don't think you would much care to see the King either. You will not, I hope, be angry, dear Mama, at my last sentence; but it is the only way that I can express what dear Alix really feels.

The Queen, however, was not prepared to be so tolerant of the Princess's personal feelings. Nor were her daughters. The Crown Princess stigmatized her sister-in-law's behaviour as 'neither wise nor kind', and Princess Alice of Hesse tried to persuade her brother to order his wife to see the King. The Prince of Wales enlisted the help of Queen Louise of Denmark, who came over to the house at Wiesbaden to say that she herself would see the King but that she was not prepared to distress her daughter by trying to persuade *her* to do so. So it was left to the Prince, who had by now seen both the King and Queen of Prussia on his own, to talk to her again himself. He 'used every argument, but in vain, to persuade the Princess . . . She would not listen to reason of any kind. After a long discussion the Princess ended it by getting up and walking out of the room by the aid of her stick.'

The Prince then decided that he would precipitate a meeting whether or not the Princess agreed. So he wrote a telegram inviting the King of Prussia to breakfast the next morning, took it to his wife's room and then handed it to Knollys and asked him to send it off. Eventually, after the

Princess had done her utmost to prevent the threatened meeting and further telegrams had been dispatched and received, the King of Prussia accepted an invitation to breakfast at Wiesbaden on 11 October.

Anxiously waiting his arrival in the drawing-room, Knollys stood up as the Princess came into the room, leaning on her stick and looking very pale. Knollys, who had done his best to avoid her during the past few days, was rather embarrassed and made some tactless remark about her pallor, expressing the fear that 'she had caught cold'. 'Maybe I *am* pale,' she replied sharply, 'but it is not from cold but from anger at being obliged to see the King of Prussia.' And what she minded most, she added, was that she would not have been obliged to do so had it not been for the interference of 'those two old women, the Prince of Wales's sisters'—the Crown Princess, who was twenty-six, and Princess Alice, who was twenty-four.

Princess Alexandra was still talking to Knollys when the King of Prussia was shown into the room. To everyone's relief she controlled her feelings and greeted him much more gracefully than anyone had dared to hope. He, in turn, was almost effusively friendly, remaining at Wiesbaden for luncheon and, so Knollys heard subsequently, expressing himself as being 'quite satisfied with his reception'.

The whole episode, however, had made Queen Victoria 'extremely angry'. If only Princess Alexandra 'understood her duties better', she complained to the Crown Princess. 'That makes me terribly anxious.' She asked the Prime Minister to take an opportunity 'of expressing *both* to the Prince and Princess of Wales the *importance* of *not* letting any private feelings interfere with what are their public duties. Unfortunately the Princess of Wales has *never* understood her *duties of this nature* . . . It is a great source of grief and anxiety to the Queen for the future.'

7
Rounds of Pleasure

You will, I fear, have incurred immense expenses.

The Queen not only criticized her daughter-in-law for not understanding her duties better, she also complained of her not even making her husband's home life comfortable. She was notoriously unpunctual for one thing, never being 'ready for breakfast, not being out of her room till eleven; and often Bertie [had his breakfast] alone, and then she alone'. Of course their whole way of life was 'unsatisfactory'.

The Prince hated the sight of a blank page in his engagement book as much as he hated being kept waiting before he could fulfil any engagement that *had* been made. Needing little sleep, he got up early and went to bed late, and spent most days energetically hurrying about from house to house, club to theatre, hunting field to card table, spa to yacht, grouse-moor to race-course, persuading friends to drop anything else they might have arranged to do, and to join him at some impromptu party whenever any of his engagements had been cancelled. The letters of Lady Carrington, whose son Charles was frequently called for by the Prince to dine with him or to stay with him when he had arranged to go to his parents, are full of complaints about the 'great disappointments' caused by the Prince's urgent summonses. 'Oh dear!' Lady Carrington lamented on hearing that her son had received yet another of these summonses. 'What a bore the Prince is!'

In the London season there were banquets and balls, garden parties and dinner parties, evenings at Covent Garden and Drury Lane. There were more informal nights spent enjoying an evening of baccarat—or, as he called it, a 'baccy' at Marlborough House; going to the Cremorne Gardens in Vauxhall; watching, from a reserved, screened box, the performances at Evans's Music Hall in Covent Garden; attending wild parties with chorus girls at Wynn-Carrington's where he was transported one night all over the house in a sedan chair, the pole of which broke and sent him crashing to the ground; or visiting a night-club where—to the dismay of the Archduke Rudolf of Austria, who ordered the waiters out of the room, since they 'must not see their future King making such a fool of himself'—he once danced a can-can with the Duchess of Manchester. There were race meetings at Epsom, Doncaster, Ascot, Newmarket and Goodwood, all of which he attended assiduously—despite repeated requests from his mother to reduce the time he devoted to them—arguing that it was much better to elevate a national sport by granting it royal patronage than 'to win the approval of Lord Shaftesbury and the Low Church party' by abstaining from it. After Goodwood there was yachting at Cowes. In the autumn there was grouse-shooting followed by deer-stalking at Abergeldie in Scotland. When the spring came round again there would be a visit to the French Riviera; after the summer, three weeks or so at a German or Austrian spa. Twice or some-times three times a year he would slip away to Paris for a few days without his wife. Accompanied by the Princess he sometimes went to Denmark to see her relatives, and then he would go on to Germany to visit his. At the beginning of November he returned to Sandringham.

The Prince's letters to his friend, Sir Edmund Filmer, provide a com-mentary on his restless social life in the middle of the 1860s. They refer to days of 'wonderfully good shooting', on one of which the Prince himself accounted for '229 head of which 175 were pheasants'; to successful bets placed at Goodwood and Ascot; to 'very pleasant' afternoons sailing off the coast of the Isle of Wight in his 'little yacht (only thirty-seven tons)'; to expeditions to Scotland with two new rifles provided for him by James Purdey & Sons; to the 'gaieties and frivolities of the great city of London' where, Filmer was advised, it was quite right for an '*homme marié*' to amuse himself occasionally 'on a tack by himself'; and to numerous weekends in country houses which were invariably followed by exchanges of photo-graphs:

> The groups that were taken have now come but the photos might have been better—however, such as they are, I suppose your better half would like to have them . . . I am having them mounted and will send them to her . . . I enclose some more photos for Lady Filmer—for which I must almost apologise—as she will be quite bored possessing so many of me—but the waste paper basket is always useful . . . I send the new photos . . . *of course*, the ladies moved . . . please thank Lady Filmer for hers and I hope she won't forget to send me one in her riding habit—as she promised.

At Sandringham the Prince's daily routine varied little from day to day, except on Sundays when the guests were expected to attend the church in the park, the ladies arriving at the beginning of the service, the gentlemen, having left their walking-sticks against a tombstone, often not appearing before the sermon as the Prince could not bear to sit still for so long. He eventually took to placing his watch on the back of the pew in front of him so that the rector should not be tempted to prolong his sermon for more than the prescribed ten minutes, and he was obviously relieved when the time came to stand up and sing the hymn in which he invariably joined in his loud and powerful voice.

Sunday was also the day for the guests to be conducted over the estate; to be shown the farm and the stables where, as Gladstone's secretary noticed, the Princess liked to feed 'almost all the horses severally with her own hands'; to walk round the kitchen gardens and the hothouses, the Italian garden, the Alpine garden and the lavender walk, the small menagerie, the joss-house, brought back from China and given to the Prince by Admiral Sir Henry Keppel, the kennels where the Princess's dogs were kept, and the nearby cemetery where they would be buried when they died. The ladies would then be taken over the house and into the Princess's private rooms with their clutter of small tables and photographs in silver and tortoiseshell frames; of ornaments and boxes in glass-fronted display cases; of dressing-tables so crowded with miniatures and bibelots that, as Lady Randolph Churchill was to notice, there was no room for brushes or toilet things; of wardrobes and cupboards containing those exquisite, simple dresses which she accumulated in such numbers and with which she could never bear to part. On a perch in the centre of the room was a rather fierce-looking white parrot which made disconcerting pecks at ladies who got too close.

The inspection over, guests would assemble for tea at five o'clock, either in the Princess's special tea-room next to the farm dairy or, more usually, in the hall, the ladies having discarded the clothes they had worn at luncheon for elaborate tea-gowns. They would change again for dinner and, with the men in full evening dress with decorations, would come downstairs to await their Royal Highnesses before proceeding in pairs to the dining-room, 'each lady in turn having the privilege of being taken in by her royal host'. 'The Prince arranged the list himself,' Lady Randolph Churchill recorded, 'and was very particular that there should be no hitch as to people finding their places at once. An equerry with a plan of the dining-table would explain to each man who was to be his partner and where he was to sit.'

After dinner on Sundays, party games like 'General Post' were played and commonly went on until two or three o'clock in the morning with oc-casional breaks for a game of bowls, but not before midnight, it being con-sidered an unseemly game for the Sabbath. On weekday evenings there were card games and dancing which often continued quite as late. The Prince was an extremely energetic dancer, urging his partner to let herself go if she seemed too stiff and inhibited, declaring, 'I like to dance to the tune'. At the three annual balls, the County, the Farmers' and—most enjoyable of all—the Servants' Ball, the jigs and reels continued almost until dawn. On other evenings, when the ladies had gone up to bed, the Prince and his cronies might retire to the bowling alley or to the billiard room, where they would light cigars beside the screen upon which the likenesses of such eminent Victorians as Lord Salisbury and Matthew Arnold were displayed in 'very dubious attitudes' in the company of naked women.

Yet the Prince never neglected his staider guests. Edward Hamilton, who felt it was 'a little shy work going in' to the entrance hall on his arrival, was soon made to feel completely at home. The Prince was 'a model of hosts', and nearly always went upstairs with the new arrivals on their first visit to make sure that they had everything they wanted before they went to bed, even putting more coals on the fire and making sure that the water in the jugs was hot enough.

On most weekday mornings, accompanied by about eight or ten of his male guests, the Prince would go out shooting, an occupation to which he devoted a great deal of time and money. The day's sport began promptly at 10.15 a.m. by the Sandringham clocks, that was to say at a quarter to ten. The Prince's clocks in Norfolk were always kept half an hour fast, a practice—also adopted at Holkham Hall—which the Prince followed partly to economize daylight, so that he could spend more time in the open air, but also, it was said, in the vain hope that the Princess might be induced to become more punctual.

The Prince enjoyed few activities more than a grand *battue;* and once, after shooting as a guest of the Bavarian financier, Baron von Hirsch auf Gereuth, at St Johann, where 20,000 partridges were killed by about ten guns in ten days, he declared that that certainly beat 'everything on record' and would 'quite spoil' him for 'any shooting at home'.

All the same he managed very well at Sandringham where the light and sandy soil was particularly suited to the rearing of partridges and pheasants; where there were also woodcock and wild duck to be had; where hares and rabbits abounded; and where his game-keepers were as efficient and smartly dressed as any in Germany. They turned out on shooting-days wearing green velveteen coats and bowler hats with gold cords, accompanied by regiments of beaters in smocks and black felt hats decorated with blue and red ribbons. Formed up in a vast semi-circle, the beaters advanced, driving the birds into the air towards the fence behind which the guns were concealed. Behind them, rows of boys waving blue and pink flags prevented the birds from flying back. A farmer who used to watch them wrote:

> On they come in ever increasing numbers, until they burst in a cloud over the fence . . . This is the exciting moment, a terrific fusillade ensues, birds dropping down in all directions, wheeling about in confusion between the flags and the guns, the survivors gathering themselves together and escaping into the fields beyond. The shooters then retire to another line of fencing, making themselves comfortable with camp-

stools and cigars until the birds are driven up as before, and so through the day, only leaving off for luncheon in a tent brought down from Sandringham.

Servants carried out the food to the tent in a portable stove; and the ladies, some on foot, others in carriages, would join the party and listen to the Prince reading out the morning's scores, pausing for applause when a gun was credited with a good bag, looking with mock severity at one whose tally was embarrassingly low. He was not a particularly good shot himself, being, so Lord Walsingham said, rather erratic and *journalier;* but he often gave the impression of being better than he was for he usually had the best position, never fired at a difficult bird, and was always equipped with a magnificent gun. Yet his critics had to admit that even when masses of pheasants were being driven over his head, he was never flustered by the number of them, or by the people who were watching him, and that he was particularly adept at killing birds behind him at an angle which most men find difficult. He was sometimes rather careless, though. George Cornwallis-West used to relate the story of a shooting-party at which the Prince, 'enjoying an animated conversation with a lady friend who unwisely pointed out a hare to him', swung round suddenly and shot an old beater in the knee.

Although the food was plentiful and excellent at these shooting-day luncheons many of the ladies did not much enjoy them, for the Prince, in his passion for fresh air, insisted that the flaps of the tent should be folded up; and, despite the straw which was scattered over the ground, it was often dreadfully cold. In the afternoons the ladies were expected to remain outside to watch the shooting and to sit behind hedges, as the Duchess of Marlborough once complained, 'with the north winds blowing straight from the sea'.

At the end of the day the bag was laid out neatly for the Prince's inspection before being taken away to the game larder which, after Baron Hirsch's, was believed to be the biggest in the world. And it had need to be; for as the years went by, the amount of game killed each year at Sandringham grew enormous: a day's shooting would sometimes yield 3,000 birds or 6,000 rabbits.

This was not achieved without constant irritation to the Prince's tenant farmers. One of these was Mrs Louise Cresswell, who had decided to continue farming the nine-hundred-acre Appleton Hall farm after her husband's death. Mrs Cresswell had cause to complain of her crops being ruined by the Prince's shooting, which was 'a perfect passion with him and nothing made him more angry than the slightest opposition to it'. His rabbits nibbled at her swedes and mangels; his hares ate her young wheat and barley; his pheasants and partridges settled on her fields like plagues of locusts; his beaters broke down her gates and fences; his game-keepers ordered her labourers to stay in the farmyard when the guns were out shooting, and forbade them to clear the weeds that grew around the game shelters for fear they disturb the nesting birds. Claims for damages were submitted only to be met with haggling or denials of responsibility by the Prince's agent.

The Prince himself was usually quite charming and friendly towards Mrs Cresswell except on those occasions when, having 'listened to tales from any quarter without taking the trouble to inquire into the truth of them', he scowled at her in his most intimidating manner. 'No one,' she decided, 'can be more pleasant and agreeable than His Royal Highness, if you go with him in everything and do exactly what he likes; on the other hand, he can be very unpleasant indeed if you are compelled to do what he does not like.' Eventually she made up her mind she could carry on no longer, answering someone who asked her at the local market why she was leaving a farm she loved with the words, 'Because I could not remain unless I killed down the Prince's game from Monday morning till Saturday night, and reserved Sunday for lecturing the agent.' She wrote a book giving an account of her unequal struggle with the Prince, whose agent, her particular *bête noire*, bought up as many copies as he could lay hands on and burned them.

But although Mrs Cresswell was not his only outspoken critic, although the Queen urged him to stop excessive game preservation at the expense of farmers' crops, and although General Knollys feared that if he persisted in competing for the 'largest game bag' he would lose his 'good name', the Prince declined to alter his ways. In fact, he considered himself a fair and reasonable landlord: his tenants never suffered in sickness or old age; they were regularly invited to meals and dances at the house; their labourers were generously paid on shooting-days, and their houses and buildings were always kept in good repair.

Concerned as the Queen often was by accounts of the goings-on at Sandringham, reports of the Prince's behaviour elsewhere were much more worrying. There was, for instance, the matter of his gambling about which Lord Palmerston wrote to her in March 1865, warning her that the Prince was drawing large amounts of capital to pay for his losses and offering to speak to him about it privately. Sir William Knollys, it appeared, had already admonished the Prince 'in writing, having ascertained on more than one occasion that that was the best, if not the only way of making a lasting impression'. In fact, the amounts which he lost on cards were never excessive compared with the losses frequently sustained by the rich men with whom he played. It very rarely happened that he had to pay out more than £100 for an evening's whist, though he once lost a total of £700 in two nights' play at White's. Nor did he bet heavily on horses. He assured his mother that when he saw other young men betting he warned them 'over and over again' of the consequences. Yet the rumours persisted that he was losing far more than he could afford; and certainly his income was not large enough to bear any extra strain having regard to the money he was spending on the improvements at Sandringham, and on entertaining at Marlborough House, whose household numbered over a hundred persons.

Visitors to Marlborough House were admitted to the entrance hall by a Scotch gillie in Highland dress. In the hall they were met by two scarlet-coated and powdered footmen, their hats and coats being passed to a hall-porter in a short red coat with a broad band of leather across his shoulders. A page in a dark blue coat and black trousers would then escort them to an ante-room on the first floor. As they passed upstairs they were 'conscious of the flittings of many maids, all in a neat uniform, whose business it was to maintain the character of the Prince's residence as the "best kept house in London" '.

The ante-room into which they were shown was panelled in walnut, the walls being hung with swords and guns, a concealed door leading to the sitting-room where the Prince was waiting to receive them. The sitting-room was also panelled, and furnished with numerous easy chairs upholstered in leather of the same colour as the rich blue velvet curtains. A writing desk, the golden key to which the Prince always wore on his watch-chain, stood opposite the door, close to a large table strewn with documents, newspapers and reference books. A frame into whose face was set half a dozen knobs and tubes enabled the Prince to communicate with the various offices of his staff on the floor below. A shelf about five feet above the oriental carpet—on which dozed one or other of the Prince's dogs—ran around the room and was filled, as were various brackets, occasional tables, ledges and cabinets, with china, bronzes, ornaments and photographs. The tall windows over-looked Pall Mall and the commodious premises of the Marlborough Club, which the Prince himself had founded with the help of a backer described by Charles Wynn-Carrington as 'an old snob called Mackenzie, the son of an Aberdeenshire hatter who made a fortune in indigo and got a baronetcy'.

The Queen had strongly disapproved of the Prince's establishment of this club, whose members were allowed to smoke freely, which was not the case at White's, and even to enjoy the pleasures of a bowling alley until the residents of Pall Mall protested about the noise and the space was covered over and converted into a billiard room. There were four hundred members of the club, all of them known personally to the Prince; and while the Queen would have considered most of them perfectly respectable, there were some who were certainly not so. The Prince himself was President. Lord Walden, afterwards Marquess of Tweeddale, was Chairman of the Committee. Other members were the Dukes of Sutherland, Manchester and St Albans; the Marquess of Ormonde; the Earls of Rosebery and Leicester; Lords Wharncliffe, Royston and Carrington; William Howard Russell, the

war correspondent; Christopher Sykes, who was to bankrupt himself in trying to keep up with the Prince's expensive habits; and Colonel Valentine
Baker, commanding officer of the Prince's regiment, the Tenth Hussars, who
was to be cashiered and imprisoned for a year for allegedly assaulting a
nervous governess in a railway carriage.

With all these disparate men the Prince was on terms of easy friendship,
enjoying good stories and jokes with them, occasionally getting drunk with
them, yet always being quick to stifle the least hint of disrespect. Lord Carrington thought it advisable to warn his son, still one of the Prince's closest
friends, that once 'boy and university days' were over he had better 'com-
mence the proper style of Sir and your Royal Highness as royal people are
touchy on such points when they are launched into life and have taken their
place'. The Prince would cheerfully indulge a regrettable pleasure in practical jokes. According to Mrs Hwfa Williams, sister-in-law of the Prince's
friend, Colonel Owen Williams, he would place the hand of the blind Duke
of Mecklenburg on the arm of the enormously fat Helen Henneker, observing, 'Now, don't you think Helen has a lovely little waist?' And he would be
delighted by the subsequent roar of laughter—'in which no one joined more
heartily than Helen'. Similarly, he would pour a glass of brandy over Christopher Sykes's head or down his neck or, while smoking a cigar, he would
tell Sykes to gaze into his eyes to see the smoke coming out of them and
then stab Sykes's hand with the burning end. Shouts of laughter would also
greet this often-repeated trick as the grave and snobbish Sykes responded in
his complaisantly lugubrious, inimitably long-suffering way, 'As your Royal
Highness pleases.'

Yet the idea of anyone pouring a glass of brandy over the Prince's head
was unthinkable. Nor must anyone ever refer to him slightingly. A guest at
Sandringham, a friend of the Duchess of Marlborough, who went so far as
to call him 'My good man' was sharply asked to remember that he was not
her 'good man'. And once in the green-room of the Comédie Française,
while in conversation with Sarah Bernhardt and the comedian, Frederick
Febvre, the Prince was approached by a man who asked him what he
thought of the play. The Prince turned his hooded, blue-grey eyes on the
interloper and replied, 'I don't think I spoke to you.'

When a newcomer to his circle mistook the nature of its atmosphere
for a tolerance of familiarity and called across the billiard table after a bad
shot, 'Pull yourself together, Wales!' he was curtly and coldly informed that
his carriage was at the door. Similarly, when another of his guests, Sir Frederick Johnstone, was behaving obstreperously late at night in the billiard
room at Sandringham and the Prince felt obliged to admonish him with a
gently reproachful, 'Freddy, Freddy, you're very drunk!', Johnstone's reply
—made as he pointed to the Prince's stomach, rolled his *r*'s in imitation of his
host's way of speaking and addressed him by a nickname not to be used in

his presence—'Tum-Tum, you're *verrrry* fat!' induced the Prince to turn sharply away and to instruct an equerry that Sir Frederick's bags were to be packed before breakfast.

The Queen was deeply distressed that he laid himself open to such impertinent banter. She learned with dismay that he had introduced the vulgar practice of smoking immediately after dinner and that he seemed increasingly drawn to what she described as the 'fast racing set' from which she and his father had always 'kept at a distance'.

Whenever the Prince came to see his mother he was always kind, considerate and affectionate, anxious to smooth over any difficulties and disagreements between them. And after he had gone she almost invariably wrote to tell the Crown Princess how 'nice', 'affectionate', 'simple' or 'unassuming' he was, how all his 'good and amiable qualities' made 'one forget and overlook much that one would wish different'. But then there would come reports of his galloping through London in a pink coat with the Royal Buckhounds like an unruly schoolboy, chasing a deer from the Queen's herd known as 'the Doctor' from Harrow through Wormwood Scrubs to Paddington Station where, in the Goods Yard, it was cornered in front of the staff of the Great Western Railway. Or he would give offence by not writing to her when some member of the Household or family died. On the death of Sir Charles Phipps, 'the second gone of those who knelt with her in that room of death' in December 1861, she received 'many affectionate letters but not one line from her own son who owed so much to Sir Charles'. He merely sent a telegram. She felt this 'acutely'. Or the Queen would receive accounts of the Prince's being seen in the company of some well-known actress or notorious courtesan. In 1868 his favourite companion was Hortense Schneider; and for her, so it was said, he was neglecting his wife though she was again pregnant.

The Queen suggested to him that he might forsake the pleasures of the London season that year and bring the Princess into the country for a change. But he replied that he had 'certain duties to fulfil' in London and raised the sore point of her continued seclusion, which made it all the more necessary for him and his wife to do all they could 'for society, trade and public matters'.

Well, then, the Queen replied, could he not at least miss the Derby and go up to Balmoral for a few nights instead, to spend her 'sad birthday' with her and 'shed a little sunshine' over her life? So he went to Balmoral in the early summer of 1868, and all was well for a time. But that autumn there was more trouble when the Prince and Princess made plans to go abroad for several months. It was to be a holiday that would afford a rest from social engagements, an opportunity for the builders to get on with their work at Sandringham, a tonic for the Princess, whose fourth child, Victoria, had been born on 6 July, and a means of escape for the Prince from the

scandalous stories connected with Hortense Schneider and what Lady Geraldine Somerset referred to as 'his troop of fine ladies'.

The trouble began with the Princess's determination to take her three
eldest children with her as far as Copenhagen. She wrote a long letter to the
Queen seeking permission to do so, telling her that it would break her heart
if she could not take the children with her and how she had been praying
daily to God that 'nothing should arise which would hinder this hoped-for
happiness'.

The Queen was not at all disposed to agree. Eventually she consented
to the two boys going with their parents; but Princess Louise, who had not
been well and was not yet two years old, ought certainly to be left behind.
It was selfish of her mother to consider taking her.

On receipt of this reply, Princess Alexandra burst into tears, while her
husband replied to the Queen in warm support of his wife:

> I regret very much that you should still oppose our wishes but as
> you throw responsibility entirely on Alix if we take Louise, I naturally
> shall share it and have not the slightest hesitation or fear in doing so.
> Alix has made herself nearly quite ill with the worry about this but
> what she felt most are the words which you have used concerning her.
> Ever since she has been your daughter-in-law she has tried to meet your
> wishes in every way . . . You can therefore imagine how hurt and
> pained she has been by your accusing her of being 'very selfish' and
> 'unreasonable', in fact, risking her own child's life. None of us are per-
> fect—she may have her faults—but she certainly is not selfish—and her
> whole life is wrapt up in her children—and it seems hard that because she
> wishes (with a natural mother's pride) to take her eldest children with
> her to her parents' home every difficulty should be thrown in her way,
> and enough to mar the prospect of her journey, and when Vicky and
> Alice come here nearly every year with their children (and I maintain
> that ours are quite as strong as theirs) it seems rather inconsistent not
> to accord to the one what is accorded to the others.

The Queen reluctantly gave way about Princess Louise. But there were
others matters on which she was adamant. The itinerary of the holiday must
be approved by her as the Prince's every movement abroad 'or indeed anywhere [was] of political importance'; a strict incognito must be preserved
at all times; Sundays must be days of rest and worship, not amusement; invitations could be accepted only from close relations; and a strict eye must
be kept on expenses.

Knowing that these conditions would not be too rigorously observed,
the Prince readily consented to them. On 17 November 1868, the day be-

fore Mr Gladstone became Prime Minister for the first time, he left London accompanied by his wife, his three children, a doctor, thirty-three servants and a large suite including Colonel Teesdale, Lord Carrington, Captain Arthur Ellis, the Hon. Mrs William Grey, a woman of Swedish birth who was one of the Princess's favourite attendants, and the Hon. Oliver Montagu, a younger son of Lord Sandwich, an amusing, animated officer in the Household Cavalry, described by the Prince affectionately as 'a wicked boy' and well known to nurse a romantic, idealistic passion for the Princess, to whom he remained devoted for the rest of his life.

From Paris the royal party travelled through Germany by way of Cologne and Düsseldorf to Lübeck, where they embarked for Copenhagen. Just before Christmas the Prince went to Stockholm to spend a few days with King Charles XV, who, to the Queen's horror, initiated him into the Order of Freemasons. On 16 January 1869 the three children were sent home to England while their parents went on to Hamburg and thence to Berlin, where they stayed with the Crown Princess and where the Prince was delighted to be invested with the collar and mantle of the Order of the Black Eagle. Though the King of Prussia and the Prince of Wales got on well enough together, relations between the Queen and the Princess were far less cordial, the Queen scarcely deigning to notice the Princess and the Princess retaliating by addressing the Queen as 'Your Majesty' instead of 'Aunt Augusta' as she had been asked to do. The Queen rebuked the Princess at a ball, then haughtily walked off; and the Princess was not much mollified to receive a dinner service from the Queen by way of apology.

Apparently Queen Victoria did not hear about these embarrassing scenes in Berlin; but she was annoyed when told by the wife of the Ambassador to the Austrian Emperor that the incognito nature of the Prince's visit had not been observed in Vienna, that the Prince had spent a whole day being escorted round the town from one Habsburg household to another and that, as there were 'twenty-seven Archdukes now at Vienna, it was hard work to get through the list'.

Leaving Vienna for Trieste, the royal party embarked for Alexandria aboard the frigate H.M.S. *Ariadne* which had been specially fitted up as a yacht. And in Egypt the Prince gave further offence to his mother. In Cairo he was joined by friends whom she deemed wholly unsuitable companions for a voyage up the Nile or, indeed, anywhere else. First of all there was Colonel Valentine Baker's brother, Sir Samuel Baker, who had recently discovered the lake which he named the Albert Nyanza. An intrepid explorer Sir Samuel might well be, but he was certainly not a suitable travelling companion. His principles were '*not good*', and the Queen much regretted 'that he should be associated for any length of time' with her son and daughter-in-law. Then there was a party which had come out from England to witness the completion of the Suez Canal. This party included Richard Owen, the naturalist, to whom, as a friend of the Prince Consort, the Queen could, of course, have no objection; John Fowler, the engineer; and the outspoken and garrulous William Howard Russell. But it also included various relations, including two sons, of that most undesirable nobleman, the Duke of Sutherland, as well as the Duke himself. 'If ever you become King,' the Queen warned the Prince as soon as she learned who was to accompany him on the voyage, 'you will find all these friends *most* inconvenient, and you will have to break with them *all*.'

Declining to break with any of them, the Prince moved into the Esbekiah Palace in the highest spirits. The Palace had been specially furnished by the Khedive, who had provided solid silver beds and chairs of beaten gold in a bedroom a hundred and forty feet long. In the gardens illuminated fountains played all night long; and troupes of acrobats and dancers appeared from tents to perform against banks of exotic flowers.

For the voyage up the Nile the Khedive had provided six blue and gold steamers each of which, gaudily decorated with scenes depicting incidents in the lives of Antony and Cleopatra, towed a barge packed with provisions including 3,000 bottles of champagne, 4,000 bottles of claret and 20,000 bottles of soda water. The Prince's own steamer was equipped with thick carpets as well as an ample selection of English furniture which the enterprising Sir Samuel Baker had chosen for him on the Khedive's behalf. The Prince and Princess had also been provided with horses, a white donkey, four French chefs and an unspecified number of laundrymen. 'You will doubtless think that we have too many ships and too large an entourage,' the Prince wrote in apologetic explanation to the Queen. 'But . . . in the East so much is thought of show, that it becomes almost a necessity.' As for Sir Samuel Baker, whatever his principles were, he was not only a good sportsman but a marvellous organizer: 'He has really taken a great deal of trouble to make all the necessary arrangements for our comfort, in which he has most thoroughly succeeded . . . I cannot say how glad I am to have asked him to accompany us.'

The Prince was particularly glad to have Sir Samuel Baker's company because of his experience in the shooting of wild animals. The royal party visited all the usual sights which the Prince had already seen in 1862; and in a temple at Karnak near Luxor they drank champagne beneath exploding fireworks. But, as on his previous visit, it was the shooting which the Prince appeared to relish most, letting fly at all manner of wildfowl, at cranes and flamingoes, at cormorants and herons, merlins, pelicans and hawk owls. He could scarcely fail to hit a great number; and one day to his delight he shot twenty-eight flamingoes. Later he killed a crocodile; and in the tomb of Rameses IV he caught an 'enormous rat'. Seeing her husband so happy, having forgiven him now for his selfishness at the time of her illness, finding the attentions of Oliver Montagu so pleasing and flattering, and surrounded by other congenial companions in a landscape that enchanted her, the Princess felt that she had never been so happy.

On the way up to Wadi Halfa and on the voyage back to Cairo, she and the Prince collected a great variety of mementoes, including a huge sarcophagus and over thirty mummy cases. They also brought back with them a black ram which the Princess could not bear to see slaughtered by the butcher after it had taken food out of her hand and which was accordingly shipped home to Sandringham; and a ten-year-old Nubian orphan, a pretty, black, turbaned figure—or, in the opinion of the English servants, a horrid little light-fingered pest—later to be seen at Sandringham, by then a baptized member of the Church of England, serving coffee in his native costume and wearing a silver ear-ring.

From Cairo—where the Prince climbed to the top of the Great Pyramid and the Princess visited a harem and returned to the Esbekiah Palace in a yashmak to tell her husband of the gorgeous unveiled faces she had seen—the tourists went on to the Suez Canal. It was an 'astounding work', the Prince concluded, after listening to an account of its progress and potentialities by the Khedive, its chief shareholder, and Ferdinand de Lesseps, its designer. Leaving Egypt towards the end of March, the royal party arrived in Constantinople where the Sultan placed the Saleh Palace at their disposal. Hospitality here was as lavish as it had been in Cairo: an orchestra of eighty-four musicians played during every meal; cannon boomed in salute whenever the Prince and Princess left the Palace, even when they were intending to visit the bazaars in the character of Mr and Mrs Williams; guards turned out ready for inspection whenever they returned. At the Sultan's Palace of Dolmabakshi a banquet was served *à l'Européenne;* and the Sultan, who had previously never had a guest (except the Grand Vizier) sitting down at his table, broke with custom to dine with the Prince and Princess of Wales and their attendants. So this visit to Constantinople, as the Prince informed his mother, was not only 'wonderfully happy', it might even be called 'historical'.

After ten days in Turkey, the Prince and Princess set sail for Sebastopol, a tour of the Crimean battlefields, a visit to Yalta and to the Tsar's palace at Livadia. A further ten days or so were spent at Athens and Corfu with the Princess's brother King George and his Russian wife, Queen Olga; then, after a boar-hunt on the Albanian coast, the *Ariadne* sailed to Brindisi, where a special train awaited to take them to Paris for a few days at the Hôtel Bristol before returning home on 12 May.

They had been away for seven months; and the Princess, pregnant again, looked as radiantly happy now that she was reunited with her children as she had done in Egypt. Hearing a few days after her return that an English friend was engaged, she wrote to her to say, 'May you some day be as happy a *wife as I am* now with my darling husband and children. This is really the best wish I can give you for your future life.'

No sooner had he arrived home than the Prince immediately plunged into the crowded activities of the London season as though anxious to make up for having missed the first few weeks. Within three hours of his arrival he had been seen at the Royal Academy though due that evening to attend a court concert. The Queen, who had been deeply concerned about the propriety of his behaviour while he had been abroad, was even more worried about him now that he was back in London. 'There is great fear,' she told him on learning that he had taken the Duke of Devonshire's house at Chiswick for week-end visits during the Season, 'lest you should have gay parties at Chiswick instead of going there to pass the Sunday, a day which is rightly considered one of rest, quietly for your repose with your dear children.'

Apart from the parties there was the matter of his expenses, a subject that had already cropped up in their correspondence, which was in itself a matter for further complaint. The Prince's letters to his mother had been dispatched quite regularly, but they were neither long nor interesting. From Cairo he had written to impart the intelligence that Alix was 'much struck with the Pyramids but disappointed with the Sphinx'; and from Russia he had written to say how the pleasure he had taken in going over the Crimean battlefields had been marred by his 'sadness to think that over 80,000 men perished—for what? For a political object!' He could write—though, as the Queen might well have expected, he did not write—'many pages more on the subject'. It was too late now, however, to complain about the quality of the Prince's correspondence. But the Queen did feel it her duty to complain about his extravagance.

She had written to him in Paris:

> You will, I fear, have incurred immense expenses and I don't think you will find any disposition (except, perhaps, as regards those which were *forced* upon you at Constantinople) to give you any more money. I hope dear Alix will not spend much on dress in Paris. There is, besides, a *very* strong feeling against the luxuriousness, extravagance and frivolity of society; and everyone points to *my* simplicity. I am most anxious that *every possible* discouragement should be given to what, in these radical days, added to the many scandalous stories current in Society . . . reminds me of the Aristocracy before the French Revolution . . . Pray, dear children, let it be your earnest desire not to vie in dear Alix's dressing with the fine London Ladies, but rather to be *as different as* possible by great simplicity which is more elegant.

The Prince admitted:

Our journey has been rather expensive, but it won't ruin us; and I am much too proud to ask for money as the government don't propose it. But I think it would be fair if the Foreign Office were to pay some of the expenses at Constantinople [where, so the Prince told the British Ambassador to Russia, he had been expected to disburse great quantities of jewelled snuff-boxes although no one there took snuff] . . . You need not be afraid, dear Mama, that Alix will commit any extravagances with regard to dresses, etc. I have given her two simple ones, as they make them here better than in London; but if there is anything I dislike, it is extravagant or *outré* dresses—at any rate in my wife. Sad stories have indeed reached our ears from London of 'scandals in high life' which is, indeed, much to be deplored; and still more so the way in which (to use a common proverb) they wash their dirty linen in public.

Deplorable as he professed to find these scandals and their public airing, however, the Prince himself was to be involved in a particularly unsavoury one not long after his return to England.

8

The Prince Under Fire

I hear some speakers openly spoke of a Republic.

Harriet Mordaunt was an attractive young woman of twenty-one occasionally to be seen at the Prince's parties at Abergeldie and Marlborough House, 'so much liked in society,' according to Lord Carrington, 'such a pretty, pleasant, nice woman; everybody had a good word for her'. But she had always been excitable and highly strung; and after the birth of her first child, whose threatened blindness she attributed to a 'fearful disease', she began to display symptoms of eccentricity verging on madness. Yet when she confessed to her husband, Sir Charles Mordaunt, that she had committed adultery 'often and in open day' with Lord Cole, Sir Frederick Johnstone and several other men, including the Prince of Wales, he chose to believe her; and, having found a compromising diary in her locked desk, he filed a petition for divorce, adopting towards all her supposed lovers an attitude of bitter distaste. The Prince of Wales strongly protested his innocence. He could not deny that he had written several letters to Lady Mordaunt, nor that he had paid her various visits; but he did deny that he had ever made love to her and that the letters were other than harmless. And when they were published this was certainly seen to be the case. 'They were not such as to entitle the writer to a place in the next edition of Walpole's *Royal and Noble Authors*,' *The Times* commented; but they were in no sense compromising.

As soon as he learned that he could not avoid being dragged into the case, the Prince told his wife that he would have to appear in court. She loyally stood by him, appearing with him in public, cancelling none of her engagements, making it clear to the world that, whatever others might think of her husband's behaviour, she would steadfastly support him.

As soon as he informed her of his predicament, the Queen assured him by telegram that she would support him, too, though she could not forbear advising him to be more circumspect in future. But comforted as he was by his family's loyalty, by the view of the Lord Chancellor who read the letters he had written to Lady Mordaunt and thought them 'unexceptionable in every way', and by the assurances that the judge would protect him in the event of any 'improper questions' being put to him, the Prince could not but await the trial in a state of extreme agitation. He wrote apprehensively:

> I shall be subject to a most rigid cross examination by [Mordaunt's counsel] who will naturally try to turn and twist everything that I say in order to compromise me. On the other hand, if I do not appear, the public may suppose that I shrink from answering these imputations which have been cast upon me. Under either circumstance I am in a very awkward position.

The Prince—already accused in *Reynolds's Newspaper* of being 'an accomplice in bringing dishonour to the homestead of an English gentleman'— was called to give evidence before Lord Penzance and a special jury on 23 February 1870. It had been decided not to cite him as a co-respondent, but, a counter-petition having been filed to the effect that Lady Mordaunt—by this time in a lunatic asylum—was, in fact, insane, the Prince had been subpoenaed by her counsel to appear as a witness on her behalf.

When he appeared in the witness box, he showed none of the nervousness he confessed to feeling. He answered the questions put to him by Lady Mordaunt's counsel unhesitatingly, and when asked the blunt question, 'Has there ever been any improper familiarity or criminal act between yourself and Lady Mordaunt?' he replied loudly and firmly, 'No never!' to applause from the spectators in the public gallery. After seven minutes he was allowed to sit down. There was no cross-examination, and Sir Charles's petition was dismissed on the grounds that since his wife was insane she could not be a party to the suit.

'I trust by what I have said today,' the Prince wrote to his mother before setting out to dinner with the Prime Minister, 'that the public at large will be satisfied that the gross imputations which have been so wantonly cast upon me are now cleared up.'

The public, however, were not satisfied; and they made it only too plain to the Prince that they thoroughly disapproved of his conduct. *Reynolds's Newspaper* suggested:

> Even the staunchest supporters of monarchy shake their heads and express anxiety as to whether the Queen's successor will have the tact and talent to keep royalty upon its legs and out of the gutter. When, therefore, the people of England read one year in their journals of the future King appearing prominently in the divorce court and in another of his

being the centre of attraction at a German gaming-table, or public hell, it is not at all surprising that rumours concerning the Queen's health have occasioned much anxiety and apprehension.

The Princess of Wales—who looked 'lovely but *very sad*', according to Mrs Gladstone's niece, on the evening of the Prince's ordeal in the witness box—was cheered and applauded when she appeared alone. Yet when her husband was with her she was subjected to those jeers, hisses and catcalls that all too often greeted him in the streets and in the theatres. On their appearance at the Olympic Theatre with the Duchess of Manchester and Oliver Montagu a week after the Mordaunt trial, the scattered cheers of a *claque* placed in the gallery by 'that ass Newry', the owner, provoked an almost deafening roar of booing from the surrounding audience. And at a public dinner in the City the toastmaster's summons to the guests to raise their glasses to the Prince of Wales was greeted with shouts of 'To the Princess!' Feelings were still running strongly against the Prince over three months later when he was loudly booed as he drove up Ascot race-course, though, after the last race had been won by a horse in which he was believed to have an interest, he pleased the crowd that cheered him in the royal stand by raising his hat to them and calling out jocularly, 'You seem to be in a better temper now than you were this morning, damn you!'

But he could not accept the people's attitude towards him as light-heartedly as he sometimes liked to pretend. Nor could the government. Nor could the Queen. The temper of the jeering crowds was matched by caricatures in magazines, by articles in the Press, by scurrilous pamphlets and by publications such as *Letter from a Freemason* by Charles Bradlaugh, the radical atheist, who expressed the hope that the Prince of Wales would 'never dishonour his country by becoming its King'.

The Queen, who, at the time of the Mordaunt trial, had confessed to the Lord Chancellor her concern that public knowledge of the Prince's 'intimate acquaintance with a young married woman' could not but 'damage him in the eyes of the middle and lower classes', continued to reprimand her son for spending so much of his time in the company of the 'frivolous, selfish and pleasure-seeking' rich. The Queen herself, however, was far from blameless for the sad state of the royal family's reputation. While he was abroad the Prince had countered the Queen's criticisms of his own conduct by tentatively admonishing her for hers. 'If you sometimes ever came to London from Windsor,' he had written to her from Egypt, 'and then drove for an hour in the Park (where there is no noise) and then returned to Windsor, the people would be overjoyed . . . we live in radical times, and the more the *People see the Sovereign* the better it is for the *People* and the *Country*.'

The government supported this view. The fund of the monarch's credit, 'greatly augmented by good husbandry in the early and middle part of this reign', was 'diminishing', Gladstone privately commented to the Foreign Secretary. 'And I do not see from whence it is to be replenished as matters now go. To speak in rude and general terms, the Queen is invisible and the Prince of Wales is not respected.'

Indeed, the very existence of the monarchy appeared to be threatened. 'I hear some speakers openly spoke of a Republic!' the Prince wrote apprehensively to his sister, reporting the meeting of a 'tremendous crowd' in Hyde Park. 'The Government really ought to have prevented it . . . The more the Government allow the lower classes to get the upper hand, the more the democratic feeling of the present day will increase.'

There was little the government could effectively do, however, to suppress the republican feeling that had grown up in England. They could not very well silence Charles Bradlaugh, whose speeches virulently condemned the royal family; nor could they prevent the formation of numerous republican clubs, more than fifty of which were established all over England, Wales and Scotland after the fall of the French monarchy. They were powerless to interfere with Charles Dilke, one of the Members of Parliament for Chelsea and an outspoken critic of royalty, who suggested that the enormous cost to the nation of the British royal family was 'chiefly not waste but mischief' and that even the middle classes would welcome a republic if it were to be 'free from the political corruption that [hung] about the monarchy'. When, referring to the extravagant number of officials at court, Dilke said in a speech at Manchester that one of them was a court undertaker, a man in his crowded audience shouted out that it was a pity there was not more work for him to do.

If more work had been found for the Prince to do, royalists almost universally agreed, the monarchy would never have come to such a pass. It was the emphatic opinion of Laurence Oliphant, the writer and traveller whom he had met in Austria, that the Prince's defects of character were largely due to 'a position which never allowed him responsibility or forced him into action'; while W.T. Stead, editor of the *Review of Reviews*, argued that 'if the Prince of Wales had been saddled with his father's duties, he might have developed somewhat more of his father's virtues'.

Yet, even now that he was nearly thirty, the Prince was still excluded from the exercise of any real authority. For years he had had to content himself with such trivial employments as taking his mother's place at levees at St James's Palace, receiving foreign sovereigns, making visits to various provincial towns, laying foundation stones, opening buildings and exhibitions, accepting numerous governorships, colonelcies and presidencies of no very demanding nature, reviewing the troops at Aldershot, lending his support to such enterprises as the establishment of a College of Music and the erection of the Albert Hall, and driving to the opening of Parliament, to which he had been admitted a peer of the realm as Duke of Cornwall and in which he occasionally attended debates on non-controversial measures that interested him. He also delivered occasional public speeches which, with practice, he did very well, making up for any lack of originality of thought or expression by a relaxed, friendly manner and an easy fluency which were all that the circumstances normally required.

He was, of course, constantly in demand; and he rarely declined any important invitation which could be fitted in with his 'social duties' and which he felt he could accept without being regarded as 'an advertisement and a puff to the object in view'.

The Prince told his mother in April 1871:

Besides our social duties, which are indeed very numerous in the Season, we have also many to do as your representatives. You have no conception of the quantity of applications we get, in the course of the year, to open this place, lay a stone, attend public dinners, luncheons, fêtes without end; and sometimes people will not take NO for an answer. I certainly think we must be made of wood or iron if we could go through all they ask, and all these things have increased tenfold since the last ten years.

Whenever he himself offered his services in the performance of more important duties in the diplomatic field—he was not really very much interested in any other work—he was still invariably rebuffed, either by the Queen or the government, mainly on the grounds that he was so indiscreet. At the time of the Franco–Prussian War, he had openly expressed the ill-founded belief that the Prussians would receive a thoroughly deserved hiding; and when his comments were reported to Count von Bernstorff, who complained about them to the government, he told his mother that Bernstorff was 'an ill-conditioned man' and that he longed for the day when he would be removed from London. At the same time he offered to act as a kind of roving diplomat between Paris and Berlin, giving the government unsolicited advice as to how a peace settlement might be reached. The advice was dismissed as 'royal twaddle'; and soon after the French surrender of Metz and Strasbourg to the Prussians, the Foreign Secretary was once more obliged to complain of some fresh indiscretion by the Prince, who had been 'more than usually unwise in his talk'.

The Princess of Wales was even more outspokenly anti-Prussian than her husband. She had been in Copenhagen with her three eldest children on her usual summer visit at the time of France's declaration of war, and the Prince had gone out to fetch her home. She adopted quite as partisan an attitude towards the conflict as she had done during the fight for Schleswig and

Holstein. 'Alix is not clever,' the Queen lamented yet again. 'Her feelings are so anti-German and yet so little really English that she is no help.' Nor was this her only fault. Although she was pregnant again, she continued with her social round as though she were still a young, irresponsible girl rather than the twenty-six-year-old mother of five children.

The Queen was not, therefore, surprised to learn that the Princess's baby, the last child she was to have, was born prematurely on 6 April 1871 and died within two days. Both parents were heartbroken. The Princess cried bitterly, blaming herself for her poor little son's death. The Prince cried, too, 'the tears rolling down his cheeks', so the Princess's lady-in-waiting, Mrs Francis Stonor, recorded. He placed the body in the coffin himself, arranging the pall and the white flowers. Through her bedroom window the Princess saw him making his way sadly to the grave in the funeral procession, holding hands with his two sons, who walked beside him in grey kilts and black gloves.

The Queen blamed him more than the mother for what had happened, and Gerald Wellesley was told to speak to him about his care of his wife. The Prince was 'evidently deeply attached to the Princess', Wellesley reported after this talk, 'despite all the flattering distractions that beset him in society; and the Dean hopes and believes that he will be more careful about her in future.' The trouble was, as the Prince himself commented, Alix was 'naturally very active in mind and body' and he was sure that 'a sedentary life would not suit her'.

She certainly did not lead a sedentary life thereafter. A few months after the death of her baby, she was on the Continent again with her husband. They went to the Passion Play at Oberammergau together, after he had tramped over the battlefields of the recent war. Then they paid another visit to Jugenheim. And from there the Prince went by himself to Homburg, a favorite haunt, where, so English readers of *Reynolds's Newspaper* were informed, he staked 'his gold upon the chances of a card or the roll of a ball—gold, be it remembered, that he obtained from the toil and sweat of the British working-man, without himself producing the value of a half-penny.'

'These things go from bad to worse,' Gladstone remarked gloomily in a letter to the Foreign Secretary after reading the account of the Prince's gambling in *Reynolds's Newspaper*, whose guaranteed circulation of well over 300,000 copies was the largest in the world. 'I saw *What Does She Do With It?* [a widely read publication by G.O. Trevelyan attacking the Queen's alleged parsimony and hoarding of money] on the walls of the station at Birkenhead.'

Less than six months after this letter was written, however, both the Queen and the Prince, driving through the streets of London together, were accorded the most tumultuous reception. For this the credit was due not to a sudden change in the Prince's way of life but to the noisome drains of Londesborough Lodge near Scarborough.

The Prince and Princess went to stay with Lord Londesborough at the end of October on their way back to Norfolk from Scotland. The Prince arrived home at Sandringham in time for his thirtieth birthday on 9 November 1871, and soon afterwards fell ill. On the 23 November it was announced that he had typhoid fever. Just over a week later one of his fellow guests at Londesborough Lodge, the Earl of Chesterfield, died of the disease; the Prince's groom followed him; and it was feared that the Prince would die himself.

By 29 November, so Lady Macclesfield heard, his ravings had become 'very dreadful, and for *that* cause the Princess was kept out of his room one day, all sorts of revelations and names of people mentioned'. When he was calmer and the Princess was allowed in to see him he called her 'my good boy'. She reminded him that she was his wife. 'That was once but is no more,' he replied. 'You have broken your vows.' At other times he was filled with remorse, and he told his wife that he felt sure she would leave him now because he had neglected her so.

The Princess's distress was piteous; yet she behaved admirably, Lady Macclesfield thought, composed and self-controlled, never thinking of herself but 'as gentle and considerate to everyone as ever'. She had naturally been much upset by the Mordaunt trial and very cross with her 'naughty little man' for getting himself involved with it. But that was all over now. She scarcely ever left the house except to pray in the church in the park or when the doctors insisted that she get a breath of fresh air. At night she lay down sleepless in her husband's dressing-room. Her sister-in-law, Princess Alice, who had come to Sandringham for the Prince's birthday, was there to help her; but she found Alice a bossy woman, more of a trial than a comfort. Prince Alfred was there, too, though Prince Leopold, who was 'dreadfully anxious' to come as he believed he could comfort his sister-in-law, was told to keep away.

The Queen arrived on 29 November. And the next day the Prince grew suddenly worse. For the first time the Princess broke down, 'almost distracted with grief and alarm'. On 1 December, however, he seemed sufficiently recovered for the Queen to leave Sandringham; and by 7 December the Princess felt able to leave the house with Princess Alice for a drive in a sledge drawn over the snow by two ponies. But that day the fever 'lighted up' and began all over again, 'as bad as ever or worse,' Lady Macclesfield reported to her husband, adding later, 'worse and worse; the doctors say that if he does not rally within the next hour a very few more must see the end.' Lord Granville informed the Queen that there did not seem any hope left. She hurried back to Sandringham.

That Sunday, a day appointed by the Church as one of national prayer for his recovery, he seemed slightly better. Yet as *The Times* reported in a leading article next morning: 'The Prince still lives, and we may still therefore hope; but the strength of the patient is terribly diminished, and all who watch his bedside—as, indeed, all England watches it—must acknowledge that their minds are heavy with apprehension.'

The apprehension was not relieved by the doctors' bulletins, five of which were issued during the course of that day, inspiring a poet—usually supposed, though perhaps mistakenly, to be Alfred Austin—to write those lines that were to confer upon him an immortality which all Austin's later writings would certainly have denied him:

> Across the wires, the electric message came:
> 'He is no better; he is much the same.'

At seven o'clock that evening Queen Victoria was woken from a brief slumber and warned that her son was not expected to live through the night. The next morning, however, he was again a little improved, strong enough to talk and sing, to whistle and laugh in raving delirium before falling back breathless against the pillows. For thirty-six hours he continued in this state, shouting at his attendants, ordering alarming reforms in his Household now that he had—as he supposed—succeeded to the throne, calling out to Dr William Gull, 'That's right old Gull—one more teaspoonful', hurling his pillows into the air and once knocking over the Princess, who had been advised not to enter the room as her presence excited him dreadfully but who attempted to circumvent the danger by crawling through the door on her hands and knees. The Queen came into the room to watch her son from behind a screen.

By now numerous other members of the family, including Prince Leopold, had been summoned to Sandringham, which was soon so overcrowded that Princess Louise and Princess Beatrice had to sleep in the same bed. Outside it was bitterly cold. All the windows had to be kept shut, and this led to the air inside becoming so stale that the Duke of Cambridge detected what he described as an ominous smell of drains in the atmosphere. He rushed about the house, sniffing in corners, and jumping up with a startled cry of 'By George, I won't sit here!' when Knollys said that he, too, had noticed a bad smell in the library. Henry Ponsonby suggested that with so many people sitting about all day in rooms hermetically sealed there was bound to be a fusty smell. But the Duke remained 'wild on the subject' and continued to create alarm by examining 'all the drains of the house' until a man came from the gas company and discovered a leaking pipe.

Although Lady Macclesfield thought her 'charming, so tender and quiet', the Queen seemed to cause the Duke quite as much alarm as the prospect of catching typhoid. One day Henry Ponsonby was taking a stroll in the garden with Prince Alfred's equerry when they 'were suddenly nearly carried away by a stampede of royalties, headed by the Duke of Cambridge and brought up by Leopold, going as fast as they could'. Ponsonby thought that a mad bull must be on the rampage. But the stampeding royalties 'cried out: "The Queen! the Queen!" and [everyone] dashed into the house again and waited behind the door till the road was clear'.

They certainly were an 'extraordinary family', decided Lady Macclesfield, who found it 'quite impossible to keep a house quiet as long as it is swarming with people and really the way in which they all squabble and wrangle and abuse each other destroys one's peace'. Some of them were despondent, others optimistic. The Queen, obsessed by memories of 'ten years ago' when the Prince Consort died at this very same time of the year, did not have much confidence, so she confessed in her journal: 'Somehow I always look for bad news.' Prince Alfred and Prince Arthur, on the other hand, talked as if their brother 'were fit to go out shooting tomorrow'.

On 13 December it seemed for a time that he would never go out shooting again, but the 'dreadful moment passed,' the Queen recorded. 'Poor Alix was in the greatest alarm and despair, and I supported her as best I could. Alice and I said to one another in tears, "There can be no hope".' Later the Queen sat by his bed, hardly knowing 'how to pray aright, only asking God if possible to spare [her] Beloved Child'.

Her prayers were answered. The next day he was brought back from the 'very *verge* of the grave'; and on 15 December when she went into the room he smiled, kissed her hand in 'his old way', and said, 'Oh! dear Mama, I am so glad to see you. Have you been here all this time?' Soon afterwards he asked for a glass of Bass's beer.

From that day onwards, sleeping for much of the time, the Prince gradually recovered his strength. He and his wife were '*never* apart', the Princess contentedly told Princess Louise. '*Never, never*' could she thank God enough for all His Mercy when He listened to her prayers and gave her back her 'life's happiness'. All her time was devoted to her 'darling husband who thank God [was] really getting on wonderfully', she wrote to Lady Macclesfield: 'This quiet time we two have spent here together now has been the happiest days of my life, my full reward after all my sorrow and despair. It has been our second honeymoon and we are both so happy to be left alone by ourselves.'

The children had been sent to Osborne, and, at the beginning of February 1872, the Prince was well enough to join them there. Just before he left, all the tenants on the estate put their signatures to a 'very respectful and affectionate address' which the Rector, the Revd Lake Onslow, read out at a little ceremony, expressing the pleasure they all felt at his recovery. The Princess 'broke down in the speech she made in return,' one of the tenants recorded, 'and Mr Onslow nearly did the same'. The Prince was 'quite himself' again, the Queen told the Crown Princess, 'only gentler and kinder than ever; and there is something different which I can't exactly express. It is like a new life—all the trees and flowers give him pleasure, as they never used to do, and he was quite pathetic over his small wheelbarrow and little tools at the Swiss cottage. He is constantly with Alix, and they seem hardly ever apart!!!'

The possibility of some sort of public thanksgiving for the Prince's recovery had already been raised before Christmas. But Gladstone's suggestion of a public procession through London and a service in St Paul's Cathedral did not find much favour with the Queen. She considered that it would not only be too tiring for the Prince but would also make a 'public show' of feelings that would be better expressed in private. The Princess of Wales 'quite understood' the Queen's attitude; 'but then on the other hand' she also considered that the people, having taken 'such a public share' in the family's sorrow, had a 'kind of claim to join with [them] now in a public and universal thanksgiving'. This being also the government's view, it was arranged that there should be a thanksgiving ceremony in St Paul's on 27 February.

There was as much excitement in London that day as there had been when Princess Alexandra had arrived for her wedding. There were also even more accidents: numerous people were knocked down by the crowds and trampled on; several others were kicked by horses and thrown from cabs or carts; a baby was crushed to death in the arms of its parents; three women fell out of windows; two had epileptic fits; a stand collapsed opposite Marlborough House, injuring many of its occupants; and a branch of one of the tall elm trees in St James's Park, where, according to *The Times*, 'the eye of official propriety was outraged by the sight of ragged dirty youths calmly enjoying positions so conspicuous', snapped off, sending twenty of them hurtling to the ground.

Yet, despite these and other calamities, the royal carriage was greeted by deafening cheers all along the route. Having once overcome her reluctance to appear in public, the Queen was determined that 'the *people*—for whom the *show*' was being put on—should be enabled to see it properly. So she insisted on an open carriage. And as soon as the procession was on the move she obviously enjoyed herself, waving and nodding to the spectators, raising her son's hand up in her own at Temple Bar and, to their noisy delight, kissing it. He himself, the *Times* correspondent thought, looked pale and drawn; and, as he raised his hat from his head in acknowledgement of the cheers, he 'revealed an extent of caducity ill-suited to his youth'. Yet he was obviously 'deeply moved by the enthusiasm of the dense masses'.

On his return to Marlborough House after the service the Prince wrote to his mother to tell her that he could not find words to express 'how gratified and touched' he was 'by the feeling that was displayed in those crowded streets' towards her and himself. The Queen also heard from Gladstone, who thought that the celebration was perhaps the most satisfactory that the City of London had ever witnessed. It was a quite 'extraordinary manifestation of loyalty and affection'. That evening in London the streets were crowded with people looking at the illuminations and the flags, the brilliantly lit shop windows and the banners festooned across the house fronts bearing legends such as '*Te Deum*' and 'God bless the Prince of Wales'. A.J. Munby recorded:

> And amidst all this the working folk, men and women, boys and girls, merrily moving along; sometimes half a dozen decent lasses arm in arm, dancing in a row, and singing, while their prentice swains danced by them, playing the flute or the accordion. I never saw such a crowd, nor a sight so striking in England: it was like a scene out of one of Sir Walter's novels of ancient English life.

Republicanism as a significant force in British politics, already damaged by the excesses of the Paris Commune, had suffered a blow from which it was never completely to recover.

A few months before, even so convinced a royalist as Munby had been expressing doubts about the Prince of Wales, whom he had seen looking 'sleek and thoughtless' at the Botanical Gardens in June. A Norfolk friend of Munby, Joseph Scott-Chad, had been to a ball at Sandringham and, while confirming that the Prince was always 'judiciously kind and hospitable to everyone', had spoken also of his 'ill habits and gross practical jokes'. But now such talk was hushed in thankfulness at his recovery. One day before Christmas, Munby was talking to Mrs Theodore Martin at her house in Onslow Square when J.A. Froude, the historian, called with Charles Kingsley:

> They began to talk about the Prince of Wales . . . and the wide and profound interest which his illness has caused. The silent multitudes, said Froude, have had a chance of showing what the real feeling of the country is; and the few malcontents have been cowed . . . Kingsley expressed great hope and confidence in the Prince of Wales's character; and Mrs Martin exclaimed, 'After such a burst of enthusiasm, and from such a nation, what a King he ought to be!'

The enthusiasm had spread to all classes. Charles Dilke no longer found receptive audiences for his anti-monarchical speeches, which were now received with far less enthusiasm and interrupted by royalist demonstrators singing 'Rule Britannia' and 'God Save the Queen'. The Prince was not, of course, thenceforward free from attack. *The Coming K—: A Set of Idyll Lays*, which lampooned him in the character of Guelpho, appeared in 1873 and enjoyed a wide circulation, as did many other less amusing and cruder satirical pieces. There were to be times enough in the future when the Prince was forced to face the jeers of hostile crowds. But, as Lord Carrington observed, the worst was over, and the monarchy was safe.

While the Prince embarked with the Princess for three months' convalescence in the Mediterranean, the government set their mind to the problem of establishing a more permanently healthy relationship 'between the monarchy and the nation by framing a worthy and manly mode of life [with regard to] public duties for the Prince of Wales'.

For years the form which this worthy mode of life might take had been the subject of inconclusive debate. Every suggestion that had been put forward had been set aside in face of the Queen's objections. The Prince himself would have liked to have been given some employment in the army, but the Queen considered that he would not take enough interest in the troops. Gladstone thought that the Prince might be useful on the Indian Council, but the Queen doubted that there was really enough for him to do on the Indian Council. Might he not, another minister proposed, be employed in the office of the President of the Local Government Board? The Queen could not suppose that he would perform any useful function there either. Should he then be attached in succession to various government offices 'so that he might be taught the business of the different departments'? The Queen did not think he should. In fact, the Queen, so Princess Alice said, saw no point in planning for the Prince of Wales.

'She thinks the monarchy will last her time,' Princess Alice wrote, 'and it is no use thinking what will come after if the principal person himself does not, and so she lets the torrent come on.'

Some years before, Disraeli had suggested that the Prince might be bought a house in Ireland in a good hunting country where he could 'combine the fulfilment of public duties with pastime, a combination which befits a princely life'. The Queen, however, would not hear of it; it was 'quite out of the question'; once a royal residence had been established in Ireland, other parts of her dominions, such as Wales and even the Colonies, would demand why they had been neglected. Besides, '*any* encouragement of [the Prince's] constant love of running about and not keeping at home or near the Queen [was] *earnestly* and *seriously* to be deprecated'. Nevertheless, the proposal had been repeated by Gladstone two years later when it was hoped that the purchase of a royal residence in Ireland might be combined with the Prince's appointment as a kind of non-political Lord Lieutenant, spending all his winters in Ireland and performing ceremonial duties there while all official responsibility remained with the Irish Secretary in London. After all, Gladstone added in a letter to Lord Granville, the Prince 'possessed that average stock of energy which enables men to do that which they cannot well avoid doing, or that which is made ready to their hands'. Besides, the Prince would obtain 'a very valuable political education'. But the Queen was even more adamant in her opposition to this suggestion than she had been to the earlier one. She would welcome her son's removal from London for the Season, but he was not fitted for the exercise of high functions of state. If a member of her family were to be appointed to the proposed office, a younger son, Prince Arthur, had superior qualifications.

Despite the Queen's intransigence, Gladstone considered that the Prince's illness and recovery provided him with a new opportunity, perhaps a 'last opportunity', to settle the royalty question and to bring the matter of the Prince's employment before the Queen once more. Already annoyed with Gladstone for repeatedly—and rather tactlessly—urging her either to emerge from her seclusion or to let the Prince enjoy more authority in her name, the Queen could not bring herself to give his advice a patient or sympathetic hearing. In fact, she went so far as to accuse him of trying to make use of her for his own political purposes, which so utterly exasperated him that the relationship between Prime Minister and Sovereign became more painfully strained than ever.

Discussions about the Prince's future employment, nevertheless, continued. If he were not to be allowed to go to Ireland, what alternatives were there? Henry Ponsonby suggested philanthropy, arts and sciences, the army, foreign affairs or India, though he rather doubted that any of them would answer the problem. 'Nothing can be more genial than [the Prince] is for a few minutes,' Ponsonby told his wife. 'But he does not endure. He cannot keep up the interest for any length of time and I don't think he will ever settle down to business . . . To get [him] to enter into a subject or decide on it is most difficult. They have to catch snap answers from him as he goes out shooting, etc.'

Of all Ponsonby's suggestions only one seemed possible to Francis Knollys, son of Sir William Knollys, whom the Prince had recently appointed his secretary. Francis Knollys did not think the Prince possessed the qualities to concern himself in any serious way with philanthropy. 'The same objection applies to science and art,' Knollys continued. 'He has been connected, more or less, for several years with the South Kensington Museum, and with several exhibitions; but I cannot say that he has ever shown any special aptitude in that line.' The trouble was that, 'with his disposition', he was always likely to 'become irretrievably disgusted with business of every description' unless his interest in it was fully involved. Nor was he suited for the army, even if it were considered an appropriate employment for the heir to the throne. He badly wanted to be appointed Colonel of the Scots Fusiliers. But this could not be approved: as General Knollys was informed by the master of the Queen's Household, 'a good deal of dissatisfaction would arise' if he were to be appointed; besides, 'a Prince of Wales cannot make the army a profession'. So, since the Queen's mind seemed firmly shut against sending the Prince to Ireland, the only choice appeared to be foreign affairs, which had at least 'afforded occupation to even the most indolent of Princes'.

But the Foreign Secretary could not agree:

The question is of urgent importance, the solution most difficult. The Queen desired me to put the Prince on committees in the Lords. I had him named on one of a non-political character. He attended the first day. He then came to me to ask whether the committee could not be adjourned for ten days. He had some engagements and so on. I am afraid the Foreign Affairs question would be treated in the same way. If the Queen really desired his opinion, sent for him and consulted him he would probably get amused and interested. But if he only gets a few bones after they have been to the Prime Minister and the Queen, and finds nothing but dispatches telling him only what he has skimmed a week before in the paper, he will cease reading them. If all the drafts are to be submitted to him, the delay will be intolerable. If he makes a suggestion on them, it will probably be snubbed by the Queen, or necessarily argued against by me, and he will make no more. And as to really confidential matters, will they remain secret? He asked me to keep him informed during the [Franco-Prussian] War. One evening I got four messages from different friends, telling me to be careful. One of my first notes to him had been handed round a dinner party.

So once more Gladstone returned to the solution of some appointment in Ireland. But it now transpired that the Prince himself had no wish to go there; and when, several years later, he was brought round to the idea again, the Queen, after seeming to yield to the plan, decided in the end that a place there would become 'a great *trouble* and *tie* which [might] become inconvenient'. Lord Spencer, the Irish Viceroy, who had patiently attempted to reconcile the Queen to the Prince's going to Ireland and who thought that he had succeeded, felt 'inclined to throw up the sponge and retire to [his] plough in Northamptonshire'.

The Queen reluctantly agreed to the Prince's visiting Ireland for short periods. He had done so in 1865, in 1868 and 1871 and was to do so again in

1885. And on each occasion the Queen was apprehensive that some part of her own authority would be usurped, that the Prince would be used for political purposes, that he would spend too much time on race-courses or that he would be assassinated. Yet every visit was a success. Only in 1885, when an angry mob attempted to break through a police cordon round Mallow station, and black flags painted with skulls and crossbones were waved beside the railway lines leading down to Cork, were there any really alarming hostile demonstrations. On his return home from this last visit, he was justified in supposing that he deserved both the Prime Minister's congratulations on the 'sound judgement, the admirable tact and feeling' which he had displayed and the Irish Secretary's assurance that his 'great public service' had earned the 'admiration and gratitude' of the House of Commons.

When the Prince of Wales returned to Marlborough House on 1 June 1872 after twelve weeks' convalescence on the Continent, the problem of his future employment still remained unresolved. He had enjoyed his holiday and looked extremely fit, though he had put on a great deal of weight since his illness and was now a good deal stouter than a young man of thirty ought to have been. He and the Princess had stayed for a time at Cannes and, after a little cruising in the royal yacht in the Mediterranean, they had been to Rome and Florence, Milan and Venice, and then to Cadenabbia on Lake Como before returning home by way of Genoa and Paris. They had travelled incognito as the Earl and Countess of Chester and most of their time had been spent in quiet relaxation; but on more than one occasion the Prince had caused embarrassment at home by speaking indiscreetly to the various public figures upon whom he called during his travels. The Prime Minister felt obliged to get up in the House of Commons to deny a report in *The Times* that the Prince, on a visit to the Vatican, had been so injudicious as to raise with the Pope the controversial issue of his Holiness's relations with the Italian government. Indeed, the Prince's indiscretion continued to be a stumbling block to his employment in the kind of work which he would have enjoyed and to which he considered himself best suited.

At the instigation of the Foreign Secretary the Prince had made a formal call upon M. Thiers, the President of the recently established Third Republic, while he was in Paris, though it 'went very much against the grain to do so', as he chose to believe that republicanism was only a passing phase in France and some form of monarchy would soon take its place. This meeting had gone off well enough; but a subsequent chance meeting at Trouville, where the Prince had landed with his friend the Duke of St Albans while enjoying a short cruise in the Duke's yacht *Xantha*, had had serious repercussions. The

Prince's long talk with Thiers on this second occasion was observed by a German spy, who reported it to Berlin, where Bismarck expressed deep concern as to its likely content.

Yet while he annoyed the Germans by his evidently close relationship with Thiers, the Prince exasperated many French republicans by his intimate friendships with both the old French aristocracy and the family of the ex-Emperor Napoleon III. When Napoleon died at Chislehurst in Kent, where he had been living in exile, the Prince was with difficulty dissuaded from attending the funeral, which the Bonapartists intended to use as an excuse for a demonstration against both the French Republic and Germany. He could not, however, be prevented from asking several leading Bonapartists to come to stay at Sandringham after the funeral, which prompted Gladstone to lament that, while the Prince was undeniably good-natured, his 'total want of political judgement, either inherited or acquired', was a matter for grave concern.

Nor could the Prince be prevented from setting out the following year upon a tour of the Loire Valley where he intended to stay in the châteaux of various prominent members of the old aristocracy, calling on his way at Esclimont near Rambouillet, the home of the Duc de la Rochefoucauld-Bisaccia, who had recently been relieved as French Ambassador in London for having supported the Comte de Paris in his claims to the French throne. The Queen did all she could to prevent the Prince from going on this holiday. He was already on the Continent, having gone to Potsdam with the Princess to attend the confirmation of his nephew Wilhelm, the son of the Crown Princess. From Potsdam, Princess Alexandra had gone to stay with her parents in Copenhagen, leaving the Prince to go on by himself to Baden where once again he provided newspapers with stories about his addiction to gambling which, combined with rumours that he was now over half a million pounds in debt, made it necessary to issue a formal denial of his financial difficulties.

It could not be denied, though, that he was excessively fond of gambling, and for this reason Sir William Knollys had deprecated the Prince's going to Baden at all. It was impossible to say what the Prince's betting habits might lead to, Sir William solemnly told the Queen. 'And, as your Majesty was once pleased to observe to him, the Country could never bear to have George IV as Prince of Wales over again.' As for Paris, why that was

the most dangerous place in Europe, and it would be well if it were never revisited. In fact, remaining on the Continent, whenever it involves a separation of the Prince and Princess of Wales—whether Her Royal Highness is in Denmark or elsewhere—cannot be otherwise than most undesirable, and in the interests of both would be better limited to the shortest period.

But the Prince would brook no interference from either Knollys or the Queen; and when the Queen asked Disraeli, who had become Prime Minister for the second time, to stop the Prince from going to France *en garçon*, Disraeli thought it as well merely to ask the Prince to be prudent, fearing that if he attempted to prevent the Prince from carrying out any private plans he had set his heart on he would destroy what 'little influence' he already possessed.

So the Prince set off to France to visit those friends of his whose company he was beginning to find so alluring, to Mouchy-le-Chatel to see the Duc de Mouchy and his beautiful half-American wife, who was a granddaughter of Napoleon's brother-in-law, Marshal Joachim Murat, once King of Naples; to Mello to stay with the lovely and lascivious Princesse de Sagan, a banker's daughter who was supposed to have admitted the Prince of Wales to her ever-expanding train of lovers; to the Duc de la Tremouille at Serrant; to the Duchesse de Luynes at Dampierre; to the Duc d'Aumâle at Chantilly; and then to Paris where he spent many happy hours at the Avenue d'Iéna house of Henry Standish, grandson of the Duc de Mouchy and of an Englishman who had made his home in France after inheriting a fortune, and husband of the delightful, ingenuous Hélène Standish, whose extraordinary resemblance to her admired and beloved friend the Princess of Wales she emphasized with all the means at her disposal in a manner less touching than absurd. The Prince enjoyed himself enormously, and was alleged to have made love to several obliging Frenchwomen, though not to the Marquise d'Harcourt, who claimed to have promised to place a rose on the latch of her bedroom door, so that the Prince could find his way to her in the night, and then planted in her bed the ugliest kitchenmaid in the château.

The month before he embarked on his continental holiday, the Prince had given a huge party which rivalled in extravagance those splendid fêtes presided over by the Prince Regent at Carlton House. Sir Frederic Leighton had been called in to supervise the decorations at Marlborough House where, on 21 July, over fourteen hundred guests had been invited to appear in fancy dress. The Prince, in the improbable and elaborate guise of Charles I with a black felt white-plumed hat blazing with diamonds and a wig of trailing curls much fairer than the Blessed Martyr's, opened the ball with a Venetian quadrille partnered by the Duchess of Sutherland—'as usual', according to Lord Ronald Gower, 'the most beautiful and graceful woman in the place'. The music played on until dawn with a break for supper, which was served in two enormous, tapestry-hung scarlet marquees. Disraeli, who arrived rather late and not in fancy dress, having had to make a speech at the Mansion House, thought the whole affair was 'gorgeous, brilliant, fantastic'.

Less gorgeous and brilliant but more to the taste of his quieter friends were the garden parties which the Prince and Princess held in the grounds of Chiswick House. And infinitely more to the taste of the Prince's young raffish friends were those parties occasionally held in houses borrowed for the night where the Prince entertained what Francis Knollys called his 'actress friends', and where cockfights were staged for the benefit of those who preferred gambling to girls.

The Queen valiantly endeavoured to turn her son's mind to more intellectual pursuits, but with less and less hope of success. While he was still Prime Minister, Gladstone had urged her Majesty to try to persuade the Prince to 'adopt the habit of reading' since the 'regular application of but a small portion of time would enable him to master many of the able and valuable works which bear upon royal and public duty'. But the Queen had replied irritably, 'She has only to say that the P of W has *never* been fond of reading, and that from his earliest years it was *impossible* to get him to do so. Newspapers and, *very rarely*, a novel, are all he ever reads.'

Gladstone had been invited down to Sandringham to talk to the Prince, who, though strongly opposed now to the Prime Minister's Irish plans, had expressed himself as being 'very glad to have an opportunity of discussing with Mr Gladstone the subject of some useful employment'. But the Prime Minister had not so much as mentioned the subject; and, since the Prince made no reference to it either, the opportunity had been lost.

So the months passed and the few duties found for the Prince remained either social, ceremonial or civic. He acted as host and guide to the Shah of Persia, who arrived in England to stay at Buckingham Palace in June 1873; he also entertained the Tsarevich, his wife and children at Marlborough House that same summer. In January the next year he went to St Petersburg to attend the wedding of his brother Alfred, Duke of Edinburgh, to the Tsar's daughter, the Grand Duchess Marie; and in the spring he busied himself with arrangements for the Tsar's state visit to England. From time to time he would leave London to open a building or exhibition in the provinces, to make a speech in some guildhall or assembly room, to inspect a factory at Birmingham, to walk round a building estate at Coventry, or to make a tour of the docks and pierhead, the Free Library and Museum, the Assize Courts and St George's Hall at Liverpool. He performed such duties conscientiously, but without undue solemnity, sometimes adding zest to a rather tedious day's work by playing one of those jokes he found so entertaining upon a member of his entourage. For instance, in Coventry, which he visited in company with the Marquess of Hartington and Hartington's mistress, the Duchess of Manchester, he laid plans for the discomfiture of the somewhat pompous Hartington, who had recently extricated himself from an expensive affair with the delectable courtesan Catherine Walters, known as 'Skittles', a former employee in a bowling alley in Liverpool. The Prince asked for a bowling alley to be included in his tour of Coventry and arranged for the innocent Mayor to tell Lord Hartington, who could be relied upon to display little interest in it, that this unusual item had been included in the itinerary at the special request of his Royal Highness in tribute to his Lordship's love of skittles.

By such means the Prince kept boredom at bay. But frustration at being excluded from any position of responsibility was not so easily assuaged and found expression in occasional fits of childish petulance or irritating insistence on airing opinions about problems whose intricacies he had neither the patience nor the discernment to grasp. Required by the Queen and the government to decline acceptance of the honorary colonelcy of a Russian regiment offered him by the Tsar, on the grounds that it would be contrary to precedent, he flew into a rage which his friends thought wholly out of proportion to the disappointment involved in being unable to add a new uniform to his already well-stocked wardrobe. At the same time he bombarded the Foreign Secretary, whose ministry was not concerned in the matter, with violent complaints about a new uniform for the army and, simultaneously, with exhortations to be '*firm*' against Russia in central Asia. Granville commented sardonically to Gladstone that the Prince and the Duke of Cambridge (another self-appointed foreign affairs adviser) were evidently 'men of iron'. The Prince's own staff were sometimes equally exasperated by his invariable habit of altering at least '*something*' in any draft prepared for him, either of a speech or a letter, even though the alteration was apparently 'without any significance whatsoever'.

9
A Passage to India

Everyone here is fascinated with H.R.H. . . . and his amiable manners.

Unknown to both the government and the Queen, the Prince now began to plan an undertaking that would certainly not prove boring and was likely, for a time at least, to release him from all sense of frustration. His Household gathered what this plan was when the librarian at Sandringham was instructed to collect all the books he could about India.

When the Queen was approached, however, she did not think an Indian tour was a good idea at all. It was 'quite against [her] desire', she told the Crown Princess. There might be some political advantage, but not much; it was not as if there were any particular crisis in Indian affairs. Besides, even if Bertie's health were up to the strain, he ought not to leave his family for so long; and there could be no question of Alix going. In any case who was to pay for it all?

'Where is the money to come from?' Disraeli also wanted to know after 'our young Hal' had induced his mother to give her assent to the scheme 'on the representation that it was entirely approved by her ministers'.

He has not a shilling. She will not give him one. A Prince of Wales must not move in India in a *mesquin* manner. Everything must be done on an imperial scale etc., etc. This is what she said . . . [She also said] that nothing will induce her to consent to the Princess going and blames herself bitterly for having mentioned the scheme without obtaining on the subject my opinion and that of my colleagues.

In fact, the Prince had never suggested to his wife that she should accompany him; and Lord Derby, the Foreign Secretary, for one, was thankful that he had not done so. For not only would there be extremely difficult problems of protocol to overcome if she were to visit the courts of Indian princes; but, so Derby said, ' "Hal" is sure to get into scrapes with women whether she goes or not, and they will be considered more excusable in her absence.'

When she discovered what her husband's intentions were Princess Alexandra was much put out, protesting, years later, that she would '*never* forget or forgive' him for having left her behind. The Prince, himself, was much annoyed when he learned that his mother—who was already pestering him with advice about the food he should eat, the time he ought to go to bed each night, the way he must behave on Sundays—insisted on supervising all the arrangements including the composition of his suite. She had written to the Prime Minister with 'positive directions that the detailed arrangements should be considered by the government as an official question'. 'At the same time,' so Lord Salisbury, Secretary of State for India, told the Prince, 'the Queen was pleased to lay especial stress upon the number and composition of your Royal Highness's suite as a matter of public importance.' But it had been '*entirely*' his own idea, the Prince protested, and it was only natural that he should wish 'to keep the arrangements connected with it in his hands'. During an interview with Disraeli at Downing Street he 'manifested extraordinary excitement' as he angrily declined to make any alterations in the names he had chosen. He would certainly not leave his friends, the Duke of Sutherland and Lord Carrington, behind simply because the Queen disapproved of them. Nor would he withdraw his invitation to the boisterous Lord Aylesford, known as 'Sporting Joe', who was also going as his personal guest; to William Howard Russell, who was travelling as his honorary private secretary; or to Lieutenant Lord Charles Beresford R.N., who had been invited to go as one of his three aides-de-camp.

In face of the Prince's obduracy, Disraeli felt compelled to give way, afterwards assuring the Queen that he would caution Carrington and Beresford in particular 'against larks', and that, apart from the Prince's secretary, Francis Knollys, who was admittedly not always as well behaved as he might be, there could be no real objection to the other members of the suite. These included Prince Louis of Battenberg and the Duke of Cambridge's son, Lieutenant Augustus FitzGeorge, as aides-de-camp; Lord Suffield as lord-in-waiting; Colonel Arthur Ellis, Major-General Sir Dighton Probyn V.C. and Lieutenant-Colonel Owen Williams as equerries; Canon Duckworth as chaplain; and Joseph Fayrer as physician. Her Majesty would be represented by Lord Alfred Paget, her clerk-marshal; and Sir Bartle Frere would be in general control of the party, taking with him, as secretary, General Grey's son, Albert. The Prince reluctantly agreed not to include the detachment of Life Guards for which he had asked, or a Russian liaison officer, on its being pointed out to him that, if he did, other countries would expect to be asked to provide liaison officers of their own. He was, however, to be attended by his stud-groom and valet, a page, three chefs, and twenty-two other servants as well as the Duke of Sutherland's piper. In addition there was to be an artist, a botanist, and Clarence Bartlett, Assistant Superintendent of the Zoological Gardens, who was both a zoologist and taxidermist. The Prince's French poodle, 'Bobêche', was to be taken, and also three handsome horses from the Sandringham stables. So as to accustom them to the sight of wild beasts and reptiles, the horses were taken regularly to look at the animals in the zoo.

Naturally there was trouble over the amount of money to be provided for the expedition as well as over its composition. *Reynolds's Newspaper*, which attacked the whole 'notion of Albert Edward, the hero of the Mordaunt divorce suit, the mighty hunter', being interested in anything other than 'pig-sticking and women', protested that working-men were being robbed so that the Prince of Wales could enjoy himself. To loud cheers of support from a crowd of over 60,000 people in Hyde Park, Charles Bradlaugh said that the nation did not wish to prevent the brave, moral, intellectual future King of England's going to India, 'indeed they would speed him on a longer journey than that'. But they did object to having to pay for such a ridiculous jamboree. All over England similar hostile demonstrations were held. Outraged orators demanded to know why the country was being asked to pay for presents to Indian princes, while the gifts offered in return would become the Prince's personal property. Banners and placards were waved in protest against the Indian visit, and during his travels that summer the Prince himself was made aware of the strong feelings which had once more been roused against him.

Even in royal circles people spoke slightingly of his mission. At Balmoral, after a Sunday morning service, Lady Errol, a Presbyterian attendant of the Queen, remarked to Henry Ponsonby how beautiful was the prayer which had been said for the Prince of Wales. 'Well,' Ponsonby replied. 'I don't know that it was a bad one, but I didn't understand what he meant [by] "Oh bless abundantly the objects of his mission." ' Lady Errol replied, 'Oh, all the good he may do.' Ponsonby sharply observed, 'The object of his mission is amusement.' 'Yes,' agreed Lord Salisbury. 'And to kill tigers. Perhaps he meant to bless the tigers.'

In spite of all the criticism, however, and in face of strong objection from the Radicals and many members of the Liberal Party, Disraeli persuaded the House of Commons to approve the expenditure of £52,000 by the Admiralty for the transport of the Prince's suite to and from India and of a further £60,500 by the Treasury for the Prince's personal expenditure including presents to Indian rulers. An additional £100,000 was subsequently contributed by the Indian government. Yet the Prince, supported by Bartle Frere and *The Times*, maintained that this was far from enough: the Indian princes would present their guest with gifts far more lavish than any that he would be able to afford to give them in return. And, as if confident that the amount of his allowances would be increased when the importance of his mission was realized, he spoke carelessly to his 'creatures', so Disraeli recorded, 'of spending, if requisite, a million, and all that'. But although 'a thoroughly spoilt child' who could not 'bear being bored', he was also, in Disraeli's opinion, 'the most amiable of mortals'; and he soon reconciled himself to the amount which the Prime Minister had raised for him without further protest—and, in the event, did not exceed it.

Irritated by quarrels over the number and quality of his companions, over the amount of money to be allowed him, and over his official status in India—where the position of the Viceroy, so the Queen insisted, must on no account be prejudiced—the Prince was also piqued by the attitude of his wife, who, refusing to accept her husband's explanation that this was an all-male party and that 'it was difficult for ladies to move about' in India, continued to complain bitterly about being left behind and appeared to Disraeli as though she were preparing to commit suttee. Albert Grey, who had equipped himself with a derringer 'to save H.R.H. from assassination', reported her as being 'very miserable', not only because she badly wanted to see India and was hurt at being left behind but also 'because besides the not unnatural fear about his health—in its best day but flabby—there [was] the more uncomfortable dread of the fanatic's knife about the sharpness of which he has received many warning letters'. The Princess was also very upset because the Queen refused to allow her to take the children to Denmark while their father was in India. Although she later relented, the Queen insisted that a decision given by the judges in the reign of George II gave her the right to prevent the royal children from leaving the country. Taking pity on the Princess, Disraeli consulted the Solicitor-General, who gave it as his opinion that the precedent was a bad one, that the Queen ought not to exercise it even if it existed, and that 'to force the Princess to live in seclusion . . . six months in England [was] a serious matter'.

Refused permission to visit either India or Denmark, the Princess, in Dean Stanley's opinion, looked 'inexpressibly sad'. And, as the time drew nearer for his departure, the Prince seemed quite as miserable himself, confessing to Lord Granville that he 'left England with a heavy heart and was so depressed in spirits on reaching Calais' that, although he was cheered on his departure by thousands of people willing to show that antagonism to his expensive venture was far from universal, he 'felt seriously inclined to return home instead of going on'. He continued 'tremendously low' in Paris, wrote Lord Carrington, who had 'never seen him like it before'; and even after their arrival in Brindisi, where crowds on the quay greeted the Duke of Sutherland with shouts of *'l'amico di Garibaldi'*, he had still not recovered his spirits. At Brindisi he went aboard H.M.S. *Serapis*, a specially converted troopship with large square portholes, which was waiting to take him through the Suez Canal by way of Athens. It was 'comfortable but not smart', and the Prince went to his cabin looking 'decidedly gloomy'. In fact, the whole party, so Lord Carrington told his mother, were 'more like a party of monks than anything else'. There were 'no jokes or any approach to it'. Georgina Frere was given similar news by her father. No shipload of pilgrims 'were ever better behaved,' Sir Bartle told her; so far there had been 'nothing which would have been voted out of place at Windsor Castle'. Lord Charles Beresford, a jocular Irishman, attempted to keep up the party's flagging spirits, but there were no games of whist, 'no sprees, or bear fights or anything'. The day after leaving Brindisi the *Serapis* began to toss in the swelling sea, and 'several chairs were empty at dinner,' Albert Grey recorded. 'H.R.H. was the first to go and a suspicious smell of eau de Cologne outside his cabin told the tale.' On recovery he was persuaded by Beresford to go up on deck and join the others, who were being weighed. Apart from Beresford himself very few of them were less than eleven stone. The Prince turned the scales at fourteen stone twelve pounds—which made Grey wonder how he would stand up to the heat of India.

At Cairo the Prince seemed rather less dispirited. He went out of his way to call upon the widow of a former French Ambassador to London whom he had met and liked when he was a boy—a fat, old, deaf lady whose conversation 'became rather tiring in the hot weather'. And, resplendent in his new uniform of field marshal (a rank to which the Queen had raised him on her last birthday), he invested the Khedive's son with the Order of the Star of India with such 'dignity of manner and grace' that Albert Grey thought that 'every Englishman, had he been there, would have been proud of him'.

By the time the *Serapis* had entered the Red Sea on her way down to Aden, the Prince's gloom had been quite dispersed. 'His temper is most amiable,' Grey wrote home. 'He sits mopping away as we steam along with the thermometer at 88 on the bridge at midnight, not complaining like the others of the discomfort of the heat—but congratulating himself as he throws away one wet handkerchief after another—"What a capital thing is a good wholesome sweat!"' He even found the energy to play deck tennis.

On the eve of the Prince's thirty-fourth birthday, 8 November 1875, 'to the tune of much gunpowder and brass bands', the *Serapis* entered Bombay harbour between two lines of English battleships. The Prince stood on the bridge, acknowledging the cheers and bowing to each ship as he glided past it. He was met by the Viceroy, Lord Northbrook, by numerous less exalted officials and by about seventy Indian princes and their attendants. Also there to greet him were two one-armed British officers, Major General Sir Sam Browne V.C., inventor of the sword-belt, who was to take charge of the transport of the royal party, and Major Edward Bradford, the 'head of the secret police in India', who was to be responsible for its security.

Bradford insisted that the Prince must never be allowed to walk anywhere on his own and that at night at least one member of his suite must sit on guard outside his bedroom or tent. Unsure of the reception likely to be accorded him, the police were already keeping various possible trouble-makers under surveillance and had imposed a censorship on some Indian journals. In fact there was no need for such precautions. A few derogatory comments did appear in the Indian press; one paper was published with black mourning bands round the edges of its pages; and a farce, *Gayadananda*, in which the Prince appeared in a particularly ludicrous light, was suppressed after a few performances. But, on the whole, the Indians were to accord the Prince a friendly reception and to make him feel welcome.

Large crowds cheered his progress from the Bombay docks to Government House and energetically waved banners on which were written such friendly mottoes as 'Tell Mama We're Happy'. *The Times* reported a few days later:

There can no longer be any doubt of the extraordinary effect which the visit of the Prince of Wales has produced in India. From the moment the Prince set foot on the shores of India there has been one continuous demonstration, surpassing all that could be expected or imagined of an Asiatic people. It was not only the Princes and Chiefs who assembled to welcome him, but the whole population of Bombay swarmed along the road, and as the royal procession slowly made its way through the dense masses which rose from the ground to the housetops . . . a welcome was given such as an Indian city has seldom seen.

From Bombay the Prince went on to Poona and Baroda, then to Goa and Ceylon, Madras and Calcutta. After Christmas at Barrackpore, he travelled northeast to Lucknow. He went to Delhi in January, then north again to Lahore, then on to Agra, Jaipur and Nepal. He reviewed parades of native troops; he inspected buildings and railways, coffee and cocoa mills; he visited prisons and the palaces of princes; he attended firework displays and banquets; held durbars, receptions and levees; he watched army manoeuvres and led his own regiment, the Tenth Hussars, in a simulated cavalry charge. He presided at a chapter of the Star of India and admitted several princes to the Order. At Benares he inspected the Maharajah's palace where the sofa on which he sat was afterwards pointed out to visitors with great reverence. 'A broad space (half the sofa) was covered carefully with tissue paper,' Grey noted in his journal, 'and thus the impress of the royal and broad seat of H.R.H. is ever hereafter to be preserved as a holy and sacred relic.'

At Kandy, so the correspondent of the *Times of India* reported, he 'seemed highly pleased with the novel, splendid and peculiar' calvacade which was presented for his entertainment.

First came about thirty men in rich dress beating the tom-tom and blowing (for it cannot be called playing) a sort of squealing, ivory-necked pipe. These were followed by forty elephants, not painted (as at Baroda) but richly caparisoned in cloth of gold or other equally brilliant covering. On every elephant were men waving fans and banners, and each animal also bore a richly decorated howdah which contained the arms and other relics of the gods . . . As each elephant approached the Prince it was made to do obeisance either by kneeling or crouching which His Royal Highness rewarded by feeding the monsters with sugar cane . . . At intervals were dancers, who, though they looked very much like women, were, I am assured, men.

They all wore bells and bangles; some sang 'strange, weird' songs; others turned somersaults; a few were covered with bright steel armour and wore 'helmets with faces of devils'.

At Delhi, Albert Grey recorded, 'a vast crowd of mingled races were herded in silent expectation . . . on the magnificent mountain of stairs [which] approached the gate of the mosque . . . At the Prince's approach they all arose at the same moment as if by instinct . . . like a flight of birds.'

The day before he arrived in Madras, readers of the *Native Public Opinion* were advised:

The advent of the Prince is an important event, and it is one which must be celebrated with rejoicings by all classes. The distinction between the conquering and the conquered must be forgotten *at least* for the time being . . . Our complexions, costumes, manners, usages and religions are different. We have yet one thing in common . . . We are all *free-born British subjects*.

The rather admonitory tone of the article was unnecessary. The Prince's welcome in Madras was unrestrained, the enthusiasm of the people 'past all description'. The *Madras Mail* reported:

He appears in evening dress to even better advantage than in his field marshal's uniform. He has grown stout of late years, and looks therefore somewhat older than thirty-four, especially as, like his father, he is threatened with premature baldness. But his face is his fortune. He has a winning smile that delights both sexes and all classes . . . It is gratifying to see how much the natives of high rank have been struck by what they rightly call his affable manner.

His suite were equally pleased with him. 'His health, courage, spirit, tact and power of memory have been wonderful,' Lord Carrington wrote home. 'He has proved himself a man in 100,000 . . . He wins golden opinions wherever he goes.' He 'is always so kind and thoughtful', Lady Frere assured Albert Grey's mother; while Grey himself wrote:

> Everyone here is fascinated with H.R.H. . . . and his amiable man-
> ners . . . ; both natives and Europeans comparing him with the Duke of
> Edinburgh [who had visited India a few years before] and Lord North-
> brook in a manner that is by no means favourable to these last . . . He is
> never idle for a moment and [exists] on a small allowance of sleep that
> would make children of many men . . . Everything he has had to do, he
> has done with such courtly dignity that he has at all times commanded
> the respect at the same time that he has enlisted the affection of those
> present . . . He is *most particular* in always being most civil to those
> whom he hears are deserving of notice from the trouble they have taken
> on his behalf . . . He gives them all a few kind words of thanks coupled
> with a little offering as a keepsake.

There was, however, a problem with these presents which—as had been feared in England—were far less valuable than those he received in return. Indeed, the idea was generally prevalent that the Prince's gifts were 'inadequate and of deficient value'. But when the Prince's suite mentioned this to the Viceroy, he 'disagreed altogether', maintaining that 'the value of the presents received by the Prince would not exceed much over £40,000' and that the value of the presents given by him would amount to the same figure. 'Of course,' Grey commented, 'a Viceroy's statement should be accepted as final . . . and he will be in the House of Lords next session to support his statement . . . yet at Madras [alone] the value of presents given *to* H.R.H. —£20,000 [while] those given *by* H.R.H.—£8,000.'

The Prince was not to blame for this. But he *was* culpable, Grey had to admit, in paying insufficient attention to the susceptibilities of Europeans who clung to the 'dignity of precedence' with 'a rigidness almost inconceivable to the home-confined Englishman'. The wife of the Collector, for example, was 'a bigger swell' than the wife of the Deputy Collector, since every woman ranked in life 'according to the salary and position of her husband'.

> The head woman therefore thinks [Grey noted in his journal]—and
> her whole training has made it part of her creed which she thoroughly
> believes in—that if any woman in the station in which she reigns supreme
> is to receive any honour, undoubtedly and assuredly it is to be she. Ac-
> cordingly when the Prince came to India every old Commissioner's wife
> assured herself that—[even if she looked] like a housekeeper—she would
> be the woman who could boast hereafter of having valsed with the

Prince. The Prince comes. He opens the ball with a duty dance—that done, in his opinion, duty has been done, too. Conversation with local bosses all day has not made him particularly anxious to continue conversation with local bosses' wives, particularly as they look frumpy and dull. His eyes search round for youth, a sparkling eye, a laughing mouth and a merry face, and not finding them in the Commissioner's wife, he at last discovers them in the wife of the Commissioner's underling, Jones, the junior clerk. Mrs Jones becomes famous for the evening by the royal attention bestowed upon her, and wins a short-lived position of envy, to be hated ever hereafter by the Commissioner's wife. And this perhaps is the reason why poor honest Jones, who besides being pitied most unrighteously for having so giddy and fast a wife, is retarded in obtaining his promotion, and lingers on on small pay long after his bachelor contemporaries are comfortably provided for.

Grey said that he had heard 'cries of protest from the mighty' in Benares, Lucknow, Delhi and—loudest of all—in Calcutta, where society was particularly angry with his Royal Highness and, Grey was 'sorry to say, not without reason'. His hostess there, Lady Clarke, had invited 'all the Calcutta swells who were pining for royal notice . . . so the dinner was more official than private. Calcutta appreciated this fact, not so the Prince,' who asked that the comedian, Charles Mathews, who was appearing there in the farce, *My Awful Dad*, should be asked to join the party with his wife after dinner. Mathews left the theatre in the middle of the performance, explaining that the abrupt termination of the piece was 'inevitable in consequence of a royal command'. And soon afterwards, he arrived at Lady Clarke's with his pretty wife, Lizzie, who had been an actress at Burton's Theatre, New York. The Prince immediately retired 'with Mrs Mathews to the verandah and sat there chaffing and smoking cigarettes from directly after dinner until 2 a.m.—the official Indignants kicking their feet in impatient and envious rage, not thinking it respectful to go before the Prince. Calcutta was furious at this.'

Fortunately there were no more than hints about the Prince's neglect of his social duties in the newspapers, and he continued to enjoy his tour with undiminished zest. He wrote rather boring letters to his mother, and more lively, ill-spelled ones to his sons, telling them of the maddening jungle leeches which 'climb up your legs and bight you' and of the fights between wild animals which were staged for his entertainment, making these sound far less unpleasant than most European spectators found them. His former gloom now quite dispelled, he was unfailingly cheerful and tirelessly energetic, showing less susceptibility to the heat and sun, according to Bartle Frere, than any member of his suite, yet causing constant anxiety to the Queen, who, convinced that he was overdoing things, dispatched telegram after telegram urging him to take more care of himself.

As those who knew him might well have predicted, to no activity did he bring more zest than big-game hunting. He killed wild pigs and cheetahs, black bucks, elephants, jackals, bears and several tigers, two of them over ten feet long. One day in Nepal, in a forest where the local ruler had assembled 10,000 men to act as servants and beaters, he shot six tigers from the vantage of a howdah, some of them 'very savage', so he told his sons, and two of them man-eaters. On another occasion he 'shot an elephant and wounded severely two others', he announced by telegraph to the Queen. He thought at first that he had also killed one of the wounded ones which fell to the ground. He cut its tail off, as custom required, while Lord Charles Beresford danced a hornpipe on its back; but it suddenly 'rose majestically and stalked off into the jungle'.

The tail was taken back to England, when the *Serapis* steamed out of Bombay on 13 March, together with an extraordinary variety of other trophies including seven leopards, five tigers, four elephants, a Himalayan bear, a cheetah, two antelopes, two tragopans, three ostriches, an uncertain number of heads which Mr Bartlett was kept busy stuffing, skins and horns, orchids and other rare plants, countless presents from Indian princes—precious stones, necklaces, anklets, gold bangles, carpets, shawls, teapots, cups and ancient guns—a Madras cook, expert in the preparation of curry, two Indian officers as additional aides-de-camp, and, for the Queen, a copy of her *Leaves from the Journal of My Life in the Highlands* translated into Hindustani with covers of inlaid marble.

The Prince's tour, Sir Bartle Frere assured the Queen, had however borne fruits far more valuable than these. The Prince, who had behaved perfectly throughout—and was warmly commended by Lord Salisbury—had succeeded in winning the affection and regard of the ordinary people of India as well as the respect of the princes. He had made an impression of 'manly vigour and power of endurance' and had encouraged Indians to believe that he stood to them in the same relationship as that in which he stood to the British.

The Times confirmed:

If there were any doubts as to the success of the visit these have been completely dissipated, and even those who are least disposed to attach much importance to courtly vanities recognise that in the particular circumstances of India, and having regard to the character of its princes and people, the visit of the heir of the British crown is likely to prove a great political event.

It certainly had one good result. What struck the Prince 'most forcibly', he told his mother, was the 'rude and rough manner with which the English "political officers"' treated the native chiefs. The system was much to be deplored, for Indians of all classes would be more attached to the British if they were 'treated with kindness and with firmness at the same time, but not with brutality or contempt'. 'Because a man has a black face and a different religion from our own,' he added in a letter to the Foreign Secretary, 'there is no reason why he should be treated as a brute.' And to Lord Salisbury, he later strongly protested about the 'disgraceful habit of officers . . . speaking of the inhabitants of India, many of them sprung from the great races, as "niggers" '.

The Prince's protests were not unavailing. Instructions were sent out to check the arrogance of those army officers and civil servants whose attitude towards Indians the Prince deplored; and one of them, the Resident in Hyderabad, was recalled 'in consequence of his offensive behaviour to princes and people'. Some years afterwards the new Viceroy's efforts to maintain a more sympathetic attitude towards the people of India by British officials was, so Lord Salisbury commented ironically, attributed to the 'malign influence of the Prince of Wales'.

The Queen warmly supported the Prince on this issue, but while he was on his way home another issue came between them and threatened to drive them apart once again. This was the Royal Titles Bill which passed its third reading in the House of Commons on 7 April and proposed to confer on the Queen the additional title of Empress of India. Neither his mother nor the government had troubled to let the Prince know of this measure; and, 'as the Queen's eldest son', he felt he had 'some right to feel annoyed' that the first intimation he had had of the subject should have come from a column in a newspaper. When the Prime Minister made the lame excuse that he did not know the Prince's address and endeavoured to placate him by suggesting that he might receive an additional title himself such as Prince Imperial of India, he brusquely replied that he was quite content with the titles he already possessed. And although he readily accepted the apologies offered him; although he assured his mother that on his return to England he had 'not the slightest wish but to receive Mr Disraeli in the kindest manner possible'; and although subsequently—without complaint—he assumed the title of Emperor of India himself, the slight to which he had been subjected rankled with him to such an extent that on his mother's death he initialled documents 'E.R.' rather than follow the example of the Queen, who had written 'V.R.I.' There was, however, another matter on his mind at the moment far more disturbing than this.

10

Exclusion

The Prince of Wales has no right to meddle and never has done so before.

Some weeks before his return to England, while in camp on the Sardah River, the Prince learned that his friend Lord Aylesford had received a short letter from his wife announcing her intention of eloping with the Duke of Marlborough's eldest son, the Marquess of Blandford. It transpired that the Marquess had, with Lady Aylesford's 'knowledge and sanction', obtained a key to her house where he had 'passed many nights with her.'

On hearing of his wife's intentions Lord Aylesford had left for England immediately, 'broken hearted at the disgrace', according to Lord Carrington, but comforted by the Prince's sympathy and his outspoken denunciation of Blandford as 'the greatest blackguard alive'.

It was natural that the Prince should support his friend. But Aylesford, though he had written perfectly friendly letters to his wife from India, had long since ceased to display much affection for her; and his mother, so the Duke of Marlborough was informed, seemed 'to impute some at least of the blame to her son'. His reputation according to Lady Aylesford's brother, Owen Williams, was most 'unsavoury'.

Lord Blandford's reputation, in fact, was not much better. His sister-in-law, Lady Randolph Churchill, considered him 'worthless'; while Churchill himself, though he came to his elder brother's defence at once, reached the conclusion before the affair was over that Blandford, clever and eloquent as he was, was nevertheless 'a horrid bore'.

On his arrival home, Lord Aylesford, who was determined to divorce his wife and was dissuaded with difficulty from challenging his rival to a duel, let it be known in society exactly what the Prince of Wales's opinion of Blandford was. Provoked by these reports, Lord Randolph insisted that the Prince was nothing but a hypocrite: he had known all about his brother's love for Lady Aylesford but this had not prevented him from issuing a pressing invitation to Lord Aylesford to accompany him on the Indian tour despite Lady Aylesford's pleas that her husband should stay behind for fear of what she might be tempted to do in his absence. Lady Aylesford, in fact, had offered no objection to her husband's accompanying the Prince but was now alarmed by the consequences of her passion for Blandford and recoiled from the prospect of a scandalous divorce. So she gave Blandford a bundle of extremely imprudent letters, 'containing improper proposals', which she had received from the Prince of Wales when he himself had been flirting with her in a relatively light-hearted way a few years before. Blandford, 'wildly infatuated' with Lady Aylesford, passed them on to his brother, Lord Randolph, who threatened to make them public if the Prince of Wales did not use his influence with Lord Aylesford to stop his divorce proceedings. Lord Randolph, accompanied by Lady Aylesford and Lord Alington, 'an excitable man worked on by Lady Aylesford's sisters', went so far as to call upon Princess Alexandra to warn her what would happen if the Prince refused to cooperate.

Princess Alexandra, having misheard her servant's message and consequently expecting a visit from Lady Ailesbury, was very much surprised to see Lady Aylesford enter the room and profoundly shocked to hear Lord Randolph Churchill tell her that he was 'determined by every means in his power to prevent the case coming before the public and that he had those means at his disposal' in the shape of letters of the 'most compromising character'. These letters, if published, would ensure that the Prince 'would never sit on the throne of England'.

Distressed beyond measure by this painful interview, Princess Alexandra sent for Sir William Knollys; but while she was telling him what had happened, her cousin, the Duchess of Teck, called to see her. She could not very well refuse to admit her, nor could she give the real reason for her unmistakable agitation. So she told the Duchess that her deafness had just led her to receive the notorious Lady Aylesford, and what on earth ought she to do to rectify her mistake?

'Order your carriage at once,' the Duchess advised; 'go straight to the Queen and tell her exactly what has happened. She will understand and entirely excuse you from any indiscretion. It will be in the Court Circular that you were with the Queen today and any comment will be silenced.'

Knollys agreed that this was the best course to follow; so the Princess left immediately to see the Queen, who—as she had been at the time of the Mordaunt case—was understanding and sympathetic, regretting that Alix's 'dear name' should ever 'have been mixed up with such people' and telegraphing to India to assure the Prince of Wales that she had perfect confidence in his innocence.

Innocent though the Prince may have been, 'any letter from a person in high position, written in a strain of undue familiarity and containing many foolish and somewhat stupid expressions, must, when displayed to the public,' as the Lord Chancellor wrote to Lord Hartington, 'be injurious and lowering to the writer'. The Queen, therefore, regretted that 'such a corre-spondence harmless as it [was] should be in existence'. But she did not think that the Prince need delay his homecoming—as he had offered to do—since it was to be hoped that there was no prospect 'of a public scandal into which his name could be dragged by these villains'.

The prospect of a public scandal nonetheless continued to worry the Prince, who, outraged by Lord Randolph Churchill's unforgivable approach to the Princess, had sent Lord Charles Beresford ahead of him to England with instructions to make arrangements for a duel with pistols between the Prince and Churchill somewhere on the north coast of France. Churchill briefly, dismissively and insultingly replied that the idea of a duel between himself and the Prince of Wales was quite ridiculous and that the Prince was obviously aware of this when he issued the challenge.

Thus the matter stood when the Prince arrived home on 11 May 1876 to face rumours, which had reached the Queen's ears, that it was Lady Aylesford the Prince admired 'as Ld A. was too gt a *fool* to be really agree-able to the P. of W.' Before his arrival the Prince had written to the Princess —'a very dear letter from my Bertie', as she described it—asking her to come aboard the *Serapis* '*first* and *alone*', leaving the rest of the family at Ports-mouth where a special train would be waiting to take them all back to London. After driving home in an open carriage from the station to Marl-borough House, the Prince and Princess went out again that same evening to see a Verdi opera at Covent Garden. The Queen had advised them not to do so; but as the Prince told her, though he himself would 'infinitely' have preferred to be alone with his wife on their first evening together again, he believed it would be better, in view of all the gossip in society about the Aylesford scandal, to show themselves in public as a happy, united family. The decision was justified. The audience stood up to clap them not only before the performance began, but also at the beginning of every act and after the final curtain. 'The shouts, the cheers, the "bravos" were as vocifer-ous and long-continued as they were hearty and spontaneous,' *The Times* reported. 'The whole assembly rose; and it seemed as if the demonstrations of welcome would never cease. The Prince bowed and bowed repeatedly, till he must have been fatigued with bowing; but the cheering went on.'

The next day the Prince was told that Lord Aylesford had decided not to divorce his wife after all. He later separated from her privately, while Lady Blandford also obtained a deed of separation from her husband. The Prince was thus saved any further embarrassment. He could not, however, bring himself to forgive Lord Randolph Churchill for his behaviour during the sad affair. And Churchill, for his part, refused to make an acceptable apology to the Prince. He wrote to the Princess 'unreservedly to offer' his 'most humble and sincere apologies' if it were felt that he had been 'guilty of the slightest disrespect . . . by approaching her on so painful a subject'.

But this, he added, was 'the only apology' which circumstances warranted his offering.

Churchill, accompanied by his wife, left for a tour of the United States in July, sending beforehand a curt letter of apology which the Prince did not deign to acknowledge. And it was not until pressed to do so by the Queen and the Prime Minister that the Prince agreed to accept a more humble letter of apology drafted by the Lord Chancellor. Even then he declined to do more than send in reply a formal acknowledgement, since Churchill—who, with ostentatious irony, had signed the letter at Saratoga— had added a postscript to the effect that it was only 'as a gentleman' that he had been obliged to accept the Lord Chancellor's wording of the document.

The Prince let it be known that he would never again set foot in any house that offered hospitality to Lord and Lady Randolph Churchill; that he would not meet anyone who chose to accept invitations from them; and that, should he be forced into contact with him at court, he would merely bow to him without speaking. People who continued to entertain him in defiance of the Prince's wishes were severely reprimanded.

Churchill's father, the Duke of Marlborough, thought it advisable to withdraw his family from English life altogether; and when Disraeli suggested that he might like to go to Ireland as Viceroy, the Duke agreed to accept the appointment although the salary covered only half the expenses and he had to sell some of the contents of Blenheim to meet them.

Sorry for the Duke but implacable in his attitude towards Lord Randolph, the Prince refused to have anything to do with him for several years. In the summer of 1880 Sir Stafford Northcote, a prominent member of the Conservative Opposition, asked Lord Beaconsfield, as Benjamin Disraeli had by then become, 'whether Randolph Churchill was forgiven yet in high quarters'. Beaconsfield 'said he was all right so far as the Queen was concerned,' Northcote recorded in his diary,

> but that the Prince of Wales had not yet made it up with him; which Lord Beaconsfield thought very unfair, as Randolph [had made] an apology . . . under the full impression that the matter was to end there, but the Prince having got the apology kept up the grievance. But nothing, said the Chief, will help Randolph into favour again so much as success in Parliament. The Prince is always taken by success.

So it was not until 1883, when Lord Randolph had established himself as one of the dominant figures in the Conservative party, that the feud was settled. On 11 March that year the Prince and Princess went to dine with the Churchills at their London house; and their two little boys, Winston, aged eight, and John, aged three, were brought down before dinner to be given a present by the Prince. Three days later Lady Randolph attended a drawing-room given by the Queen; and in March 1884 it was announced that 'a full and formal reconciliation' had been effected between the Prince and Lord Randolph at a dinner given by Sir Henry James.

After the excitement of India, and the gratifying sense he had had there of doing something both pleasurable and worth while, the Prince found it more frustrating than ever on his return home to be once more relegated to performing those public engagements at schools and hospitals, exhibitions and dinners, which might just as well have been carried out by any other person in the public eye or even by some local dignitary. Dutifully he held levees, attended drawing-rooms and state concerts; and occasionally he went to the House of Lords. Once he spoke briefly in the Lords in favour of a bill to legalize marriage with a deceased wife's sister—a measure which appeared to him all the more desirable since it would enable Princess Beatrice to marry the Grand Duke of Hesse, whose wife, their sister Princess Alice, had died of diphtheria in December 1878. And another day he spoke at rather greater length, and with considerably more force, of the appalling conditions which he had witnessed in the slums of St Pancras, comparing them, rather inappropriately it was considered in some quarters, with the housing provided for his own work-people at Sandringham.

The expedition to St Pancras and other London slums had been undertaken at the suggestion of Lord Carrington, a fellow-member of a Royal Commission on the Housing of the Working Classes. He, Carrington and the Chief Medical Officer of Health in the Local Government Board, all of them dressed in workmen's clothes, had left Carrington's house in a four-wheeler escorted by a police cab. The Prince had wandered about the narrow streets, dismayed and sickened by the appalling poverty, squalor and misery to which he was introduced, the background to so many thousands of Londoners' lives. He found a shivering, half-starved woman with three ragged, torpid children lying on a heap of rags in a room bereft of furniture. Asked by her landlord where her fourth child was, she replied, 'I don't know. It went down into the court some days ago and I haven't seen it since.' Distressed by her plight, the Prince took a handful of gold coins from his pocket and would have handed them over to her had not Carrington and the doctor warned him that such a display of wealth might lead to his being attacked by the woman's neighbours.

On their way back to Marlborough House, they were joined by one of the doctor's subordinate medical officers. Not recognizing the Prince, and supposing him to be some rich man out for a morning's slumming, and evidently irritated by his reflective silence and aloof demeanour, he slapped him on the back with some such familiar jocularity as 'What do you think of that, old Buck!' The Prince 'kept his temper and behaved very well',

Carrington recorded. 'We visited some very bad places in Holborn and Clerkenwell, but we got him back safe and sound to Marlborough House in time for luncheon.'

Although the Prince was moved by this experience to speak out in favour of housing reform, his friend Lord Hartington, who was appointed Secretary of State for War in 1882, found it difficult to persuade the Prince that army reform was equally urgent. Devoted to the Duke of Cambridge, to whom all change was for the worse, the Prince found it impossible to sympathize with the reformist zeal of the Quartermaster-General, Sir Garnet Wolseley, a clever, ambitious officer who had served with distinction in China and Ashanti, had fallen foul of the Prince's friend, Sir Bartle Frere, in South Africa, and was now the Duke of Cambridge's main bugbear in London. The Prince, to whom loyalty to his friends was more a way of life than a virtue, owed his appointment as Colonel-in-Chief of the Household Cavalry to the Duke of Cambridge, who in May 1880 had at long last over-come the Queen's objection to the fulfilment of one of the Prince's principal ambitions. And the Prince, as he often protested, could scarcely be expected to do anything to upset a dear old uncle who had always been so kind to him.

The Duke of Cambridge, however, was quite unable to persuade the Queen or the government to allow the Prince to go out to Egypt in 1882 to serve with the British army which had been sent there to suppress a national-ist revolt. Exasperated by taunts that his passion for uniforms was as excessive as his dread of cannon, and that, though a field marshal, his experience of war began and ended with the Battle of Flowers at Cannes, the Prince did all he could to obtain permission to go out to join the forces in Egypt. But the Cabinet was adamant and so was the Queen, who 'conclusively' decided that it was necessary to ask him 'to abandon the idea'. So the Prince had to be content with presiding at various dinners in honour of the generals and admirals who had been allowed to fight, and with opening an exhibition of war photographs in Bond Street and a panorama of the battle of Tel-el-Kebir.

Like his efforts to be present on that battlefield, his subsequent attempts to have his old friend Valentine Baker appointed Commander-in-Chief of the new Egyptian army met with implacable opposition from the Cabinet, which followed the British public in supposing that this was an entirely inappro-priate post for an officer who, seven years before, had been sentenced to twelve months' imprisonment and dismissed from the army for his indecent activities in a railway carriage.

The disagreement with the Queen over the Prince's going out to Egypt was but one of several differences he had recently had with her. There had been trouble over his being required to relinquish his appointment as Colonel-in-Chief of the Rifle Brigade to his brother, the Duke of Connaught, when being made Colonel-in-Chief of the Household Cavalry. The Queen had asked him to say nothing about this, as she wanted to give the good news to Arthur herself; but the Prince had forestalled her by making an arrangement with his brother so that he could retain the right to wear the black buttons of the Rifle Brigade, which no true rifleman ever willingly surrenders. The Queen had been cross about this arrangement's being made without her knowledge; and the Prince had been equally cross when he had replied to her letter of remonstrance: 'I do not think that I am prone to "let the cat out of the bag" as a rule, or to betray confidences; but I own it is often with great regret that I either learn first from others or see in the newspapers, hints or facts stated with regard to members of our Family.'

The trouble was that the Queen continued to believe that he was, in fact, still far too prone to let the cat out of the bag. She had been warned by Disraeli that the Prince ought not to see confidential papers as he was still far too inclined to 'let them out and talk to his friends about them'. So that when war with Russia had appeared imminent in 1877, she had seen to it that he was shown no secret papers, though he had been at that time as strongly anti-Russian as herself, and though a key to the Cabinet boxes had been made available to Prince Leopold. He complained, without avail, to Lord Granville about the Queen's ban and further annoyed her by frequently inviting to Marlborough House and Sandringham Granville's Under-Secretary of State, Sir Charles Dilke, whose republican views had been modified since meeting the Prince in 1880 at a dinner at Lord Fife's where, so Dilke said, 'the Prince laid himself out to be pleasant, and talked to me nearly all the evening—chiefly about the Greek question and French politics', his knowledge of which, Dilke thought, suffered from believing everything he read in the *Figaro*.

Irritated as she was by the Prince's familiarity with Dilke—who, she felt sure, was being plied with hospitality in return for information he ought not to divulge—the Queen had been even more exasperated to learn that, after the defeat of the Conservatives at the General Election of March 1880 and her consequent loss of Disraeli, her son had taken it upon himself to consult his friend, Lord Hartington. The Prince, so he had informed his mother through Henry Ponsonby, had more than one 'long conversation' with Hartington, who had been '*more* anxious than ever that the Queen should send for Mr Gladstone to form a government instead of sending for Lord Granville or himself . . . Far better that she should take the initiative than that it should be forced on her.'

Infuriated that her son should presume to tell her how to act and, in particular, to advise her to appoint Gladstone—which, in the end, she had been obliged to do—the Queen had reminded him '*very shortly*' what the constitutional position was. It was, in fact, '*quite* clear': The Prince of Wales 'has *no* right to meddle and *never* has done so *before*. Lord Hartington must be told . . . that the Queen cannot allow any private and intimate communications to go on between them, or all confidence will be *impossible*.'

Even this rebuff was less severe than that delivered to the Prince in 1884 when he wrote to thank the Queen for an advance copy of her *More Leaves from a Journal of Our Life in the Highlands*, adding tactlessly that he entertained grave doubts as to the propriety of her exposing her private life to the world, meaning, in particular, her association with the tiresome gillie, John Brown. She would not agree, he knew, but he held 'very strong views on the subject', and urged her to restrict the book to private circulation. The Queen passed the letter on to her secretary with a cross note to the effect that she thought it 'very strange that objections shd come from that quarter where grt strictness of conduct [was] not generally much cared for [and where there was so] much talk and want of reticence'. As for her son's advice that she should restrict the book to private circulation, to do so would be to limit the readership to members of society, who were just the very people least qualified to appreciate it. Changing tack, the Prince again wrote to protest that, although he was well aware that the main purpose of the book was to describe her life in the Highlands, it might create surprise that the name of her eldest son never occurred in it.

To this the Queen riposted by asking if he had actually read the volume in question or asked his 'so-called friends' to do so for him. If he had been kind enough to read it himself, he would have found that his name was mentioned on pages 1, 5, 8, 331 and 378. It would have been mentioned more often, the Queen did not forbear to add, if he had come to Balmoral more frequently.

But then, as she complained on other occasions, he was far too preoccupied with the pleasures of his social round to spare much time for that. Even when her dear friend Dean Stanley died, still mourning the loss, five years before, of his beloved wife, Lady Augusta, and arrangements were made to bury him in Westminster Abbey, the Prince felt obliged to point out that on the date proposed for the funeral there was racing at Goodwood and that it would be better, therefore, if the ceremony were held a day earlier. The Queen was deeply shocked that such a consideration should have interfered with the arrangements for the funeral of a man who had earned an 'immortal name for himself', who was 'more than any Bishop or Archbishop', who had shown himself worthy both of the Prince's high regard and of his deep affection. Nor was this the only reprimand which the Queen felt compelled to administer at the time of Dean Stanley's death.

That month King Kalakaua of Hawaii was in England on an official visit; and the Prince, hoping to persuade the King that the British would be more understanding and helpful friends than the Americans, had been unremitting in his attentions to him. He escorted him to banquets, invited him to luncheon at Marlborough House and to a ball where the Princess opened the royal quadrille with him. He urged his friends to give dinners for him, insisting on his taking precedence over the Crown Prince of Germany, and rejecting the Germans' protests by observing, 'Either the brute is a king or else he is an ordinary black nigger, and if he is not a king, why is he here?' Dean Stanley's death occurred in the middle of King Kalakaua's visit, and the Prince rejected the Queen's request that he should postpone his ball at Marlborough House because of it.

Nor could the Prince be dissuaded from making such frequent trips abroad that it was sometimes suggested that he spent almost as much time on the Continent as he did at home. To be sure, many of these trips were to family weddings or funerals. In February 1881 he had gone to Berlin to the wedding of his nephew Prince William to Princess Augusta Victoria, a daughter of Duke Frederick of Schleswig-Holstein-Sonderburg-Augustenburg. The next month he was in St Petersburg attending the funeral of the Tsar Alexander II and investing his successor, Alexander III, with the Order of the Garter. Back in England for Disraeli's funeral in April, he was off again in May, this time to Vienna for the wedding of Crown Prince Rudolph and Princess Stephanie of Belgium. In March 1883, after nearly two months in Cannes—preceded, the previous summer, by several weeks at Homburg— the Prince went to Berlin for the silver wedding celebrations of the Crown Prince and Princess, then back to Homburg, then to Baden, then to Homburg again, then to the autumn manoeuvres of the Germany army which, to the Princess of Wales's distress, he watched in the uniform of a Colonel of the Fifth Pomeranian Hussars. Altogether he was away on the Continent for over two months that year, though he had to forego his usual visit to Paris because of French anger over the British intervention in Egypt. The next spring, however, he was back at Cannes faced with the melancholy task of bringing home the body of his brother, Prince Leopold, Duke of Albany, the Queen's 'dearest son', who had died of a brain haemorrhage at the Villa Nevada, having fallen down in a club. Three weeks after his brother's funeral he was in Darmstadt for the wedding of his niece, Princess Victoria of Hesse, to Prince Louis of Battenberg. He remained on the Continent for eight weeks, thankful to escape from an England in gloomy mourning for the Duke of Albany.

Although she considered that the Prince spent too much time abroad, the Queen continued to deny him the satisfaction of knowing that she fully trusted him when he was at home. She was not blind to his virtues. He was generous and affectionate, she admitted; she was very fond of him and had more than once said so. 'It gives me such pleasure to hear you speak so lovingly of dear Bertie,' she had once written to his sister Victoria, 'for he deserves it. He is such a good kind brother—a very loving son and true friend—and so kind to all below him, for which he is universally loved—which poor Affie [the Duke of Edinburgh] is not at all, either by high or low.' Similarly, in the autumn of 1887, she praised his good nature in her journal after a visit he had made to Balmoral—'a most pleasant visit which I think he enjoyed and said so repeatedly . . . He is so kind and affectionate that it is a pleasure to be a little quietly together.'

Yet in dealing with delicate affairs of state his judgement was not to be relied upon, so that whenever he offered to perform some important public duty he was more likely than not to be told that he was disqualified either by his rank, his inexperience, or his lack of the particular natural talents required. In 1870, for instance, his proposal to act as mediator between France and Prussia had elicited the dispiriting response that his position would make it quite impossible for him to undertake the mission even if he were 'personally fitted for such a very difficult task'. And he certainly was not fitted, in the Queen's opinion. He was still far too indiscreet and impressionable.

The Queen was not alone in considering him so. Both Lord Granville and Lord Hartington thought so, too. And in 1885 Charles Hardinge, at that time Third Secretary at the British Embassy in Berlin, was 'shocked by the indiscreet language of the Prince of Wales to the Russian military attaché in the hearing of a crowd of diplomatists'. Charles Dilke, commenting on his impressionability, and of his being 'a good deal under the influence of the last person who [talked] to him', said of him,

> He is very sharp in a way . . . with more sense and more usage of the modern world than his mother, whose long retirement has cut her off from that world, but less real brain power . . . It is worth talking seriously to the Prince. One seems to make no impression at the time . . . for he seems not to listen and to talk incessantly except when he is digesting [his food] . . . but he does listen all the same, and afterwards, when he is talking to somebody else, brings out everything you have said.

Dilke himself never found it too difficult to change the Prince's mind. When, for instance, work began on a Channel tunnel in 1881, the Prince was most enthusiastic and inspected the early workings near Dover. But Dilke persuaded him that the proposed tunnel might endanger the safety of the country in time of war, and the Prince was soon as strongly opposed to the idea as he had previously been in favour of it.

Denied the Queen's confidence, the Prince complained in vain about the continuing ban on important information being supplied to him. 'Needless to say' he was 'kept in perfect ignorance as to what [was] going on,' he wrote resentfully when trouble in Afghanistan almost led to war between Russia and England in the spring of 1885. His position was much the same as it had been ten years before when he had been left completely in the dark about the intention to proclaim the Queen Empress of India. He had been certain on that occasion, so he told Disraeli, 'that in no other country in the world would the next Heir to the Throne have been treated under similar circumstances in such a manner'. The Prime Minister sympathized with the Prince's attitude. 'He certainly has great quickness of perception and a happy knack of always saying the right thing,' Gladstone told Edward Hamilton in April 1885. 'He would make an excellent sovereign. He is far more fitted for that high place than her present Majesty now is. He would see both sides. He would always be open to argument. He would never domineer or dictate.' But, as Hamilton said, Gladstone did not like to act behind the Queen's back in releasing information to him. Francis Knollys told Hamilton that Disraeli had occasionally let the Prince have 'tit bits of Cabinet secrets'. So as to keep on good terms with both his sovereign and the heir apparent, he had, however, done so without telling the Queen, who subsequently declined to believe that Disraeli had 'ever made such communications'. And, as Hamilton had to admit, Disraeli 'could do a good many things connected with the Queen which Mr Gladstone could not do and certainly would not do'.

So it was not until 1886, when his friend Rosebery became Foreign Secretary, that the Prince received copies of various secret Foreign Office dispatches. Even then, Rosebery acted on his own initiative without the Queen's specific authority. Indeed, it was not until 1892 that the Prince was at last given the Prince Consort's gold key which opened the Foreign Office boxes and received from the Prime Minister's private secretary reports of Cabinet meetings of much the same character as those that were sent to the sovereign.

But the Queen still refused to allow him to exercise any real authority. Thus, in September 1896, when the Tsar came to Balmoral for important conversations with the Queen and Lord Salisbury, the Prince had been 'so anxious,' as he told the Queen's private secretary, Sir Arthur Bigge, 'that the arrival should be marked with every possible compliment' that he had returned from Homburg to supervise personally all the arrangements for the visit. He had stood on the dockside at Leith to welcome the Tsar to Scotland in the pouring rain and had put himself out, as the Queen's lady-in-waiting, Lady Lytton, said, to be 'very nice to everyone . . . and the greatest help all the time'. But he had not been invited to join any of the conversations.

Even his repeated attempts to give advice on diplomatic and other appointments were as likely as ever to be ignored. In 1896, for instance, his nominee for the appointment of British Minister in Stockholm was not only rejected in favour of another man but he was not even told to whom the post had been given. His views on a suitable successor to Sir Edward Malet as Ambassador in Berlin were not so much as sounded, while his proposal that Lord Pembroke should be promoted Lord Chamberlain was followed almost immediately by the appointment to that post of the Earl of Hopetoun.

He was no more influential with regard to appointments to the Cabinet. He was not the slightest use to the Queen, he unhappily told Francis Knollys when Gladstone was forming his last administration. Everything he said or did was 'pooh-poohed'; his sisters and brothers were 'much more listened to' than he was.

Yet when he was given work to do, he showed that he could offer more than charm, tact, influence and a wide range of acquaintance. In the first place he was an excellent organizer, as he had shown in a minor way at an appallingly haphazard City ball held in honour of the Sultan of Turkey in 1867.

It was enormously overcrowded and the authorities were quite ignorant of West End ways [reported Henry Ponsonby, normally no great admirer of the Prince]. At the chief supper Lord Raglan was not included [although he was] the lord-in-waiting representing the Queen with the Sultan. Raglan gave it to one of the aldermen pretty freely afterwards. The Duke of Beaufort tried to get in. They wouldn't let him in—another row. On the dais they tried [unsuccessfully] to clear a place for dancing. The Duke of Beaufort saw Djemil Bey struggling with a policeman—he remonstrated with an alderman who was giving the order and at last Djemil Bey was allowed in. Immediately afterwards came Apponyi. Beaufort said, 'You must let *him* in.' Alderman wouldn't, at last did sulkily and said, 'There you'd better take my place and do duty here.' 'If I did,' said the Duke, 'my first duty would be to throw you out.' So you see the amenities were numerous . . . Of course, the Lord Mayor read an interminable address. The Sultan then spoke . . . in Turkish, and Musurus [the Turkish Ambassador] read [a speech] in fearful English. If it had not been for the Prince of Wales the civic authorities would have done all sorts of absurdities, but he kept them in order very well indeed.

The Prince's tact and organizational abilities were given more scope at the time of the Queen's Golden Jubilee, when he was allowed to supervise the ceremonial details and the reception of the numerous foreign representatives. His talent for organization was equally appreciated that year, during the preparations for the Colonies and India Exhibition, as his chairmanship of the Executive Council of the Royal College of Music had been in 1883. 'He makes an excellent chairman,' Edward Hamilton had noted in his journal then, 'businesslike, sensible and pleasant.' Also, while still inclined to lose interest in projects which ran into complicated difficulties or public apathy, he was much more conscientious than he had been in the past. As he had been abroad so often in 1884 he managed to attend no more than nineteen of the fifty-one meetings of the Royal Commission on the Housing of the Working Classes. But when in December 1892 he was asked to serve on a Royal Commission on the Aged Poor he accepted immediately, abandoned his usual visit to the South of France the next year, and missed few of the Commission's sessions. He informed his son, without complaint, that he didn't think he had ever been so busy in his life and impressed James Stuart, a radical fellow-member of the Commission, not only by his regular attendance at the proceedings—during which he doodled Union Jacks with red and blue pencils as he listened to the evidence—but also by asking 'very good questions'. 'I thought at first that he had probably been prompted to these,' Stuart recalled in his *Reminiscences*, 'but I soon found out that they were of his own initiative, and that he really had a very considerable grasp of the subjects he dealt with.'

Yet the opportunities allowed the Prince to demonstrate these capabilities were very few. He rarely made a direct protest to the Queen, although remarks about other heirs, such as Crown Prince Rudolph of Austria's being treated 'almost like a boy by his Parents', were, no doubt, intended to convey allusions to his own predicament. He knew from experience how stubborn his mother could be, and was consequently disinclined to approach her again after an initial rebuff unless he could do so at Balmoral, where she was 'always in a better way'. Elsewhere her wrathful displeasure was too high a price to pay for offending her. Baron von Eckardstein, the German diplomat, recalled how, owing to the Kaiser's insistence that they finish a race at Cowes which had been interrupted by the wind suddenly dropping, they had all arrived at Osborne late for dinner. The Kaiser unconcernedly apologized; but the Prince 'took cover for a moment behind a pillar, wiping the sweat from his forehead before he could summon up courage enough to come forward and make his bow. The Queen only gave him a stiff nod, and he retreated behind the pillar again.' Everyone was afraid of his mother, the Prince once told Margot Asquith 'with a charming smile', everyone 'with the exception of John Brown'. Henry Ponsonby agreed with him, but added, as the only other exception, Napoleon III's son, the Prince Imperial. Nevertheless, the Prince did occasionally defy the Queen, as when, for instance, he acted as pall-bearer at Gladstone's funeral. What advice had he taken? the Queen wanted to know. And what precedent had he followed for doing such a thing? The Prince replied that he had not taken any advice and knew of no precedent.

Also, towards the end of the Queen's life, the Prince did sometimes persuade her to change her mind on matters of little importance. She reluctantly allowed him to receive the salute at her birthday parade on the retirement as Commander-in-Chief of her cousin, the Duke of Cambridge, who had formerly represented her. Also, after assuring her son that her decision against it was final, she eventually gave way to his suggestion that the Kaiser—who had delighted him by giving him a commission in the Prussian Dragoon Guards—should be granted an honorary colonelcy in a British regiment since it was well worth while paying a reciprocal compliment to the 'finest army in the world'. But when, two years later, the Prince was so incensed by the Kaiser's congratulatory telegram to President Kruger on the failure of Dr Jameson's raid into the Transvaal that he proposed 'a good snubbing', she rebuked him sternly. 'Those sharp, cutting answers and remarks only irritate and do harm, which one is sorry for,' the Prince was informed. 'Passion should be carefully guarded against. [The Kaiser's] faults come from impulsiveness, as well as conceit. Calmness and firmness are the most powerful weapons in such cases.'

And calmness and firmness, she made it clear, were not to be expected of the Prince.

11

'Other Ladies'

Suddenly I saw him looking at me in a way all women understand.

If the relationship between the Queen and the Prince of Wales continued to be imperfect, all differences between her and the Princess were now forgotten. They had come close together at the time of the Prince's illness; and, after the death of Princess Alice, the Prince's favourite sister, when 'dear Alix' proved to be a 'real devoted sympathizing daughter' to the Queen, they remained deeply attached to each other up till the day the Queen herself died.

The Princess was much affected by her mother-in-law's death. She was the only woman seen to be in tears at the private funeral service at Frogmore. And afterwards she told Lady Downe how sad and strange Windsor Castle seemed without her: 'I feel as if she were only gone abroad and I keeping house for her in her absence.'

The relationship between the Princess and her husband was more difficult to understand. Lady Antrim, who knew her well, thought that if she had loved him as much as he loved her he would have been more faithful to her. No one doubted, though, that she did love him. 'I miss my little Man terribly,' she told Lady Downe when he was abroad after the Mordaunt divorce case; and it was obvious that, although her children came first in her life, she did miss him terribly. It was obvious, too, that despite his affairs and many intimate female friendships, he loved her in return. 'After all,' she said of him when he was dead, 'he always loved me the best.'

He seems, all the same, never to have found her particularly attractive sexually. Perhaps no man did so, not even Oliver Montagu, for she was evidently not in the least a sensual woman. She inspired admiration, respect, and, usually, affection in almost everyone who knew her, but never the passion aroused by those whom Lord Carrington referred to as 'the Prince's other ladies'. 'Every time one sees her,' wrote Edward Hamilton soon after her thirty-ninth birthday, 'one is more struck by her refined beauty and her extraordinarily youthful appearance.' Such comments were commonplace.

So were tributes to her still 'lovely figure' and 'straight back', 'her fresh red lips which were never painted and always moist', her gaiety, her sense of fun and of the ridiculous. Charming stories were told of her suddenly exploding with irresistible laughter as, for instance, she did in St Petersburg when the Prince entered the Throne Room of the Anitchoff Palace followed by five members of his staff, solemnly bearing on velvet cushions the insignia for the Tsar's installation as a Knight of the Garter and looking 'exactly like a row of wet-nurses carrying babies'. There was also that well-remembered occasion when, having asked Tennyson to read aloud the *Ode of Welcome* which he had written for her wedding, she could not contain her laughter, which proved so infectious that soon Tennyson, too, was laughing helplessly and dropped the book on the floor. Yet, even when romping about at Sandringham, making rather childish jokes, squirting her son with a soda-water syphon, or trying on everyone else's shoes on the dance floor at Chatsworth, she never lost her poise and dignity. As Lady Frederick Cavendish said, she could gather up her stateliness at any moment.

Extravagantly generous with her money, handing out cheques and cash to anyone who seemed in need of help, or pressing a pair of gold cuff-links into the hand of an unhappy-looking footman, she was not in the least discriminating, giving her nieces presents which were nearly always 'inappropriate'. Often thoughtless, sometimes obstinate and always unpredictable, she could also be distressingly inconsiderate, particularly to her maids of honour, most of whom had cause to feel at some time during their service that the Princess paid little heed to their own welfare, and one of whom was seen to receive a sharp blow from her mistress's long, steel umbrella for some offence during a drive in an open carriage. Utterly unimaginative, she was also in no sense clever, although her deafness, which grew progressively worse after her illness, occasionally made her seem more stupid and less interesting than she really was, especially when she attempted to conceal it by a continuous stream of talk which allowed of no comment or reply. Her deafness also prevented her from enjoying many of those social activities in which, in company with her husband, she had formerly delighted. After the onset of middle age, they spent more and more time apart.

She never became the least bitter, though, and never displayed any jealousy she may have felt when her husband, who, in the later years of their marriage, treated her always with the greatest courtesy and respect, made it obvious to the world that he preferred the company of 'his other ladies' to that of his wife. She sometimes referred to them disparagingly. The lovely American debutante, Miss Chamberlayne—with whom Edward Hamilton, in the summer of 1884, saw the Prince 'occupying himself entirely' at a party at Mrs Allsopp's—she nicknamed 'Chamberpots'. But she was always perfectly polite to her when she met her. And when her husband, having finished flirting with 'Chamberpots', embarked upon a much more serious affair with

Mrs Edward Langtry, the Princess sensibly accepted the situation and raised no objection to his new *inamorata's* being invited to Marlborough House.

The Prince had first met Lillie Langtry on 24 May 1877 while the Princess was in Greece staying with her brother and convalescing after an illness. The meeting took place at a small supper party given especially for the purpose by the Arctic explorer, Captain Sir Allen Young, an unmarried friend of the Prince who had a house in Stratford Place. The Prince was immediately captivated by the tall, graceful, glowingly voluptuous woman who had recently established herself as one of the most celebrated and sought-after beauties in London. The daughter of the Revd William Le Breton, Dean of Jersey, she had been married three years before, at the age of twenty-one, to Edward Langtry, a widower of twenty-six whose family had made money as shipowners in Belfast and whose yacht, his bride later confessed, interested her more than its owner. Edward Langtry was, indeed, a rather nondescript character, kind and amiable but indecisive and suggestible, the victim of moods of deep despondency—no match, in their frequent differences, for his wilful and determined wife. Persuaded to move to London he set up house in Eaton Place where, though he had sold his yacht, his income was insufficient for the kind of life his wife proposed to lead. He was like a fish out of water, Mrs Langtry said; and consoled himself by drinking while she set about making their entry into society.

She experienced no difficulty in doing so. Helped by Lord Ranelagh, whom she had met occasionally in Jersey, where he had a house, the Langtrys were soon introduced into the kind of drawing-rooms where she wished to be seen and where her beauty, her confident bearing and her deliciously proportioned body could not fail to be admired. Lord Randolph Churchill met her at Lord Wharncliffe's and told his wife, 'took in to dinner a Mrs Langtry, a most beautiful creature, quite unknown, very poor, and they say has but one black dress'.

Within a few months Mrs Langtry was quite unknown no longer. She was painted by Millais and Edward Poynter, by Whistler and Edward Burne-Jones, one of whose portraits of her was bought by the young Arthur Balfour. Photographs of her were to be seen everywhere. And, once her intimate friendship with the Prince of Wales became common knowledge, crowds gathered to stare at her whenever she went shopping or rode in the park on a horse which had been given to her by another admirer, Moreton Frewen. 'It became risky for me to indulge in a walk,' she recalled with pride. 'People ran after me in droves, staring me out of countenance and even lifting my sunshade to satisfy their curiosity.' The young Margot Tennant saw 'great and conventional ladies like old Lady Cadogan and others standing on iron chairs in the park to see Mrs Langtry walk past'.

The Prince took no trouble to disguise his love for her. He let it be known that he would like her invited to certain country houses where he was going for the week-end; he took her to Paris where he was reported to have kissed her on the dance floor at Maxim's; he was often to be seen with her at Ascot; he arranged for both her and her husband to be presented to the Queen. She became, in fact, almost *maîtresse en titre;* and felt quite secure in that position even when Sarah Bernhardt, with whom the Prince often dined in Paris, came to London in 1879 and was invited to Marlborough House. 'London has gone mad over the principal actress in the Comédie Française who is here, Sarah Bernhardt—a woman of notorious, shameless character,' wrote Lady Frederick Cavendish disapprovingly in her diary. 'Not content with being run after on the stage, this woman is asked into people's houses to act, and even to luncheon and dinner; and all the world goes. It is an outrageous scandal!'

The Prince himself once arranged for a supper to be given for her by the Duc d'Aumâle 'at which all the other ladies present . . . had been invited at [his] request.' But it was 'one thing to get them to go,' observed Charles Dilke, one of the male guests, 'and another thing to get them to talk when they were there; and the result was that, as they would not talk to Sarah Bernhardt and she would not talk to them, and as the Duc d'Aumâle was deaf and disinclined to make a conversation on his own account, nobody talked at all . . .'

Other evenings arranged by the Prince for Sarah Bernhardt were, however, more entertaining than this. And after one summons to Marlborough House she sent a note to the manager of her company: 'I've just come back from the P. of W. It is twenty past one . . . The P. has kept me since eleven.'

When asked what exactly was the relationship between the Prince and Sarah Bernhardt, her granddaughter replied, 'They were the best of friends.' Others supposed them to be occasionally lovers as well. But, in any case, Mrs Langtry displayed no jealousy and thus retained his fond affection, so that when her alleged affairs with other men, the birth of a daughter (fathered by Prince Louis of Battenberg), rumours of her impending involvement in what the scandalous weekly magazine, *Town Talk,* referred to as 'about the warmest divorce case' ever likely to come before a judge, all contributed to Mrs Langtry's name being crossed off their invitation lists by many hostesses, the Prince did his best to save her from total ostracism.

Gladstone was induced to visit her, much to the distress of his secretary, who was already deeply concerned by his habit of walking the streets at night and talking to prostitutes. Mrs Langtry 'is evidently trying to make social capital out of the acquaintance,' Edward Hamilton wrote in his diary after Gladstone had presented her with a copy of his 'pet book', *Sister Dora.* 'Most disagreeable things with all kinds of exaggerations are being said. I took the occasion of putting in a word [as Rosebery also did] and cautioning him against the wiles of the woman whose reputation is in such bad odour that, despite all the endeavours of H.R.H., nobody will receive her in their houses.' But Gladstone paid no attention. He told Mrs Langtry that she might write to him, enclosing her letters in double envelopes which, as Hamilton said, secured them from the 'rude hands' of his staff; and she made much use of this privilege.

She also made much use of the Prince's generous support when in 1881 she decided to go on the stage, appearing with a professional company at the Haymarket Theatre in *She Stoops to Conquer*. The Prince attended that performance, and praised her part in it to the actor-manager, Squire Bancroft, who agreed to let her play a leading role in a new play which he was putting on the next month. The Prince went to see this play three times, persuaded all his friends to go to see it as well, and was largely responsible for its success. Thus launched on a profitable stage career, Lillie Langtry saw less of the Prince than she had done in the past; but they remained good friends, arranged meetings when she returned from her tours in America, and wrote each other friendly letters—those from him, like most of his other letters, containing little of interest, being addressed to '*Ma Chere Amie*', 'The Fair Lily' or 'My dear Mrs Langtry' and being sent by the ordinary post.

Towards the end of the 1890s, however, these letters became more and more infrequent, for the Prince had fallen in love with someone else. For a time he had adopted 'a strange new line', according to the Duke of Cambridge, of 'taking to young girls and discarding the married women'. And Lady Geraldine Somerset, who said that he was 'more or less in love' with Mrs Francis Stonor's daughter, Julie, also spoke of two other 'reigning young ladies . . . Miss Tennant and Miss Duff'. But these girls, 'H.R.H.'s virgin band', as Edward Hamilton called them, seem to have meant little to him compared with the passion he developed, as he approached his fiftieth birthday, for the wife of Lord Brooke, heir to the cantankerous fourth Earl of Warwick.

Frances Brooke, or Daisy as she came to be called, was twenty years younger than the Prince. Strikingly good looking, intelligent, fascinating and extremely rich, she was the owner of estates worth more than £20,000 a year which she had inherited from her grandfather, the last Viscount Maynard. There had been a suggestion that she should marry Prince Leopold; but this had come to nothing, either because her mother and step-father refused the match on her behalf, as she maintained in her first book of memoirs, or because, as she contradicted herself by claiming in the second, she had already fallen in love with Lord Brooke and Prince Leopold was in love with someone else. In any case, she had married Lord Brooke at Westminster Abbey in April 1881, in the presence of the Prince and Princess of Wales. Thereafter she had settled down happily to married life with her good-natured husband, first at Carlton Gardens in London and then at Easton Lodge, the Maynard family home in Essex where, pregnancies permitting, she indulged a passion for hunting, for driving a four-in-hand and for giving house-parties. After a time, however, such pleasures proved insufficient for her; and, her husband, 'good old Brookie', being a complaisant man—who remained always devoted to his erring wife but confessed that he found 'a good day's fishing or shooting second in point of pleasure to nothing on earth'—she began to seek excitement elsewhere.

She met the Prince of Wales at a ball in 1883. But at that time, though he asked her to dance and spent a few minutes talking to her in a corridor, he seemed much more interested in Lady Randolph Churchill. Not long afterwards, however, Lady Brooke found a lover in the Prince's friend, Lord Charles Beresford, brother of the manager of the Prince's stud, Lord Marcus Beresford, and a notorious adulterer who claimed, as one of numerous escapades, to have tip-toed into a dark room in a country house, and to have leaped joyfully into what he believed to be some obliging lady's bed, only to find himself in the protesting arms of the Bishop of Chester. Beresford's was not a kindly nature. He confessed that he enjoyed making women cry, because it was 'such fun to hear their stays creak'. And he made no secret of the fact that he did not regard very highly the allurements of his wife, who was ten years older than he was and whose elaborate make-up included not only rouge and false hair but also false eyebrows one of which, mistaken for a butterfly, once came off in the hand of a child into whose pram she was foolhardy enough to poke her painted face.

Lady Charles's mettlesome husband and Lady Brooke fell passionately in love. Indeed, there was talk of elopement and divorce. But such steps, which would have placed the lovers beyond the pale of society, were fortunately never taken. For Lord Charles discovered that Lady Brooke 'was not content with his attentions alone'; while Lady Brooke found out that Lord Charles's wife was pregnant, and—the morals of Lady Charles Beresford being beyond reproach—there could be no doubt that the father was the husband.

Enraged by this evidence that her lover had not abandoned his wife's bed, Lady Brooke wrote him a letter of furious reproach which arrived at Lord Charles's house while he was abroad. His wife, who said that she had been asked to open all his correspondence during his absence, read it with horror. In it, Lady Brooke stated that he must leave home immediately and join her on the Riviera; that one of her children was his; that he had no right to beget a child by his wife, 'and more to that effect'. Other people, who read the letter later, agreed that its contents were utterly shocking; and that, as Lord Marcus Beresford commented, it 'ought never to have seen the light of day'.

When Lady Brooke heard that it had found its way into the hands of

Lady Charles and thence into those of George Lewis—a solicitor said to know more about the private lives of the aristocracy than any other man in London—she was inclined to agree with Lord Marcus's verdict. Distressed by what she had done, she turned to the Prince of Wales, trusting that his influence and hatred of scandal would enable her to extricate herself from her appalling predicament.

Since that ball in 1883, when he had been preoccupied with Lady Randolph Churchill, the Prince had entertained the Brookes at Sandringham and had stayed with them once or twice at Easton Lodge. He had been attracted to Lady Brooke, and now responded readily to her call, agreeing to see her in private at Marlborough House. 'He was more than kind,' she later wrote of the subsequent interview, 'and suddenly I saw him looking at me in a way all women understand. I knew I had won, so I asked him to tea.'

Losing no time in his eagerness to help her, the Prince of Wales, at two o'clock that morning, went to see George Lewis, who was persuaded to show him the letter. The Prince, who thought it the 'most shocking' one he had ever read, afterwards tried to persuade Lady Charles to have it handed over to him so that it could be destroyed. Lady Charles declined to hand it over. Instead, she instructed Lewis to inform Lady Brooke that if she kept away from London that season the letter would be given back to her. Lady Brooke refused to consider such a solution, so the Prince went to Lady Charles a second time and 'was anything but conciliatory in tone'. He 'even *hinted,*' so Lady Charles claimed, 'that if I did not give him up the letter, my position in society!! and Lord Charles's would become injured!!'

Whether or not the Prince did, in fact, make such a threat, he certainly made it clear to society that he was now the close, trusted and devoted friend of Lady Brooke. He saw to it that she and her husband were invited to the same houses as himself. And according to the by no means reliable recollections of his new mistress, 'when that sign of the Prince's support didn't stop the angry little cat, the Prince checked her in another way. He simply cut her name out and substituted mine for it and wrote to the hostess that he thought it would be better for me not to meet the angry woman till she had cooled off and become reasonable.'

Lord Charles, who had himself been trying to have the letter destroyed, was quite as angry with the Prince as was his wife. At the beginning of January he went to see him, warned him of the consequences of taking any further action against Lady Charles, with whom he was now reluctantly reconciled, and, as everyone who knew him would have expected, lost his temper. It seems that he furiously pushed the man who had taken over his former mistress against a sofa into which the Prince fell, murmuring, 'Really, Lord Charles, you forget yourself.'

Relieved as he must have been that, immediately after this painful scene, Lord Charles left England to go to sea again in the armoured cruiser *Un-*

daunted, the Prince's peace of mind was not restored. For another and even more disquieting problem had yet to be resolved.

In September the year before, the Prince had gone to Yorkshire for Doncaster races; but instead of staying as usual at Brantingham Thorpe with Christopher Sykes, who could no longer afford to entertain him there, he went to Tranby Croft, the country house of Arthur Wilson, a rich ship-owner. Lieutenant-Colonel Sir William Gordon Cumming, a baronet in the Scots Guards who enjoyed a private income of £80,000 a year, was also of the party. After dinner the first evening, while several of the guests, includ-ing the Prince, were playing baccarat, two of them suspected Sir William of cheating, a suspicion which had been entertained in various other houses in the past. The next night he was watched by other guests, who confirmed that he was, indeed, manipulating his counters dishonestly. Sir William was confronted with their accusation; and on the understanding that all those who knew of his conduct would 'preserve silence', he was asked to sign a document agreeing never to play cards again so long as he lived. Sir William, protesting his innocence, objected that to sign the document would be tanta-mount to an admission of guilt. But, under pressure, he did sign it; and the Prince added his signature to those of the nine other men who had played baccarat with him.

The next day the Prince left Tranby Croft for York where, on the day after that, Lord and Lady Brooke, who had been prevented from joining the party by the death of Lady Brooke's step-father, joined him at the rail-way station on their way to Abergeldie.

It was widely supposed afterwards that the Prince told the Brookes in confidence what had happened at Tranby Croft; and that Lady Brooke, known to irreverent journalists as 'the Babbling Brook', could not keep the fascinating story to herself. She denied the charge; and George Lewis, now acting for the Prince's friends, the Brookes, rather than for the out-of-favour Beresfords, was instructed to issue an announcement to the effect that pro-ceedings would be taken against anyone repeating the lie. What could not be denied, however, was that someone had revealed the Tranby Croft secret; and, hearing that this was so, Gordon Cumming told his solicitors to bring an action against his accusers. In an effort to spare the Prince the ignominy of appearing in a civil court, attempts were made to have a military court inquire privately into the affair and thus render a civil action much more difficult to bring. But the Judge Advocate-General advised that this would be unfair to Sir William; and, to the Prince's dismay, the Adjutant-General, Sir Redvers Buller, accepted that advice.

'It is enough to make the great Duke of Wellington rise from his tomb,' the Prince protested to the Duke of Cambridge, 'and point his finger of scorn at the Horse Guards . . . The conduct of the A[djutant] G[eneral] is inexplicable but he cannot have the interests of the Army at heart, acting in the way he has. I always knew he was a born soldier—and equally imagined he was a gentleman, but from henceforth I can never look upon him in the latter category.'

An attempt by the Prince and his friends to avoid a public scandal by a private inquiry at the Guards Club also failed. A civil action was, therefore, inevitable.

Waiting for it to be brought, the Prince grew more and more anxious and irritable, deciding not to go to France that year, 'not knowing what might turn up', refusing to go to Windsor unless his mother promised not to talk about baccarat, constantly talking to his friends about the impending action and asking for their advice as to what he ought to do, if anything, in the meantime. Both Lord Hartington, a recognized arbiter of social questions, and Francis Knollys were against any attempt at compromise since 'a great number of people [would] think and say that it [had] been arranged to screen the Prince of Wales'. Knollys gave it as their opinion, therefore, that it was in the Prince's interest that the action 'should be allowed to take its course'. The Queen also thought that the action ought to go ahead as, although it was 'a sad thing [that] Bertie [was] dragged into it', people thought good might come of it and it would be a 'shock to Society and to gambling'.

So the Prince could do nothing but await the trial, which he did in extreme trepidation, condemning the conduct of Gordon Cumming, who had been reported as having been seen playing baccarat in France, as 'simply scandalous throughout'. Gordon Cumming's version of the affair 'was false from beginning to end'. He did not have 'a leg to stand on and his protestations of innocence were useless'. The Prince's certainty about the man's guilt did not, however, make it any easier for him to face the prospect of the forthcoming trial with equanimity. The Princess—who loyally castigated Gordon Cumming as 'a brute', a 'vile snob' and 'a worthless creature' whom she had always thoroughly disliked and who was now behaving *'too abominably'*—said that her husband was making himself 'quite ill' with worry.

This was obvious when he appeared at last in court at the beginning of June looking tired and tense and increasingly nervous as the proceedings dragged on. He listened with evident anxiety as Sir Edward Clarke, representing Gordon Cumming, skilfully made it appear not only that his client had been unjustly condemned on bad evidence but that he was also the victim of a conspiracy to save the Prince from exposure in a public scandal. And the Prince looked dismayed as Sir Edward also maintained that he had deliberately ignored army regulations which, applying to him as a field marshal as they did to every other officer, required all cases of alleged dishonourable conduct to be submitted to the accused's superior officer.

In contrast to Gordon Cumming, who responded to all the questions asked him in a firm, clear voice, the Prince, when it came to his turn, gave his answers in so low a tone that only a few of them could be heard. This, as the editor of the *Daily News* said, caused an unfavourable impression.

There had been a murmur of disapproval in court when Gordon Cumming ostentatiously turned his back on the Prince as he took his place in the box. But the spectators generally were on Gordon Cumming's side; and when, on the seventh day of the trial—taking their cue from a four-hour summing up by the Lord Chief Justice in the defendants' favour—the jury brought in a verdict against him, there was an angry outburst of prolonged hissing.

The demonstrations in court were an accurate reflection of the feelings of the people outside, many of whom wrote to the Gordon Cumming family to express their sympathy with them. The Prince was loudly booed that month at Ascot; and the attacks upon him in the Press were quite as vituperative as they had been at the time of the Mordaunt divorce case. According to the *Review of Reviews*, the various country gentlemen whom the editor interviewed gave it as their unanimous opinion that the Prince ought to be condemned as 'a wastrel and whoremonger' as well as a gambler, it being not so much baccarat as 'the kind of life of which this was an illustration that was the cause of their disgust'.

The Queen well understood this feeling. It was not just 'this special case —though his signing the paper was wrong (and turns out to have been contrary to military regulations),' she told her eldest daughter, 'but the light which has been thrown on his habits which alarms and shocks people so much, for the example is so bad . . . The monarchy almost is in danger if he is lowered and despised.' American as well as English newspapers agreed with her. 'The scandal cannot fail to add,' the *New York Times* advised its readers, 'to the growing conviction that "royalty" is a burden to the British tax-payer for which he fails to receive any equivalent.' *The Times* ended a long article on the case on 10 June:

We profoundly regret that the Prince should have been in any way mixed up, not only in the case, but in the social circumstances which prepared the way for it. We make no comment upon his conduct towards Sir William Gordon-Cumming. He believed Sir William had cheated; he wished to save him; he wished to avoid scandal; and he asked him to sign the paper. This may have been, and probably was, a breach of military rule; but with that the public at large does not concern itself. What does concern and indeed distress the public is the discovery that the Prince should have been at the baccarat table; that the game was apparently played to please him; that it was played with his counters [a set given him by Reuben Sassoon, marked from 5s. to £10, engraved with the Prince of Wales's feathers and] specially taken down for the purpose; that his 'set' are a gambling, a baccarat-playing set . . . Sir

William Gordon-Cumming was made to sign a declaration that 'he would never touch a card again'. We almost wish, for the sake of English society in general, that we could learn that the result of this most unhappy case had been that the Prince of Wales had signed a similar declaration.

In an effort to allay these adverse comments, the government was approached with the suggestion that 'some public utterance in defence or apology for the Prince should be made'. But Lord Salisbury, who had succeeded Gladstone as Prime Minister, expressed the opinion 'very earnestly' that it was not right that any minister of the Crown should make any such pronouncement.

We may be examined as to all matters that fall within the scope of our duties [Salisbury wrote to Hartington on 16 June] but the private morals of the Prince of Wales do not come within that scope; and we ought not to be questioned about them. If we are questioned we should refuse to discuss them. There is a further question in which I understand you have interested yourself. Whether the Prince of Wales himself should make any such pronouncement . . . I confess if I had the advising of him (which I am not likely to have) I should recommend him to sit still, and avoid baccarat for six months: and at the end of that time write a letter to some indiscreet person (who would publish it) saying that at the time of the Cumming case there had been a great deal of misunderstanding as to his views: but the circumstances of that case had so convinced him of the evil that was liable to be caused by that game, that since that time he had forbidden it to be played in his presence. Such a declaration—referring to what he *had* done would suffice to deodorize him of all the unpleasant aroma which this case has left upon him and his surroundings: but nothing else would be sufficient.

The Queen suggested that an open letter, expressing the Prince's disapproval of gambling, might be written to the Archbishop of Canterbury. But the Prime Minister did not agree with this suggestion either. And when approached again by Lord Hartington on the Prince's behalf, he clung to his opinion that 'anything' in the nature of a public statement or correspondence would not be judicious. So Francis Knollys, who had just been about to leave Marlborough House to catch the 12.29 train to Chenies to see the Archbishop, stayed in London. And two months later the Prince wrote a private letter to the Archbishop expressing a rather disingenuous 'horror of gambling', gambling being a term which, as he had already made clear in conversation with him, he did not apply to a little harmless flutter by those who could afford to lose their stakes, on either cards or horse-racing, 'a manly sport' which was 'popular with Englishmen of all classes'.

Condemning the Press which had been 'very severe and cruel, because,' as he put it to his sister Victoria, 'they know I cannot defend myself', the Prince was equally displeased with the government for not protecting him from Sir Edward Clarke's attacks as Gladstone had protected him during the Mordaunt case by taking, as Knollys put it, 'all the *indirect* means in his power (and *successfully*) to prevent anything being brought out in the course of the trial that could be injurious to the Prince and the crown'. The Prince was also still angry with Sir William Gordon Cumming, a 'damned blackguard' who crowned his infamy, in the Prince's eyes, by marrying, on the very day after the trial, 'an American young lady, Miss Garner (sister to Mme de Breteuil), with money!' The Prince hoped he would never have to see the man again; and, according to Gordon Cumming's daughter, 'said that anyone who spoke to him would never be asked to Marlborough House again, also no Army or Navy Officer was to accept invitations to shoot at [Gordon Cumming's country estates] Altyre or Gordonstoun'. When he went down to Eastbourne that summer the Prince was seen to be in a 'very bad temper'.

So was Lord Charles Beresford. In his cabin aboard the *Undaunted*, letters of complaint had reached him from his wife, who, still cold-shouldered by the Prince, had been outraged to hear that the Princess had publicly received Lady Brooke at Marlborough House. The continuing humiliation was too much for her, Lady Charles announced to her husband: she would sell her house in London and go to live on the Continent.

Angrier than ever now with the Prince, Lord Charles sat down on 12 July to write a letter to him in which he told him bluntly:

> For some months I have received letters, not only from Lady Charles but from many of my friends, that you have systematically ranged yourself on the side of the other person against my wife . . . [in such an] ostentatious way . . . that some people believe [my wife] is entirely [in the] wrong . . . I have no intention of allowing my wife to suffer for any faults I may have committed in days gone by. Much less have I any intention of allowing any woman to wreak her vengeance on my wife because I would not accede to her entreaties to return to a friendship I repudiated.
>
> I consider that from the beginning by your unasked interference and subsequent action you have deliberately used your high position to insult a humbler by doing all you can to elevate the person with whom

she had a quarrel . . . The days of duelling are past, but there is a more just way of getting right done . . . and that is publicity . . . The first opportunity that occurs to me I shall give my opinion publicly of Y.R.H. and state that you have behaved like a blackguard and a coward, and that I am prepared to prove my words.

Lord Charles did not send this letter direct to the Prince of Wales, but to Lady Charles, with instructions to show it to the Prime Minister first with a warning of the 'grave events' now likely to follow unless a '*public* apology' were forthcoming. Lady Charles accordingly sent her husband's letter, together with her own detailed account of the whole business, to Lord Salisbury, who was warned not only that 'the highest legal authority' had advised her husband that he was in a position to force 'damning' publicity upon the Prince of Wales, but also that Lady Charles's sister, Mrs Gerald Paget, had prepared for publication a pamphlet which had 'already been shown, as an interesting episode in the Prince of Wales's mode of life, to several people who want to make use of the story at the next General Election for purposes of their own'.

Unwillingly dragged once again into the Prince of Wales's affairs, Lord Salisbury nevertheless at once accepted the fact that he must try to limit the reverberations of the quarrel. He urged Lady Charles not to send on her husband's letter to the Prince; and he wrote himself to Lord Charles to point out that such a letter would, 'if published', do the sender 'endless harm', since, 'according to our social laws', no gentleman must ever be the means of bringing any lady 'into disgrace because she yielded' to him. Furthermore, Lord Salisbury continued,

I do not think the letter was fair to H.R.H. So very grave a charge as that of insulting your wife should—if made at all—have been expressed in clear detail, so that H.R.H. might either show you that you were mistaken as to some matter of fact or apologise if his action had been misunderstood . . . Of course, if he actually insulted Lady Charles, there is nothing to be said in his defence; but I gather that you complain of a sudden cessation of acquaintance . . . [After the] stormy interview you had with him, in which your language to say the least was very plain, I quite understand why the Prince has fought shy of any meeting with Lady Charles. If any person had addressed you in similar language I think you would from that time forth have abstained from speaking to the third person or the third person's wife. If I may give advice . . . the acquaintance of *no* illustrious person is necessary to one's happiness . . . Your position in society is in your profession and not affected by the friendship of anyone however highly placed . . . Ill-considered publicity

would be of no possible service to Lady Charles: it would do you most
serious harm . . . I strongly advise you to . . . do nothing.

Thus warned of the harm he might do himself, and of his obligation to
protect Lady Brooke, Lord Charles agreed that his letter should not be sent
to the Prince, and that he would write instead a less inflammatory one, not
involving Lady Brooke and giving the Prince an opportunity to apologize.
But although this might have settled the matter quietly, Lord Salisbury could
not prevent the circulation that autumn of Mrs Gerald Paget's type-written
pamphlet which, under the title *Lady River*, gave details of Lady Brooke's
intimacy with the Prince and provided a copy of her letter to Lord Charles
which had precipitated the whole unpleasant affair.

Copies of this pamphlet were passed excitedly from hand to hand. According to the magazine *Truth*, it caused so much interest that hostesses who
managed to get hold of a copy had but to announce a reading from it to
find their drawing-rooms more crowded than if a dozen prima-donnas were
on the bill of fare. The Duchess of Manchester was evidently one of these
hostesses; and the Prince was so offended that he refused to talk to her for
more than ten years, being reconciled only when the Duchess's son, on meeting him by chance in Portman Square after his accession, knelt down, kissed
his hand and afterwards invited him to meet the Duchess again at dinner.

Warned by her brother-in-law, Lord Marcus, and others, that the pamphlet would do much more harm to her than to Lady Brooke, Lady Charles
sent a telegram to her husband asking him to come back to protect her. Lord
Charles had already warned Lord Salisbury that it might be imperative for
him to come home for this purpose as he was 'determined not to allow Lady
Charles to be annoyed and made unhappy in his absence by anyone no
matter how high their position'. So he packed his bags and arrived home just
before Christmas to find his wife demanding that Lady Brooke should withdraw from London for at least a year and his brother complaining of the
disgrace that was being brought upon the family name. Lord Marcus asked:

Can anything be more terrible or damning to you, to your family and
to your children, than this pamphlet being circulated high and low by
your wife and your sister-in-law? . . . You expressed no horror at the
letter being published—but you . . . utter threats about what you intend
to do against a man who has been the greatest friend to you in the world,
because people had written and told you that he says and does things
which I can swear he never has said or done.

Undeterred, Lord Charles demanded an apology from the Prince, failing
which he would 'no longer intervene to prevent these matters becoming
public'.

'I am at a loss to understand how Lady Charles can imagine that I have in any way slighted or ignored her,' the Prince protested. 'Lady Charles was invited to the garden party at Marlborough House this last summer . . . and . . . I have made a point on all occasions of shaking hands with her, or of bowing to her, as the opportunity presented.'

The reply to this was sharp and short: 'I cannot accept your Royal Highness's letter as in any way an answer to my demand, Your Royal Highness's behaviour to Lady Charles having been a matter of common talk for the two years that I have been away from England.'

Having delivered himself of this retort, Lord Charles then announced that he would call a Press conference at his house, and that, after giving details of the Prince's private life, he would resign his commission and go to live in France with his wife.

The Prime Minister, who had previously been told that Lady Brooke was willing to withdraw from court for a time but that the Prince would not allow anyone to approach her on the subject, was now informed that a temporary withdrawal had after all been approved. He was, therefore, able to draft letters which both the Prince and Beresford felt able to accept, Beresford merely placing on record that 'circumstances had occurred which led Lady Charles Beresford and her friends to believe it was [His] Royal Highness's intention publicly to wound her feelings'; the Prince putting his signature to a denial that he 'had ever had any such intention', and to a regret that 'she should have been led to conceive an erroneous impression upon the point'.

The Prince was not disposed, however, to forgive the Beresfords yet. On hearing in March the next year that the troublesome letter had at last been burned, he told Lady Charles's brother-in-law, Lord Waterford, to whose care it had been entrusted, that he could never forget and would never forgive her conduct nor that of Lord Charles. 'His base ingratitude, after a friendship of about twenty years', had hurt the Prince more than words could say. It was not until June 1897, when the King's horse, *Persimmon*, won the Ascot Gold Cup that he was prevailed upon to speak to Lord Charles again; and even then he felt impelled to write immediately to Lady Brooke to apologize for having done so.

My own lovely little Daisy [his letter ran], I lose no time in writing to tell you of an episode which occurred today after you left—wh. was unpleasant and unexpected—but I hope my darling you will agree I could not have acted otherwise, as my loyalty to you, is I hope, a thing that you will never think of doubting!—Shortly before leaving Ascot today, Marcus B. came to me, & said he had a gt. favour to ask me—so I answered at once I should be delighted to grant it. He then became much affected, & actually cried, & said might he bring his brother C.

up to me to offer his congratulations on 'Persimmon's' success. I had no alternative but to say yes. He came up with his hat off, & would not put it on till I told him, & shook hands. We talked a little about racing, then I turned and we parted. What struck me more than anything, was his humble attitude and manner! My loved one, I hope you won't be annoyed at what has happened, & exonerate me from blame, as that is all I care about.

Throughout the final stages of the distressing Beresford affair, the Princess of Wales, although naturally upset that her husband's passion for Lady Brooke had led him to become so reckless a champion, had stood by him as loyally as she had done during the Gordon Cumming trial. Knollys told the Prime Minister's private secretary that the Princess was even more angry with Beresford than the Prince, that she warmly supported her husband 'in everything connected with this unfortunate affair' and was 'anxious to do all in her power to assist him'.

Comforted by this support, the Prince was also consoled by Lady Brooke, who, on her father-in-law's death in December 1893, became the Countess of Warwick. The Prince was still passionately in love with her, gazing at her longingly, so she afterwards claimed, giving her numerous little sentimental presents and tokens of his affection, writing to her regularly. And despite the warning administered to him by the Mordaunt case, he wrote her far more intimate letters than any he seems to have composed for other women, addressing her as his 'darling Daisy', his 'own adored little Daisy wife'. 'He wrote me a letter twice or three times every week,' she said, 'telling me everything that had happened to him. He expected me to write frequently, and if I didn't he used to say I had hurt him.'

In Lady Warwick's subsequent accounts of their relationship, she makes him appear far more in love with her than she was with him, describing him once as having been 'bothersome as he sat on a sofa', holding her hand and 'goggling' at her. Six years after the Prince's death, she told the journalist Frank Harris, 'He was remarkably constant and admired me exceedingly . . . He had manners and he was very considerate and from a woman's point of view that's a great deal . . . He was indeed a very perfect gentle lover. I think anyone would have been won by him . . . I grew to like him very much.'

By then Lady Warwick had become a dedicated socialist; and she liked to emphasize the part she had played in interesting the Prince in worthy causes, being at pains to point out the taste they shared for the simple pleasures of country life. She said that he had advised her 'against giving expensive entertainments' and had added that, for his part, he was much happier to come down to Easton Lodge to see her quietly with a couple of friends. All the same, they had both enjoyed house-parties on the grand scale; and she had spent a great deal of money in giving them. One of them, attended by the Prince, lasted a week, the guests being transported by a special train which ran from London and back every day; and actors being engaged to play the parts of chessmen in the gardens, arrayed in fantastic costumes.

At Easton Lodge house-parties, according to Elinor Glyn, who lived nearby at Durrington House and often attended them, those with a taste for sexual intrigue and illicit liaisons found their hostess an ever-willing and resourceful collaborator, always careful to warn her guests that the stable yard bell rang at six o'clock in the morning, thus providing them with a reliable alarm in case they had to return to a previously unoccupied bed.

In the staircase hall, Mrs Glyn wrote,

> there was a tray, on which stood beautifully cleaned silver candlesticks . . . one of which you carried up to your room, even if you did not need it at all. It might be that in lighting it up for you, your admirer might whisper a suggestion of a rendezvous for the morning; if not, probably on your breakfast tray you would find a note from him, given by his valet to your maid, suggesting where and when you might chance to meet him for a walk . . . Supposing you had settled to meet the person who was amusing you in the saloon, say, at eleven, you went there casually at the agreed time, dressed to go out, and found your cavalier awaiting you. Sometimes Lady Brooke would be there too, but she always sensed whether this was an arranged meeting or an accidental one. If it was intended, she would say graciously that Stone Hall, her little Elizabethan pleasure house in the park, was a nice walk before lunch, and thus make it easy to start. Should some strangers who did not know the ropes happen to be there, too, and show signs of accompanying you on the walk, she would immediately engage them in conversation until you had got safely away.

Once the intending lovers had come to an understanding, it would usually be agreed that something would be left outside the lady's bedroom door to signify that she was alone and that the coast was clear; but a pile of sandwiches on a plate, formerly a favourite sign, had fallen into disfavour since the greedy German diplomat, Baron von Eckardstein, seeing some in a corridor at Chatsworth, had picked them up and eaten them all on the way to his room, much to the consternation of the countess who had placed them there.

These clandestine arrangements were perfectly acceptable to the Prince, of course, provided there was no hint of scandal or even of open discussion of what everyone knew was going on. Discretion was insisted upon as *de rigueur*, disclosure unforgivable. A gentleman's behaviour was not to be measured in terms of his sexual activities but by the strictness with which he observed the rules that polite society imposed upon their conduct. Certain practices were not to be tolerated. On hearing reports that Lord Arthur Somerset, the superintendent of his racing stables, had been apprehended by the police in a homosexual brothel in Cleveland Street frequented by Post Office messenger boys, the Prince had at first refused to believe it of a friend of his 'any more than [he would have done] if they had accused the Archbishop of Canterbury'. He had sent emissaries to the Commissioner of Police, the Director of Public Prosecutions and the Prime Minister in an effort to clear Lord Arthur Somerset and to get 'something settled'. The Assistant Director of Public Prosecutions was informed by these emissaries that the Prince was in a 'great state' but that he 'didn't believe a word of it'. It was, as the Prince told Lord Carrington, 'simply inconceivable': if Somerset were guilty of such an offence, who on earth could they trust? Finally he was forced to conclude that Somerset, like anyone capable of such behaviour, must be an 'unfortunate Lunatic' and the less one heard 'of such a filthy scandal the better'. But, aberrations like this apart, a gentleman's infidelities were his own affair so long as he kept them to himself and did not allow them to become the subject of public discussion. This being understood, lovers who had spent part of the night together were expected next day to betray not the least hint of their previous intimacy.

Lady Warwick's own affair with the Prince of Wales seems to have ended a year or so after she became chatelaine of Warwick Castle. Contemporaries believed that he had grown bored by her lectures. As she herself wrote,

> only a sincere democrat desires to know the uncomfortable things of life. In [the Prince of Wales] there was a perpetual struggle between his sense of duty and a desire to conceal from himself that all was not well with the best of all possible worlds. Queen Victoria did not lend a listening ear to recitals of the wrongs of the people; he, on the other hand, did listen, but he would not seek to hear. Those who revealed unpleasant things were not liked the better for it.

He would murmur to them, 'Society grows; it is not made.'

He and Lady Warwick remained friends, and continued to see each other often at country house-parties; but since they were no longer lovers, Lady Warwick began to fear that, as her influence over him waned, she might lose it altogether. So, at the beginning of 1898, just before she gave birth to another child after an interval of over twelve years, she thought it as well to assure the Princess of Wales, who had never accepted her in the way she had accepted his other mistresses, that her relationship with the Prince was now purely platonic. She sat down to write to them both, contritely assuring the Princess of her great respect for her and addressing the

Prince in a more formal tone than usual so that he could show the letter to his wife.

My own lovely little Daisy [the Prince replied immediately], It is difficult for me to describe how touched I was by your beautiful letter which reached me at Chatsworth this morning . . . I gave it to the Princess to read. She was moved to tears, and said she felt very sorry for you and that 'out of evil good would come'.

She kept the letter to read it again and return it to me at tea-time, and begged me to thank you for the letter she received from you . . . . She really quite forgives and condones the past, as I have corroborated what you wrote about our friendship having been platonic for some years. You could not help, my loved one, writing to me as you did—though it gave me a pang—after the letters I have received from you for nearly nine years! But I think I could read 'between the lines' everything you wished to convey . . . But how could you, my loved one, imagine that I should withdraw my friendship from you? On the contrary I mean to befriend you more than ever, and you cannot prevent my giving you the same love as the friendship I have always felt for you. Though our interests, as you have often said, lie apart, still we have that sentimental feeling of affinity which cannot be eradicated by time . . . I know my darling that [the Princess] will now meet you with pleasure, so that your position is, thank God! better now than it ever was since we have been such friends, and I do not despair in time that you and she might become quite good friends.

In his relief that it had all ended so satisfactorily, the Prince even thought that this proposed friendship between his wife and former mistress might be brought about by finding some charity in which they could share a common interest. But the Princess, quite prepared to be friendly from a distance, was certainly not willing to become as closely involved with Lady Warwick as this. She did, however, undertake to send a brief note of forgiveness. And the Prince was duly thankful. 'Certainly the Princess has been an angel of goodness through all this,' he told Lady Warwick, 'but then she is a Lady and never could do anything that was mean or small.'

Yet, despite the Prince's protests that he would never feel less than affectionate towards Lady Warwick, her ardent socialism, her indiscreet attempts to make use of her supposed influence over her former lover, as well as her undiminished appetite for other men, imposed too great a strain on a friendship which, if never entirely broken, was never fully resumed. For several years, presents and letters continued to be exchanged on appropriate anniversaries. But one day, four years after the birth of her last child, she was told by a messenger from Windsor, 'with charming courtesy and frankness', as she had to admit, that 'it would be as well for all concerned if [her] close association with great affairs were to cease as it was giving rise to hostile comment'.

By then two other women had entered the Prince's life, both of whom were universally considered to be far more suitable companions for him than Lady Warwick. One of them was Agnes Keyser, daughter of a rich stockbroker, who, with her sister, ran a nursing home for army officers in Grosvenor Crescent which was supported by donations from the King's rich friends. A handsome, governess-like woman of strong yet understanding personality, forty-six years old in February 1898 when the Prince first came to know her, Agnes Keyser shunned the kind of society which the Prince had enjoyed at Easton Lodge. And, when he felt disinclined to exert himself in more demanding company, Miss Keyser was prepared always to welcome him to a quiet dinner where, as though in a nursery far more agreeable than any he had known as a child, he was given such plain fare as Irish stew and rice pudding.

The other woman, whom the Prince first met in that same month of February 1898, was to love him and be loved by him for the rest of his life. This was the bright and vivacious, stately and Junoesque Hon. Mrs George Keppel, 'a memorable figure in the fashionable world', in the opinion of Osbert Sitwell, who greatly enjoyed listening to her talking when 'she would remove from her mouth for a moment the cigarette which she would be smoking through a long holder and turn upon the person to whom she was speaking her large, humorous, kindly, peculiarly discerning eyes.' The daughter of Admiral Sir William Edmonstone, she was then twenty-nine years old and had married George Keppel, a son of the seventh Earl of Albemarle, some years before. Keppel was an extremely handsome, tall army officer with a bristling moustache, an aquiline nose and a hearty laugh. Very fond of women himself, he raised no objection to the Prince's friendship with his wife, to whom he was deeply attached; and when his income proved inadequate for the sort of life he was called upon to lead—and his wife's bank managers to whom she was, as her daughter said, 'irresistibly attractive', could help no more—he cheerfully went to work for Sir Thomas Lipton, who obligingly found him employment at the Prince's instigation. Almost everyone, in fact, was devoted to Mrs Keppel, of whom scarcely anything worse was said than that during animated conversations her voice, usually so delightfully deep and throaty, became unnecessarily loud, and that, as Lord Carrington observed, she seemed to enjoy being 'much toadied by everyone'. Well aware of the importance of her position, she never took advantage of it. Both kind and amusing, she was as discreet as she was disarming. Ministers, trusting in her circumspection and knowing her to be completely loyal to the Prince, while aware of his failings, reposed in her a unique trust, making use of her as a kind of invaluable liaison officer. Rules of precedence were disregarded in her favour: Count Mensdorff, the Austrian Ambassador in London, and a second cousin of the Prince of Wales, noticed that at a dinner party at Crichel Down, 'the *Favorita*', as Mensdorff called her, was actually seated next to the Kaiser so that 'she might have the opportunity of talking to him'. Mensdorff would have loved to have known 'what sort of report she sent back to Sandringham'.

With very few exceptions, such as the Marquess of Salisbury and the Dukes of Portland and Norfolk, members of society accepted her and, when it became known that the Princess of Wales accepted her too, invited the Keppels and the Waleses to the same parties. But although the Princess of Wales tolerated her, she naturally found it impossible fully to share the general admiration. She was grateful to Mrs Keppel, no doubt, for keeping her husband entertained and, therefore, good-tempered; but her family knew that she found her constant presence irksome, while her attendants were sometimes given the impression that she even found it absurd. One day after she had become Queen, glancing out of a window at Sandringham, she caught sight of Mrs Keppel returning from a drive with the King in an open carriage. Mrs Keppel had become rather stout by then and the sight of her imposing bosom in such close proximity to the corpulent figure of the King suddenly struck the Queen as ludicrous. She called to her lady-in-waiting to come to share the view, and burst into peals of laughter.

Yet Mrs Keppel's reputation was such that the Archbishop of Canterbury was invited to sit down at the same table with her. By then, of course, King Edward's relationship with Mrs Keppel may have changed as his relationship with Lady Warwick did. Certainly, the Archbishop told the Earl of Crawford and Balcarres that he

never believed the Keppel affair was anything more than platonic. The King showed this to the Archbishop by always placing him next to her at table: something he would never have done if she had been, as generally supposed, his mistress—it would have been an insult to the Church and utterly unlike him. The subtlety of this approach, the Archbishop said, was very characteristic of the King.

After the death of the King, who made provision for her through Sir Ernest Cassel, Mrs Keppel bought a villa in Tuscany, where Sir Harold Acton remembers her enormous charm and her still fine figure. 'One of the secrets of her success,' Sir Harold says, 'was that she could be amusing without malice; she never repeated a cruel witticism. Above all, she was not snobbish.' Her husband, 'well matched as to height', looked 'every inch a colonel'. 'I remember how shocked he was to find my mother reading a book about

Oscar Wilde,' Sir Harold writes. ' "A frightful bounder. It made me puke to look at him," he muttered. . . . To a certain extent the Colonel shared his wife's aura. A guide once pointed him out to a group of inquisitive tourists as "*l'ultimo amante della regina Victoria*".'

12

'Inconvenient' Friends and 'Ill-bred' Children

It is the greatest bane in one's life saying good-bye, especially to one's children, relations and friends.

'If you ever become King,' the Queen had warned the Prince of Wales in 1868, 'you will find all these friends *most* inconvenient, and you will have to break with them *all*.' He had long since become used to such criticisms and had grown tired of rebutting the allegation that almost all his friends were the 'fashionable bad set and betting people'. It could not be denied, though, that a good many of them were. There was, for instance, a certain handsome young man who called himself Count Miecislas Jaraczewski, whose scarcely pronounceable surname was translated into English by his cronies at the Turf Club as 'Sherry and Whiskers'. Jaraczewski had been admitted to the Marlborough Club by the Prince, who entertained him frequently at Sandringham and was often to be seen with him in Paris where the police described Jaraczewski as the Prince's 'faithful and inseparable friend and one who, incidentally, never had a good reputation for honesty as a gambler'. The Queen must have been distressed to learn that this young friend of her son, after giving a splendid supper party one evening at the Turf Club, had returned home to take a lethal dose of prussic acid rather than face arrest and ruin.

The Queen was not alone in her disapproval of the Prince's friends. After another member of the Marlborough Club turned out to be an American swindler wanted by the police, *The Times* condemned his patronage of 'American cattle-drovers and prize-fighters', while other critics spoke harshly of his intimate friendships with men distinguished by riches rather than birth. They condemned, for example, his intimacy with Sir Thomas Lipton, who had begun work at the age of nine in his Irish father's grocery shop in Glasgow; with Sir John Blundell Maple, proprietor of a furniture store in Tottenham Court Road; and with the ruthless, self-made adventurer Cecil Rhodes, whose blackballing by the Travellers' Club induced the Prince to resign from it himself. Most of all they disapproved of his close friendships with affluent Jews. 'We resented the introduction of the Jews into the social set of the Prince of Wales,' Lady Warwick said; 'not because we disliked them individually . . . but because they had brains and understood finance. As a class, we did not like brains. As for money, our only understanding of it lay in the spending, not in the making of it.' The Prince, on the contrary, was fascinated by the operations of capitalists and talk of high finance. And he delighted in the company of rich Jews like the Sassoons, whose ancestors had been settled in Mesopotamia for many centuries and whose immense wealth was derived from the profits of the great merchant house of David Sassoon & Company of Bombay. Arthur Sassoon lived in great splendour at 8 King's Gardens, Hove, waited upon by forty servants. His half-brothers Reuben and Alfred had almost equally sumptuous houses nearby. Arthur also had a large house, Tulchan Lodge, in Invernessshire; and at all these places the Prince was welcome to stay for as long as he liked.

The Prince was on quite as intimate terms with the Rothschilds. He had known the gruff and despotic Nathan Meyer Rothschild at Cambridge, and had subsequently often gone to stay with him at Tring Park. He was also a frequent guest of Nathan's brothers, the extravagant and urbane bachelor, Alfred, who lived in sybaritic luxury at Halton House; and the kindly Leopold of Ascott and Palace House, Newmarket. Their uncle, Sir Anthony de Rothschild, the first baronet, advised the Prince on his finances and, on occasions, arranged for the family bank to advance him money when he was in difficulties. Similar services were offered to the Prince by Baron Maurice von Hirsch auf Gereuth, an enormously rich Jewish financier known as 'Turkish Hirsch' because a large part of his fortune had been derived from the building of railways for the Sultan. Hirsch's social ambitions in Germany and Austria had been thwarted by racial prejudice despite his lavish gifts to charity. Knowing that the Prince of Wales was afflicted by no such prejudice, and that the company of millionaires was highly congenial to him, Hirsch had approached the Crown Prince Rudolph of Austria for an introduction. Having obtained one in exchange for a loan of 100,000 gulden, Hirsch, who had a house in Paris as well as an estate at St Johann, called at the Hôtel Bristol one day when the Prince was staying there. The Prince took to him, understood his predicament, accepted an invitation to luncheon at his house and agreed to stay with him at St Johann. And when Hirsch came to England and rented a house in London, a country house near Sandringham and a shoot near Newmarket, the Prince undertook to sponsor his entrée into English society, becoming '*dreadfully* annoyed' when the Queen declined to invite his protégé to a state concert at Buckingham Palace and sharing the Baron's pleasure when a yearling filly, *La Flèche*, which Hirsch had bought on the recommendation of Lord Marcus Beresford, won the One Thousand Guineas and the Cambridgeshire as well as the Oaks and the St Leger in the single season of 1892. Before long, however, the Prince began to find Hirsch's company rather tiresome, and after the Baron's death in 1896 he was glad to recognize in his executor another multi-millionaire whom he could not only trust as a financial adviser but also value as a close personal friend.

Ernest Cassel was ten years younger than the Prince, to whom he bore a marked resemblance. Born in Cologne, the youngest son of a Jewish banker in a modest way of business, he had left for England at the age of sixteen and obtained employment with a firm in Liverpool. A few months later he moved to Paris as a clerk in the Anglo–Egyptian Bank; and, on the outbreak of the Franco–Prussian War, returned to England, where he joined the staff of the financial house of Bischoffsheim and Goldschmidt, one of whose partners, Louis Bischoffsheim, was Hirsch's brother-in-law. By the time he was twenty-two, Cassel was manager of the firm at a salary of £5,000 a year. Before he was thirty, by industry, acumen, and a deserved reputation for unassailable integrity, he had accumulated capital of £150,000. He had also married an English girl, becoming a British subject himself on the day of the wedding and being received into the Roman Catholic Church three years later in obedience to his beloved wife's dying wish. Cautious and reticent in human relations, Cassel was more interested in power than in people. He was a well-known figure in society; he was careful to join the right clubs; and he was as indefatigable in his pursuit of British as he was of foreign decorations, once coolly informing Francis Knollys, who passed the message on to the Prime Minister's Private Secretary, that he was 'anxious to have the G.C.B. conferred upon him without loss of time'.

It was felt that, except when he was in the hunting field, or inspecting his horses in the stud or on the race-course, Cassel's attention never wandered far from the world of finance, of international loans, of percentages and profits. Yet, unlike most men of comparable riches, he derived as much pleasure from spending money as in amassing it. Though his own tastes were restrained, he was the most generous of hosts both at Moulton Paddocks, Newmarket, and at his London houses in Grosvenor Square and Park Lane, both of which were filled with old masters, with all kinds of *objets d'art* from Renaissance bronzes to English silver and Chinese jade, and with equally decorative women whose company Cassel, like the Prince, preferred to that of men.

Finding Cassel on occasions a trifle dispiriting, the Prince never tired of the Marquis de Soveral, the lively, stimulating Portuguese Minister in London whose charming presence was welcome at every party. Known as the 'Blue Monkey' because of his animated manner, blue-black hair and dark complexion, Luis de Soveral was recognized, indeed, as being 'the most popular man in London', except at the German Embassy, where he was known as 'Soveral-Überall' and strongly disliked for his known anti-German sentiments. The Princess of Pless, the former Daisy Cornwallis-West, treated him as a rather distasteful joke.

> He imagines himself to be a great intellectual and political force and the wise adviser of all the heads of the government and, of course, the greatest danger to women! . . . [But surely] even those stupid people who believe that every man who talks to a woman must be her lover, could not take his Don Juanesque pretensions seriously. Yet I am told that all women do not judge him so severely and some even find him *très seduisant*. How disgusting!

The Princess of Pless apart, virtually everyone in London, even the husbands of his mistresses, and both the Princess of Wales and Alice Keppel, delighted in the sight of his tall figure approaching, a white flower in his buttonhole, a monocle firmly fixed in one glittering eye, his large moustache neatly brushed, his regular teeth revealed in a warm and happy smile, ready to greet an old friend with enthusiasm or to charm a new acquaintance. 'As a talker he was quite wonderful in keeping the ball rolling,' Henry Ponsonby's son, Frederick, thought. 'And without being exactly witty his conversation was always sparkling and amusing. It was only when he had to talk seriously that one realised how clever he was.' Yet he did all he could to disguise his cleverness, having found by experience that 'both men and women fight shy of a clever man'.

Certainly the Prince fought shy of clever men whose intelligence was on permanent display. He preferred the company of actors to authors; and authors as a rule did not regard him highly. To Rudyard Kipling he was a corpulent voluptuary; to Max Beerbohm a fat little boy kept in a corner by a domineering mother; to Henry James an 'ugly' omen for 'the dignity of things'. He was once prevailed upon by Sir Sidney Lee to give a dinner at Marlborough House to celebrate the publication of the *Dictionary of National Biography*. He had evidently not been very keen to do so; and at the dinner was not in his brightest mood, 'embarrassed by the effusive learning of Lord Acton on one side and the impenetrable shyness of Sir Leslie Stephen on the other'. It is said that on looking round the table his eye fell on Canon Ainger, who had written the entries on Charles and Mary Lamb. 'Who is the little parson?' he asked. 'Why is he here? He is not a writer.' It was explained to him that Ainger was 'a very great authority on Lamb'. At this the Prince put down his knife and fork, crying out in bewilderment, 'On *lamb!*'

Actors viewed the Prince more kindly, for he took the trouble to gain their regard. One evening in 1882, for example, after Lillie Langtry's appearance on the stage of the Haymarket Theatre, the Prince, as a gesture of thanks to the kind cooperation of her more experienced colleagues, gave a large dinner party at Marlborough House where a number of actors were, so Lord Carrington told his wife, 'sandwiched between ordinary mortals with more or less success'. The only regrettable incident occurred when William Kendal, 'a good-looking bounder', 'distinguished himself' late in the evening by singing 'a very vulgar song which was not favourably received in high quarters, after which the party rather collapsed'.

The Prince might well have let the vulgarity pass unremarked in other circumstances, but he evidently considered Marlborough House an unsuitable stage for the comedian's performance. Yet, while he was ever careful to remind the forgetful that he was regal as well as *roué*, few people ever accused the Prince of being a snob. Certainly he preferred the company of the rich to the poor, judged riches as useful a method of grading people as any other, and obviously chose to associate with those who could entertain him in the comfortable surroundings to which he had grown accustomed. But although newly established millionaires such as J.B. Robinson were invited to Sandringham almost as a matter of course, the Prince also offered hospitality to men who would never be in a position to return it. One of these was Henry Broadhurst, a former stonemason and trade union leader who was Liberal Member of Parliament for Stoke on Trent and who had served with the Prince on the Royal Commission on the Housing of the Working Classes. Broadhurst had no evening clothes and was relieved when the Prince, 'in order to meet the difficulties in the matter of dress', made arrangements for him to have dinner served in his bedroom. Yet he did not feel neglected or deprived. He had several long conversations with his host and his family, and left Sandringham 'with a feeling of one who had spent a week-end with an old chum of his own rank in society'.

As few people ever accused the Prince of being a snob, so everyone agreed that his eagerness to help his friends was one of the most pleasing traits of his personality. It often took him a long time to forgive those who had offended him; but most of them were forgiven in the end, as was Sir Frederick Johnstone, who had insulted him when drunk in the billiard-room at Sandringham. He was sometimes slow to realize that the financial ruin of certain men was due to their attempts to keep up with him and to fulfil the kind of obligations placed upon Christopher Sykes, who was constantly being told to arrange a dinner or a party for the Prince and his friends. Lord Hardwicke, known as 'Glossy Top' from his habit of brushing his beaver hat until he could see his face in it, ruined himself like Christopher Sykes. So did the charming Charles Buller, who was obliged to resign his commission in the Household Cavalry when he could no longer pay his mess bills and was eventually sent to prison for issuing a worthless cheque. But when told of such friends' distress, the Prince did what he could to help them. On the appearance of Christopher Sykes's forthright sister-in-law at Marlborough House with the sad news of Sykes's imminent bankruptcy, arrangements were made for the most pressing debts to be paid. And on Lord Arthur Somerset's fleeing the country rather than face a charge of 'gross indecency', the Prince wrote to the Prime Minister asking that the poor 'unfortunate Lunatic' might be allowed to return to England to see his family without fear of arrest.

The Prince's correspondence is replete with requests that desirable political and diplomatic appointments should be offered to friends of his or to men to whom he had cause to feel obliged, and with recommendations for promotions, preferments, honours, titles and decorations. A whole series of letters were addressed to three separate prime ministers on behalf of the Revd Charles Tarver, his former tutor, who was living in poverty in a small parish in Kent. He was almost equally importunate on behalf of a Norfolk neighbour who had once acted as his agent and who, in the Prince's opinion, ought to be knighted, having been six times Mayor of King's Lynn. And he ardently pressed the claims of Dean Liddell of Christ Church to be considered a worthy successor to Arthur Stanley as Dean of Westminster. He was determined that a diplomat whom he much admired, Sir Robert Morier, should be appointed British Ambassador in Berlin despite the objections of Bismarck; that Mrs Gladstone ought to receive a peerage and become Mistress of the Robes, though this could hardly be expected to meet with his mother's approval; that, since he was 'a good fellow' and his family owned half the county, Lord Rothschild ought to succeed the Duke of Buckingham as Lord Lieutenant of Buckinghamshire whatever other local notables might have to say on the subject; and that Sir Ernest Cassel ought to be elected to the Jockey Club, which did not want to admit him. He pressed for the appointment of Charles Dilke as President of the Local Government Board; of Lord Carrington as Viceroy of India; of Canon Dalton as Dean of Exeter; of Ferdinand Rothschild as a Trustee of the British Museum; of Valentine Baker as Wolseley's chief intelligence officer in Egypt; and of Rosebery— whom he later successfully persuaded to go to the Foreign Office and to whom, in retirement, he gave the memorable advice, 'to rise like a Sphinx from your ashes'—as Secretary of State for Scotland.

To the Prince's chagrin, his recommendations were more often disregarded than not. And to the government they were sometimes embarrassing, even suspect. In February 1881 Gladstone was worried by an approach from the Prince, who wished to recommend for baronetcies four men, not one of whom was considered worthy of the honour. Gladstone's secretary, Edward Hamilton, noted in his journal:

It is perhaps hardly fair to say so, but these recommendations have rather an ugly look about them. A respectable clergyman [the Revd H.W. Bellairs] wrote not long since to say that he was in possession of information, to which he could swear, that there were certain persons scheming for hereditary honours in consideration of bribes, and bribes to people in very high life . . . that a gentleman had told him that he had been offered a baronetcy by the Prince of Wales . . . on condition that he would pay £70,000 to the Prince's agent on receiving the title.

Only one of the men recommended by the Prince was 'known to ordinary fame', Hamilton added. This was a rich building contractor, C.J. Freake, and for him a knighthood would have been quite sufficient, 'having regard to the reported wild habits of Freake *fils* and the political proclivities of Freake *père*'. Yet the Prince 'persistently and somewhat questionably (if not fishily)' pressed Freake's name upon Gladstone; and his baronetcy was, in fact, approved by the Queen a few months later.

Then, in 1884, there was the case of

Mr Francis Cook who gave such a huge sum . . . towards the Alexandra Home for Female Art Students [and] got the Prince of Wales to back his claim for a baronetcy [which he received in 1886]. How is it possible to advise the favourable consideration of such a claim? It is munificence, given with every sort of [assurance], of disinterestedness, but really intended as a bribe.

Just as the Queen was highly critical of the kind of people with whom the Prince associated, so she was critical of the way he brought up his children.

'They are such ill-bred, ill-trained children,' she wrote in a spasm of irritation when they were young. 'I can't fancy them at all.'

Others, more predisposed to like children generally, agreed with her. Lady Geraldine Somerset thought them 'wild as hawks'. The daughters— though the eldest was '*very* sharp, quick, merry and amusing'—were 'rampaging little girls', while the boys were 'past all management'. Certainly guests at Sandringham were never for long unaware that there were children in the house. A game of croquet or even a tea-party was likely to be interrupted by excited screams and running boots which, in most other country houses, would have led to a severe reprimand for the governess. When they were taken to other houses—which they rarely were—their unwilling infant hosts and hostesses were well advised to put away their best toys in the nursery cupboard, as the Duchess of Teck's children always did.

There were five of them in all, ranging in age, on their father's thirtieth birthday, from seven to three, the three girls, Louise, Victoria and Maud, being the youngest. They appeared to be devoted to each other and to their parents, hating to be parted, and disliking in particular having to go to stay with their grandmother at Balmoral. A proposed visit there once reduced all the girls to tears and induced a fit of defiance in the youngest, who stamped her foot and declared that she wouldn't go.

Their mother adored them, though even she had occasion to complain to the boys' tutor of their 'using strong language to each other' and of their habit of 'breaking into everybody's conversation' so that it became 'impossible to speak to anyone before them'. She took the greatest delight in giving them their baths—and inviting favoured guests at Sandringham to watch her doing so—reading undemanding books to them, saying their prayers with them, then tucking them up and kissing them goodnight. She hated to be parted from them as much as they disliked leaving her, treating them as children, and writing childish letters to them, long after they had become adult.

Apart from insisting that they did not quarrel with each other or assume attitudes of superiority with anyone else, Princess Alexandra paid little attention to the way her daughters were educated. They were taught music; but those who knew them well in later years could find little evidence of their having been given any other formal instruction or even of their having many other interests, apart from the various country pursuits in which most of their leisure hours were spent. They were all rather shy and gave the impression, despite their high spirits when young, of being rather apathetic and unimaginative women. None of them was good looking, although they all had pleasant features and did not deserve the nickname by which they were widely known, 'The Hags'. Their mother, who did not want to lose them, gave them no encouragement to marry and, of course, actively discouraged all possible suitors from Germany. Her selfish possessiveness worried Queen Victoria, who spoke to her son about it; but the Prince of Wales explained that he was 'powerless' in the matter, that 'Alix found them such companions that she would not encourage their marrying, and that they themselves had no inclination for it'. When she was twenty-two the eldest, shyest and most uncommunicative of them all, Princess Louise, did, however, get married. The husband selected was the sixth Earl of Fife, a Scottish landowner and businessman, eighteen years older than herself, one of those few of her father's friends of whom her grandmother approved, though the Queen—who needed some persuasion when it was proposed to create Fife a Duke—would have been more severe had she known that, amongst the Parisian *demi-monde*, he was known as *'le petit Écossais roux qui a toujours la queue en l'air.'* After her marriage, Princess Louise retired to the fastness of her husband's estates where she indulged a passion for salmon-fishing, at which she was said to have developed exceptional skill.

It was not until seven years after Princess Louise's marriage that a husband was found for her sister Maud, whom Queen Victoria had long supposed would have liked one much earlier. Princess Maud was then in her late twenties; and, although she had been the most lively and venture-

some of the Prince's daughters as a child—when she had been nicknamed
'Harry' after her father's friend, Admiral Harry Keppel, whose courageous
conduct in the Crimean War was legendary—she had become rather gloomy
and disgruntled. Marriage made her more so. Her husband, a first cousin,
Prince Charles of Denmark, who was crowned King Haakon VII of Norway
in 1905, was 'a very nice young fellow', in Lord Esher's opinion; but Princess Maud did not like living abroad and strongly resented being left alone
when her husband, who was a naval officer, had to go to sea. Making no
secret of her grievances, she returned to England every year to stay near
Sandringham at Appleton House which her father gave to her. Then, after
this annual visit, she would return reluctantly to Bygdo Kongsgaard where
she laid out an English garden which, apart from her horses, dogs and only
son, was one of her few real interests.

Princess Victoria, the middle daughter, never married. There were two
men she would have liked but both, being commoners, were forbidden her.
Lord Rosebery, broken by the death of his wife, also intimated in a rather
uncertain way that he and Princess Victoria might find happiness together.
But this proposal was not to be considered either, to the infinite regret of
Victoria, who, years later, lamented, 'We *could* have been so happy.' So
Victoria was kept at home, following her parents about from one country
house to the next, at the beck and call of a far less intelligent mother who, as
a Russian cousin, the Grand Duchess Olga, said, treated her just like 'a glori-
fied maid', ringing a bell to summon her and then, as her daughter ran to her
side, forgetting what it was she had wanted. Often unwell and constantly
concerned about her health, she grew increasingly resentful of her lot and
prone to making waspish comments about her dull relatives and those friends
of her parents in whose restricting society she felt herself confined.

The Prince had left his daughters' upbringing entirely to their governesses and their mother, maintaining that a child was 'always best looked
after under its mother's eye' and that if children were too severely treated
they became shy and fearful of those whom they ought to love. And though
he was extremely fond of his three girls, as he was fond of children generally, taking them on his ample knee and allowing them to pull at his beard
and play with his watch-chain and cigar-case, he never formed with any of
them the kind of emotional attachment that his father had formed with the
Empress Frederick. In many ways he was closer to his sons.

The elder of the two, Prince Albert Victor, known as Prince Eddy, was
rather a worrying child, amiable, slow, lethargic and dull, or, as his loving
mother put it, well-disposed but 'dawdly'. His kindness and good nature
seemed due not so much to positive virtue as to a lazy rejection of vice.
The Prince had hoped to send him to Wellington College, which, opened in
1853, had been founded as a memorial to the great Duke for the sons of
officers and for boys who, it was hoped, would become officers them-

Lady Randolph Churchill.

Lady Brooke.

Hélène Standish.

Daisy, Princess of Pless.

The Prince and Princess of Wales in May 1888.

A house-party at Lady Brooke's house, Easton Lodge, in October 1891.
Standing, left to right: *Lord Algernon Lennox, Count Mensdorff, Lady Eva Greville, the Prince of Wales, Lady Brooke, Princess Victoria Mary of Teck, the Duchess of Teck;* seated, left to right: *Prince Francis of Teck, Lady Kaye, Lord Brooke, Lady Lilian Wemyss, the Marquis de Soveral.*

A family group in 1896. Standing, left to right: *Princess Louise (Duchess of Fife), the Prince of Wales, the Duchess of York, Princess Maud, Prince Charles of Denmark;* seated, left to right: *the Duke of Fife, the Duke of York (holding Prince Edward), the Princess of Wales, Princess Victoria.*

King Edward VII, soon after his accession, with George, Prince of Wales.

Queen Alexandra with Little Marvel
at Mar Lodge, her daughter
the Duchess of Fife's house
in Scotland, in 1904.

King Edward and Queen Alexandra
at Cowes in 1903.

A house-party at Elveden, Lord Iveagh's house, in January 1908. Back row, left to right: *Sir George Holford, Sir Arthur Davidson, Count Mensdorff, the Marquis de Soveral, Sir Schomberg McDonnell, the Duke of Abercorn, Lady Churchill, Lady Savile, Sir Ernest Cassel, the Duchess of Abercorn, the Hon. Mrs George Keppel, Lord Londonderry;* middle row, left to right: *Georgiana, Countess of Dudley, Lady Iveagh, the King, Consuelo, Duchess of Manchester, Lady Rossmore, Lady Sarah Wilson, Mrs Arthur James;* front row, left to right: *Mrs Ernest Guinness, Ernest Guinness, the Duke of Marlborough, Lord Iveagh, Lord Churchill, Mr Blain (Lord Iveagh's agent).*

Postcards on sale in Paris at the time of the Boer War. Following complaints by English residents and the British Embassy, these two, and others like them, were confiscated by the French police.

(Archives de la Préfecture de Police de Paris)

The Hon. Mrs George Keppel by Ellis Roberts.

The King with Tsar Nicholas II at Revel in 1908.

The King with the Kaiser and the Duke of Connaught at Windsor in November 1907.

Lord Marcus Beresford.

The King towards the
end of his life.

selves. But, as the boys' tutor, the Revd John Neale Dalton, soon observed, Prince Eddy was not at all suited for such an education and could never have kept up with the other boys. He could never 'fix his attention to any given subject for more than a few minutes consecutively', his mind being at all times in an 'abnormally dormant condition'. Prince Eddy was therefore sent, together with his younger brother, George, as a naval cadet to the training-ship *Britannia*.

The two boys left for Dartmouth in 1877, Eddy being thirteen and George twelve, both of them crying bitterly as they said good-bye to their mother, who was quite as unhappy as they were themselves. Queen Victoria was not at all sure that a training-ship would provide an adequate curriculum for her grandsons, particularly with regard to foreign languages which were of the 'greatest importance' and in which they were both 'sadly deficient'. She had favoured the idea of a public school. But she was at least thankful that the two boys would be far removed from possible contamination by contact with the Marlborough House set, a danger which she mentioned to their father several times, warning him of the 'vital importance' of the *dear Boys* being kept . . . above all apart, from the society of fashionable and fast people', and not being completely convinced when her son assured her that he entirely agreed with her, that his 'greatest wish' was to keep the boys 'simple, pure and childlike as long as possible'.

Prince George got on well in the *Britannia*. He was a bright, affectionate child, high-spirited but obedient, adored by his 'Motherdear' who wrote him deeply affectionate letters to which 'little George dear' responded in the same loving, childish tone. He passed his examinations and pleased his tutors, whereas poor Prince Eddy was so utterly incapable of mastering a single subject that the desirability of removing him from the ship had to be discussed. Dalton considered that the only answer was to separate the two brothers after two years aboard the *Britannia* and to send the elder on a cruise round the world attended by various tutors specially trained to deal with backward children. Their father did not agree. The two boys were devoted to each other; if they were kept apart he feared that Prince Eddy would lapse permanently into that slough of lethargy from which his brother seemed alone sometimes capable of arousing him. So in September 1879 both boys sailed for the West Indies aboard the *Bacchante*—with a carefully selected complement of officers and a staff of tutors under Dalton's direction —leaving their mother so unhappy at parting with them for so long that her husband kindly gave up his holiday at Homburg that year and went with her to Denmark. Seven months later the boys returned but only to sail away again shortly afterwards, once more in tears, for an even longer period.

Their father was almost as miserable at having to part with them, particularly with the younger boy, as was their mother. He wrote to Prince George after one parting:

On seeing you going off by the train yesterday I felt very sad and you could, I am sure, see that I had a lump in my throat when I wished you good-bye . . . I shall miss you more than ever, my dear Georgy . . . Now God bless you, my dear boy, and may He guard you against all harm and evil, and bless and protect you. Don't forget your devoted Papa, A.E.

'When I wished you good-bye on Thursday in your cabin I had a lump in my throat which I am sure you saw,' the Prince wrote after yet another parting a year later. 'It is the greatest bane in one's life saying good-bye, especially to one's children, relations and friends . . .'

Although he was often homesick—writing home to his 'dearest Papa' to tell him that he missed him 'every minute of the day' and confessing to his mother that he sometimes almost cried when he thought of Sandringham— Prince George assured his parents that he liked the navy and was perfectly happy to make it his profession. He was progressing well, and it was expected of him that were he free to continue in the service he might achieve high rank. It was all the more galling to him, therefore, that he just failed to obtain the marks necessary for a first-class pilot's certificate. But his father wrote to comfort him: 'You have, I hope, got over your disappointment about a First. It would of course have been *better* if you *had* obtained it; but being only within twenty marks is *very* satisfactory, and shows that there is no favoritism in your case.'

Prince Eddy afforded his father no such satisfaction. He 'sits listless and vacant,' Dalton reported, 'and . . . wastes as much time in doing nothing, as he ever wasted. This weakness of brain, this feebleness and lack of power to grasp almost anything put before him, is manifested . . . also in his hours of recreation and social intercourse.' After disembarking from the *Bacchante* for the last time the boy, then aged eighteen, was sent to Lausanne to learn French, an undertaking totally beyond his powers. He was then entered at Trinity College, Cambridge, although in the opinion of J.K. Stephen, who had gone to Sandringham to help to cram him for the ordeal, he could not 'possibly derive much benefit' from attending university lectures, since he hardly knew 'the meaning of the words *to read*'. However, as a tribute to his birth rather than his intellect—which was not in the least stimulated by university studies and no doubt hampered by his being rather deaf—he was granted an honorary LL.D. in 1888.

He was not an unattractive young man. Edward Hamilton, who played bowls and billiards with him at Sandringham when he was twenty, described him as 'a pleasing young fellow, natural and un-stuck-up'. Sir Lionel Cust thought that he had inherited much from his mother, to whom he was devoted, and that he might one day win the nation's heart as she had done. Prince Eddy confessed, however, to being rather afraid of his father, and aware that he was not quite up to what his father expected of him. He was extremely polite in his manner, modest, equable and deferential to his elders, particularly to his grandmother. In her turn, Queen Victoria regarded him with affection: he was a 'dear good simple boy', dutiful and even 'steadily inclined'; she loved him *so dearly*, she told Lady Downe, 'an affection he returned *so* warmly'. The Queen's secretary, Sir Henry Ponsonby, thought that, although his sentences were inclined to 'tail off' as though he had forgotten what he was going to say, Prince Eddy could talk quite sensibly when he chose and would be popular when he got 'more at his ease'. But he was certainly incapable of applying himself to anything for 'a length of time', and when he was bored his perpetual fidgeting seemed like a nervous tic. He was, in fact, constitutionally incapable of concentration, except on whist, which he played quite well, and on polo, at which he was adept. As he grew older, he appeared only to be fully alive when indulging his strongly developed sensuality. Despite a somewhat droopy cast of countenance, he was quite good looking and was undoubtedly attractive to women.

Since he had evinced not the least enthusiasm for either the navy or for Cambridge, it was now decided that Prince Eddy should go into the army. But at first he showed no aptitude for that either. His instructor at Aldershot was 'quite *astounded* at his utter ignorance'. When the Commander-in-Chief came down on a tour of inspection he expressed the hope of seeing him perform 'some most elementary movement'; but the Colonel 'begged him not to attempt it as the Prince had not an *idea* how to do it! And the [Commander-in-Chief] not wishing to expose him let it alone!' His slowness was overlooked, however, and in time he did become moderately efficient. When he was twenty-two he was given a commission in the Tenth Hussars. He did at least like the uniform, since he had always taken a great interest in clothes and, despite his lackadaisical demeanour, dressed himself with the utmost care. Always smart to the point of dandification, he was nicknamed 'Collar and Cuffs'.

Prince Eddy returned from a trip to India in 1890 worn out and 'really quite ill' from the dissipated life he had been leading. Then, to compound his folly, he fell in love with Princess Hélène d'Orléans, who was not only a Roman Catholic but daughter of the Comte de Paris, a pretender to the French throne. Before falling in love with her, Prince Eddy—or the Duke of Clarence and Avondale as he became in May 1890—had wanted to marry Princess Alix of Hesse, but she would not consider him. He had then been asked to think about another cousin, Princess Margaret of Prussia, but he declined to consider her.

Princess Alexandra was naturally not disappointed that neither of these German marriages materialized. On the other hand she liked Princess Hélène, who was, indeed, a most pleasant, warm-hearted and entirely unexceptionable girl, and she undertook to help her son overcome the difficulties which

Princess Hélène's birth and religion placed in the way of the match. As soon as she heard that they had become engaged while staying with her daughter, the Duchess of Fife, at Mar Lodge, she encouraged them to go immediately to Balmoral, rightly supposing that, as Princess Hélène was prepared to renounce her religion, Queen Victoria's affection for Prince Eddy and the romantic appeal of young lovers in distress would lead her to support a marriage which prudence frowned upon. Princess Alexandra was right: the Queen did give the young couple her blessing. But the Comte de Paris was aghast to learn that his daughter had even considered the possibility of becoming a Protestant in order to marry such a dissolute young man; while the Pope, to whom Princess Hélène ill-advisedly appealed, refused to entertain the already doomed proposal. So, as Princess Alexandra resignedly admitted, there was nothing for it but to 'wait and see what time [could] do'.

It was not, however, in Prince Eddy's nature to wait and see. Obliged to separate from Princess Hélène, he found that, although 'quite wretched' for a time, absence did not make his heart grow fonder and that he was, after all, in love with Lady Sybil St Clair Erskine. But this was not an acceptable match either; so the search continued for a suitable bride who might help to keep the dissipated bachelor out of further trouble. Where, though, his father asked, was 'a good sensible wife' with the necessary strength of character to be found?

Despite the formidable objections, the Prince of Wales had favoured the possibility of his son's marrying the French princess. He liked her; and he liked her mother, too, despite the Comtesse de Paris's distressing habit of smoking a pipe and helping herself to his cigars. So, in the hope of reaching a settlement on the religious issue, he had approached the Prime Minister to ask if the problem might be resolved by Princess Hélène's giving an undertaking that any children there might be would all be brought up in the Church of England while the mother remained a Roman Catholic in accordance with her father's wishes. Informed by the Prime Minister that this would be quite out of the question, the Prince had decided that, since no other suitable candidate presented herself, Prince Eddy would, as a punishment for his ever more disconcertingly scandalous behaviour, have to be sent on a tour which would take him as far away from England as South Africa, New Zealand and Canada.

But Queen Victoria, only partially aware of the reasons why a foreign tour was considered desirable, thought that Prince Eddy would benefit more from travelling about the cultivated European courts; and she reminded her son that there were as many 'designing pretty women in the Colonies' as anywhere else. To add to the Prince of Wales's troubles his wife, who had of late been much upset by her husband's affection for Lady Brooke, considered that their son ought not to be sent abroad at all, but ought to remain with his regiment so that she could keep an eye on his behaviour.

Rather than discuss the problem with his wife in her present disapproving mood, the Prince sailed for Homburg, instructing Knollys to deal with Princess Alexandra, who was to be left to decide what was to be done with their erring son. Fortunately by this time another possible bride had entered the lists, Princess May of Teck, a sensible, dutiful young woman whose virtues were held to outweigh the disadvantages of having a mother who was excessively slapdash and a bad-tempered father whose mind had been unbalanced by a stroke. So Princess Alexandra decided that Prince Eddy should marry Princess May and, in the meantime, remain with his regiment as she had wanted. The next day she sailed for Denmark. Then, rather than return home to England where the Lady Brooke affair was becoming common gossip, she went on to Russia for the silver wedding of her sister, the Tsarina, leaving her husband to celebrate his fiftieth birthday by himself.

In her absence negotiations for Prince Eddy's marriage progressed smoothly. Amenable as always, he complaisantly accepted Princess May, proposed to her at a house-party at Luton Hoo and was accepted. The wedding was fixed for 27 February 1892, a few weeks after the bridegroom's twenty-eighth birthday.

His father expressed the greatest satisfaction and relief. He had spent a most unhappy winter. At the beginning of November Prince George had fallen seriously ill with typhoid fever, which he had contracted while staying at Lord Crewe's; and the Prince of Wales, worried about his elder son's behaviour and by his wife's disapproval of Lady Brooke, had feared for a time that he might be called upon to bear the loss of his beloved younger son. But then the heavy gloom had suddenly lifted. Princess Alexandra had hurried home; and in their shared anxiety for Prince George—who was announced to be out of danger on 3 December—his parents had forgotten their differences.

The Prince's contentment did not, however, last long. Soon after Christmas Prince Eddy, pale and shivering, returned early from a day's shooting with his father at Sandringham and went to bed with a bad headache that presaged the onset of influenza. He came downstairs on his birthday to look at his presents but felt too ill to stay long and went back to bed. His mother watched him climb the stairs and never afterwards forgot the way he turned to give her 'his friendly nod'. Soon afterwards, seriously ill with pneumonia, he became delirious; and on 13 January his mother, who had sat by his bedside all night, woke her husband to tell him that she believed their son was dying.

The Prince would not at first believe it. Taking comfort from the specialist who felt that there was still some hope, he constantly appeared at the door of the small sick-room, looking anxiously in upon his son, who never stopped talking, but 'with great difficulty and effort,' as his mother said, 'and with that terrible rattle in his throat'. From time to time it seemed that the Prince's hope might be justified; subcutaneous injections of ether and strychnine brought the patient momentarily round; but then he relapsed again. Princess Alexandra wiped the sweat from his face and neck, and the nurses placed packs of ice on his forehead. At last he cried out, 'Something too awful has happened. My darling brother George is dead.' He then asked, 'Who is that? Who is that? Who is that?' murmuring the question repeatedly until he died.

The Prince was grief-stricken, quite 'broken down', as his mother said. He burst into tears when the Princess's devoted friend Oliver Montagu came down to Sandringham to comfort her. Until the day of the funeral he kept returning to gaze upon the body. At the funeral he 'broke down terribly', sobbing uncontrollably. In a printed copy of the sermon preached at Sandringham the next Sunday he wrote, 'To my dearest Wife, in remembrance of our beloved Eddy, who was taken from us. "He is not dead but sleepeth." From her devoted but broken-hearted husband, Bertie.'

For years the hat which Prince Eddy had been wearing when he went out shooting for the last time, and which he had waved to his mother as, glancing back, he had caught sight of her at a window, was kept hanging on a hook in her bedroom. And for years, too, his own room was kept exactly as it had been when he was alive to use it, his tube of toothpaste being preserved as he had left it, the soap in the washbasin being replaced when it mouldered, a Union Jack draped over the bed, and his uniforms displayed behind the glass door of a wardrobe.

'Gladly would I have given my life for his,' the Prince told his mother, 'as I put no value on mine . . . Such a tragedy has never before occurred in the annals of our family.' Yet he knew in his heart that Prince Eddy had been hopelessly ill-qualified for the position for which his birth had destined him. And it was of inestimable comfort to his father that his new heir, Prince George, who was quite content to marry Princess May, seemed, on the contrary, suited in every way to kingship.

When Prince Eddy died, Queen Victoria was seventy-two and had already celebrated her Golden Jubilee. In 1897, on the occasion of her Diamond Jubilee, she was driven through six miles of London's streets and accorded such an ovation, so she recorded in mingled pride, surprise and delight, as no one had ever received before: 'The crowds were quite indescribable, and their enthusiasm truly marvellous and deeply touching. The cheering was quite deafening, and every face seemed to be filled with real joy.' Tears of gratitude had fallen from her eyes, and the Princess of Wales had leaned forward in the carriage to touch her hand.

Now her sight was failing, and her limbs were stiffened by rheumatism. But on her eightieth birthday in 1899 her cheeks were still rosy and friends commented on her good spirits. The Boer War broke out, however, a few months later; and her next birthday was her last. She felt 'tired and upset' by all the 'trials and anxieties' she had had to endure.

On 18 June 1901, the Prince of Wales and her other surviving children were summoned to Osborne. The Prince arrived on 19 June, but his mother had rallied by then and he did not stay the night. Three days later he was back again and as he entered her room she looked up for a moment and held out her arms. She whispered 'Bertie', then lapsed into the unconsciousness from which she never emerged. The Prince put his head into his hands and wept.

Later that day his mother died. He was King at last. The Edwardian Age had begun. And, as though to herald its beginning, the Kaiser, the King of the Belgians and the King of Portugal, waiting for the funeral of the Queen to start, stood by a fireplace in a corridor in Windsor Castle, where smoking had always been strictly forbidden, puffing at cigars.

Part II

KING
1901-1910

13

King of the Castle

During my absence Bertie has had all your beloved Mother's rooms dismantled and all her precious things removed.

Emerging from the Reform Club on his way to dinner with the tenants of his De Vere Gardens flat, Henry James was shocked to see a newspaper placard proclaiming 'Death of the Queen'. The streets seemed 'strange and indescribable', the people in them dazed and hushed, almost as though they were frightened. It was 'a very curious and unforgettable impression'; and James, sensing London's fear that the Queen's death would 'let loose incalculable forces for possible ill', was himself 'very pessimistic'.

Writing later to friends in Austria on the black-bordered paper of the Reform Club, he had not expected to feel such grief for the 'simple running down of an old used-up watch'. But he deeply lamented the passing of 'little mysterious Victoria' and the succession of that 'arch vulgarian', 'Edward the Caresser', who had been 'carrying on with Mrs Keppel in so undignified a manner'. 'His succession, in short, [was] ugly and [made] all for vulgarity and frivolity'. At dinner he heard John Morley say that the King had made a 'good impression' at his first Privy Council meeting, to which James added the doubtful comment, '*Speriamo.*'

The Times shared Henry James's gloomy outlook. It admitted that King Edward had 'never failed in his duty to the throne and the nation'. But there must have been many times when he had prayed, 'lead us not into temptation' with 'a feeling akin to hopelessness'. *The Times*, in fact, could not pretend that there was nothing in the King's long career which those who respected him 'would wish otherwise'.

The new King was fifty-nine. His fair beard was turning grey, and although a lotion was vigorously applied to his scalp twice a day, he was nearly bald. Exceedingly portly, he still walked as if he were late for some appointment, his stout legs full of energy. He entered upon his inheritance with appealing enthusiasm and zest. At Windsor Castle and Buckingham Palace he strode about with his hat on his head, his dog trotting after him, a walking stick in his hand, a cigar in his mouth, giving orders; opening cupboards; peering into cabinets; ransacking drawers; clearing rooms formerly used by the Prince Consort and not touched since his death; dispatching case-loads of relics and ornaments to a special room in the Round Tower at Windsor; destroying statues and busts of John Brown; burning the papers of his mother's pretentious and wily Indian attendant, the Munshi, whose letters from the Queen were eventually retrieved from his widow; throwing out hundreds of 'rubbishy old coloured photographs' and useless bric-à-brac; setting inventory clerks to work at listing the cluttered accumulations of half a century; rearranging pictures. His Surveyor of Pictures recorded:

> He lost no time in decision. I found it useless to ask the King if I should hang this *there* or another *here* and so on. His mind could not take it in . . . 'Offer it up,' he would say and when 'offered up' he would come to see and perhaps put his head on one side, all with a twinkle in his eye, and say, 'That is not *amiss*,' or perhaps he would at once say that he did not like it. He enjoyed sitting in a room with the men working about him, and liked giving directions himself as to the actual position of pictures.

'I do not know much about art,' he would say, rolling his *r*'s in that characteristic German way of his, 'but I think I know something about ar-r-rangement.' He certainly knew a great deal about the family portraits, 'and was seldom at fault, even with almost unknown members of various Saxon duchies'.

He gave instructions for new bathrooms and lavatories to be installed; for the telephone system to be extended; for various coach houses to be converted into garages for the motor-cars which now came rattling and sputtering through the gates; for rooms to be redecorated, supervising the work himself, as the Queen 'had little interest in such matters', having all the varnish stripped off the oak panelling.

He would brook no opposition to his plans, overcoming any resistance with good-natured firmness, determined not to allow inconvenient sentiment to stand in the way of necessary overhaul. 'Alas!' Queen Alexandra lamented to her sister-in-law in Berlin. 'During my absence [in Copenhagen] Bertie has had all your beloved Mother's rooms dismantled and all her precious things removed.' He caused even greater offence to his sisters by disregarding his mother's will, which had provided for Osborne House to be kept in the family, and by presenting the place to the nation for use as a Royal Naval College and a convalescent home for naval officers.

As well as reorganizing the royal palaces, the King also transformed the court, drastically reforming both the Lord Steward's and the Lord Chamberlain's offices. He appointed new grooms-in-waiting and gentlemen ushers, making Sir Dighton Probyn Keeper of the Privy Purse; retaining Sir Francis Knollys as his private secretary; and taking more and more into his confidence Lord Rosebery's clever, subtle, handsome friend, Lord Esher, who eventually, in the words of the Secretary for War, St John Brodrick, 'constituted himself the unofficial adviser of the crown'. As a supposedly self-seeking *éminence grise*, Esher was disliked and distrusted by those who suspected his motives for so sedulously acquiring authority and influence to be less disinterested than they were. Lord Carrington recognized him as an 'extraordinary' and 'clever' man, but added that he might be dangerous and was certainly unscrupulous. 'He seems to be able to run about Buckingham Palace as he likes,' Carrington noted in his journal. 'He must be a considerable nuisance to the Household . . . He is not trusted by the general public who look on him as an intriguer.' Margot Asquith described him as 'a man of infinite curiosity and discretion, what the servants call "knowing" . . . He has more intelligence than most of the court pests. Slim with the slim, straight with the straight, the fault I find with him is common to all courtiers, he hardly knows what is important from what is not.'

An exceptionally ceremonious man, Lord Esher was doubtful at first that all the King's changes in the running of the Household were for the better. The King was 'kind and debonair and not undignified', Esher thought, but 'too *human*'. The sanctity of the throne was gradually disappearing, and Esher could not help but 'regret the mystery and awe of the old court'. The 'quiet impressive entrance' of the monarch before dinner was 'as obsolete as Queen Elizabeth'. The King came down unannounced, and dinner itself was 'like an ordinary party' with 'none of the "hush" of the Queen's dinners'.

Before long, however, Esher was pleased to note that the etiquette 'stiffened up very much'; ladies were required to wear tiaras and men to appear in court costume with decorations.

Decorations for the King were of transcendent significance, and he took a quite touching delight in awarding them. Lord Carrington remembered how the King, especially dressed in field marshal's uniform for the occasion, had expressed—and had obviously felt—'the greatest pleasure' in giving him the Order of the Garter, the 'finest Order in the world'. 'His Majesty had gone to the trouble' of doing so in a room filled with reminiscences of their Indian tour, turning the occasion into a memorable little ceremony and breaking with tradition to make a short and apposite speech as he held his friend's hand. 'I was so much moved,' Carrington recorded in his journal, 'that I left the Garter behind at Buckingham Palace, but Elsom (my old footman) now a "Royal" came running out with it and saved the situation.'

It pained the King beyond measure to see decorations incorrectly worn, particularly those which he had awarded himself. Very occasionally he would be amused by some peculiarly atrocious solecism as, for instance, Henry Ponsonby's wearing two Jubilee Medals at once at a dinner in Germany. But the normal response was a pained rebuke such as that delivered to Sir Felix Semon, who was informed at Chatsworth that the Star of the Victorian Order was '*usually* worn on the *left* breast'.

He could not forbear correcting any error his sharp eye detected, though he generally contrived to do so as tactfully as possible. Noticing an English diplomat wearing his G.C.B. incorrectly, he informed him quietly of his mistake in German, employing a Bavarian dialect which no one in the room, other than the diplomat himself, who had a Bavarian mother, would have understood. Similarly, at a ball at Devonshire House, he waited until it was time to wish his host good night and to congratulate him on the 'magnificent manner in which everything had been done', before informing the Duke confidentially that there was, however, one thing that had not been quite right. What was that? the Duke asked anxiously, and was told, 'You have got your Garter on upside down.'

Taking care to be exceptionally tactful with foreign diplomats, the King was seen to draw aside the Swedish Minister, who had appeared at court with his medals in the wrong order, and was heard to whisper in his ear—as though imparting a state secret of the utmost significance—the name of the court jewellers, 'Hunt and Roskill, 148 Piccadilly'.

The King was equally distressed to see men wearing their uniforms improperly or turning out in civilian clothes which he considered inappropriate to the occasion. On embarking upon a continental tour in 1903 he had his suite paraded on the deck of the *Victoria and Albert* in full dress uniform. 'The sea was rough,' recorded Charles Hardinge, Assistant Under-Secretary of State for Foreign Affairs, who was one of the party, 'and it was somewhat painful staggering about the deck in full uniform, but it seemed to amuse the King to see us. Our clothes were all criticized without exception.'

Scarcely anyone who came into contact with the King escaped such criticism. Even a woodwind player who was seen to be wearing a black tie instead of a white at Covent Garden was sharply reprimanded by an equerry. 'He could not endure a button being even an inch out of place,' as the Duke of Manchester said, 'and thought nothing of calling down any person, no matter who they might be, if the slightest item was wrong.' The Duke went on to cite one of the King's extremely rare mistakes when he told an Austrian nobleman at Marienbad that he was doing something he ought not to do. 'What was that?' the Austrian enquired, much perturbed. He was wearing, 'quite inadvertently', the King was sure, the tie of the English Guards. How long had these been the Guards' colours? the nobleman asked and, on being told for over three hundred years, was able to reply, 'Sir, they have been my family's colours *for over seven hundred years*.'

The King was intensely annoyed to find himself wrong in such matters. Discovering the French Ambassador wearing an unfamiliar ribbon to his Grand Cordon of Charles III at a reception at the Spanish Embassy, he took him aside to advise him that his valet ought to be more careful. On being told by the Ambassador that the ribbon had lately been changed by the Spanish court, he evinced the deepest shock. 'Impossible! Impossible!' he said in so loud and agitated a voice that other guests at the reception imagined some dreadful catastrophe had befallen Europe. 'Impossible! I should know about it!' He made it his first duty the next morning to find out whether or not the ribbon had been changed; and, being told it had been, he immediately summoned the Spanish Ambassador to reprimand him gravely for not having informed him.

Ladies were not immune from the King's rebukes. The Queen was a law unto herself and had been known to wear her Garter star on the wrong side when she felt it clashed with her other jewels. But the Queen's eccentricities were no excuse for anyone else's. The Duchess of Marlborough, who appeared at dinner with a diamond crescent instead of the prescribed tiara, was sharply reprimanded for having done so. In the King's opinion there was a suitable manner of dress for every conceivable occasion, even on board the royal yacht where a minister was scolded for wearing knee-breeches instead of trousers and a race-horse trainer for having a black scarf round his neck rather than a white one. Catching sight of R.B. Haldane, whose German sympathies were well-known, in an unsuitable hat at a garden party, he exclaimed, 'See my War Minister approach in a hat he inherited from Goethe!' And at Coburg in the middle of some instruction to Henry Ponsonby, suddenly noticing the man's dreadful trousers, he broke off to ask where on earth he had found them: they were quite the ugliest pair he had ever seen in his life. Lord Rosebery, always unpredictable in his choice of attire, was a particular irritant. The King contented himself with eyeing Rosebery angrily 'all through dinner' when he had the temerity to present himself aboard the royal yacht wearing a white tie with a Yacht Squadron mess-jacket. But he could not contain himself when Rosebery came to an evening reception at Buckingham Palace in trousers instead of knee-breeches. 'I presume,' the King growled at him, 'that you have come in the suite of the American Ambassador.'

'My dear fellow,' he once said, 'more in sorrow than in anger', to a groom-in-waiting who was to accompany him to a wedding, 'where is your white waistcoat? Is it possible you are thinking of going to a *wedding* in a black waistcoat?' And to a secretary who had thought it odd to be told to present himself in 'a sort of Stock Exchange attire' for a visit to see the pictures at the Salon in Paris and who had thought it prudent to question the instructions, the King replied, 'I thought everyone must know that a *short* jacket is always worn with a silk hat at a private view in the morning.' He himself was infallible. He even knew what the answer was when the Russian Ambassador asked him if it would be proper for him to attend race-meetings while in mourning: 'To Newmarket, yes, because it means a bowler hat, but not to the Derby because of the top hat.'

He selected his own clothes with the nicest care, and earnestly discussed with his tailor the exact manner in which he thought the cut of the evening dress waistcoat could be improved or the precise reduction that ought to be made in the length of the back of a tail coat. Austen Chamberlain, accompanying the King on a cruise as Minister in Attendance, was 'very much amused' to overhear an instruction issued to a Swiss valet as the yacht approached the Scottish coast: '*Un costume un peu écossais demain.*'

The King's taste in clothes was generally conservative: he attempted to prevent the demise of the frock-coat and to revive the fashion of wearing knee-breeches with evening dress. He refused to wear a Panama hat and derided those who did; he continued to wear a silk hat while riding in Rotten Row long after this was considered old-fashioned. Yet he made several new fashions respectable. His adoption of a short, dark blue jacket with silk facings, worn with a black bow tie and black trousers, on the voyage out to India led to the general acceptance of the dinner jacket. Twenty years later, so Winston Churchill told his mother, 'everyone wore tweed suits' at Goodwood Races following the King's 'sensible example'; while his appearance at Longchamps Races in an unusually tall, peculiarly shaped top hat started a hunt in London for similar headgear by fashion-conscious Frenchmen, who subsequently discovered that the King's hat was made at a shop in the Place Vendôme and that its shape was attributable to its designer's anxiety to conceal the baldness at the back of his head. Nevertheless, many other similar hats were soon to be seen on the Paris boulevards. The King's adoption of the loose, waist-banded Norfolk jacket made this type of jacket popular all over England; while photographs of him wearing a felt hat with a rakishly curved brim brought back from Homburg, or a green, plumed Tyrolean hat from Marienbad, led to thousands of others being sold at home. He found it more comfortable—then decided it looked elegant—to leave the bottom button of his waistcoat undone, and soon no gentleman ever did that button up.

Sometimes he went too far. The sight of the King on a German railway station in a green cap, pink tie, white gloves and brown overcoat induced the *Tailor and Cutter* to express the fervent hope 'that his Majesty [had] not brought this outfit home'. Other observers were driven to complain about the tightness of his coats, and the excessive size of his tie-pins, as well as the ungainly figure he cut in those foreign uniforms which he loved to wear even when their short coats, as those of the Portuguese cavalry, 'showed an immense expanse of breeches', or when their huge, shaggy greatcoats, as those of the Russian dragoons, made him look 'like a giant polar bear'. But despite these lapses the King was the acknowledged arbiter of sartorial taste as well as a recognized expert on uniforms, decorations and medals, of which he had an immense collection. When he was at Marienbad, continental tailors came with notebooks and cameras to record any changes in style he might have favoured since the previous season. And in the West End of London, there were often to be seen in the streets short, stout pedestrians who copied not only his clothes but also his beard and way of moving so faithfully that other passers-by respectfully raised their hats to them.

Apart from clothes, sport, food and women, the King had few other interests outside his work. He enjoyed the ritual and regalia of Freemasonry; he liked pottering about in the gardens of his friends, pointing out with his walking stick arrangements and vistas that appealed to him, commenting on alterations that had been made since his last visit. He often went to the theatre and the opera, his arrival at the Royal Opera House, Covent Garden, being preceded by that of a chef and six footmen and by numerous hampers filled with cloths, silver, gold plate and food for the ten- or twelve-course meal which was served in the room at the back of the royal box during the hour-long interval.

The King's favourite theatrical performances were plays about modern upper-class society, musical comedies and light opera rather than classical tragedies, Shakespeare or anything more intellectually demanding. Queen Alexandra, on the other hand, preferred grand opera, and once at Windsor gave instructions for the band to play Wagner. At the same time the King sent a request for Offenbach to the dismayed bandmaster, who thought it advisable to compromise with a selection from Gilbert and Sullivan operettas and thus got into trouble with them both. According to Lady Warwick, 'the King's retort to the attempt [by Sir Walter Parratt, Master of the King's Musick] to introduce more serious musical compositions at the state concerts was to have a performance by Sousa and his band'.

Because of its connections with the court, he took an interest in the Poet Laureateship, and had urged the claims of Swinburne against those of Alfred Austin, whose eventual appointment as successor to Tennyson was due to his services to the Conservative Party. But the King seems rarely to have even so much as opened a book, and almost never to have finished one, a notable exception being Mrs Henry Wood's romantic novel, *East Lynne*, which he had read in Egypt as a young man, had recommended to his travelling companions, and about which he subsequently asked them questions to test their familiarity with the plot. On receiving a book he would say how much he was looking forward to reading it; but Winston Churchill, whose mother sent the King a copy of *The Malakand Field Force*, seems to have been uniquely fortunate in being assured that the book had actually been read with 'the greatest possible interest'. When supervising the alterations at Buckingham Palace after his mother's death, he airily gave instructions to the librarian at Windsor to 'pack up' his father's fine collection of books and to 'get rid of those which were not required'. And when furnishing the library at Sandringham he summoned a man from Hatchard's bookshop, instructing him to fill the shelves with whatever volumes might be considered suitable for a country house.

Nor did the King display much interest in the visual arts, particularly not in anything which smacked of the *avant-garde*. In painting he insisted on the strictest accuracy in representation, and far preferred portraits to landscapes. On being shown Holman Hunt's picture of the London Docks on the night of his marriage, he looked at it closely for a few seconds and then, by way of comment, asked the single question, 'Where am I?'

He far preferred to be in the open air, although his outdoor activities were now rather limited. Riding not very well, he had still gone out with the West Norfolk Hounds in the 1880s, but his hunting days were over long before he came to the throne. Still weighing over sixteen stone, he was also both too heavy and too old for fencing, which he had practised as a younger man, or for lawn tennis, which he had begun to play in the early 1880s as an additional means of losing weight. He had never been much of a swimmer, and had never taken to cricket, which he had once played on the Curragh, dropping two easy catches and failing to score a single run. Later, he did occasionally play at Sandringham, where he liked it rather better, as it was the common practice to bowl him a few easy balls so that he could score some runs and thus be kept in a good temper. He did not have the patience for fishing, which was, in any case, too lonely an occupation for him. Nor did he greatly care for golf, though he had courses made at both Windsor and Sandringham on which Queen Alexandra and Princess Victoria enjoyed playing a wild game of the Queen's own invention; this involved a race from tee to hole to see who could get a ball in first. The game usually ended in a hockey-like scrimmage on the green, where the cut and battered balls were once found by the King, who thought someone was trying to play a trick on him.

Towards the end of his life the King took the greatest pleasure in riding a specially made tricycle up and down the drive at Sandringham. He also much enjoyed motoring, provided he was not accompanied by the Queen, 'whose one idea was not to run over a dog' and who tapped the chauffeur on the shoulder whenever she thought his speed excessive. Her husband, on the contrary, liked to be driven extremely fast, and could not bear the sight of a car in front of him on a stretch of country road. Motorists, therefore, became accustomed to being overtaken by a large Daimler or sixty-five horsepower Mercedes in which a bearded figure sat on the blue morocco back seat, smoking a large cigar, as he urged his chauffeur on, with impatient gestures and gruff commands, to ever greater speeds. After 1907 motorists also became used to the uncouth sound of a special horn in the shape of a four-key bugle which was always carried in the royal cars after their owner had admired a similar device employed by the Kaiser.

The King had been introduced to the pleasures of motoring in 1898 at Warwick Castle, whence he had made a brief excursion in a six-horse-power Daimler. The next year, while staying with Mr and Mrs George Cavendish-Bentinck at Highcliffe Castle in Hampshire, he had been taken out by John Douglas-Scott-Montagu, later second Lord Montagu of Beaulieu, in a twelve-horse-power Daimler which, to the consternation of the ladies sitting in the back, reached a speed of forty miles an hour. At that time very severe restrictions were imposed upon the speed of cars, and it was not until 1903 that the limit was raised to twenty miles an hour on roads deemed suitable for such fast-moving traffic. Yet the King, unaffected by the traffic laws of his realm and driving in cars which bore the Royal Arms on the door-panels but carried no number plates, paid no attention to the regulations. He often congratulated himself on having driven along the Brighton road in 1906 at sixty miles an hour, three times as fast as the law allowed, though he professed himself to be uncompromisingly opposed to motor racing, which he thought 'would be very dangerous for the occupants of the motors and still more so for the Public'. His motor engineer, C.W. Stamper, who rode in front next to the driver, ready to jump down with his tool-bag if there were any trouble with the engine, recorded that the King's Mercedes was once rattling up to Newark at 'a good pace' when the chauffeur failed to notice a culvert in the road which the car's wheels struck with a fearful bump. 'Stop! Stop!' the King called out. 'Do you want to kill me?' But he seemed more disturbed by the dent in his brown bowler, which he showed indignantly to Stamper, than by the threat to his own safety. Generally as he got out of the car he would say to Stamper with satisfaction, 'A very good run, Stamper; a very good run, indeed!'

At Queen Alexandra's instigation, so it was said, the King gave up the cruel practice of shooting pigeons released from traps. But to the end of his life he continued to derive the greatest pleasure from most other forms of shooting. He was always seen to be in excellent spirits when, dressed in a rough country suit with heavy boots and an Inverness cape, and accompanied by his favourite retriever, Diver, he left the house with the prospect of a day's good sport. After tripping over a rabbit hole at Windsor in 1905 he was unable to walk out with the other guns, but he solved the problem by bringing into use a low pony carriage in which he was drawn to his stand, where the pony was taken out of the shafts so that the King could shoot from his seat.

As he grew older the King seemed to enjoy a day's racing even more than shooting. He relished the company of racing people and what he himself termed the 'glorious uncertainty of the turf'. Before the middle of the 1890s he had had very few successes as an owner. But his fine horse *Persim-*

mon won the Derby in 1896—prompting Rosebery to remark that everyone would say that all the other horses had been stopped—and four years later, after another splendid royal horse, *Ambush II*, had won the Grand National, *Persimmon*'s brother, *Diamond Jubilee*, also won the Derby. As well as the Derby, *Diamond Jubilee* won the Newmarket Stakes, the Eclipse Stakes, the St Leger and the Two Thousand Guineas, after which last success its owner appeared to be 'delirious with joy'.

Admiring success in others, the King revelled in the glow of triumph himself. He seemed never happier than when a victory on the turf was welcomed by the crowd as an opportunity to cheer him and wave their hats at him, shouting 'Good old Teddy!' In the last year of his life, *Minoru* won the Derby for him for the third time, and racing correspondents reported that there had 'never been such cheering', that tens of thousands of people sang 'God Save the King', and that even the policemen on duty, infected by the almost hysterical atmosphere of the occasion, threw their helmets in the air and joined in the roars of acclaim. That night the King gave his usual Derby Day dinner at Buckingham Palace to the members of the Jockey Club. His chefs had excelled themselves with their turtle soup and whitebait and those sugary concoctions made up in the royal racing colours of purple, scarlet and gold. And the happy host, who had returned from the Continent a fortnight before looking tired and ill, now seemed suddenly to have recovered his health and spirits in the excitement of his success.

Criticisms of the King's extravagance as a racing man were not altogether just. He was certainly impulsively lavish in his presents to his jockeys and stablemen after a win: when *Ambush II* won the Grand National he gave £500 to the jockey, £250 to the head stableman and £50 to the lad who looked after the horse. But his prize-money was considerable. In 1896 and 1897, when he earned a total of nearly £44,000, he was second in the list of winning owners; and in the single year of 1900 he earned almost £32,000. *Diamond Jubilee*, who won the Derby that year, was eventually sold for £31,500. Altogether, between 1886 and 1910, from stud fees and stake money, his stables took well over £400,000. Nor was he, contrary to many reports, an extravagant gambler. It seems that the largest bet he ever placed on a horse to win was £600; and although he could not have afforded to lose such a sum in his youth, by 1894—when he did lose it by backing the favourite, Baron Hirsch's *Matchbox*, to win the Paris Grand Prix—his finances were in a less perilous condition.

As early as 1869 Queen Victoria had noted in her journal her son's hopes and expectations of being granted a larger income. But Gladstone had contended that it was up to the Queen to make provision 'in consideration of the extent to which she [allowed] him to discharge her social duties for her'. Twelve years later Francis Knollys told Lady Spencer, so Gladstone's secretary recorded in his diary, that the question of the Prince of Wales's debts could not be postponed much longer. That will be an awkward matter for the government to deal with. It is sure to raise a very strong feeling against the Queen who (it will be thought and not unfairly thought) should have made some allowance to H.R.H. in consideration of the extra expenses which fell upon him by reason of her seclusion.

But it was not until 1889 that the House of Commons increased his income by £36,000 and granted him a capital sum of £60,000 so that he could make provision for his children. And even then, having spent £300,000 on the improvements at Sandringham, he had found it impossible to carry on without recourse to borrowing from friends and even, so it was supposed, from moneylenders whom French detectives reported as being perpetual visitors to his various hotels. He was apparently also reduced from time to time to selling various possessions. Joseph Duveen recalled a man coming into his shop with a piece of jewellery for which he asked £100. Duveen claimed to have told the man it was worth much more than that and to have given him £500. He was 'pretty sure' that his customer had been the Prince of Wales.

When the King came to the throne he had no private capital left, nor any to expect under the terms of his mother's will which provided for her own private fortune to pass to her younger children. Parliament, however, came to his help by granting him the handsome income of £470,000; and in the hands of men, including Sir Ernest Cassel, who were more capable of administering it than he was himself, that income, which was £85,000 more than Queen Victoria had received and to which was added £60,000 from the Duchy of Lancaster, proved adequate to withstand the strain that his way of life placed upon it.

Certainly the King's guests never had cause to complain about their host's hospitality. His reforms of the Household had included pensioning off many under-employed servants such as the Indians—whose sole duty it had been to cook the curry for luncheon whether anyone wanted it or not—and several of Queen Victoria's huge kitchen staff of nineteen chefs and numerous cooks, bakers, confectioners, apprentices and underlings. But the food in the royal palaces, under the supervision of M. Menager, was still as plentiful as it was excellent.

Some of the Queen's former guests objected to the less formal atmosphere as Lord Esher did. But most of them welcomed the relative informality which even at Windsor permitted impromptu dances to be held in the crimson drawing-room under the energetic supervision of that tireless waltzer, Lord Fisher.

Relaxed as the atmosphere at Windsor was, though, and 'extraordinarily comfortable' as Haldane found all the arrangements, no one was allowed to be late for anything if the King were not to be deeply offended, perhaps even enraged. Once when Asquith, as Prime Minister, was late in joining a party in the Castle courtyard, the King 'looked first at his watch and then at the Castle clock', so Mrs Asquith said, 'and fussed crossly about the yard'. Angrily turning to his gentlemen-in-waiting, he asked, 'What have you done? Where have you looked for him? Did you not give him my command?'

The arrangement had been to meet in the courtyard at four o'clock, to motor first to the gardens and then to Virginia Water for tea. And it was now ten minutes past four.

The distracted gentlemen-in-waiting flew about, but I could see in a moment that Henry was not likely to turn up, so I begged the King to get into his motor [Margot Asquith recorded]. He answered with indignation, 'Certainly not. I cannot start without the Prime Minister . . .' Seeing affairs at a standstill I went up to the Queen and said I feared there had been a scandal at court, and that Henry must have eloped with one of the maids of honour. I begged her to save my blushes by commanding the King to proceed, at which she walked up to him with her amazing grace, and, in her charming way, tapping him firmly on the arm pointed with a sweeping gesture to his motor and invited [Lady Londesborough] and Alice Keppel to accompany him: at which they all drove off . . . When we returned to the Castle we found that Henry had gone for a long walk with . . . one of the Queen's maids of honour, over which the King was jovial and even eloquent.

The Queen of course was frequently late, and although the King's usual reaction was to sit drumming his fingers and then to swallow his anger when she at last appeared with an insouciant, 'Am I late?', on one occasion at least, according to a royal chef, he took his revenge. It was during a luncheon party at Windsor where thirty guests had been kept waiting for a quarter of an hour by the Queen's non-appearance. It was the custom at Windsor for the dining-room staff to serve the King and Queen first, then work their way down the table to the other end. When everyone had finished a bell was rung and the plates were cleared away for the next course. At this particular luncheon, however, the King gobbled each course and rang the bell as soon as he had cleared his own plate.

When the roast was reached the guests were beginning to give up hope of managing more than a few mouthfuls during the whole meal. All of them had hearty appetites, and there were downcast expressions before the dessert stage was reached. As the King had expected, Queen Alexandra was aware of their plight, but she could do nothing to help them, for it was to some extent her fault that the meal had been hurried.

At Balmoral, after the deer-stalking, grouse-driving and salmon-fishing, there were gillies' balls as well as card-games and even the occasional cinema show, which was 'jolly bad' in the opinion of one frequent guest, Sir Felix Semon, a nose and throat specialist of German descent, but at least it had the charm of novelty and was certainly much to be preferred to the 'deafening tribe of royal pipers in Highland garb, who, when game was served, solemnly marched three times round the table and made a hellish noise with their bagpipes'.

The King was much less tolerant of drunkenness among his Highland servants than his mother had been, and summarily dismissed one of them who appeared in front of him one day barely able to stand. But life at Balmoral was otherwise much freer than it had been in his mother's time, and for most of the guests it was more enjoyable. Winston Churchill, who went there as a twenty-seven-year-old Member of Parliament in 1902, told his mother how 'pleasant and easy-going' it was (adding that she must 'gush' to the King about his having written to say how much he had enjoyed himself). Edward Grey, the Foreign Secretary, gave similar testimony to the pleasures of Balmoral. He 'always groaned' when he had to go there; but it was 'observed with amusement' how he immediately succumbed to the King's charm and how, on arriving home—provided with a hamper containing a venison pie, fruit and a bottle of champagne for the journey—he invariably confessed that he had had a most agreeable time. Like every other guest, though, Grey was rather dispirited by Balmoral's interior decorations and was much relieved when even Queen Alexandra—who had insisted that, as this was Queen Victoria's favourite home, it must remain exactly as it had been in her time and that none of the dreadful wallpapers must be touched—could not tolerate the tartan carpets and curtains in the drawing-room.

Most of the King's friends preferred Sandringham to any of his other homes. It had not been improved in appearance either by the rebuilding which had been carried out in 1869 or by the new wing which had been added after the fire of 1891 had completely destroyed thirteen bedrooms in the upper part of the house. There was little worth looking at inside, apart from the tapestries designed by Goya which were a present from the King of Spain and were hung in the dining-room. But there was a special *Gemütlichkeit* at Sandringham not to be found elsewhere. Strangers felt quite as much at ease there as they had done when the King was Prince of Wales. Like Henry Broadhurst, Joseph Arch, the working-class founder of the Agricultural Labourers' Union and Liberal Member of Parliament for the North West division of Norfolk, was a contented week-end guest. And a deputation of trade union leaders was also made to feel welcome.

The guest list at Sandringham was not quite as varied as it had been in the days when Lord Alington's daughter—surprised to find that she had been invited at the same time as George Lewis, the solicitor—had been shocked that the royal family played baccarat, 'an illegal game, every night . . . [with] a real table, and rakes, and everything like the rooms at Monte Carlo'. But although bridge had taken the place of baccarat, Gottlieb's orchestra played in the hall, and the barrel-organ, previously brought into use for dancing, was now usually silent, Lord Carrington thought it was just like the 'old days'. He wrote:

> I could hardly realize that the Prince of Wales was King. He seemed so entirely himself . . . his own kind dear self. The Queen walked out alone after dinner, and the King remained in the dining-room and smoked as he used to do . . . When the Queen retired we all went into the smoking-room, which was the same as ever. The Leech pictures, the same furniture, the table where the Equerry wrote the stable orders for the morning, the bowling alley next door, and the whole thing brought back memories of Blandford, Oliver Montagu, Christopher Sykes . . . Charlie Beresford, Charlie Dunmore, and old Quin.

14
The King at Work

There is no use in ministers liking the King if he is treated like a puppet.

Immediately on his accession, the King took up his new duties with obvious relish, conscious of the importance of his vocation and enjoying to the full its responsibilities. Lord Redesdale described how he once called at Marlborough House during the early months of the new reign before the King had moved to Buckingham Palace:

> I found him in his private sitting-room all alone, and we sat smoking and talking over old times for a couple of hours. Towards midnight he got up and said, 'Now I must bid you good night, for I must set to work,' pointing to a huge pile of familiar red boxes. 'Surely,' I said, 'your Majesty is not going to tackle all that work to-night!' His answer was, 'Yes, I must! Besides, it is all so interesting,' and then he gave me one of his happy smiles.

Lord Esher also described the enthusiasm with which the King came to his new work, how he would ask question after question, interrupt the answers with his quick, 'Yes . . . yes . . . yes', give orders, scribble notes on bits of paper in his scarcely legible handwriting, and then stand in front of the fire with one of his immense cigars between his teeth, 'looking wonderfully like Henry VIII, only better tempered'. The impression he gave Lord Esher was 'that of a man, who, after long years of pent-up action, had suddenly been freed from restraint and revelled in his liberty'. He insisted on having all his letters 'brought to him unopened, about 400 a day', and sorted them by himself. 'He tried at first to open them all but found that impossible.' He also insisted on signing the 6,600 army commissions which had accumulated during the last months of his mother's reign; and he then embarked on the Royal Navy commissions, which had formerly been signed at the Admiralty as traditionally being the responsibility of the Lord High Admiral, but he found that additional task beyond him.

He was too restless and impatient, however, for prolonged desk-work. Soon he took to summoning secretaries and giving them outlines of what he wanted to say rather than writing long letters himself as his mother had done. He was far more at home in fulfilling those public engagements which he was called upon to carry out in such numbers and which he performed so well. He gave the impression of being really interested in what he was doing and displayed an ability to listen to officials telling him things he knew already, or did not want to know at all, with every sign of absorbed concentration. According to some observers, though, he was not at his best at levees. But then, those who attended levees did not care for them either. They could be tedious, and even on occasion embarrassing. An official was posted at the door leading into the throne room to turn away anyone who was incorrectly dressed. The absent-minded Arthur Hardinge, for instance, once appeared before the horrified King with a buttoned boot on one foot and an evening shoe on the other, a blunder he weakly excused on the grounds that he was very short-sighted. Edward Marsh, then a junior clerk in the Colonial Office, wrote of a levee in St James's Palace in 1902:

> The levee was a most wearisome performance and I don't know whether to laugh or cry when I think of the manner in which 1,500 of the educated classes spent their morning. It took about an hour to get round, through the successive pens in which one is shut up with the same little group of people . . . and when one reached 'the Presence' one was rushed through with just time to make one's bow to the red, bored, stolid sovereign.

If bored at levees at St James's, the King rarely displayed any lack of interest at equally tedious functions elsewhere. Every year there were reports of his laying foundation stones, opening exhibitions, attending dinners, visiting hospitals and schools, inspecting new libraries and art galleries with the same assiduity he had displayed as Prince of Wales. And even those whose comments were not for publication spoke of his geniality and *bonhomie*. Osbert Sitwell, as a boy at Eton, was present when he opened the School Library, a memorial to boys killed in the Boer War, and was struck by the 'very individual and husky warmth' of his voice: 'There was, as he spoke in public, a geniality in its sound, as of one who found in life the utmost enjoyment, and in spite of a rather prominent and severely attentive blue eye, and a certain appearance of fatigue, the chief impression was one of good humour.'

Every summer, between Ascot Races and Cowes Regatta, he went to an industrial town, usually in the Midlands or the North, to undertake the duties of an official visit. And every winter he opened Parliament in state, resuming a ceremonial which Queen Victoria had abandoned, and renewing the practice of reading the speech from the throne.

He was an effective speaker. At the first Privy Council meeting of his reign he had, as John Morley said, impressed his audience by his ability to speak fluently and spontaneously without a prepared script. On that occasion, after almost breaking down on referring to the irreparable loss he and the whole nation had suffered by the death of his 'beloved mother, the Queen', he spoke with what Lord Carrington described as 'dignity and pathos' for eight minutes without reference to a single note. It was a facility which he perfected. He told Lord Fisher that he had once learned a speech off by heart to welcome the French President to England. But when the time came to deliver it, he could not remember the words he had so laboriously memorized and was forced to 'keep on beginning at the beginning'. So, except when he had to say a few words in Danish or Russian, he had never tried to learn a speech again; and his delivery was all the better for it, whether in English, French or German. It was remembered with pleasure how, on a visit to Germany, he had been quite equal to the occasion when the Kaiser had risen to make an impressive speech at a dinner at which it had been agreed no speeches should be made. On completing his prepared oration, the Kaiser invited the King to reply. Undeterred, the King did so; and, apart from a moment's embarrassing silence when he tapped the table in an effort to recall a particular German word, which Prince von Bülow supplied for him, he made quite as effective a speech as his host had done. Very rarely did he make a mistake in one of these more or less impromptu speeches; and when, calling in at an Italian port during one of his Mediterranean cruises, he caused brief embarrassment in Rome and London by referring to a non-existent 'alliance' between England and Italy when he should have said 'friendship', it was admitted that the slip—which was not reported in the Press —was of a kind that the King scarcely ever made.

Admirably as he carried out his ceremonial and social duties, the King soon made it clear that he was not prepared to confine himself to making speeches, signing documents and laying foundation stones. He was not much concerned with domestic policies or with colonial affairs; he was bored to death by talk about free trade and tariff reform; but he evinced a deep interest in the army and the navy; in hospitals and medical research; and, above all, in foreign policy.

He told St John Brodrick, Secretary for War, that he expected to be consulted about the appointment and promotion of senior officers, about every important question of policy, and particularly about the reform of the army medical system which, so Brodrick said, 'he pressed forward from the first day of his reign'. He was equally insistent that matters of naval policy should be brought to his attention; and, when the time came, gave his unhesitating support to Lord Fisher, whose reforms, as Fisher himself recognized, might well have been scuppered by his opponents had not the King made it so forcibly obvious where his own sympathies lay in the First Sea Lord's bitter quarrel with the vain and tiresome Lord Charles Beresford.

As it was with the army and navy, so it was with medicine. Numerous hospitals had cause to be grateful for the attention he paid to their welfare. He helped to found the National Association for the Prevention of Consumption; he started King Edward's Hospital Fund which eventually had an annual income of over £150,000; and he assured one of his several medical friends, Sir Frederick Treves, that it was his 'greatest ambition not to quit this world until a real cure for cancer' had been found.

Concerned as he was with all these matters, however, he devoted only a fraction of the time to them that he gave to foreign affairs. Once a week he asked Charles Hardinge to have breakfast with him at Buckingham Palace, and he discussed foreign politics 'most of the time at these interviews with great breadth and interest'. He read through every dispatch that came from abroad, his secretary observed, 'often when the subject was very dull. Any inaccuracy annoyed him: even a slip of the pen put him out'. And he paid the same close attention to those private letters which he liked British ambassadors to write to him as supplements to their official dispatches. He studied draft treaties carefully, and occasionally made suggestions for alterations in their wording. He received foreign representatives alone in his room; and, when abroad, with the agreement of the Foreign Office, undertook diplomatic discussions both with other sovereigns and with their ministers.

His usefulness in this respect was widely recognized: as Disraeli had said of him, 'he really has seen everything and knows everybody'. So, too, was his conscientiousness appreciated. Charles Hardinge wrote:

> Often I had to suggest a visit which I knew would be irksome to him, or that he should see somebody that I knew he would not want to see, and he would exclaim, 'No, no, damned if I will do it!' But he always did it, however tiresome it might be for him, without my having to argue the point or in fact say another word. He had a very strong sense of the duties which his position entailed and he never shirked them.

Yet he was constantly given cause to complain that the government did not take him into their confidence, that he was consulted only when it suited their convenience, that he was often ignored, and that the excuses which ministers made to him when they failed to keep him informed of their actions were 'often as "gauche" as their omissions'. Uneasily aware that ministers had been far more punctilious in keeping the monarch informed of their problems and proposed solutions in Queen Victoria's time than they now were in his, he was deeply offended at what he took to be the least sign of slighting neglect. In the first few months of his reign he had reason to rebuke Lord Halsbury, the Lord Chancellor, for having, without reference to him, published a report about a new form of declaration against the doctrine of transubstantiation which, according to the Bill of Rights of 1689, the monarch was required to make before reading the speech from the throne. Since the King himself had suggested a modification in the wording of the declaration, which he took to be insulting to his Roman Catholic subjects, he was 'naturally much surprised that he had received no intimation, previous to his having read it in the newspapers, of the report, as it was an important matter concerning the Sovereign regarding which he ought to have been consulted'.

This was the first of numerous rebukes he felt obliged to administer. Throughout his reign he fought to maintain the Crown's right to be consulted, to prevent the Sovereign's becoming a 'mere signing machine', to retain those few remaining royal prerogatives which he felt were being gradually eroded. Yet he could not prevent their erosion. He was forced to accept not only Parliament's authority to cede territory, but also the Prime Minister's power to appoint and dismiss ministers without reference to the Sovereign, as well as the Cabinet's right to take over the patronage of so-called 'Crown' appointments, including the appointment of bishops which, in the last few years of his reign, was left in the hands of Campbell-Bannerman, born of Presbyterian parents in Glasgow, and Asquith, the son of a noncomformist Lancashire wool-spinner.

Although eventually he lost interest in the selection of bishops, he never did so in the case of diplomatic appointments. But his suggestions about these were quite as likely to be disregarded as they had been when he was Prince of Wales. In 1904, for example, his proposal that Arthur Herbert should go to Sweden and Sir Rennell Rodd to Morocco was followed by Rodd's being retained at Stockholm and Herbert's being despatched to Norway.

As though intent upon reminding his ministers of his concerned and watchful eye on their affairs, the King was as ready to offer his comments on the papers that were sent to him as he was to call attention to points which the ministers appeared to have overlooked or underestimated. One day complaining about the 'trash' which the Poet Laureate, Alfred Austin, sent to him, the next about papers being initialled instead of signed, or addressed to him in an incorrect manner, the King was determined not to be disregarded. Sometimes his interferences was fruitful: after his insistence that a grant of £50,000 to Lord Roberts on being created an earl on his return from South Africa was disgracefully mean, the grant was doubled. And although his objection to the appointment of the American Admiral Mahan as Regius Professor of Modern History at Cambridge—on the grounds that the chair ought to be held by an Englishman—did not result in the selection of the King's nominee, John Morley, it did bring about the appointment of a compromise candidate, the classical scholar John Bagnell Bury. Usually, however, the King's inconvenient views were, if possible, ignored in the hope that he would—as frequently he did—not continue to press them once they had been stated.

He never, however, ceased to press his right to be informed of government decisions before they were implemented. He appreciated that there might be some constitutional objection to his being allowed to see Cabinet papers while important matters were under discussion; and was evidently not surprised to learn that the Prime Minister considered it 'impossible . . . to yield in a matter of this kind'. But he did insist that it was his 'constitutional right to have all dispatches of any importance, especially those initiating or relating to a change of policy, laid before him prior to their being decided upon'. This right, 'always observed during Queen Victoria's reign', was certainly not always observed during his. In April 1906 he had reason to complain that the Prime Minister never brought anything before him, never consulted him in 'any way'. The perfunctory reports of Cabinet meetings that were sent to him really made 'an absolute fool of the King,' Francis Knollys protested the following year. 'There is no use in ministers liking the King if he is treated like a puppet.'

Under the next administration the situation did not much improve. When, in July 1908, the King asked to see 'a copy of Winston Churchill's Army Scheme', the Secretary for War passed the letter on to the Prime Minister, who sent it back with the comment, 'I return this. I have replied to Knollys in the sense which you suggested. It is, in any case, an impertinent request. These people have no right to interfere in any way in our deliberations.'

Most of the King's disagreements with his ministers were attributable to his being 'completely left in the dark'. Since the ruin of Sir Charles Dilke by the scandal of his divorce, and of Lord Randolph Churchill by disease, the King had no close political friends other than the Duke of Devonshire and Lord Rosebery. He did not get on with his Conservative Prime Minister, Arthur Balfour, with whom he had almost nothing in common. Nor did he relish the company of the three ministers, Lord Lansdowne, Lord Selborne and St John Brodrick, with whom, as Foreign Secretary, First Lord of the Admiralty and Secretary for War, he was principally concerned. Arnold-Forster, who succeeded Brodrick in 1903, was even worse, 'obstinate as a mule', according to Lord Esher, opposing everything which the King proposed. Nor were Balfour's opponents any better, in the King's opinion. Their leader, Sir Henry Campbell-Bannerman, had given particular offence by his criticisms of the conduct of the Boer War, speaking of British 'methods of barbarism in South Africa', a phrase that so annoyed the King that he had with difficulty been dissuaded from sending for the Liberal leader and telling him to avoid such remarks in future. Since then Campbell-Bannerman's 'gratuitous and ungenerous' attacks on the Prime Minister had continued to exasperate the King, who remarked to Knollys that it was 'curious' that he hardly ever opened his mouth 'without saying something in bad taste'.

When Campbell-Bannerman succeeded Balfour in 1905 and the King got to know him better, he became quite fond of him. But he continued to annoy the King by his speeches on foreign policy, a subject about which—like Lloyd George—he knew 'nothing'. 'Between ourselves,' Knollys confided to Esher in 1907, 'I don't think the King ever will like "C.B." politically.' As for Campbell-Bannerman's Under-Secretary for the Colonies, Winston Churchill, the King decided that he was *almost more* of [a] cad in office than he was in opposition' when he had 'showed a great want of taste' and talked 'simple nonsense'. He liked Churchill well enough as a man—though Francis Knollys did not—but Churchill's conduct towards Lord Milner was, in the King's opinion, 'simply scandalous', while his later comments on the 'richer classes' were 'unforgivable'.

There were, indeed, very few politicians whom the King fully trusted. He thought John Morley, Secretary for India, 'wonderfully agreeable and sensible'. He liked Arnold-Forster's successor, Haldane, who was 'always acceptable', though he described him as a 'damned radical lawyer and a German professor' when it fell to Haldane's lot to reduce the army estimates. He got on well, too, with the ebullient, working-class President of the Local Government Board, John Burns, whose appearance in knee-breeches, Esher said, was 'a revelation' and whose summary of his relationship with the King was expressed in the words, 'Me and 'im get on first-rate together.' The King was also particularly attached to Lord Fisher, a man of commanding personality, who whole-heartedly returned the King's affection and remained forever grateful for his support against his enemies. '*They would have eaten me but for Your Majesty*,' Fisher once told the King, who was delighted that his dear friend had triumphed over that 'gasbag' Beresford.

The King did not enjoy many victories himself. He did get his own way with the Order of Merit which he insisted, against all objections, should be open to military and naval officers despite the great number of other honours available to them. He was equally and successfully insistent that the Kaiser should be allowed to decorate all the British officers and men who had been in attendance on him while he was in England at the time of Queen Victoria's death, although his ministers much regretted the growing practice of British citizens accepting foreign decorations. The King also occasionally managed to wrest a written promise from a minister by declining to sign a paper until the required undertaking had been given. He refused, for example, to sign a Royal Warrant concerning army pay and allowances until Arnold-Forster had assured him in writing that no serving officer would have his pay cut, unless, at the same time, his duties were to be reduced. The King was again victorious when an attempt was made to limit the time an equerry could remain in his service to five years and to stop their army pay for that period. And when the government, which had agreed to pay the expenses he incurred in entertaining foreign sovereigns, asked that a distinction should be made between political and private visits, the King refused to allow that such a distinction could be made. He had his own views, Knollys told the Treasury, 'respecting the importance, from a political point of view, of visits of foreign sovereigns to this country which might not coincide with those of the Secretary of State'; and there might, therefore, be 'constant conflicts between the King on one side, and the Treasury and Foreign Office on the other'. This argument proving ineffective, the King said that he would send for the Prime Minister and tell him personally that he would not stand for 'such an attempted evasion by the Treasury of what was agreed upon' at the time of his accession. And at this threat, the Treasury gave way.

It was usually, however, the King who had to give way; and he rarely did so without a struggle. Determined to outgrow his reputation for being over-impressionable, in his later years he was often obstinate. And even when he had been convinced that he must yield to pressure he would not do so immediately, saying, 'I will consider the matter,' which his staff learned to translate as, 'I recognize that I will shortly have to surrender.'

In the first year of his reign a young officer who had been cashiered for cowardice by surrendering to the enemy in South Africa appealed to him to exercise his royal prerogative of mercy. The King read the papers, decided that the officer had been harshly treated, and approached the Commander-in-Chief, Lord Roberts. Roberts agreed with the King and asked the Adjutant-General to hold a special court of inquiry. The court recommended that the sentence should be quashed and that the officer should be convicted of an error of judgement and allowed to resign his commission. But the Secretary of State for War, who was concerned by the number of times officers had surrendered unnecessarily in the war and had considered it his unpleasant duty to make an example of this particular officer, threatened to resign if the harsher punishment were not imposed. The King's apparent willingness to pardon the young man anyway brought from the Prime Minister a warning of the possibility of the entire government's resignation in order to defend the principle of collective Cabinet responsibility. So the officer had to be sacrificed; and the King had to yield to the government's pressure.

The King also had to yield when the war was over and it was proposed to appoint a Royal Commission to enquire into its conduct. He wrote to the Prime Minister:

This system of 'washing our dirty linen in public' the late Queen had a horror of. The Government is a strong one with a large Parliamentary majority. Why, therefore, should Ministers pledge themselves, or give way to demands from unimportant M.P.'s? The proposed Inquiry will do the Army and also the Country harm in the eyes of the civilised world.

The Prime Minister replied that he was already pledged to the Commission and that he could not overrule the Cabinet; and the King was left to complain gloomily to Knollys about the apparent power of a body which neither the King nor the Prime Minister could gainsay.

The King was no more successful when he attempted to prevent the publication of an *Army Journal* in which officers were to be free to express their feelings on military subjects. This, the King maintained, was totally opposed to the army's tradition of silence. He would 'neither sanction nor support' the *Journal* in any way; 'this should be clearly understood'; he washed his hands 'of the whole matter'. But the *Journal* was established all the same.

Nor did the King's views prevail when he suggested that the age for admittance of subalterns into the Guards might be reduced to eighteen; nor when he proposed that on the fiftieth anniversary of the Indian Mutiny the occasion should be marked 'by a judicious distribution of honours'; nor when he tried to obtain an earldom for Lord Curzon; nor when he asked that the band of the Coldstream Guards should be sent to play in Germany, a request turned down by the Foreign Office, whose 'extraordinary conduct' of the 'whole transaction' caused him 'much annoyance'. Nor did the King succeed in preventing the admission of native members to the Viceroy of India's Council, which he considered a 'step fraught with the greatest danger to the maintenance of the Indian Empire under British rule'. When Satyendra Prassano Sinha, a distinguished Hindu lawyer, was suggested as a suitable member of the Council, the King wrote to protest 'most strongly'. He told Lord Minto, the Viceroy:

> To take a very clever native on to your Executive Council must necessarily be a source of much danger to our rule in the Indian Empire. I am afraid it is the 'thin end of the wedge', and it will require a most resolute Viceroy to avoid being forced to nominate one if not two native members of the council. I can hardly believe that the present appointment of a Hindoo will not create great and just indignation among the Mahomedans and that the latter will not be contented unless they receive an assurance that one of their creed succeeds to Mr Sinha.

A week later, however, he was obliged to sign 'the objectionable paper'. 'Do try and induce Morley not to be so obstinate by appointing another Native,' he asked Esher on Sinha's resignation. 'He knows how strong my views are on the subject, and so does Minto; but they don't care what I say, nor does any member of my precious (!) Govt.'

One of the most painful of all the King's disagreements with his government was over his determination, during Balfour's premiership, not to confer a Knighthood of the Garter upon the Shah of Persia, who had been persuaded by the British Minister in Teheran that if he made the journey to England, which he was reluctant to do, the King would admit him into that most noble order of chivalry. The King contended that it was a Christian order and could not, therefore, be bestowed upon an infidel even though his mother had conferred it upon the Shah's father as well as upon two Sultans of Turkey. The government, on the other hand, maintained that were the Shah not to receive the Garter which he had been led to expect would be bestowed upon him, he was quite likely out of pique to ally himself with Russia, a consequence as much to be dreaded as it was easy to avoid. The Foreign Secretary, Lord Lansdowne, endeavoured to solve the problem by preparing a memorandum of a proposed revision in the statues of the Order to enable it to be conferred upon non-Christians. This document, so Lansdowne said, the King had read in his presence and, having done so, had nodded twice as if he approved of it. But this the King denied, though he admitted that he had taken the document from Lansdowne and had put it to one side intending to read it later. Anyway, Lansdowne went ahead with his plan and ordered from the court jewellers special Garter insignia from which the Christian emblems were to be removed. At the same time he sent a letter to the King explaining what he had done, and attached to it coloured illustrations of the proposed new Garter Star from which the Cross of St George was to be omitted.

The King at the time was on board the royal yacht, the *Victoria and Albert,* at Portsmouth; and Frederick Ponsonby described the dreadful scene when the King opened the harmless-looking Foreign Office box and took out the contents. He was already annoyed with the Shah, who, put out by the delay in conferring the Order upon him, had rejected a gold-framed miniature of the King surrounded by diamonds which had been offered him and had told his suite not to accept the English decorations which it had been proposed to confer upon them. Consequently, as the King picked up Lansdowne's letter and—in its recipient's eyes—its scarcely less than blasphemous enclosure, there was an immediate 'explosion. He was so angry that he flung the design across his cabin'. It went through the porthole and, so Ponsonby thought, into the sea. Furiously, the King dictated 'some very violent remarks' to be addressed to Lord Lansdowne. Ponsonby softened the tone of the letter; but, even so, Lansdowne recognized that he would have to resign unless the King gave way. While Knollys urged the King to stand firm, the Duke of Devonshire advised the Prime Minister to support Lansdowne, and the Shah became thoroughly disgruntled.

'We have a very difficult game to play,' Balfour wrote to the King, who continued to protest that it was 'an unheard of proceeding, one sovereign being dictated to by another as to what order he should confer on him'. Balfour persisted:

> Russia has most of the cards, yet it would be dangerous to lose the rubber. Our well-known fidelity to our engagements is one of our few trumps. We must not waste it . . . Lord Lansdowne, erroneously believing himself to be authorized by Your Majesty, has pledged your Majesty to bestow the Garter upon the Shah—has indeed pledged your Majesty repeatedly and explicitly. If he be prevented from carrying out these pledges, what will be his position? . . . And, if he resigned, could the matter stop there in these days of governmental solidarity?

Faced once again with the threat of the government's resignation, the King felt obliged to give way. He was 'much depressed about it all', Knollys told Balfour; but his 'high sense of duty' and 'patriotic motives' overcame his great reluctance. He insisted, however, that no decorations should be given to the Shah's suite in view of their earlier refusal of them, and that this must be the last time the Garter was conferred upon a person who was not a Christian. But even these conditions were not observed. The King was persuaded in the end to give decorations to the Shah's grumpy entourage, and though he would not agree to the Order being conferred upon the King of Siam five years later, he agreed to bestow it upon the more important Emperor of Japan.

If King Edward often found his successive governments tiresome and difficult, he was not an easy man to do business with himself. By the end of 1905 he had virtually stopped giving formal audiences to his ministers, preferring to talk to them when he happened to meet them at dinner parties or upon other social occasions, or dealing with them through people he knew well and trusted including Sir Charles Hardinge, Sir Ernest Cassel, Lord Fisher, de Soveral, Knollys and Esher, the last five of whom all worked closely together and met frequently at Brooks's Club.

Most of his personal staff were devoted to him; some loved him; but none could pretend that working for him was always a pleasure. When a subject interested him he was scrupulous, even pedantic in his attention to its smallest and most insignificant detail. 'He is . . . a good listener, if you aren't too long,' Asquith, Campbell-Bannerman's successor, told his wife. 'He has an excellent head and is most observant about people . . . He is not at all argumentative and understands everything that is properly put to him.' Yet with matters that bored him he would not make the slightest effort to comprehend them. Frederick Ponsonby commented:

He had a most curious brain, and at one time one would find him a big, strong, far-seeing man, grasping the situation at a glance and taking a broad-minded view of it; at another one would be almost surprised at the smallness of his mind. He would be almost childish in his views, and would obstinately refuse to understand the question at issue.

He never troubled to conceal his annoyance at even the most trifling grievances. Ponsonby recalled accompanying him to the Anglican church at Biarritz, where they sat in the front pew. When the time for the collection came, Ponsonby discovered that the only coin he had in his pocket was a gold louis; so he put it in the plate next to the King's donation, also a gold louis. After the service the King crossly asked Ponsonby if he always gave a louis. 'I hastily explained that I had nothing else,' Ponsonby commented, 'but he seemed to think I had spoilt his donation. He considered it only right to put in a gold piece, but when *I* did the same people thought nothing of his generosity.'

He was often 'distinctly peppery in his temper', speaking so sharply to those who asked him what he considered trivial questions that they dared not approach him a second time, sending the servants 'flying about in all directions'. Once the very able English Consul at Marseilles came aboard the royal yacht to deliver telegrams and letters from a large portfolio which, on being opened, proved to be empty. The King shouted at the man so loudly that he fled from the yacht terrified and, during the hour that it took the Consul to retrieve the missing correspondence, he marched up and down the deck, abusing him as a half-wit. When some order of his had not been fully understood, the King would repeat it very slowly and precisely, word by carefully enunciated word, while the listener stood before him, dreading the possibility that the bottled-up anger might suddenly burst forth before he was allowed to escape from the room.

If more seriously provoked, the King's rages were ungovernable. Ponsonby recalled numerous occasions of his master's 'boiling with rage', 'breaking into a storm of abuse', 'shouting and storming', 'shaking the roof of Buckingham Palace', 'becoming more and more angry and finally exploding with fury'. There was the time when Ponsonby advised him not to give several Victorian Orders on going to Portsmouth as this would lead naval officers to expect decorations whenever he went to any other naval base. Ponsonby said:

He was furious and shouted at me that I knew nothing about such matters, and that, being a soldier, I was, of course, jealous of the navy. I, however, stuck to it, and said that the Victorian Order would be laughed at if it were given on such occasions. He was still more angry and crushed me with the remark that he didn't know that the Victorian Order was mine to give. After this explosion I at once retired, but I was interested to see that when he did visit Portsmouth he gave no decorations.

A similar explosion erupted on board the royal yacht when the King and Queen were cruising in the Mediterranean in May 1909 and it was decided to pay a visit to Malta. The King was looking through the programme arranged for his reception at Valetta when a telegram arrived from the Commander-in-Chief of the Mediterranean to the effect that all ships in the area had been ordered off to make a demonstration. King Edward was 'perfectly furious and in his rage became most unreasonable'. Captain Colin Keppel, commander of the royal yacht, could do nothing with him and suggested that Frederick Ponsonby be sent for. Ponsonby recorded:

> When I entered the King's cabin I at once grasped that there was thunder in the air. 'What do you think of that?' the King shouted at me as he tossed me a telegram, and before I had time to answer he stormed away at the disgraceful way he was treated. He ended a very violent peroration by saying he had a good mind to order the Fleet back to Malta.

Ponsonby succeeded in calming the King's anger by pointing out that the navy, no doubt, had very good reasons for requiring the Mediterranean Fleet to make a demonstration; but when he went on to say that it was extraordinary that neither the Prime Minister nor the First Lord of the Admiralty had had the courtesy to keep him informed of the situation, the King's fury burst out afresh, and 'after breaking into a storm of abuse of the government', he instructed Ponsonby to send messages in cipher to both ministers which, 'had they been sent as he directed them, would certainly have startled both recipients and would probably have entailed their resignation'.

The King was equally angry when, on arriving in Naples, he found that the Queen had ordered donkeys to transport the royal party up to the summit of Vesuvius from the end of the railway. He refused to risk placing his great weight on the back of a small donkey; and, while the Queen and others of the party set off, he went for a short walk. According to her sister, the Empress Marie of Russia, who had been invited to join the party, the Queen did not trust herself to a donkey either but was carried up in a chair while the Empress walked. But Frederick Ponsonby remembered them all as having been on donkeys which were still a long way from the summit when the King returned from his walk to the train. Eager to begin a picnic luncheon, he had the train's whistle sounded at regular and increasingly frequent intervals to summon the riders back for the return journey. By the time the last rider had returned on his weary donkey, the King was 'boiling with rage' and 'unable to let off steam' on Queen Alexandra or on Fehr, the courier, who had wisely disappeared, the King poured 'the vials of his wrath' on Ponsonby's innocent head.

The King was also very demanding. Ponsonby recalled a day at Malta when, summoned to the King's cabin after breakfast, he was told to prepare a list of names for decorations and given fifteen letters to write as well as two to copy. On being released, Ponsonby rushed off to a review. Then he had to go to a luncheon in an army mess. After that there was a levee to attend, and he did not get back on board the royal yacht until half past five. Ponsonby recorded:

> The King sent for copies of letters to show the Queen at tea. Answer, not yet done. Afterwards he sent for me to discuss decorations and asked for a *typed* list. Answer, not done. Had I written yet to so-and-so; answer, no. Then the King said, 'My dear man, you must try and get something done.' So I got a list of decorations typed by a petty officer on board. He spelt two names wrong and left out a third, all of which the King found out . . . Although I sat up till 1.30 to get straight, the King is left with the impression that nothing is done.

With his work the King neither received nor asked for any help from the Queen. Occasionally the Queen's hatred of Germany or concern for her Danish relations would induce her to make some suggestion or protest. In 1890, for instance, during the government's negotiations to secure a protectorate over Zanzibar in exchange for Heligoland, she strongly protested about this 'knuckle-down to Germany' and prepared a memorandum in which she stressed that, before Britain came into possession of Heligoland during the Napoleonic Wars, the island had 'belonged from time immemorial' to Denmark and that 'in the hands of Germany it would be made the basis of operations against England'. The Queen also offered her services in translating letters from her brother, the King of Greece, and in making his difficulties well known to her husband and the government. But these were rare interpositions. As Charles Dilke said, the Queen never talked politics; and the King would not have had it otherwise.

He was even unwilling to let the Queen play an important part in the ceremonial duties of the monarchy or to attend official functions without him, insisting that such work was his responsibility and that she ought not to carry it out without his being there as well. Sometimes she complained, but she did not press the point. And while her husband spent more and more time away from her, she was quite content to retreat to Sandringham. She seemed perfectly happy on her own there; and when her husband did join her, she made it clear that whatever freedom or authority he might enjoy outside the home she was the mistress inside it. Lord Esher remembered how when he and the King, then Prince of Wales, had been discussing some important topic, a message had come from his wife asking him to go to her. He had not gone immediately; but a second summons had sent him scurrying from the room, leaving the business unfinished. And the Countess of Airlie recorded the Princess's cheerfully irreverent comment to Sir Sidney Greville, who, anxious not to keep his Royal Highness waiting any longer for an important engagement, pressed her to join him: 'Keep him waiting. It will do him good!'

The contents of official boxes which were never shown to the Queen were, however, readily made available to his son and his daughter-in-law. This was, the King explained, a 'very different matter'.

Prince George and his father were—and were always to remain—on excellent terms. 'We are more like brothers than father and son,' the King once wrote, a sentiment which his son later echoed in a letter to Lord Dalkeith; and although Prince George held his father in too much awe for this to be really so, there was between them an intimacy which in royal relationships was so rare as to be almost unique. Recognizing his son's diffidence, his need of reassurance and sympathy, the King gave him the confidence that he would otherwise have lacked by a constant affirmation of love and trust, by an obvious pride in his reliability. He made it clear that he trusted him in a way that he himself had never been trusted and that he regarded him with an unreserved affection with which his own parents had never been able to look upon him.

He hated to be parted from him. Within a week of Queen Victoria's death he abruptly cancelled a long-standing arrangement for his son to make an official visit to Australia on the grounds that neither he nor Queen Alexandra could spare him so soon for so long. The King was persuaded to change his mind by the Prime Minister, but he parted from his son with sorrow, confessing to Lord Carrington that he 'quite broke down as he said good-bye', and he welcomed him home with unconcealed joy. Lord Esher recalled how the father, on the many occasions on which he spoke of his son, '*always*' did so 'with that peculiar look which he had—half smile, and half pathos—and that softening of the voice, when he spoke of those he loved. He used to say the words "my son" in quite a different tone from any which were familiar to me in the many tones of his voice.' For his part the Duke of York, as Prince George became in 1892, was utterly devoted to his father, consulting him about every aspect of his life, 'even as to whether his footmen ought to wear black or red liveries at dinner', and 'complaining terribly' when his father was not available for consultation that he had 'no one to go to or advise him'. After the King's death he could scarcely bring himself to speak of him without tears starting to his eyes. Though he recognized his faults, he admired him intensely and would never allow a word of criticism of him ever to be spoken. The only criticism he himself ever made of him in his voluminous correspondence with his mother was of a decision he had made to convert the bowling alley at Sandringham into a library.

It was the greatest comfort to the King in the last years of his life that his son and his son's family lived in a small house in the grounds of Sandringham—York Cottage, formerly known as the Bachelor's Cottage, which had been built as an annexe for male guests at Sandringham and which he had given to Prince George as a wedding present. Although this was not altogether pleasing to the Duchess of York—who was much more aware than her husband of the house's inconvenience and lack of character and who had to submit to perpetual visits from her mother-in-law—the King delighted in the intimate propinquity, and seemed never more content than when his grandchildren with their parents came up to the big house for tea.

The grandchildren loved to do so, and in later life they remembered their grandfather with unclouded pleasure and affection. They retained memories of being taken to see him in his robes before he left for Westminster Abbey on the day of his coronation. 'Good morning, children,' he had said to them. 'Am I not a funny-looking old man?' They were too overwhelmed by the sight of him in his strange costume to offer any opinion in reply on that occasion, but they were not usually in the least in awe of him. His eldest grandson, Prince David—later King Edward VIII—recalling the contrast between life at York Cottage and that other world, redolent of cigar smoke and scent, which his grandfather inhabited, described him as being 'bathed in perpetual sunlight'. Prince David was so little afraid of him, in fact, that he was even capable, on one occasion at least, of interrupting his conversation at table. He was reprimanded, of course, and sat in silence until given permission to speak. 'It's too late now, grandpapa,' Prince David said unconcernedly. 'It was a caterpillar on your lettuce but you've eaten it.'

Both the King and Queen delighted in looking after their grandchildren when their parents were away. They encouraged them to romp about the house, even in the dining-room, and to show off to the guests, who were required to pretend they were elephants and to give the children rides on their backs. And, so as to enjoy them all the more, the King once contrived to leave their governess in London for a fortnight while he spoiled them to his heart's content at Sandringham.

With the small children of close friends he was equally indulgent, allowing Mrs Keppel's to call him 'Kingy'. The younger of the Keppel daughters, Sonia, was rather frightened of him at first. Instructed to curtsy to him whenever she saw him but never daring to 'look higher than beard-level', she 'played safe and curtsied to the cigar and rings'. But

Sir Ernest Cassel, too, had a beard, wore rings and smoked cigars; 'so, more often than not, he came in for the curtsy'.

In time, though, Sonia overcame her nervousness, and when the King came to tea with her mother she was delighted to be allowed down into the drawing-room at six o'clock to see him. Together they devised a 'fascinating game' with bits of bread and butter which were sent, butter side downwards, racing along the stripes of his trousers. Bets of a penny each were placed on the contestants, Sonia's penny being provided by her mother. 'The excitement was intense while the contest was on . . . and Kingy's enthusiasm seemed delightfully unaffected by the quality of his bets.'

On Princess Victoria's birthday a children's party was given each year by the King and Queen at Buckingham Palace where balloons were shot up into the sky and, on bursting, discharged presents all over the lawn while excited children raced about to pick them up. They were not in the least intimidated by the presence of their host, as most of their parents were; and when he asked one boy what he would like, he received the brusque command, 'More jam, King.'

15

The King at Home

The pleasure of giving seemed never to leave their Majesties, as it so often does with rich people.

Perpetually alarmed by the prospect of boredom, the King was as anxious as ever to ensure that each day held for him the promise of some interesting activity. To make this easier to achieve, his yearly programme followed an almost unchangeable plan, largely regulated by the need to be in London in January or February for the State Opening of Parliament; by the social obligations of the London season, which began after Easter and ended with the races at Ascot in late June; and by those other race-meetings at which his Majesty's presence was expected as a matter of course. After the yachting at Cowes in early August he liked to be at Bolton Abbey, the Duke of Devonshire's Yorkshire house, for the opening of the grouse-shooting season on the twelfth. October would normally find him shooting at Balmoral. On 9 November he would invariably be at Sandringham for his birthday.

Although guests at Sandringham were pleased to find that life there was fairly informal, the King's taste for regularity and punctuality imposed upon it an almost immutable routine. Breakfast began at nine and ended promptly at ten. The Royal Family did not appear, having breakfast in their own rooms; but those who chose to come down for it would find small round tables laid in the dining-room and a menu as ample and varied as that demanded by the King's own voracious appetite. Indeed, the quantities of food consumed by the King, at breakfast as at every other meal, astonished those who, unapprised of his capacity, observed for the first time his zestful gourmandism.

After drinking a glass of milk in bed, he would often content himself with coffee and toast when he was to spend the morning indoors; but to fortify himself for a morning's shooting he could devour platefuls of bacon and eggs, haddock and chicken, and toast and butter, in as short a time as it would take a less hungry man to drink two cups of coffee. Soon afterwards, an hour or so in the cold fresh air would sharpen his appetite for hot turtle soup. Yet this would in no way impair his appetite for luncheon at half past two, just as a hearty luncheon would not prevent his appearing for tea in a short black jacket and black tie in the hall where, as his band played appropriate melodies, he helped himself to poached eggs, *petits fours* and preserved ginger as well as rolls and scones, hot cakes, cold cakes, sweet cakes and that particular species of Scotch shortcake of which he was especially fond.

The dinner which followed at half past eight consisted usually of at least twelve courses; and it was not unknown for the King to take a liberal sample of every one, to the horror of the Queen, who confessed to his doctors that it was just 'terrible' the amount of food he got through, that she had 'never seen anything like it'. He would enjoy several dozen oysters in a matter of minutes, setting the fashion for swallowing them between mouthfuls of brown bread and butter; and would then go on to more solid fare. He had an exceptional relish for caviare, plovers' eggs and ortolans, for soles poached in Chablis and garnished with oysters and prawns, for chicken and turkey in aspic, quails and pigeon pie, grouse, snipe, partridge, pheasant and woodcock; and the thicker the dressing, the richer the stuffing, the creamier the sauce, the more deeply did he appear to enjoy each mouthful. No dish was too rich for him. He liked his pheasant stuffed with truffles and smothered in oleaginous sauce; he delighted in quails packed with *foie gras* and garnished with oysters, truffles, mushrooms, prawns, tomatoes and croquettes; he never grew tired of boned snipe, filled with forcemeat as well as *foie gras*, grilled in a pig's caul and served with truffles and Madeira sauce. He declared 'delectable' a dish of frogs' thighs served cold in a jelly containing cream and Moselle wine, and flavoured with paprika, which was especially prepared for him at the Savoy by Ritz and Escoffier, who named it *Cuisses des Nymphes à l'Aurore*. Yet he appeared to derive almost equal enjoyment from more simple dishes: roast beef and Yorkshire pudding invariably appeared on the menu for Sunday luncheon at Sandringham, though he himself far preferred lamb. At Balmoral a stag-shooting party would be offered Scotch broth, Irish stew and plum pudding. And when once the King was noticed to frown upon a bowl of boiled ham and beans, it was not, he hastened to explain, because he despised such homely fare but because 'it should have been bacon'. Almost the only dish he did not like was macaroni.

His appetite was not in the least affected by the huge cigars and the Egyptian cigarettes he smoked in such quantities. By the time he sat down to breakfast he had already had two cigarettes and one cigar; and often by dinner time he had smoked twenty more cigarettes—exhaling the smoke slowly and contemplatively through his nose—as well as twelve vast and pungent Corona y Corona, Henry Clay's 'Tsar', or Uppmanns' cigars. He never learned to smoke a pipe, which he said was something he had always wished

to do as it was by far the most convenient form of smoking when out shooting, especially in a high wind. Frederick Ponsonby gave him one as a present,
having taken

> an enormous amount of trouble to get one with a top fitted . . . but he
> was so long putting the metal top on when he had lit the pipe that it
> always went out. He had three tries and the more he hurried the more
> clumsy he became. After the third try proved a failure he produced a
> cigar and said, 'This is, after all, far simpler', and explained that it was
> the fault of the tobacco.

If tobacco did not blunt his appetite, neither did alcohol. In earlier years
he had drunk a good deal of champagne, preferably Duminy *extra sec*,
1883, which he had had decanted into a glass jug from which he helped himself; and he had been fond of making a powerful cocktail to a recipe sent to
him from Louisiana and comprising champagne, whisky, maraschino, angos-
tura bitters and crushed ice. But, as King, he rarely had more than two or
three glasses of champagne at a time and he drank little other wine. He might
enjoy a small cognac by way of a *chasse-café* but spirits held little appeal for
him and he rarely drank port. Once the ladies had retired he was anxious to
rejoin them as soon as possible, preferring their company to that of men;
and for a short time he instituted the practice of taking the men away as
soon as their hostess had 'collected the eyes' of the ladies. Indeed, any pro-
longation of the meal was tiresome for him. He grew impatient with guests
who dawdled over their food and did not like the menu to be interrupted by
sorbet or iced punch, though when his favorite rum-flavored sorbet was on
the menu he could not resist it. Nor did he like his concentration on his food
to be distracted by intellectual conversation, which always made him fiddle
with the cutlery. Such talk, he considered, should be limited to the intervals
between the courses, if tolerated at all. He preferred to listen to a good anecdote retailed by one of his amusing friends or a whisper of gossip from a
pretty woman.

He was not a gifted conversationalist himself, rarely speaking more than
a dozen words at a time and usually framing these in the form of questions.
He was extremely tactful, though, in asking the sort of questions which the
guest to whom they were directed would have pleasure in answering. For
he made a point of remembering people's tastes and interests; and it was frequently noticed how, during those Sunday afternoon inspections of his
estate at Sandringham, he would find in a cup or plate, or some other trophy
he had won at a race meeting or regatta, a reason to talk about horses or
yachts to a sportsman who had felt unable to comment sensibly on the
fuchsias and tomato plants in the greenhouse. He was also exceedingly adept
at bringing a difficult conversation to an end with a murmured, 'Quite so,

quite so'; and then immediately, and in as natural a way as possible, diverting it on to easier lines.

Although everyone agreed with Lord Sandwich that he had 'a marvellous memory' and could—as he often did—recite the entire list of guests at house-parties he had attended years before, the King was an indifferent raconteur. He told his stories with too ponderous an emphasis on their introductory scene-setting, choosing to relate those which required a lightness of touch not at his command, and sometimes grasping a button on the coat of the man to whom they were principally addressed as though he sensed a wandering attention. He was also inclined to repeat his favourite stories until they became all too familiar. Whenever the name of the Shah of Persia was mentioned, for instance, he was as likely as not to remind his companions of the time he and the Shah had been fellow-guests of the Duke of Sutherland at Trentham and how the Shah had observed disapprovingly of their rich host, 'Too grand for a subject. You'll have to have his head off when you come to the throne!'

Another of his favourite stories concerned an English officer who had been shot through the head during the Boer War and had been sent home to be operated on by Sir Frederick Treves. Finding the damage extensive, Treves had been forced to remove a large part of the brain; and, although the operation had been successfully performed, he felt obliged to reveal to his patient his apprehension as to the young man's prospects in his career. 'It's very kind of you to take so much interest in my welfare, Sir Frederick,' the officer replied, 'but thank God my brain is no longer wanted. I have just been transferred to the War Office.'

Such stories were well received since it was the King himself who told them. But a less courtly audience would, no doubt, have been less indulgent. The King's tendency to jovial banter would also have been found less amusing in other men. Occasionally the King really was amusing, as when a neighbour, Somerville Gurney, inadvertently shot a hen pheasant one day late in the season when instructions had gone out that only cocks were to be killed. 'Ah, Gurney,' the King admonished his guest as the hen fell to the ground, 'what a one you are for the ladies!' The laughter his Majesty's sallies aroused, however, encouraged him to continue the chaff to the point where the responses became dutiful rather than spontaneous.

Sir Felix Semon was a common butt for the King's insistent banter after he had shot a young stag below the minimum admissible weight. Ashamed of his action, Semon had retreated to a corner of the drawing-room where the guests assembled before dinner. But immediately on entering, the King went up to him and in a hoarse stage whisper, clearly heard throughout the room, accused him of being a 'chicken butcher'. The remark was greeted by prolonged laughter which continued to punctuate the subsequent exchanges:

'Oh, Sire, that is hard!'

'Not too hard. It is thoroughly merited! How could you shoot such a miserable staggie? Defend yourself!'

Semon protested that he had not intended to kill so young an animal.

'That won't wash. If you were a young lad who had gone out stalking for the first time I might possibly accept such an excuse. But you, you have killed hundreds of stags. Be ashamed of yourself! You will have to hear of this until your life's end.'

'I hope your Majesty will not be as good as your word.'

"Won't I? Well, you will see!'

For several days the bantering continued with persistent references to 'Sir Felix's babies' until Semon was reported to have caught a 15-pound salmon. The King publicly congratulated him; then, after a long pause, added the question, 'Did it have horns?'

More loud laughter broke out immediately; and there was further merriment the next day when Semon shot three fully grown stags before luncheon, during which the King told his eldest grandson to go up to Sir Felix and enquire 'if he had killed a little staggie to-day'. At this there was 'general laughter'.

"Who set you on to this?' Semon asked.

'Grandpa,' came the reply, 'which set the laughter going again, the King shaking with mirth the whole time'.

Tiresome as some guests found what the Duchess of Teck termed the King's 'odious chaffing', everyone who knew him well agreed that he had a kind heart. This was never more obvious than it was at Christmas when he and the Queen spent hours together in the ballroom at Sandringham arranging presents on the trestle tables which were laid out around a big Christmas tree.

He delighted in giving presents, whether chosen with care—like the huge silver-gilt inkstand he gave to the Gladstones on their golden wedding anniversary to make up for the impersonal telegram of congratulations from Queen Victoria—or given impulsively, like the gold cigarette-case he presented to Margot Tennant for having picked him out a winner at Ascot. When staying with friends he would often be driven to a nearby antique shop to choose them something he thought they would like; or, when special services had been rendered, he would order a commemorative present to be specially made. To Sir Walter Campbell, Deputy Ranger of Windsor Park, who had cleared the park of rabbits which had become a pest there, he presented a silver model of a rabbit with the remark that there would at any rate be one rabbit left at Windsor. And to Lord Burnham of Hall Barn, Beaconsfield, he gave a silver pheasant 'as a recollection of the best day's shooting' he had ever had. Friends going abroad were liable to be asked to buy him a selection of suitable gifts, as was a visitor to the Paris Exhibition to whom he sent 5,800 francs to spend 'on any *bibelots* or *objets d'art*' which took her own fancy and which he would find 'useful as birthday and Xmas presents'.

At Christmas at Sandringham guests were required to wait in the corridor outside the ballroom before dinner and to come in one by one to receive the gifts which had been wrapped up for them. Frederick Ponsonby thought this was

a rather trying experience as one found the King on one side and the Queen on the other explaining who gave what present and giving particulars about the various articles. One stood gasping one's thanks to each alternately, and it was always a relief when the next person was called in. It was impossible to make a set speech, and most people, including myself, continued gasping, 'Thank you so much.'

Ponsonby himself was quite overcome by the number of presents he received: 'There were prints, water-colours, silver cigarette-cases, a silver inkstand, pins, studs, and several books.' But it was all 'beautifully done, and the pleasure of giving seemed never to leave their Majesties, as it so often does with rich people'.

On Christmas Eve it was the turn for the families on the estate to gather near the coach-house door where the King and Queen sat to wish them a Merry Christmas and to give each family a joint of beef. And on New Year's Eve all the servants collected outside the ballroom where huge piles of presents, about eight hundred in all, and each one numbered, were massed around the Christmas tree. As the servants entered the room they drew two numbers each and were handed the corresponding presents by one of the princesses or a member of the household. It was not a very satisfactory method of distribution, as 'a housemaid might get a razor and a footman a powder-puff'; but it 'seemed to give much pleasure. At the conclusion the Christmas tree was stripped and all the toys and sweets were given to the children'.

The ballroom was also the setting for those occasional theatricals and musical performances which were intended to form one of the highlights of the Christmas festivities but which many of the guests found extremely boring. Indeed, a week-end at Sandringham, despite the informality of the atmosphere and the King's efforts to make his guests feel at home, was sometimes a rather tedious affair, particularly as solitary pursuits and pleasantly lazy idling were discouraged. 'What are you going to do to-day?' the King would ask; and if no satisfactory answer were forthcoming, there would follow a recommendation of some activity which the guest might well feel totally disinclined to pursue. So, rather than be sent off to play billiards, to watch a game of golf or to join one of those games which were played after tea, the wary and experienced guest would say that he was on his way to read a book in the library or to have a look at the collection of fire-arms in the gun-room. Any excuse would satisfy the host; but some plan of action had to be given, otherwise the King would immediately propose one or endeavour to entertain the indolent guest himself. And his efforts in this respect were not always successful. Sir Felix Semon cited the example of an antiquated bishop who could not be sent off to play billiards or croquet and who, when his host endeavoured to engage him in conversation, seemed to share not a single interest with him. The King switched in despair from one subject to another without arousing the least response. At length, catching sight of a photograph of himself on a side table, he thought he would try that as a last resort. What did the bishop think of the likeness? The bishop put on his spectacles, peered at the photograph, then shook his head in a melancholy manner before replying, 'Yes, yes, poor old Buller!'

For those who did not play cards, the evening after dinner often seemed excessively long; while for those who did, it could seem even more so if they happened to be playing with the King. He was very fond of bridge, which he nevertheless did not play very well, soon losing interest when his cards were bad, yet never failing to criticize his partner's mistakes without the least equivocation or apology. He soon recovered his temper, however, after even the most unsatisfactory game, accepting his winnings with complacent satisfaction and paying out his losses as though he were bestowing upon his opponent a most valuable present. And when he was ready to go to bed, between one o'clock and half past one, he was usually as affable as he had been during the day, making sure that everyone had a good supper, recommending the grilled oysters which were his own favourite refreshment at that time of night, going upstairs, as he had done in his youth, to escort the men guests to their rooms, to make sure that they had all that they could possibly require and to give a token poke to the fire in the grate.

No one, however, was allowed to go to bed before the Queen retired at about midnight. One evening, finding the number of people downstairs to be one short, and imagining that the absentee must be one of the younger guests, he rang for a page and told him to go and fetch back the culprit, who turned out to be General Sir Dighton Probyn, the seventy-five-year-old Keeper of the Privy Purse, who had gone to bed because he was not feeling well. Ponsonby thought that the King was 'very much amused by this episode; but Sir Dighton was not'.

On leaving Sandringham the King frequently went to stay for a week or so with the Duke of Devonshire at Chatsworth, or with Lord Iveagh at Elveden, the first of those several country house visits which he liked to make each year. In 1872 the then Duke had written a rather breathless letter from Chatsworth to his son Lord Hartington, who was staying at Sandringham: 'Glad you are staying at Sandringham, for you will be able to get answers to several things I want to know. How long do they stay? How many servants do they bring? How many maids for the Princess? Do you think they could bring any horses? Am so afraid that our own may not stand the cheering . . .'

A generation later the answers to these and other similar questions were well known at Chatsworth as they were in many other large country houses in England, the owners of which were put to a good deal of trouble and expense in providing the King with the comfort he had grown accustomed to expect.

In the first place, his hosts were often required to accommodate an entourage of almost Elizabethan proportions. It was not unknown for the King to travel with two valets, a footman and a brusher; with a lord-in-waiting, a groom-in-waiting, a private secretary and two equerries, all of whom had their own servants; with two chauffeurs, two loaders for the King's guns and a loader each for the guns of the gentlemen attendants; with a gentleman-in-waiting and two ladies-in-waiting for the Queen, who also brought a hair-dresser and two maids; with two detectives, two police sergeants and three constables; and with an Arab boy whose sole duty it was to prepare the royal coffee, which he served to his master on bended knee. The number of pieces of attendant luggage was likely to be equally prodigious. In the King's trunks alone there would be as many as forty suits and uniforms and twenty pairs of boots and shoes even for a visit which was to last for no more than a week.

Despite the cost and trouble of entertaining the King and his entourage there were, however, few places where they were not welcome. And hostesses whose houses were never included in the royal progresses were deeply jealous of those his Majesty favoured: the Saviles of Rufford Abbey with whom he often stayed for Doncaster Races and the Grevilles of Reigate Priory became known to the disappointed as the Civils and the Grovels.

The King's intimation of a proposed visit would be followed by a notification from a member of his Household as to the length of the stay. A list of guests would then be submitted for his approval; and occasionally he would add a name or, more rarely, cross one out. Except in the case of houses which were visited regularly, there would then ensue a lengthy correspondence about the arrangements for the reception of the royal party, the number of attendants and servants to be expected, the sort of accommodation to be provided for the detectives, the provision of a guard of honour, the speeches of welcome to be made at the railway station and the addresses to be handed to the King by various local dignitaries. When, for instance, the King proposed to visit Alnwick Castle to stay with the Duke of Northumberland in 1906, a cascade of letters, orders, *questionnaires*, invitations and prohibitions issued from the castle to ensure that all the arrangements were conducted in an efficient and seemly manner. Instructions were given for the railway station to be closed to ordinary traffic and to be decorated. The entrance gate to the castle was also to be decorated, while the front of the barbican was to be illuminated at night by gas flood-lighting. Triumphal arches were to be erected in the town, and tickets to be printed so that the Duke's tenants would have the best view of his Majesty's progress. Medals were to be issued so that the local schoolchildren would have a suitable memento of the auspicious event. Orders were given that the loyal addresses from the county council and urban authority should be inscribed and handed to the King, not spoken; and that no more than four members of the council were to be presented to him. Arrangements were made for a guard of honour from the Fifth Northumberland Fusiliers and for a sovereign's escort. 'There is one very important point to bear in mind,' the Duke warned the councillor in charge of the civic welcome. 'The Alnwick mob is all right till a procession has passed, but they have no idea of not breaking up and rushing after the carriage . . . [So] a considerable part of the escort must be placed behind the King's carriage.'

Arrangements also had to be made for a band to play before dinner; for a singer to perform after dinner; for rooms to be prepared not only for the King and Queen and their servants but for the minister in attendance as well. Accommodation was also required in the castle for an inspector, a sergeant and three constables of the Household Police, as well as an inspector and a sergeant from Scotland Yard. These policemen would wear ordinary clothes and mingle with the indoor servants when the King and Queen were in the castle and with the gardeners, game-keepers and beaters when they were in the grounds or out shooting.

Alnwick Castle, which had been extensively restored in the previous century, was in good order and no alterations or redecorations had to be carried out in the suite of rooms allocated to the King and Queen. But the owners of other houses which they visited were put to great expense in painting, papering and refurnishing rooms which were considered insufficiently imposing for royal habitation.

'We came to Mount Stewart at Whitsuntide,' wrote Lady Londonderry after arrangements had been made for a royal visit there in 1903. 'And looking over the house . . . the place looked extraordinarily shabby; and we felt that it must be tidied up for the great occasion.' So the billiard-room was transformed into an additional drawing-room; twelve other rooms were re-papered; the main drawing-room was provided with specially embroidered upholstery and cushions; the suites of upstairs rooms to be given to the King and Queen were redecorated in green and yellow silk and equipped with new furniture, including some 'nice little bits of Sheraton' and with 'masses of flowers both in baskets and on the tables'.

Once he had spent a week-end in a country house the King liked to be given the same bedroom, sitting-room, dressing-room and bathroom on each succeeding visit; and he liked to follow the same sort of daily routine. If he were not going out shooting, he would have breakfast in his room and then attend to any correspondence there might be, his letters being opened for him by a servant who stood behind his chair and slit the envelopes with a long paper-knife. Towards midday he would go down to join the other guests and perhaps go for a stroll in the garden, making comments on any alterations his sharp eye noticed as having taken place since his last visit, or play a game of croquet which he and his partner usually won as everyone knew how cross he got if he was beaten. When staying with Sir Ernest Cassel he was often pitted against the Duchess of Sermoneta, who was not only extremely pretty but also a very bad player so that a game with her always put him in a good mood. One day, however, a lucky hit sent her ball flying 'right across the ground,' she recorded in her memoirs, 'and straight through the right hoop (I didn't even know it was the right one) and, continuing its glorious career, hit the King's ball straight into the rose bushes . . . By the icy stillness that prevailed I realized that never, never was such a thing to happen again.'

During his walks in the garden the King was usually accompanied by his dog, a brown and white long-haired fox terrier who bore on his collar the legend, 'I belong to the King.' Despite the ministrations of the footman whose duty it was to wash and comb him, Caesar was a peculiarly scruffy animal and was often to be seen with his mouth covered with prickles after an unsuccessful tussle with a hedgehog. The King loved him dearly, took him abroad, and allowed him to sleep in an easy chair by his bed. Once in Bohemia, when the dog fell ill, he was only dissuaded from spending £200 on a visit by his English vet on learning that there was a first-class man in Vienna. Taken to rejoin his master after a brief parting, Caesar would always jump up in excitement at seeing him, and the King would say with gruff affection, 'Do you like your old master, then?' He could never bring himself to smack the dog, however reprehensible his behaviour; and 'it was a picture', so Stamper, the motor engineer, said, 'to see the King standing shaking his stick at the dog when he had done wrong. "You naughty dog," he would say very slowly. "You naughty, naughty dog." And Caesar would wag his tail and "smile" cheerfully into his master's eyes, until his Majesty smiled back in spite of himself.' Devoted as he was to the King, though, Caesar showed not the least interest in the advances of other human beings who bent down to fondle him, disdaining to notice the staff when he accompanied the King on an inspection of the kitchens from which, on less important occasions, he was nevertheless eager to accept any bones. 'Whenever I went into the King's cabin,' recalled Charles Hardinge, who accompanied the King on the royal yacht during his continental excursions in 1903, 'this dog always went for my trousers and worried them, much to the King's delight. I used not to take the slightest notice and went on talking all the time to the King which I think amused His Majesty still more.'

As the hour chosen by the King for serving dinner approached, a gentleman-in-waiting informed the host that his Majesty would be ready in fifteen minutes. The guests were then asked to assemble in the drawing-room to await the arrival of the King. They presented themselves in full evening dress, the men in white ties with carnations or gardenias in their button-holes, the ladies in dresses with trains, wearing, perhaps, a spray of orchids on their well-corseted bosoms, and carrying ostrich feather fans. The King appeared with exact promptitude at the time he had stipulated. Having taken stock of the company to make sure there were no absentees, he walked across the room to his hostess, offered her his arm, and escorted her immediately into the dining-room, where his footman in scarlet livery stood behind his chair. If the Queen were present the men wore frock dress and knee-breeches, and it was she who led the way to the dining-room on the arm of her host.

The King was usually an easy and agreeable guest. Even when he arrived in an exceptionally grumpy mood, he could normally be won over by a dish that pleased him or a remark that amused him. Sir Osbert Sitwell recorded an occasion when the King went to stay with Lord and Lady Brougham 'in a mood that rendered him difficult to please. Plainly something had gone wrong; and at dinner he was silent'. But Lady Brougham, 'an old lady of rare beauty and of infinite charm' renowned for her 'unfailing shrewdness of judgement and her use of the appropriate but unexpected adjective', was quite equal to the challenge.

' "Did you notice, Sir, the soap in your Majesty's bathroom?" '

' "No!" '

' "I thought you might, Sir . . . It has such an amorous lather!" '

'After that, the King's geniality returned.'

On the day of his departure, having sat for the inevitable group photograph and planted the almost equally inevitable tree, the King would sign his name in the visitors' book, and perhaps bestow a minor decoration, such as the Coronation Medal, on a senior servant. And while a member of his Household presented a suitable sum to be distributed amongst the other servants, he would give a present to his hostess. Often it was a present at least as valuable as that 'most lovely bracelet', with the King and Queen's miniatures 'set in diamonds with the royal crown and ciphers and green enamel shamrocks at the sides', which was given to Lady Londonderry after the King's visit to Mount Stewart. If he had no suitable jewellery with him he would send to London for a selection from Hunt and Roskill. And once, having stayed at a house in the north where his own servant had been taken ill, he called for his host's servant who had looked after him instead.

'Which do you think is the handsomest of these rings?' he asked him as they examined the case which had arrived from Piccadilly. 'I am sure you are a good judge of these things.'

The servant indicated the one that he preferred. The King picked it up and handed it to him with the words, 'Keep it.'

16
The King Abroad

I have crossed the Channel six times this year.

When he went abroad the King's entourage was not usually as large as
it was when he travelled in England. Nor did he make his journeys in so
grand a style as his mother, who would book an entire hotel which she filled
with a hundred of her own servants as well as numerous pieces of her own
furniture and favourite pictures. Yet, although he usually contented himself
with a doctor, two equerries, two valets and two footmen—one of the footmen, a tall Austrian named Hoepfner, to wait at table and open the door,
the other an Englishman, Wellard, whose duties included cleaning the boots
and brushing the dog—he had been known to travel abroad with no less than
thirty personal servants in addition to his suite and his doctor. He had taken
thirty-three with him when he went to Paris in 1868 to visit the Emperor
Napoleon III. And in 1901, on going to stay with his sister at Friedrichshof,
the royal yacht had thirty-one servants aboard as well as a crew of three
hundred. Journeys by rail were undertaken in a special train, the King's
private carriages being equipped with well-upholstered furniture, commodious cupboards, thick carpets and heavily tasselled curtains. There were
fully equipped bathrooms and a smoking-room where the King could enjoy
a game of cards or read a newspaper in one of the Spanish leather arm-chairs.
In later years short journeys on the Continent were made in one or other
of the three claret-coloured motor-cars which were driven out in advance
by the royal chauffeurs.

The prospect of a trip abroad almost always put the King in a good
mood. He would first send for his Swiss-born courier, the well-informed and
loud-voiced M. Fehr, who had formerly worked for Thomas Cook, and
with him he would discuss all the details of the journey. He would ensure
that Chandler, the Superintendent of the Wardrobe, knew what suits and
uniforms would be required; that his Austrian first valet, Meidinger, had all
the correct accessories; that his favourite crocodile dressing-case contained
his diary, jewellery, a miniature of the Queen, photographs of his children

and of his mother (seated at a table, signing a document); that his ragged silk dressing-gown, to which he had become so devoted that he refused to have a new one, was not forgotten; that Stamper, the motor engineer, had received proper instructions with regard to the motor-cars; that the luggage contained an ample supply of presents and decorations, particularly of the ribbons and insignia of the Victorian Order, to be bestowed upon attentive officials and obliging friends.

The last item was most important, since the King liked to be able to reward those who had helped him or pleased him wherever he went. Indeed, few acts gave him greater pleasure than making presentations of medals and decorations and of expensive miniatures, snuff-boxes, photographs in silver frames and gold cigarette-cases without regard to their value which, in any case, he never really appreciated. Frederick Ponsonby had scarcely ever known the King so angry as when all that could be found to present to an important member of the French Jockey Club, who had made arrangements for him to be conducted over some model racing stables near Paris, was a relatively inferior plain silver cigarette-case. Ponsonby deemed this inadequate as so many much more expensive presents had been handed out during the visit, and he had the temerity to send a message to the King pointing this out. Soon afterwards the King appeared before Ponsonby in a state of suppressed fury. Having put his hat, glove and stick slowly and deliberately on the table, he asked in a menacingly quiet voice, 'Did you send a message that the cigarette-case I had chosen was not good enough?' On Ponsonby's admission that this was so, the King burst forth in a deafening 'flood of oratory' that shook the whole hotel and reduced Ponsonby 'to a state of speechless terror'. Regaining the use of his tongue, Ponsonby pleaded that as such beautiful presents were usually given to his Majesty's friends, it seemed 'a pity that he should give such a cheap thing to du Bois, who would no doubt show it to everyone in Paris'. This raised a fresh storm, and Ponsonby began to think that the King might have a fit. Eventually, however, he picked up his hat, stick and gloves and left the room, slamming the door. Ponsonby commented:

> It was usual with the King after he had let himself go and cursed someone to soothe matters by being nice to them afterwards. But in this case he resented my being so outspoken and made no attempt to forgive me. It was not till years later that I understood that he had really agreed with me but had been much annoyed at not being able to give something good. During the visit to Berlin [in 1909] when the King was ill with a chill and quite unable to attend to anything, he said, 'I must leave the presents entirely to you to do, and I know you will do everything perfectly and not give anything shoddy like I did in Paris.'

As Ponsonby observed, the King's rages soon cooled, particularly when he was abroad and enjoying himself as—while on the Continent—he usually was. Indeed, he was never at home for long before he began to look forward eagerly to his next foreign visit. In the year before he died he told his son with the deepest satisfaction, 'I have crossed the Channel six times this year!'

He was particularly fond of France. He paid regular visits to the Riviera where he engaged with relish in the annual battle of the flowers, once dressed as Satan complete with scarlet robes and horns, and where he played roulette *'comme d'habitude'*. He was even more frequently to be seen in Paris, where he sometimes stayed at the Ritz or the Hôtel de l'Ambassade, but usually at the Bristol, being known there as the Earl of Chester or the Duke of Lancaster, a title which Lord James of Hereford, for one, considered him unjustified in using as it properly belonged to the descendants of John of Gaunt and did not go with the Duchy.

As Prince of Wales he had loved to go for walks in the Bois de Boulogne and down the Champs Elysées, to sail up and down the Seine, to stroll along the boulevards, looking into the shop windows in the rue de la Paix, buying shirts at Charvet's, jewellery at Cartier's, handkerchiefs at Chaperon's and hats at Genot's. He had enjoyed meals at his favourite restaurants—Magny's, Léon's and Durand's, the Voisin, the Bignon, the Café Américain, the Café des Ambassadeurs and the Café de la Paix. He had wandered into one or other of the clubs of which he was a member—the Jockey Club, the Yacht Club de France, the Cercle des Champs Elysées, the Union Club, the Nouveau and the Rue Royale. Almost every evening he had been to the theatre —the Théâtre Français, the Théâtre des Variétés, the Gymnase, the Vaudeville, the Odéon, the Palais Royal, the Nouveautés, the Renaissance or the Porte St Martin. Afterwards he had paid calls backstage with friends from the Jockey Club, or he had gone to the Épatant for a game of baccarat, or to 16 rue de la Pépinière for *'une soirée intime'*, or to the cabaret at the Lion d'Or, the Bouffes-Parisiens or the Moulin Rouge. Once he had played the part of the murdered prince in Sardou's *Fedora* while Sarah Bernhardt wept over him. And he had entertained Bernhardt and other actresses in the Café Anglais in the 'Grand Seize', an exotic private room hung with red wall paper and gold hieroglyphics, furnished with gilt chairs and a crimson sofa, and softly lit by gasoliers.

He had made elaborate efforts to give the slip to the indefatigable French detectives who, to his extreme annoyance, followed him everywhere, suitably disguised, even to the extent of wearing clothes appropriate to the different parts of the theatres to which they were assigned and taking their wives with them to restaurants. Occasionally the Prince's carriage had suddenly rattled off at such a pace from the Hôtel Bristol that the police had lost track of him. But generally they managed to keep up with him and

were able to submit reports of meetings with celebrated beauties in the
Jardin des Plantes, of long afternoons spent with his intimate friends, the
Comtesse Edmond de Pourtalès in the rue Tronchet, the Baronne Alphonse
de Rothschild in the Faubourg St Honoré, and the Princesse de Sagan on the
corner of the Esplanade des Invalides.

The police had watched him on his visits to Mme Kauchine, a Russian
beauty who rented a room in the Hôtel du Rhin; to 'the widow Signoret',
mistress of the Duc de Rohan; to a certain 'Dame Verneuil' who had an apart-
ment on the second floor at 39 rue Lafayette; to the Baronne de Pilar at
the Hôtel Choiseul; to Miss Chamberlayne (described in 1884 as his *'maîtresse
en titre'*) at the Hôtel Balmoral; to unidentified ladies in the Hôtel Scribe
and the Hôtel Liverpool in the rue de Castiglione. The police had been
particularly concerned by his visits to the Hôtel de Calais, where he often
spent most of the night with a mysterious woman known to the chambermaid
as Mme Hudrie, 'a very beautiful woman, aged about thirty, tall, slim,
blonde, remarkable for her magnificent colouring and her perfect elegance
. . . usually dressed in white satin, but always in black when she meets the
Prince'. This turned out to be the Comtesse de Boutourline, wife of the
Prefect of Moscow, sister-in-law of General Boutourline, formerly military
attaché at the British Embassy in London, and granddaughter of Princess
Bobinska, with whom she claimed to be staying in the rue de Chateaubriand,
though the police discovered that she was actually living in a house belonging to the Comte de Guinsonnas.

The Prince had spent other evenings with the delightful English courtesan, Catherine Walters; and had visited his favourite brothel, Le Chabanais,
where the chair upon which he sat with his chosen young women was still
displayed over a generation later to the brothel's customers. He had gone
to the Maison Dorée with the Duc de Gramont to meet the generous, pas-
sionate and consumptive Giulia Beneni, known as La Barucci, who arrived
very late and, on being reprimanded by the Duke, turned her back on the
royal visitor, lifted her skirts to her waist and said, 'You told me to show
him my best side.' He had asked also to meet La Barucci's rival, Cora Pearl,
who had appeared before him naked except for a string of pearls and a
sprig of parsley.

On one occasion, when Queen Alexandra was feeling depressed and out
of sorts, the King asked her if she would like to go with him to Paris. Immediately she accepted the invitation with the excited eagerness of a little
girl. They stayed at the British Embassy; and, for the first time in her life,
the Queen was able to dine in public in a restaurant. She had been *'delighted'*
with Paris on a previous visit many years before, and she was equally en-
tranced by it now.

Although they were very rarely in Paris together, the King often went
with the Queen on her annual visit to her family in Denmark. He did so out

of kindness, for he was overcome by boredom and restlessness while he was there, having to dine with his ancient father-in-law at six o'clock or half past six at the latest and then to play boring games of whist for very low stakes. He pretended to enjoy it all for the Queen's sake. But the enclosed, provincial atmosphere, sometimes enlivened by a huge family party at the castle of Fredensborg where seven different languages were spoken, he found desperately tedious. Once, after visiting every museum, art gallery and house of historical interest which Copenhagen had to offer, he was driven to going over a farm which sold butter to England. He always longed to be back in Paris again and to take on once more the persona of the Duke of Lancaster.

The incognito was scarcely necessary for almost everyone in Paris knew who the Duke was; and he seemed quite content that this should be so. 'Ullo Wales!' La Gouloue, the famous dancer, would shout at him on his appearance at the Moulin Rouge, and he would smile indulgently and order champagne for the dancers and the members of the orchestra. Those who did not recognize him were soon made aware of his identity, as was 'a prosperous-looking American with a large cigar in his mouth' who stood waiting for the lift in the lobby of the Grand Hotel. The King also stood waiting to be taken up to the floor on which the ex-Empress Eugénie had taken a room. When the doors opened the American moved forward to enter first as he had been waiting the longer. The King, so accustomed to having everyone else wait for him that he took no notice of his neighbour, strode forward at the same time, collided with him, knocked him off his balance with the superior weight of his great bulk and sent the cigar shooting out of the American's mouth.

Occasionally on his foreign visits the King would be upset by some display of anti-British feeling. At the time of the Boer War he was deeply offended by being forced to listen to renditions of the Boers' national anthem on his way to Friedrichshof; and he cancelled his usual spring holiday on the Riviera and refused to open an International Exhibition in Paris because of hostile articles about his country and rude caricatures of himself which had appeared in French newspapers. But normally he was greeted respectfully wherever he went. Sometimes, indeed, he was forced to complain of the all too enthusiastic welcome accorded to him by cheering crowds or inquisitive tourists who pressed about him with clicking cameras, anxious to obtain a snapshot of a man so famous and revered that people collected cigar stubs that had touched his lips, bones that had been left on his plate, and bowed towards the chair upon which he was accustomed to sit in a favoured shop.

In his later years his continental visits began to assume a set pattern. He would leave England at the beginning of March for France, spending a week or so in Paris before going on to Biarritz for three weeks. He then would embark on a month's cruise, in the royal yacht, usually with the Queen and preferably in the Mediterranean. Although he once told Lord Morley, while they were driving together through the forests near Balmoral, that 'if he could have chosen his life he would have liked to be a landscape gardener', he did not usually seem to take much notice of his surroundings and certainly rarely made a comment on the scenery. At Biarritz, however, he was struck by the beauty of the Basque coast-line and wrote to his friend, Lady Londonderry, of the 'splendid views' and of the pleasure he derived from listening to the 'continual roll of the Atlantic'. He wrote one day in the early spring of 1906:

> Though this place is quieter than the Riviera it is more bracing and I am sure healthier. I have charming rooms in a very big hotel close to the sea [the Hôtel du Palais] . . . Golf is the principal pastime, but the roads are excellent and I take continually long motor drives into the country and to Spain. I shall meet the Queen at Marseilles in the yacht . . . There are a great many English here.

One of the principal advantages of Biarritz was that the air suited him far better than the more sultry air of the Riviera. Towards the end of his life he was troubled by coughing fits so severe that he found it difficult to get his breath and seemed to be choking. But once installed at the Hôtel du Palais he found his breathing much more easy, and only regretted that Biarritz was so smelly. It was bad enough in 1907, but so much worse in 1908 that he instructed the British Ambassador in Paris to make representations to Clemenceau himself about 'the effects of defective draining', otherwise some other resort would 'have to be thought of'. Assurances were given that something would be done, and so the next year the King returned as usual.

At Biarritz he was called at seven, and after his glass of warm milk and his bath, he would have breakfast at ten, usually in a small tent on the terrace outside his apartments. The Corsican detective, Xavier Paoli, who was assigned to guard him, reported that he had grilled bacon, boiled eggs and fried fish for breakfast with a large cup of coffee, and that, having finished this meal, he would sit at his writing-table till a quarter past twelve when he went out for a walk. Lunch was served in his large private dining-room overlooking the sea at one o'clock and invariably included hard-boiled plovers' eggs with a touch of paprika, followed by trout, salmon or grilled sole, a meat dish (preferably chicken or lamb with asparagus), and strawberries or stewed fruit. As in England he drank very little either at luncheon or dinner, contenting himself with a glass or two of Chablis or dry champagne or, possibly, claret and Perrier water. Occasionally between meals he would have a whisky and soda.

Paoli complained of the difficulties of maintaining the King's privacy. He managed to reduce the swarm of beggars that habitually descended upon Biarritz in the season to two blind and ragged mendicants who took up the same position every day and, at the sound of Caesar's bark, held out their bowls into which the King dropped his daily contribution with the words, '*A demain!*' But newspapermen were a more serious problem. Paoli found a retired detective who bore such a marked resemblance to the King that he was known as 'Edouard'. He tried dressing this man up in clothes like the King's; but although the resemblance was more striking than ever, 'Edouard' could not manage a remotely convincing imitation of the King's smile or his highly characteristic way of walking or bowing, and the experiment had to be abandoned.

Despite his occasional failures, Paoli believed that he earned the King's respect, even his friendship; and he proudly recorded in his memoirs how one day he had ventured to admire the tiny gold matchbox with the royal crown which the King wore on his watch-chain. 'Accept it, my dear Paoli, as a souvenir,' the King immediately replied with his usual impulsive generosity. 'I should like you to have it.'

Although Paoli complained of the newspapermen, they discreetly omitted to mention in their reports the presence in Biarritz of Mrs Keppel, who was usually there staying, with her two daughters and their governess, at the Villa Eugénie as a guest of Sir Ernest Cassel and his sister. Mrs Keppel's daughter Sonia has described how exciting these annual journeys to Biarritz were, and how respectfully her mother was always treated: 'At Victoria a special carriage was reserved for us; and a special cabin on the boat. And at Calais, Mamma was treated like royalty. The *chef de gare* met her and escorted us all through the customs, and the car attendant on the train hovered over her like a love-sick troubadour.' Once at Biarritz, Sonia and her sister saw 'Kingy' frequently, accompanying him on picnics which, 'for some unfathomed reason', he chose to have by the side of the road, where other cars were sure to park nearby and where footmen unpacked chairs and tables, linen tablecloths, plates, glasses and silver, and 'every variety of cold food'. 'Much of "Kingy's" enjoyment of these picnics was based on his supposed anonymity and, delightedly, he would respond to an assumed name in his deep, unmistakable voice, unaware that most of the crowd was playing up to him.'

Every year, after the Regatta at Cowes, the King also went to Germany or Austria to take the waters at a spa. Formerly he had favoured Homburg which, in the season, had been full of foreign visitors 'most of whom [he knew] more or less'. These included Reuben Sassoon, a 'curious old gentleman', in George Cornwallis-West's opinion, who 'never opened his mouth except to put food in it'; but who gave the most entertaining picnic parties for as many as seventy guests; Mrs Arthur James, whose humour and high spirits always put the King in a good temper; and the dear old Duke of

Cambridge with his son, Colonel FitzGeorge, and the Duke's friend, Mrs
Robert Vyner. The King had stayed at the Ritters Park Hotel and had
drunk the waters conscientiously between half past seven and nine o'clock
in the morning before breakfast of a cup of coffee and a boiled egg.

In 1899 the King had transferred his favour to Marienbad, a small town
in a pleasant valley in Bohemia, two thousand feet above the sea. The springs
of healing waters at Marienbad belonged to the nearby abbey of Tepl, whose
monks spent alternating periods of two years in seclusion followed by two
years in the outside world and—as though in doubt as to which side of the
abbey wall their life's work lay—wore black top hats with white cassocks.
The monks had been profiting by the sale of their waters for more than
twenty years when the King, as Prince of Wales, had gone there for the
first time. And by 1899 it had become extremely fashionable, the chosen
spa of numerous members of Europe's oldest families: of Grand Admiral
Tirpitz and Lord Fisher; of Sir Ernest Cassel and the faded Lillie Langtry; of
the Gaekwar of Baroda, the Turkish Grand Vizier and the King of Greece;
of the dissolute Duke of Orléans and the celebrated French cavalry officer,
General Galliffet, whose wounded stomach was covered by a silver plate;
of Princess Dolgorouki, who had morganatically married the Tsar of Russia;
of Madame Waddington, the attractive American widow of a French Ambassador in London; and of numerous ladies who, as one English visitor disapprovingly noted, 'either have already been, or are qualifying themselves
for being, divorced'. Most of them were extremely fat when they arrived;
and many not much less so when they left.

There were several excellent hotels in the town, the most fashionable
being the Weimar where from 1903 to 1909 the King took a suite of rooms
which were specially furnished for him in a different style for each succeeding visit, all the pieces being sold for much more than their intrinsic value
after he left.

Every morning at the Weimar, the King's valet, Meidinger, himself
awakened by a band which began to play under his window at half past six,
entered his master's bedroom to draw the curtains. And, without fail, he
would be asked the same question phrased in the same six words: 'What's
the weather doing to-day, Meidinger?'

Having heard the subsequent report, the King got up and dressed himself. Soon after half past seven, with his secretary on one side and an equerry
on the other, he could be seen strolling briskly up and down on the prome-
nade by the spring known as the Kreuzbrunnen, smartly dressed in a hard,
curly-brimmed pale grey felt hat worn at a slight angle to the left, a stiff
white collar, neat grey pin-striped suit with all three buttons done up, and
yellow suede gloves sewn with black stitching. In warmer weather he would
wear a light-weight, dark blue coat and white trousers which were always im-

maculately creased, sometimes in front and at others down the sides. He was invariably closely shadowed by six Austrian detectives and two detectives from London, Patrick Quinn and Quinn's assistant, Hester. Even at that hour of the morning crowds of sightseers gathered to watch him stride by, his left arm bent as though he were about to put his hand into his pocket, his right hand grasping a gold-knobbed malacca cane or an ebony walking stick adorned with an E in brilliants, surmounted by a crown. As in Paris he liked to be known as the Duke of Lancaster, and was infuriated when the courier, Fehr, had his luggage labels printed, 'Lord Lancaster', a mistake that led him to expostulate angrily that people would think he was an ennobled gunmaker. Also, as in Paris, the incognito was scarcely worth while since everyone knew who the Duke of Lancaster was, the Burgomaster advertising his arrival by putting up notices asking people to respect his privacy, and photographs of him being on display in every shop window.

Although Frederick Ponsonby asserted that the King's 'one idea of happiness was to be in the middle of a crowd with no one taking any notice of him', others, more discerningly, supposed that he had no objection to being looked at and admired—he was rather annoyed, in fact, if he was not recognized. When dining incognito in restaurants, he became excessively impatient with waiters who failed to accord him the special treatment to which he was accustomed and treated him as an ordinary person who had to take his turn. And, once, paying an unexpected call on friends in Paris, he was exasperated to be asked at the door who he was. 'You do not know me? Well, you ought to know me,' the King expostulated, adding as proof of his own remarkable memory for faces, 'I know you. Last year you were third footman with the Duchess of Manchester.'

What the King did object to was being hampered or inconvenienced by inquisitive people who lacked the good manners to remain at a respectful distance. The crowds at Marienbad became so obtrusive that the King felt obliged to complain to the Emperor, whose officials saw to it that in future he was allowed to stroll about the town in peace, raising his hat in those varying degrees of respect which he had adopted to convey the exactly appriate measure of esteem to those whom he encountered. The gestures of civility due to the Grand Duchesses of Saxe-Weimar and Mecklenburg-Schwerin were rather more elaborate than those due to Mme Waddington, and considerably more so than those used to indicate recognition of the English actors who visited Marienbad as regularly as he did himself. Servants off duty were also recognized; and staid Austrian aristocrats were astonished to see him raise his hat to them, a condescension strongly criticized as unbecoming in a monarch. Similarly shocking was the friendliness with which he greeted Fräulein Pistl, an exceptionally good-looking young woman who had a shop under the colonnades by the Kreuzbrunnen where she sold those

Styrian hats which members of the King's entourage were urged to buy and which he bought himself, requiring Fräulein Pistl to deliver them to his hotel personally.

The King usually had his first tumbler of mineral water at his hotel, and two others sitting on a bench which was reserved for his use near the Kreuzbrunnen, both glasses being brought to him by the head waiter of the Weimar. After his second glass he went to have a mud bath in the Neubad. Then he would settle down to lunch, conscious of the fact that he was at Marienbad for a cure which ought to involve the loss of a good deal of weight, yet, as an Austrian journalist noticed, evidently without intending 'to subject himself to any severe regime'. Certainly, he did not eat as much as he did at home, and dispensed with the cold chicken which in England normally stood on his bedside table in case he woke up hungry in the night. He professed himself to be extremely dismayed by other people's lapses, particularly those of his friend Harry Chaplin, who, having dieted for several days, would suddenly find fattening food and drink irresistible; and he became very cross when something which was strictly forbidden, such as champagne, was handed round in his presence. Nevertheless, he enjoyed the local trout; he did not decline grouse with fried aubergines; and he ate a large number of peaches, his favourite fruit, which the suave and elegant Marienbad doctor, Ernst Ott, advised were better for him than oranges. He never seems to have claimed to have lost more than eight pounds in a fortnight and considered even this highly satisfactory.

Occasionally he would have luncheon at the Rübezahl restaurant on a hillside overlooking the town, and after the meal would go for a walk in the surrounding pine forests or for a drive in a motor-car. He once went for a drive with the English War Minister, Haldane.

He proposed that we should go in plain clothes as though we were Austrians [Haldane recalled]. And the first thing he did was to make me buy an Austrian hat [from Fräulein Pistl, of course] so as to look like a native ... As we were passing a little roadside inn, with a wooden table in front of it, the King stopped and said, 'Here I will stand treat.' He ordered coffee for two ... He said Austrian coffee was always admirable, and you could tell when you had crossed the frontier into Germany, because of the badness of the coffee ... 'Now I am going to pay,' he said. 'I shall take care to give only a small tip to the woman ... in case she suspects who I am.' We then drove to a place the King was very fond of—a monastery inhabited by the Abbot of Teppel— where we had a large tea and where the King enjoyed himself with the monks very much, gossiping and making himself agreeable.

Knowing how fond the King was of shooting, the Abbot once invited him to shoot on the monastery lands. Normally while at Marienbad the King went shooting at Bischofteinitz with Prince Trauttmansdorff, who arranged his guns and four hundred beaters to perfection. But the Abbot, inexperienced in such matters, thought that all he had to do was buy a few partridges, put them down in a field and drive them over the guns. So as to prevent their flying away before the guns were ready, two kites, which the partridges were rightly expected to mistake for big, predatory birds, were set up over the field. But the kites were left in position when the beaters began the drive, which meant that the birds would only fly for short distances in front of the beaters before alighting again. This made the shooting both difficult and dangerous; and one old monk, who appeared with an antiquated gun, thought he would be better off behind the beaters. 'It will all be quite safe,' he assured the nervous English guests. 'But of course if anyone shoots at me, I shall shoot back.' The King, who was used to being given the best position, was for some reason placed right at the end of the line and was scarcely able to get a single shot all day.

On Sundays the King attended morning service at the Anglican church in the Jägerstrasse; and on the Emperor's birthday, 18 August, wearing a splendid Austrian military uniform, he went to the thanksgiving service in the Roman Catholic church, after which, standing on the Weimar's wide balcony in his green plumed hat with the ribbon of the Order of St Stephen on his chest, he took the salute of a parade of veterans. On the evening of that day he always gave a dinner, either in the banqueting hall of the Weimar or in the hall of the Kurhaus, for important local dignitaries, distinguished visitors to Marienbad and British residents in Vienna such as Henry Wickham Steed, *The Times*'s correspondent.

Almost every other evening there was some sort of party in the King's hotel suite. This was sometimes a gay, relaxed gathering, at others, so one disgruntled guest complained, 'a trying mixture of court restraint and jollity', with the 'dismal mysteries of bridge' for those who played the game and 'difficult conversation' for those who did not. Occasionally the King went to the theatre to attend some light-hearted piece such as Oscar Strauss's *Walzertraum* or Lehar's *The Merry Widow*, or to listen to Yvette Guilbert, the *diseuse* whose performances he had much admired since an American friend, Mrs Ogden Goelet, had paid her £600 to break a contract in Paris in order to sing for him at Cannes. And once he went to what was billed as *Die Hölle* ('The Underworld') thinking it was a melodrama. It turned out to be a rather tiresome series of rude songs and recitations performed by a company from a Viennese music-hall. When the second act threatened to be no better than the first the King got up and left, as he had left a much coarser performance by a Viennese cabaret singer—who sang a song about a monk who says to a lascivious countess, 'Were it not for my holy robes' and receives the reply, 'Then take off your holy robes'—which the King had thought disrespectful to the Abbot and monks of Tepl.

The day after he had walked out in boredom from *Die Hölle* the papers congratulated his Majesty on having made a stand against immorality by having refused to see an improper performance; and soon afterwards a letter arrived from England from William Boyd Carpenter, Bishop of Ripon, expressing the satisfaction of the whole Church at the protest the King had made against obscene musical comedy. The King's secretary wanted to know how to reply to this letter. 'Tell the Bishop the exact truth,' the King replied. 'I have no wish to pose as a protector of morals, especially abroad.'

The King was certainly more used to being criticized for depraving morals at Marienbad than praised for protecting them. He was only too liable to pick up curious people and ask them to luncheon, Frederick Ponsonby admitted.

Monsieur and Madame de Varrue came one day. She had been a noted beauty in Paris, and had late in life married a young man who suddenly called himself Baron de Varrue . . . Mrs Dale Lace, with an eye glass, short skirts and a murky past, also came to luncheon and some of the habitués were shocked, although she amused the King . . . Life at Marienbad was very hard work, as I spent so much time seeing people who were difficult to get rid of. For instance . . . a beautiful lady from the half-world in Vienna who wanted to have the honour of sleeping with the King. On being told this was out of the question, she said if it came to the worst she would sleep with me, so that she should not waste the money spent on her ticket.

'A cloud of bluebottle flies constantly buzzed round the King,' one British visitor complained in 1904. He was 'recklessly abandoned to the society of a few semi-déclassé ladies and men to match', though he was 'civil enough to decent people' and 'followed the cure loyally'. In 1905 he was deemed to be 'less evilly surrounded than in other years' and the 'doubtful ladies' were 'rather out of it'. But it was still well enough known that doubtful ladies continued to seek his company, that he was rarely averse to theirs, and that he found Marienbad a very convenient place in which to meet them. Sophie Hall Walker, whose husband, breeder of the King's Derby winner, *Minoru*, became the first Lord Wavertree, was one of his favourite companions. And the daughter of Sir Charles Gill, another Marienbad *habitué*, remembered how in the afternoons she used to watch fascinated as Mrs Hall Walker's hotel room was prepared for a tea-time visit by the King, how flowers were placed in big vases, the air sprayed with scent and the curtains drawn.

The American actress, Maxine Elliott, who was not invited to dinner parties in London by those hostesses generally known to entertain the King, confessed that she went to Marienbad, 'where matters could be more easily arranged', with the sole purpose of getting to know him. Sailing out to Bohemia with a socially impeccable American woman friend, she took rooms in a hotel near the Weimar and soon learned the King's routine. Thus it was that one fine morning, the delightful, beautifully dressed figure of Maxine Elliott was to be seen sitting on a bench near the Kurhaus, apparently absorbed in a book. The King approached, attended by Frederick Ponsonby, Sidney Greville and Seymour Fortescue; Miss Elliott raised her eyes from her book; the King glanced into them; the royal party walked past. Then one of the King's attendants returned to the bench with a message: 'His Majesty believes you are the Miss Elliott he admired so much in your play. His Majesty would be delighted with your presence tonight for dinner. Mrs Arthur James is giving a dinner in His Majesty's honour. 7.45 at the Weimar Hotel. Your invitation will, of course, be delivered to your hotel.' After a further visit to Marienbad in a subsequent year, during which she was seen frequently in the King's company, Miss Elliott was sufficiently assured of his interest in her to buy a house in England, Hartsbourne Manor at Bushey Heath, where she spent a great deal of money on a suite of rooms above her own which she referred to as 'the King's suite'.

Every second day a bag of royal mail arrived from England together with a generous selection of English newspapers which the King read carefully, looking also through various French newspapers and the Vienna *Neue Freie Presse* so that when one of his ministers joined him at Marienbad he was found to be well informed of what was happening elsewhere.

Frequently in his company was Sir Henry Campbell-Bannerman, who, mainly for the sake of his wife, Charlotte, had been a regular visitor to the spa for many years. Campbell-Bannerman had disapproved of the King before he got to know him well, just as the King had supposed that he would have little in common with Sir Henry, whom he had expected to find 'prosy and heavy'. At first the King had taken little notice of him; but one day he asked him to luncheon and found him, contrary to all his expectations, very good company with a fund of amusing stories, 'repartees, jokes and gastronomic appreciations'. Thereafter the King sought him out and spent many pleasant hours with him—too many hours, in fact, for the taste of Campbell-Bannerman, who, having been asked to lunch or dinner almost every day in September 1905, complained, 'I got so mixed up with the King's incessant gaieties, for which his energy and appetite are alike insatiable, that it was no rest or holiday for me. Thus when at last he was gone . . . my Dr ordered me to bed and absolute rest for forty-eight hours.'

Sometimes the King talked politics to him, but more often the conversation was on less weighty subjects. A picture of them both talking earnestly in the gardens of the Kurhaus appeared in an illustrated paper. The King was shown striking his palm with a clenched fist in emphasis of some point to which Campbell-Bannerman was paying close attention. Underneath the picture was the caption, 'Is it peace or war?' When Campbell-Bannerman's private secretary showed him the paper, his master examined it for a few moments before asking the secretary if he would like to know what was being discussed. The secretary said that he would. 'The King wanted to have my opinion,' Campbell-Bannerman informed him, 'whether halibut is better baked or boiled!'

17
L'Oncle de l'Europe

He is, and this one cannot deny, the arbiter of Europe's destiny.

'The more you know of him,' Whitelaw Reid, the American Ambassador in London wrote to President Roosevelt about King Edward in 1907, 'the better I am sure you will like him, and the more you will come to the prevalent English, and, in fact, European belief, that he is the greatest mainstay of peace in Europe.'

The King's reputation as a diplomatist of unique influence was prodigious. 'He is, and this one cannot deny, the arbiter of Europe's destiny, the most powerful personal factor in world policy,' the Italian Foreign Minister told the French Ambassador in Rome. 'And, as he is for peace, his overall approach will serve above all to maintain harmony between the nations.' The King was widely supposed, in fact, to 'run the foreign policy of the country', as Frederick Ponsonby said, a supposition which, Ponsonby thought, may have made Lord Lansdowne 'a little jealous' and which, therefore, may have accounted for the rather strained relationship between the King and his Foreign Secretary.

The King's reputation as an arbiter of foreign policy stood quite as high abroad as it did in England. As the Belgian Chargé d'Affaires in London put it in a report to Brussels in 1907: 'The English are getting more and more into the habit of regarding international problems as being almost exclusively within the province of King Edward, for whose profound political instinct and fertile diplomacy they, very rightly, feel great respect.' The King's views were often considered to be decisive, while his frequent foreign travels—attributed by his detractors as being due to *Wanderlust*, his determination to emulate the Kaiser, or to a taste for playing an apparently important role in the limelight of the European stage—were followed, watched and reported upon as assiduously as his political opinions were solicited and discussed.

This belief in the King's virtual omnipotence was particularly strong in less powerful states such as Italy; and even more so in those smaller countries, like Greece, Belgium and Portugal, whose thrones were occupied by monarchs to whom the King felt sympathetically drawn not only by their membership of his own profession but also by family ties. He naturally enjoyed this reputation. The Controller of the Kaiser's Household, who, in the year before the King's death, came to the view that his influence was far less than the Germans had always imagined, pictured 'a sly and amiable smile' stealing over his face when he thought how the world looked upon him 'as the guiding spirit of . . . British diplomacy'. Under no illusions about the limits of his power, the King was nevertheless most insistent that he must be kept fully informed about the course and problems of the government's foreign policy, either by the Prime Minister, or by the Foreign Secretary if the Prime Minister left the effective control of policy in his Foreign Secretary's hands. He took particular pleasure in letting fellow-sovereigns know how well-informed he was. One day at Marienbad in 1905, according to Henry Wickham Steed, 'he chaffed the life out of Ferdinand of Bulgaria, who . . . always [prided] himself upon being more rapidly informed than anyone else', because Prince Ferdinand knew nothing about the Japanese Admiral Kaimamura's destruction of the Russian Vladivostok squadron, of which the King had received advance notice from the Counsellor of the British Embassy in Vienna.

The King's obvious satisfaction in being entrusted with important confidences, his numerous contacts with ruling dynasties and with important foreign ministers, his charm and tactful good manners, his gift for drawing men out in conversation, and his willingness to listen to them in attentive silence, all stood him in good stead as a roving diplomatist and added to his reputation as an eminent mediator. But after his death it began to be realized that his influence on the conduct of European affairs had, in reality, been far from as effective as had been supposed, and that his views on foreign policy were never consistent and always liable to be influenced by personal considerations and prejudice. The goodwill that he inspired in most European countries, except Germany, together with the dignity of his manner and the forcefulness of his personality when he represented his own country, were fully recognized; yet, as Balfour asked Lord Lansdowne to confirm after the outbreak of the First World War, 'he never made an important suggestion of any sort on large questions of policy' during the years when they were both his ministers. Nor did the King ever add the sort of detailed, considered minute which his mother's ministers had grown to expect from Prince Albert on the Foreign Office dispatches which were sent to him, usually contenting himself with a mere indication of approval or commendation.

When he disagreed with ministerial advice he did not hesitate to put forward his own views, much to the annoyance of the young Eyre Crowe, who was one day to be Permanent Under-Secretary of State for Foreign Affairs. Crowe was highly critical of the King's insistence on maintaining his royal authority, and went about maintaining that he 'must be taught that he is a pawn in the game'. But the King's obedience to constitutional propriety was far too strong for him to argue with an important Cabinet decision once it had been taken. And far more often than not he had to give way to his government, as when, for example, he endeavoured to prevent the appointment as French Ambassador in London of M. Challemel-Lacour, a supposed Communist, against whom the King had been prejudiced by his aristocratic French friends and by biased reports in *Figaro*.

Although he allowed himself to be persuaded to accept the appointment of Challemel-Lacour (whom he found on personal acquaintance to be entirely unobjectionable), the King did not always give way without a more determined struggle. This was well exemplified in 1903 when, having visited Portugal—where his presence was interpreted in Berlin as a setback for German ambitions in Africa—the King went on to Italy and decided that, on passing through Rome in April, he ought to pay a visit to the Pope as the Kaiser had twice done.

Influenced by Knollys, who was 'dead against it', he had, before leaving England, reluctantly accepted the Cabinet's advice not to pay the visit. And on 23 March, Knollys had assured Balfour that the King would go only for the day to Rome, where he was to have lunch with King Victor Emmanuel III, and 'by this arrangement he [would] get out of seeing the Pope'. 'He hopes the Pope will not be offended by his not calling [on] him,' Knollys added in a letter to Balfour's secretary, J.S. Sandars, a few days later. 'But if he is H.M. cannot help it.'

So it was that on arrival at Malta a telegram had been sent from the royal yacht to Sir Francis Bertie, British Ambassador in Rome, to the effect that owing to the short time that the King was to stay in Rome it was 'impossible for his Majesty to visit the Pope for whom he [entertained] the highest reverence and respect'. On the very day that this telegram was dispatched from the royal yacht, however, the Foreign Minister's secretary, Sir Eric Barrington, sent a message, in cipher and marked 'very confidential', from London: 'The King will receive telegram from Prime Minister about Pope. My conviction is that it is intended as a loophole in case King thinks informal visit desirable.'

The next day the Prime Minister's telegram was deciphered aboard the *Victoria and Albert*:

> Mr Balfour has the honour to report that yesterday the Duke of Norfolk and Lord Edmund Talbot [two leaders of the Roman Catholic community in England] came to see him on the subject of your Majesty's visit to Rome. They expressed with deep emotion their views on what they declared would be regarded by the Roman Catholic world as a deliberate slight put upon an old and venerable man [aged ninety-

three] by your Majesty's abstaining from visiting the Vatican. They also maintain that while this course would deeply hurt the sentiments of Roman Catholics, the opposite course would raise no widespread ill-feeling among Protestants. Mr Balfour said he deeply regretted that anything should be done to hurt the feelings of the Pope but that he still adhered to the view that there was really great danger of irritating Protestant sentiment if the King of England paid a formal visit to the Roman pontiff . . . Mr Balfour could not therefore alter the tenor of the advice already given with the concurrence of the Cabinet.

Lord Edmund Talbot was bitterly disappointed when shown a copy of this telegram which, in his opinion, did not give the King 'any lead' at all. 'The whole thing has been deplorably bungled,' he told Sandars. 'I have still faith in the King's good taste to extricate himself from this extremely pain-ful position . . . [But] I wish the Prime Minister had found it possible to give His Majesty a helping hand.'

Entirely convinced by the arguments put forward by the Duke of Nor-folk and Lord Edmund Talbot, and annoyed by the government's equivo-cation, the King gave orders for another telegram to be sent requesting less ambiguous advice. Both Balfour and Lansdowne were accordingly informed that the King felt '*very* strongly on the subject', that he attached 'great importance to the question', that on his three previous visits to Rome as Prince of Wales he had invariably visited the Pope, and that not to do so 'on this occasion would not only be a slight to a venerable Pontiff but would alienate all the King's Catholic subjects throughout the world. The King deeply [regretted this divergence of his opinion with the Cabinet], but would like to hear from [the Prime Minister] again on the subject.'

This elicited a reply from Balfour again expressing fears that 'Protestant prejudice might fasten on the visit' and make trouble in England; and a complementary message from Barrington to Hardinge confirming that Lansdowne nevertheless wanted the visit to be made. 'The Cabinet dare not recommend the King to go,' Barrington explained. 'But evidently A.J.B[alfour] wished the King in such a matter to *passer outre* of his advisers.'

The King now lost his temper. Demanding straightforward advice he dictated an enraged telegram to Hardinge, who passed it on to Frederick Ponsonby for coding and dispatch. Ponsonby read it with consternation, feeling 'instinctively that if this message was sent there would be no alterna-tive for Arthur Balfour but to send in his resignation'. Ponsonby, therefore, rewrote the message 'in conciliatory language'; and at last the King received the sort of reply from the Prime Minister for which he had been hoping:

If the proposed visit could really be made private and unofficial, Mr Balfour would think it an impertinence to offer any observations on it . . . The whole stress could be laid on the fact that . . . the Pope was very aged and in course of nature could live but a short time, that he had expressed a personal desire to see your Majesty and that as a matter of courtesy (so to speak) between gentlemen, you could not pass his door without acceding to his wishes.

The King readily accepted this advice, but great difficulty was experienced in persuading the Vatican to intimate that the Pope would like to see him. Cardinal Rampolla, the Papal Secretary of State, intent upon making it appear that the King had requested an audience, assured Monsignor Edmund Stonor, titular Archbishop of Trebizond and a resident English prelate in Rome, that 'the Holy Father, in consequence of his well-known present position in Rome, could not take the initiative in inviting a sovereign to pay him a visit, but should the King of England wish to do him the courteous attention of calling upon him, this would be acceptable and duly appreciated.'

But the King felt that he could not go to the Vatican unless he was actually invited to go; and any such invitation, Cardinal Rampolla continued to insist to Monsignor Stonor, could not possibly be issued. Faced with this impasse, the Duke of Norfolk decided to intervene personally. He did not trust Monsignor Stonor, considering him 'stupid and a bungler', so Francis Bertie told Sandars, and suspecting that he was playing along with Rampolla in the hope of 'getting his reward'. Under pressure from Norfolk the more reliable Monsignor Merry del Val, the President of the Accademia, who had been to school in England, went to see the Pope personally and, to Cardinal Rampolla's anger, returned from the Vatican with an acceptable message: 'His Holiness has personally expressed his concurrence with what the Duke of Norfolk conveyed to His Majesty as to the pleasure which His Holiness would derive from a visit from His Majesty.'

No sooner had the seemingly intractable problem of the invitation been settled, however, than other problems arose. First of all, the Vatican wanted to know, where would the visit be made from? The Pope could not possibly receive the King if he left from the Quirinale, since relations between the Papacy and the Monarchy had been severely strained by the Pope's loss of his patrimony as a consequence of the unification of Italy. Sir Francis Bertie went to consult King Victor Emmanuel on this point. The Italian King was agreeable and accommodating. He told Bertie that he thought that a visit to the Pope was 'quite natural and that though it could not be made direct from the Quirinale, there were ways of satisfying the Pope's susceptibilities'. He cheerfully suggested that King Edward might start his journey from the house of the Minister whom his nephew, the Kaiser, had accredited to the

Pope. Bertie, so he reported, 'treated this suggestion as intended as a joke'.

Meanwhile it seemed to Mr Balfour, so yet another message from London informed the King, 'that if the Pope lays down from what palaces he will, and from what palaces he will not receive a direct visit from your Majesty, he has not much real ground of complaint if he is not visited at all'. Ignoring this comment, the King decided to make his visit from the British Embassy, and Hardinge was sent to discuss the final arrangements with Cardinal Rampolla. It was not a comfortable interview.

> Cardinal Rampolla received me in a most gushing manner [Hardinge reported to Balfour]. His appearance did not impress me. He has a deceitful eye and does not look one straight in the face. He speaks Italian French. He asked if the King would come and call on him and whether he might return the visit to the King at the English College. I told him quite plainly that much as the King would like to make his personal acquaintance there could be no question of his Majesty paying him a visit since the King only paid visits to sovereigns. He at once quoted the precedent of the German Emperor to which I replied that the King of England could not possibly admit that his actions could in any way be bound by precedents set by the German Emperor. I also added that there was no question of the King going to the English College as if he did so he would have to go to the Scotch and Irish Colleges . . . He then asked if the King would visit St Peter's as he would like to receive him there . . . to which I replied that if H.M. went to St Peter's it would be 'en touriste'. He also asked if Monsignor Stonor would accompany the King from the Embassy to which I answered that the King proposed to take me in his carriage and that Stonor had better await the King at the Vatican . . . I impressed upon him that although the King would come in uniform as an act of courtesy to the Pope the visit was to be considered quite private and informal.

Sailing from Malta on 21 April 1903, the *Victoria and Albert* set course for Naples whence a telegram was dispatched to say that the King would arrive incognito, which seemed 'rather absurd' to Frederick Ponsonby since 'no other human being in the world would come with eight battleships, four cruisers, four destroyers, and a dispatch vessel'.

On stepping ashore at Naples, the first English monarch to set foot there since Richard Coeur de Lion, the King immediately alarmed the Italian police, who had planned to close to the public the museums which he was to visit and to fill the galleries with detectives. He refused to have any police protection, and when two of his suite were asked to walk closely behind him at all times to guard him from the knives and bullets of assassins, he turned round in irritation and sent them off in different directions. He even insisted on exploring the slums of Naples with Queen Amélie of Portugal and Mrs Cornelius Vanderbilt, afterwards listening complacently to a lecture from Charles Hardinge 'about exposing himself needlessly'.

Bertie reported to Sandars on 26 April:

The King has been very civilly and respectfully received in the streets here. Hats off and some clapping but no cheering. On the other hand at the Opera Gala last night he had an enthusiastic reception—vivas and cheers and clapping of hands several times and lasting some time . . . There was a great display of jewels but not much beauty. The ballet dancers had pink caleçons which gave them an odd appearance. I believe that King Victor Emmanuel [II], of holy memory, said of a ballet of that kind that if it were not for the clothes it would be paradise.

Two days later the King arrived in Rome feeling rather crotchety and out of sorts. A morose and sleepy guest, he had been entertained at luncheon the previous day by Lord Rosebery, an equally quiet as well as an unwilling host, who had a villa outside Naples and who had employed a firm of caterers to provide the seemingly interminable but indifferent meal of twenty courses which lasted until four o'clock. But although the King's bad mood worsened as he left for the Vatican and found that the private nature of his visit had been rendered suspect by streets lined with troops and cheering crowds, and although Cardinal Rampolla grumpily declined to be present, the interview with the Pope went off very well.

Hardinge reported to Balfour:

On arrival within the precincts of the Vatican, His Majesty was received with great pomp by a motley and picturesque group of ecclesiastics, chamberlains, officers of the Swiss Guard and of the Noble Guard, many of them in sixteenth century costumes. After the presentations to the King, His Majesty was taken to the Pope's private apartments where the Pope . . . a perfect marvel for a man of ninety-three . . . came to meet him in the ante-room, and took him into an inner room where they remained in conversation for about a quarter of an hour or twenty minutes. The King has told me since that the Pope talked to him of every sort of question—Venezuela, Somaliland, Lord Salisbury, some occasion when he had seen the Queen about forty years ago, etc. The King then sent for us and presented each of us in turn to the Pope.

The King had been careful to warn his suite to show the Pope the utmost respect without prejudicial veneration, to bow as often as they liked but on no account to kiss his ring if it were offered to them. But the Pope, 'a really fine and dignified old gentleman', saved them any possible embarrassment by getting out of his chair, shaking hands with everyone in turn and then making a short speech assuring them how happy he was to have had the opportunity of seeing their master.

The visit to the Pope was a happy prelude to the King's far more politically important visit to Paris the next month. He had made his plans to visit Paris, after going to Portugal and Italy, in 'the utmost secrecy', as the Marquis de Soveral told King Carlos I. He had told neither the Queen nor the government, nor even his private secretary, 'extreme discretion' being necessary in view of the effect which his journey would have on Russia and Germany. Nor had he told the French President. 'He does not wish to compromise himself,' Soveral explained, 'but wants to be in a position where he can abandon his trip should difficulties crop up.' When they were informed of the King's intentions, most of the Cabinet were extremely dubious about the wisdom of a visit to France. Lord Lansdowne warned the King that it might be dangerous in view of French feeling about the Boer War and about the incident at Fashoda in the Upper Nile Valley from which a French detachment had been forced to retreat after a protest at their presence there had been handed to them by General Kitchener. But the King was undeterred. The French President, Émile Loubet, welcomed the idea warmly, telling the British Ambassador, who also approved of it, that 'he could not lay too much stress on the influence which the King's presence in Paris would have on friendly relations between the two peoples . . . His Majesty, while Prince of Wales, had acquired an exceptional popularity; and he would find when he returned that this feeling was as warm as ever . . . [and] was general among all classes.'

So the government, without enthusiasm, gave their consent to the visit, trusting that their foreboding would not be justified and that the King's personal reputation in France would avert any serious unpleasantness, even though he was going—as he insisted on going—with 'all the honours due to the King of England'.

Certainly in earlier years, as President Loubet had said, the King had been very popular in France, where his influence was such that, as the Goncourt brothers noted, 'the style of handshake with the elbow pressed close to the body' which became fashionable in about 1895 'arose from his having an attack of rheumatism in the shoulder'. Both Queen Victoria and the British Foreign Office had been much concerned by his intimate friendship with the French nobility after the fall of the Second Empire. The Queen had thought it most imprudent of him to offer the house which he had borrowed from the Duke of Devonshire—and to which he referred as 'notre maison de campagne, "Chiswick" '—as a refuge to the exiled Empress Eugénie. The government had also been concerned about his equally chivalrous insistence

that the highest funeral honours should be paid to the Prince Imperial, who
had been killed while serving with the British army in the war against the
Zulus in 1879. Arranging for a man-of-war to bring the coffin back to
England and acting as pallbearer at the funeral, his generous display of sympathy had been deeply gratifying to the dead man's mother, the Empress
Eugénie; but Disraeli had felt compelled to express the hope that the republican government of France would feel as obliged to him as she was.

Yet the Prince of Wales's friendship with imperialists and royalists had
not in the end hampered his ability to get on well with republicans. A report
prepared by the French police in 1874 indicated that there was no political
significance in his private friendships with either Orleanists or Bonapartists.
This report ran:

> *Il est très sympathique. C'est le type du gentilhomme anglais; il a les
> instincts toriés; mais tout le monde s'accorde à dire qu'il fera un excellent
> roi. Quant à ses opinions relativement à la France, on peut citer la ré-
> ponse qu'il fit au Général Fleury, lors du voyage du Czar à Londres,
> 'Monseigneur,' disait le Général, 'on prétend que vous êtes orléaniste.'
> 'Bah! Mon cher Général, rien qu'un petit peu.'*

In 1878 the republican government had expressed the wish that the
Prince would be appointed President of the British section of the Paris
International Exhibition. He had accepted the offer, and had delighted the
Parisians by the good-humoured way in which he laughingly acknowledged
the cries of *'Vive la République!'* which were directed at him as he walked
by in the procession at the opening ceremony. He also created a favourable
impression two days later at a banquet in the Hôtel du Louvre where, in a
speech delivered half in English and half in French and without recourse to
notes, he gave moving testimony of his love of France and of his conviction
that there would now be a period of lasting friendship between that great
country and his own. 'England is very popular here at this moment,' the
British Ambassador had told the Foreign Secretary contentedly the following week. 'And the Prince of Wales's visit has been the principal cause of
this.'

The Prince had increased that popularity as time went on. He had developed an unlikely but mutually respectful relationship with the ugly, ill-
dressed Léon Gambetta, who found it 'no waste of time to talk with him
even over a merry supper' at the Café Anglais. The Prince had convinced
Frenchmen that he sincerely loved France 'at once *gaîment et sérieusement*',
as Gambetta put it, despite the colonial rivalry between their country and
his which sometimes led to his being cruelly lampooned in the French press
and execrated by the Parisian mob. And he had allayed disappointment at
his refusal in 1889 to bestow his official favour on an International Exhibi-

tion in Paris on the anniversary of the outbreak of the French Revolution—
on the grounds that its inspiration was anti-monarchical—by visiting the
Exhibition privately with his wife and children, making another family excursion to the new iron tower whose marvels were explained to them by its
designer, Alexandre Gustave Eiffel, and going to the Elysée to repay a visit
made to him by the President, Sadi Carnot. When Carnot was assassinated
he went out of his way to display his sympathy by calling in person at the
French Embassy to offer his condolences to the Ambassador and attending
the requiem Mass in the French chapel in Leicester Square. He had always
been equally punctilious in his attentions to Carnot's successors, particularly
to Loubet, who became President in 1899.

Since then, however, the former happy relationship between the King
and the French Republic—clouded first by the Fashoda crisis and then by
the vociferous pro-Boer sympathies of the French people and press—had
been further overcast by his decision not to make his annual visit to France
in 1900 as a protest against the savage ridicule of the royal family by Anglo-
phobic journalists and caricaturists. He had also declined to attend the opening of the International Exhibition in Paris that year; and when Lord
Salisbury pressed him to do so in the interests of Anglo–French relations,
he had produced an exceptionally scurrilous article in *La Patrie* and had
reiterated his determination to make his displeasure known by his absence.
The following year he had been even more exasperated by caricatures in
Le Rire.

But by 1903 the King had decided that the time had come to make the
quarrel up. Feeling against England was still quite strong, as he knew only
too well. A special number of the weekly paper *L'Assiette au Beurre*—devoted
to British concentration camps in South Africa and concluding with a rude
drawing of Britannia, '*L'Impudique Albion*', lifting her skirts to reveal but-
tocks imprinted with the unmistakable features of King Edward VII—sold
more than a quarter of a million copies. And several nationalist journals,
notably *Libre Parole, La Patrie and L'Autorité*, maintained an uncompromisingly anti-British tone in every issue. Yet he believed that he must now
make an official visit in an effort to bring about the *détente* which both
governments desired, hoping that his personal popularity amongst most
people in Paris would help them to regard his country in a more friendly
way.

His reception, as he drove from the Porte Dauphine railway station in
the Bois de Boulogne down the Champs Elysées, was not altogether encouraging. Most of the crowd watched in silence. A few hats were raised. There
was a little scattered cheering—more, however, for the President than the
King. But the loudest shouts—fortunately directed at the King's suite, particularly at Frederick Ponsonby, who was wearing a red military coat, rather
that at the King himself—were '*Vive Fashoda!*' '*Vivent les Boers!*' and '*Vive*

Jeanne d'Arc!' Once or twice a voice shouted quite a long sentence which the English visitors could not catch but which was greeted by loud laughter from the crowd.

'The French don't like us,' one of the King's suite remarked; and the King curtly observed, 'Why should they?' He seemed in excellent spirits, though, glancing to right and left, acknowledging the infrequent acclamations with a smile and polite nod of the head, sitting straight-backed as the carriage rolled by.

After paying a state visit to the President at the Elysée, he drove to the British Embassy where, in reply to an address presented to him by the British Chamber of Commerce, he made a highly effective speech which had been prepared for him by Hardinge. Dinner at the Embassy was followed by a performance of Maurice Donnay's *L'Autre Danger* at the Théâtre Français where the audience seemed rather nervous and reserved. Displaying not the least affront at his unenthusiastic reception, he left the loge during the *entr'acte*, to the evident consternation of the police, and walked about with the rest of the audience as though he felt as much at home as he would have done at Drury Lane, proudly wearing the Grand Cordon of the Légion d'Honneur on his starched shirt front. Noticing the actress Jeanne Granier, he walked up to greet her, kissing her hand and carefully enunciating in French, in a voice loud enough for others to hear, the so often quoted words, 'Ah, Mademoiselle, I remember how I applauded you in London where you represented all the grace, all the *esprit* of France.'

The next morning that remark was repeated everywhere in Paris as the people read reports in the newspapers of the King's speech at the British Embassy in which he had referred to his great pleasure at being once more 'in this beautiful city' and to the friendship and admiration which he and his countrymen felt 'for the French nation and their glorious traditions'.

Willing to respond to these sincere overtures, the Parisians greeted him more warmly as he drove out that morning to a military review held in his honour at Vincennes, where, to the crowd's obvious delight, he simulated the greatest relief and surprise when six cavalry regiments, charging headlong towards his stand with sabres and lances flashing in the air, came to a sudden halt beneath him. He turned round to the President to give him a hearty handshake.

The more extreme nationalists still shouted patriotic slogans and rude remarks; but, as the British Ambassador said, it was easy to perceive that there was in general 'a marked increase in cordiality'. Although there was little obvious enthusiasm on the road to Vincennes, which took the King through the poorer quarters of Paris, there were far fewer catcalls than there had been the day before. And it gave the people evident satisfaction to see how gravely and conscientiously the King raised his hand in salute to the flags that lined the route of the procession. At the Hôtel de Ville—where the crowds cheered as the royal standard was unfurled on the flag-staff—the King once more assured his hosts in his clear and confident French that it was always with the greatest pleasure that he returned to Paris—'*où je me trouve toujours comme si j'étais chez moi*'.

As he sat down he received 'a tremendous ovation', according to Frederick Ponsonby, who had described the atmosphere the day before as having been 'distinctly antagonistic'. 'He now seemed to have captured Paris by storm. From that moment everything was changed wherever he went. Not only the King but all of the suite were received with loud and repeated cheering. It was a most marvellous transformation.' As the British Ambassador confirmed a few days later, the visit had proved a success 'more complete than the most sanguine optimist could have foreseen'. 'Seldom has such a complete change of attitude been seen,' the Belgian Minister in Paris thought, 'as that which has taken place in this country . . . towards England and her Sovereign.'

That evening, on his way from a state banquet at the Elysée to the Opéra, the King was made to feel that all restraint had been abandoned and all reservations overcome. He seemed now to have entirely won the people over. Cheering crowds blocked the path of his carriage, shouting '*Vive Edouard!*' '*Notre bon Edouard!*' '*Vive notre roi!*' These shouts were repeated whenever he thereafter appeared; and on 4 May as the King left the Embassy for the Gare des Invalides where the royal train was waiting to take him to Cherbourg, the crowds' parting ovation was described in Paris newspapers as being '*délirant*', '*fervent*', '*passionnant*', '*excitant*'.

He had spoken of strengthening the bonds of friendship between the two countries, and of their mutual desire to 'march together in the path of civilization and peace'. And certainly most Frenchmen—supposing the King's powers to be far greater than they were—believed that whither he wished to march, Englishmen would follow and that he himself was wholeheartedly committed to bringing about a lasting friendship with their country.

In England, however, public opinion still regarded the *entente* with France suspiciously; and it was to be many years yet before that suspicion, which was never completely to disappear, began at last to dissolve. There could be no doubt, though, that King Edward's charm and personality helped to hasten its dissolution and to make the *entente cordiale* a reality.

His reputation as the sole originator of the *entente* is undeserved. It ignores the patient work of Lord Lansdowne (who had a French grandmother), Paul Cambon, French Ambassador in London, and Théophile Delcassé, who told a friend on taking office in 1898, 'I do not wish to leave this desk without having restored the good understanding with England.' It also ignores England's need to end her isolation from the continental powers and to overcome her colonial difficulties, particularly in Africa. But as Sir Sidney Lee said, 'the credit for influencing public opinion not only in

France but also in England in favour of the *entente*, the credit for lulling the French suspicions of *perfide Albion* and English suspicions of France, the credit for creating an atmosphere in which agreement could be reached, must go to Edward VII.'

The King was also to be given credit for helping to preserve the *entente* in its delicate infancy. He warmly welcomed President Loubet to England on his return visit in July 1903, making gracious little speeches in praise of Franco–British friendship, and giving orders for the *Marseillaise* to be played in full, triumphantly, on all occasions. And when twelve French battleships arrived at Portsmouth in August 1905, at the invitation of 'King Edward and his government', he ensured that they were given a reception which the French sailors would never forget and which their compatriots would appreciate as a symbol of the King's firm commitment to the long life of the *entente*.

Clearing the way for the *entente* was the King's greatest achievement. In no other sphere of foreign policy did he achieve a comparable success. The government, nevertheless, often had cause to feel grateful for his taste for foreign travel as well as for his international contacts. He was generally quite willing to interrupt a holiday when occasion demanded, to go to a royal funeral in Spain, for instance, or to distribute a few Victorian Orders in Portugal where he was on excellent terms with King Carlos, though the Portuguese nobles always reminded him of 'waiters at second-rate restaurants'. Apart from the King of the Belgians, whom he grew to despise and distrust, there were few European sovereigns with whom he could not have a useful and pleasant conversation; while his known liking for America and Americans was by no means a negligible factor in Anglo–American relations. He much enjoyed the company of Whitelaw Reid, the American Ambassador in London. And, when England and the United States had quarrelled so bitterly over a border dispute between Venezuela and British Guiana in 1895 that war had seemed imminent, he had helped to calm the storm by the tone of his reply to a telegram sent to him by Joseph Pulitzer, whom he had met at Homburg. When Pulitzer's telegram requesting his views on the critical issue had arrived in London, he had shown it to the Prime Minister, who had deprecated his decision to answer it. But the warm and conciliatory reply which had none the less been dispatched, and which Pulitzer had prominently published in his paper, the *New York World*, had soothed many ruffled tempers on the other side of the Atlantic.

Much as the King normally enjoyed travelling, the experience was not always a pleasurable one. As Prince of Wales, for example, he had been

asked to go to Ireland in 1885 when feeling in the south was running harder
than usual against the English. Understandably annoyed that the government
were neither willing to pay his expenses nor to request him officially to make
a journey from which, as he pointed out, he could hardly expect to derive
any 'personal pleasure', he was reluctant to go. But as soon as the government agreed to authorize the visit officially and to pay for it, he sailed for
Dublin with the Princess Alexandra and his elder son. Their reception in
Dublin and in the North was welcoming enough; but in Cork, where they
were booed and pelted with onions, it was, as the Prince's equerry reported,
'a nightmare'. 'The streets were filled with sullen faces—hideous, dirty, cruel
countenances, hissing and grimacing into one's very face, waving *black* flags
and black kerchiefs . . . No one who went through this day will ever forget
it . . . It was like a bad dream. The Prince of Wales showed the greatest
calmness and courage.'

So, too, he did when, despite the unrest in St Petersburg, he insisted on
leaving for Russia to attend the funeral of Tsar Alexander II, who had been
killed by a bomb which had been flung at him as he was returning to the
Winter Palace from a military review. Grave doubts were expressed for the
Prince's safety. But neither he nor Princess Alexandra, who was the new
Tsarina's sister, had any doubt that they ought to go. And Lord Granville,
the Foreign Secretary, considered that there were strong diplomatic advantages to be gained. 'I have no doubt that your Royal Highness's visit will be
productive of good,' Granville wrote to him. 'There can be no question that
a good understanding and friendly relations between this country and Russia may be of immense advantage to both.'

So the Prince and Princess sailed for St Petersburg, where they were
given the doubtful assurance by the Minister of the Interior that, provided
they did not go about in the new Tsar's company, they were unlikely to
suffer the same fate as his father.

Tsar Alexander III himself, who joined the Prince and Princess at the
gloomy and heavily guarded Anichkov Palace after the funeral, was virtually a prisoner there, taking exercise in a narrow courtyard, not daring to
go out for fear of the bombs of the nihilists. It was 'a great consolation' to
have the Prince and Princess there with him, he told Queen Victoria; and
he was obviously deeply moved when the Prince invested him with the
Order of the Garter, which he had sought permission to do before leaving
London. The British Ambassador, Lord Dufferin, thought that 'nothing
could have been in better taste, or more gracefully delivered' than the
Prince's brief speech on that occasion. Indeed, Dufferin, who had been held
responsible by Queen Victoria for any unpleasant incident and was naturally
greatly relieved when the visit was over, considered that, from a diplomatic
point of view, it had been a marked success. Apart from any other consider-

ation, the Prince had 'shown all Europe how ready he had been to do a kindness to a near relative, in spite of any personal risk to himself'.

On the death of Alexander III a few years later, the Prince again visited Russia and once more served his country well by his conduct there. The Prime Minister, Lord Rosebery, had urged him to attend the funeral and to take advantage of the opportunity to endear himself to his nephew, the new Tsar, Nicholas II, who was then twenty-six. But the Prince needed no persuasion. He had left London with Princess Alexandra immediately on hearing of Alexander III's illness, and was in Vienna when he heard of his death. He told Prince George to join him in St Petersburg not only out of respect for 'poor dear Uncle Sasha's memory', but also because 'the opportunity to see the great capital of Russia' was 'not one to be missed'. 'Poor Mama is terribly upset,' he added. 'This is indeed the most trying and sad journey I have ever undertaken.'

Once in St Petersburg the Prince uncomplainingly performed all the duties that were expected of him with the utmost conscientiousness. He attended the daily and appallingly tedious services in the fortress church of St Peter and St Paul; he displayed no sign of fatigue or restlessness during the final four-hour-long funeral service, nor any distaste when he was required to kiss the lips of the evil-smelling corpse, which had not been embalmed until three days after death. He made himself agreeable to everyone, winning 'golden opinions', Princess Alexandra's woman-of-the-bedchamber, Charlotte Knollys, said, 'by all the kind feeling he [had] shown', even to the King of Serbia—whom all the Russian high nobility ignored because he was so uncouth—and particularly to the young Tsar, whom he described as 'shy and timid' and, despite his autocratic views, 'weak as water'. All the same, he had grown quite fond of him and, in return, the Tsar was now prepared to inscribe himself to his 'dearest Uncle Bertie' as 'ever your most loving nephew, Nicky'.

Lord Rosebery warmly congratulated him on his arrival home, assuring him that he had never stood so high in national esteem, that he had made the most of his opportunity, justified the highest anticipations and rendered a 'signal service' to his country 'as well as to Russia and the peace of the world'.

Thereafter, although he disapproved of the Tsar's autocratic outlook and was frequently suspicious of Russia's 'promises and protestations', he strove as King towards *détente* with Russia, stressing in his correspondence with the Tsar his desire to come to a 'satisfactory settlement . . . similar to the one . . . concluded with France'. Hearing, in Scotland in 1906, that Baron Isvolsky, the Russian Foreign Minister, was in Paris, the King returned to London at once in the hope that a meeting might be arranged. Responding to the King's overture, Isvolsky came to London for discussions which, as Hardinge said, 'were entirely due to King Edward's initiative [and]

helped materially to smooth the path of the negotiations then in progress
for an agreement with Russia'. This, Hardinge added, 'was just one of those
many instances when King Edward's "flair" for what was right was so good
and beneficial to our foreign relations'.

The King's diplomatic skills were again appreciated in 1908 when he
met the Tsar at Tallinn, then known as Revel, a meeting arranged—after
the signing of the convention with Russia—in the hope that better relations
might be established between the King and the Tsar, who, uneasy about
England's ties with Japan, had not long before condemned the King as 'the
greatest mischief-maker and the most deceitful and dangerous intriguer in
the world'. Hardinge was worried on this occasion by the King's intention
both to raise the delicate question of the persecution of Russian Jews, about
which he had received a memorandum from Lord Rothschild, and to mention Sir Ernest Cassel's interest in the flotation of a Russian loan. To raise
the question of the Jews was considered not to be 'constitutionally right or
proper', while to become involved at the same time in a business transaction
on behalf of a Jewish financier was held 'to be unwise to say the least'. His
concern for the welfare of the Jews, however, and his desire to oblige an old
friend overrode considerations of prudence. So both the pogroms and the
loan were mentioned. But although the King clearly questioned Sir Arthur
Nicolson, British Ambassador in St Petersburg, on all sorts of subjects which
he thought might crop up in discussions with the Tsar, little else of political
importance was discussed. And neither were the pogroms halted, nor did the
loan materialize. Yet, as Nicolson acknowledged, the meeting was a notable
success. The Russian Prime Minister, Stolypin, was greatly impressed by the
King's unexpected knowledge of Russian affairs which, thanks to Nicolson,
he had been able to parade. '*Ah*,' Stolypin commented, '*on voit bien que
c'est un homme d'état!*' At the same time, the Tsar 'repeatedly expressed his
great satisfaction at the visit of the King and Queen'. It had, he said, 'sealed
and confirmed the intention and spirit of the Anglo–Russian agreement,' so
Hardinge reported to Edward Grey; and the Tsar was convinced 'that the
friendly sentiments which now prevailed between the two governments
could only mature and grow stronger . . . A glance at the Russian press of
all shades and opinions shows conclusively how extremely popular throughout Russia the King's visit had become, and how it was welcomed as the
visible sign of a new era in Anglo–Russian relations.'

The King was criticized for declining to take a Cabinet minister with
him on the grounds that to have done so 'would have made him feel like a
prisoner handcuffed to a warder while conversing with his relatives through
a grille'. And he was also censured for having made the Tsar an Admiral of
the Fleet without consulting Reginald McKenna, the First Lord of the Admiralty. He accepted the criticism in good part. As Knollys explained to the
Prime Minister, Asquith:

He had never thought of proposing that the Emperor of Russia should be appointed an Admiral of the Fleet until the idea suddenly struck him at Revel. [He explained] that he was totally unaware of the constitutional point or else he certainly would not have said anything to the Emperor without first consulting you and Mr McKenna and that he regretted he had, without knowing it, acted irregularly . . . He was always anxious to keep on the best of terms with his ministers . . . Nothing could have been 'nicer' or more friendly than he was.

The King's errors, in fact, such as they were, were minor in comparison with the *rapport* established at Tallinn with the Tsar, who openly admitted to having got on much better with the King than he had done the year before with the Kaiser at Björkö. But reading reports of the King of England's friendly conversations with the Tsar, the Germans, alarmed by the possible consequences of the meeting, spoke again of 'encirclement' and 'English machinations'.

18
The King and the Kaiser

Thank God, he's gone.

The King's relations with Germany had never been easy. Persistent trouble in the past had been caused by his frequent displays of sympathy for the family of the last King of Hanover, whose son, the Duke of Cumberland, had married Queen Alexandra's youngest sister, Thyra. Hanover had found itself on the losing side in the Austro–Prussian War of 1866, and had subsequently been incorporated in the German Empire. The King, as Prince of Wales, had constantly supported the Hanoverians in their attempts to regain their confiscated fortune and territories. Nor had he hesitated to raise the awkward question of their restitution whenever opportunity offered or, when the old King of Hanover died in exile in Paris, to walk at the head of a long procession of mourners at the funeral. This occasion, attended by numerous of the Prince's Royalist and Bonapartist friends, had assumed the nature of an anti-Prussian demonstration.

There had also been trouble over the Prince of Wales's known sympathy for France during the Franco–Prussian War. He had been reported as having actually expressed his hopes of a Prussian defeat at a dinner at the French Embassy soon after the War began; and although Francis Knollys had assured Count von Bernstorff, the Prussian Ambassador in London, that the close family connection which the Prince 'enjoyed with Prussia' made it impossible for him 'to entertain the opinion which he was alleged to have expressed', Bernstorff had not been convinced. Nor had Prince Bismarck, the Imperial Chancellor, who had gone so far as to complain in public that their country had an enemy in the heir to the British throne.

The Prince of Wales had given further offence to Bismarck a few years later when the Prince's nineteen-year-old niece, Princess Victoria, daughter of the Crown Princess of Prussia, had fallen in love with Prince Alexander of Battenberg, who had been chosen to rule Bulgaria, after its liberation from the Turks, as a Russian nominee. He was a most charming young man, handsome and gifted; but there had not only been strong political objections to the marriage, there had also been the dynastic objection that Prince Alexander was the child of a morganatic marriage between Prince Alexander of Hesse and a Polish countess. Princess Victoria's mother, however, had dismissed these obstacles as of little importance. And so had her brother, the Prince of Wales. He had considered that Prince Alexander was just the husband for his young niece; and, after long and pleasant conversations with him at Darmstadt, where they had both attended the wedding of Prince Alexander's brother, Prince Louis of Battenberg, the Prince of Wales had taken Prince Alexander on to Berlin where the Crown Prince had been persuaded by his wife and brother-in-law that Prince Alexander was, indeed, a worthy suitor.

The Crown Prince's father, the old Kaiser Wilhelm I, had certainly not been persuaded, though. Nor had the Crown Prince's son, Prince Wilhelm, then aged twenty-five, and strongly opposed to his parents' liberal outlook. Nor had Prince Bismarck, who had spoken to the Prince of Wales about the insignificance of romantic love in comparison with a country's destiny. Disregarding both Bismarck's rebuke and the Kaiser's ban on any further discussions about the possibility of such an unsuitable match, the Prince of Wales and his sister had arranged for a secret meeting between the two young lovers, who had been encouraged to believe that, although the marriage could not take place while the Kaiser was still alive, the situation would be transformed once the old man was dead.

Queen Victoria had been entirely on Prince Alexander's side. At the Darmstadt wedding of her granddaughter, Princess Victoria of Hesse, to Prince Louis of Battenberg, she had fallen under Prince Alexander's spell herself. She had found him not only 'very fascinating' and 'a person in whose judgment' she 'would have great confidence', but even to be compared with Prince Albert. 'I think he may stand next to beloved Papa,' she had written at that time. 'I think him (as in beloved Papa's case) so wonderfully handsome.' So annoyed had she been, indeed, that the marriage between this paragon and her granddaughter, Princess Victoria, had been forbidden in Berlin that when Prince Wilhelm had proposed to visit England, she had let it be known that he would not be welcome at Windsor. Delighted to have an excuse not to have the tiresome young man at Sandringham either, the Prince of Wales had explained to him that he could hardly go to England to stay with his uncle if he could not call on his grandmother: so the visit had better be cancelled. Prince Wilhelm had, therefore, remained in Germany where he had gone about making insulting remarks about his uncle and referring to his grandmother as an 'old hag'. He had come to England with his father for Queen Victoria's Jubilee two years later; but his uncle, that 'old peacock', had virtually ignored him.

Within a year of the Jubilee, however, it was impossible to ignore the egregious young man any longer. For in March 1888 his grandfather had died at last; less than four months later his father, Frederick III, had also died; and on 15 June 1888, at the age of twenty-nine, he had become Kaiser himself.

Impulsive and theatrical, Kaiser Wilhelm II was capable of exercising great charm. He was undoubtedly clever and could be lively and amusing in conversation, although the encouraging laughter of his entourage would often drive him on to excessive hilarity and to that kind of boisterous, bullying banter into which so many of Queen Victoria's descendants all too easily lapsed. John Morley wrote after meeting him at luncheon:

> He is rather short, pale, but sunburnt; carries himself well; walks into the room with the stiff pride of the Prussian soldier; speaks with a good deal of intense and energetic pleasure, not like a Frenchman, but staccato; his voice strong but pleasant; his eye bright, clear and full; mouth resolute, the cast of face grave or almost stern in repose, but as he sat between two pretty women he lighted up with gaiety and a genial laugh. Energy, rapidity, restlessness in every movement from his short, quick inclinations of the head to the planting of the foot.

A compulsive exhibitionist, he was insatiably fond of talking, determined in his efforts to bring all those in his company to agree with what he said, and ever on the watch for an opportunity to demonstrate the breadth of his knowledge or the retentiveness of his memory. Frederick Ponsonby recalled one embarrassing occasion when the Kaiser asked him across the dinner table how many members there were of the London County Council and how many years elapsed between elections. Ponsonby, not very certain of his facts, answered as best he could. 'I don't think you're right,' the Kaiser commented and thereupon gave the exact figures. Presumably he had committted them to memory, as he learned by heart the statistics of all the most modern ships in the Royal Navy so as to impress any British Admiral with whom he might find himself in conversation, but his easy and irritating display of detailed information was nevertheless 'effective', as Ponsonby said, 'and everyone present marvelled at his knowledge'.

Disliking the Kaiser, to whom he referred as 'William the Great', and dismayed that so sudden an end had been put to his hopes of regulating Anglo–German relations in partnership—as senior partner—with his good-natured, amenable brother-in-law, the Prince of Wales had taken little trouble to disguise his dislike or to guard his tongue when speaking of his nephew. He compared him unfavourably with his father, Frederick III, and maintained that his 'illustrious nephew' needed to learn that he was 'living at the end of the nineteenth century and not in the Middle Ages'. The Prince also disliked the Kaiser's Foreign Minister, Count Herbert Bismarck, son of the Chancellor, who, in turn, made no secret of the fact that he 'hated the Prince of Wales'. When Bismarck quarrelled with Sir Robert Morier, British Ambassador in St Petersburg who had been a friend of the Empress Frederick when serving in the British Legation at Darmstadt in the Franco–Prussian War, the Prince intervened in the quarrel so vigorously that the Prime Minister, Lord Salisbury, was forced to conclude that the Prince had been impulsive and indiscreet and that he persistently offended the Kaiser—as he put it on another occasion—by treating him 'as an uncle treats a nephew, instead of recognizing that he was an emperor'. Soon afterwards the Kaiser was reported—later, he said, falsely reported—to have made it plain that, on a forthcoming state visit to Vienna, the continued presence of his uncle at the Grand Hotel, where the Prince was then staying on holiday, would not be acceptable to him. And the British Ambassador in Vienna, Sir Augustus Paget, was therefore given the unpleasant duty of informing the Prince that the Austrian Emperor would be grateful if he left the city before the Kaiser arrived. Paget subsequently reported to the Prince:

I am perfectly certain, from what has been told me, that all the present trouble comes from stories having been repeated to [the Kaiser] of what Your Royal Highness has said. Some of those stories have been repeated to me. I need not say that I do not believe them, but it is necessary to avoid saying anything *whatsoever* which may be made use of as a foundation for the gossip of the malevolent or idle . . . [I must emphasize] the *all importance* of Your Royal Highness being *more than guarded* in anything you say about the Emperor William.

The Queen had had a good deal of sympathy for her son in this squabble with the Kaiser and in his insistence that he ought to receive from him a written apology for having said that he did not wish to meet the Prince of Wales in Vienna. She had told Lord Salisbury that it was 'really too *vulgar* and too absurd to suggest that the one treated the other as a nephew rather than as an emperor'. It showed 'a very unhealthy and unnatural state of mind'; and the Kaiser 'must be made to feel that his grandmother and uncle [would] not stand such insolence'. The Queen would 'not swallow this affront', and the 'Prince of Wales must *not* submit to such treatment' by 'such a hot-headed, conceited, and wrong-headed young man' who was 'devoid of all feeling'. Yet she was forced to agree that the political relations of the German and British governments ought 'not to be affected (if possible) by these miserable and personal quarrels'; and she sent her son-in-law, Prince Christian, to Berlin to see what he could do to bring about a family reconciliation.

On his arrival in Berlin, Prince Christian was assured by the Kaiser that he had never said he did not want to meet his uncle in Vienna; but since, as he continued to insist, this was 'not a simple affair between uncle and nephew, but between Emperor and Prince of Wales', he was not prepared to send a written explanation. Nor did he do so, merely writing in reply to a letter from the Queen—which the Prince deemed 'rather too mild'—that the whole Vienna affair was 'absolutely invented, there not being an atom of a cause to be found'. The whole thing was 'a fixed idea which originated either in Uncle Bertie's imagination, or in somebody else's.' And with this, the Prince had to be content. 'What a triumph for the Bismarcks, as well as for Willy,' the Prince commented gloomily to his sister. 'Lord Salisbury was consulted by [the Queen], and he gave her the worst possible advice, making us virtually to "eat humble pie"!'

Yet despite this quarrel, when the Kaiser came to England in the summer of 1889, he showed himself so determined to be pleasant that Knollys was able to assure the Prime Minister that he and the Prince of Wales had succeeded in getting along perfectly well together. The Kaiser had obviously been delighted to be made an honorary Admiral of the Fleet and to be proposed for membership of the Royal Yacht Squadron; while the Prince—though his temper was rather frayed by an attack of phlebitis and he still thought that 'Willy [was] a bully'—had decided that his nephew was certainly a good deal less combative than he had been formerly. On the day of the Kaiser's departure, Joseph Chamberlain declared in a speech at Leicester that 'no far-seeing English statesman could be content with England's permanent isolation on the continent of Europe', and that the 'natural alliance' was between England and 'the great German Empire'. The Prince of Wales would not have put it as strongly as that, but he was now more inclined to assent to an Anglo–German understanding. Accordingly, the Prince's return visit to Berlin the next year was as successful as the Kaiser's visit to England. The Prince—who had shown no resentment that his nephew was now an Emperor while he was still a powerless heir—told Queen Victoria that he had been treated 'quite like a sovereign' in Germany and that his only regret was that his expenses had 'in consequence been heavy'.

It was almost the last time that the Prince wrote well of his nephew, about whom nothing annoyed him more than his determination to shine at Cowes as a brilliant yachtsman and as master of an increasingly powerful navy. Until the Kaiser decided to become what the Prince, in the hearing of Baron von Eckardstein, called 'the boss of Cowes', it was the Prince himself who was the star of the annual regatta. He was Commodore of the Royal Yacht Squadron as well as of the Royal Thames Yacht Club; he was President of the Yacht Racing Association; and he was extremely proud that his own racing cutter, *Britannia*, with himself aboard, had won many an important race and was, indeed, in his own estimation, 'the first racing yacht afloat'. But the Kaiser had spoiled all that. In 1893 he had appeared at Cowes with a new yacht of his own, *Meteor I*, with which he had the satisfaction of beating the King in the race for the Queen's Cup. And thereafter he had bombastically set about using Cowes as a showplace for the latest warships of the German navy.

In 1895 he arrived in the imperial yacht, *Hohenzollern*, escorted by Germany's two newest warships, *Wörth* and *Weissenburg*, both named after German victories during the Franco–Prussian War. And on 6 August, the twenty-fifth anniversary of the victory at Wörth, he chose to address his sailors in a vainglorious speech which the Prince of Wales denounced as an affront to his hosts and which provoked journalistic warfare between the English and German press.

Having already antagonized the regatta committee by ostentatiously withdrawing *Meteor I* from the race for the Queen's Cup on the grounds that the handicapping was unfair to him, the Kaiser exasperated his uncle two days later at a dinner party aboard the *Osborne*. A quarrel had broken out between France and England over a border dispute in the Far East, and there was even talk of war. The Kaiser was in an exceptionally boisterous mood that evening; and, heedless of his uncle's excessive sensitivity about never having been on active service, slapped him on the back—on the front, one eye-witness told Baron von Eckardstein—and cried out, 'So, then, you'll soon be off to India to show what you're good for as a soldier.'

Before leaving Cowes that year the Kaiser approached George Lennox Watson, the designer of the three-hundred-ton *Britannia*, and ordered a yacht which would be even bigger than that and even faster than *Meteor I*. The Prince could not cope with this. He sold *Britannia*, in which he had taken such pride, to John Lawson-Johnston, who had made a fortune out of Bovril; and, although he bought the yacht back when he became King and attended Cowes with unfailing regularity, he never took part in a race there again. 'The regatta at Cowes was once a pleasant holiday for me,' he complained. 'But now that the Kaiser has taken command it is nothing but a nuisance . . . [with] that perpetual firing of salutes, cheering and other tiresome disturbances.'

Having won the Queen's Cup with his unrivalled *Meteor II* in 1899, the Kaiser added insult to injury not only by repeating his complaint about the 'perfectly appalling' system of handicapping but also by insisting on bringing to England with him, as his naval aide-de-camp, Admiral Baron von Senden und Bibran. This overbearing *Junker* had irritated the Prince by his haughty manner on previous visits to England and, piqued by the Prince's dismissive attitude towards him, had spread reports in Berlin about the Prince's anti-German sentiments. As soon as the Prince saw Senden's name on the Kaiser's list, he sent for Baron von Eckardstein to tell him that 'after what had happened, the Kaiser could not possibly be accompanied on his visit to England by this person' for whom he had 'a quite peculiar aversion'.

He absolutely declined to receive such a cad as the Admiral had shown himself to be. Eckardstein did his best on the Prince's behalf, but the Kaiser was adamant, flatly declaring that if he went to England at all he would take with him anyone he liked. It seemed, in fact, that the visit would have to be cancelled until the German-born Duchess of Devonshire, 'one of the cleverest and most capable women' that Eckardstein had ever met, persuaded the Prince to accept Senden if he apologized for his past conduct and if it was clearly understood that he would be invited to Windsor only to attend the official dinner in honour of the Kaiser and, in no circumstances at all, to Sandringham.

In spite of this ominous beginning, the Kaiser's visit to England in 1899 was a notable success. It was recognized that his coming at such a time, accompanied by his Foreign Secretary, was proof to the world that, if there were a European coalition in favour of the Boers, Germany would not be party to it. And the Kaiser received much credit in England for this gesture which was made in defiance of public opinion in Germany. The Prince, who supervised the arrangements with his habitual attention to detail in such matters, went out of his way to be agreeable to his guest; while the Princess of Wales, who cordially disliked him and considered that he got 'more foolish and conceited every day', succeeded in disguising her distaste for his company at Sandringham, though in private she ridiculed the 'fool's' having thought it necessary to arrive there with three valets and two hairdressers, one of whom was responsible for the upward-sweeping wings of the imperial moustache. 'The German visit is going off very well,' Francis Knollys reported to his friend, Lord Rosebery. 'The German Emperor is much pleased with . . . England, and he evidently wishes to be very civil to everybody.'

The Kaiser also created a good impression in England by his behaviour when Queen Victoria died. And after her death, in defiance of the wishes of his ministers, he declared that he would stay on in England as a private member of her family until the funeral. The Prince, who had, in fact, been rather put out by the Kaiser's officious attempt to lift his grandmother's body into her coffin, told the Empress Frederick that he had been kindness itself

and touching in his devotion without a shade of brusquerie or selfishness . . . [His] touching and simple demeanour, up to the last, will never be forgotten by me or anyone. It was indeed a sincere pleasure for me to confer upon him the rank of field-marshal in my army, and to invest Willy [the German Crown Prince, aged nineteen] (who is a charming young man) with the Order of the Garter.

Delighted by the compliments that had been paid to him in England, the Kaiser returned to Germany an evidently dedicated Anglophile. 'We ought to form an Anglo–German alliance,' he had declared on the last day of his visit at a luncheon at Marlborough House. 'You would watch over the seas while we would safeguard the land. With such an alliance not a mouse would stir in Europe.' His recently appointed Chancellor, Count von Bülow, wrote:

> I found him completely under the spell of his English impressions. As a rule he could not change his military uniform often enough, but now he wore civilian clothes as he had done in England. He wore a tie-pin with his deceased grandmother's initials on it. The officers who were summoned . . . to dine with him . . . did not seem very pleased by his constant enthusiastic allusions to England and everything English.

It seemed for a time that some sort of agreement might be reached with Germany; and, although the King was sceptical, he agreed to do what he could to help. But he was not enthusiastic, and became even less so as the months went by.

The King and the Kaiser met again in Germany in February 1901 when the King went out to see his sister who was dying of cancer at Friedrichshof. Having expressed the hope that it would be regarded as a purely family visit, the King was disconcerted, on stepping down from the train at Frankfurt, to find his nephew in full-dress uniform waiting to greet him with a military escort.

Six months later, the King had to return to Germany for his sister's funeral. Expecting that he would have to talk to the Kaiser about the possibility of an Anglo–German alliance which their respective governments had been considering, the King asked Lord Lansdowne to give him a set of notes which he could use as a basis for private discussions. But when the time came, the King was so deeply upset by the loss of his sister; so annoyed by the Kaiser's recent reference to British ministers as 'unmitigated noodles'; so exasperated by the Kaiser's long letters of gratuitous advice about the conduct of the Boer War; and, in any case, so sceptical about the prospect of an Anglo–German alliance, that he impatiently and imprudently handed Lansdowne's notes to the Kaiser without attempting to discuss any of the points mentioned in them.

Having thus avoided any unpleasant conversation at Homburg, the King went on to Wilhelmshöhe near Cassel, where he was irritated to find 15,000 troops to welcome him to further official talks with the Kaiser which had been arranged to take place in the castle. These conversations got off to a bad start. The Kaiser, in his knowing way, said that he was interested to hear that the British government were thinking of granting independence to Malta, a proposal of which the Colonial Office had not troubled to inform the King, who was naturally at first embarrassed by his ignorance and then furious with the government for having failed to consult or enlighten him. Nothing of importance was thereafter discussed at Wilhelmshöhe, from which the King was thankful to escape to Homburg. He seemed even more relieved when, soon after his return home to England, he was told that the government had decided to break off the negotiations for an alliance with Germany.

The next year, 1902, the Kaiser was again in England; and this time the visit was an utter failure. At Sandringham, to which the Kaiser was asked by his uncle to travel in plain clothes since it was 'not customary to wear uniform in the country in England', the most strenuous efforts were made to entertain the Kaiser and his suite. Musicians were brought up from London for him; Horace Goldin displayed his remarkable gifts as a conjurer; Albert Chevalier came to sing his funny songs; Sir Henry Irving arrived with a company of actors to perform Sir Arthur Conan Doyle's *A Story of Waterloo;* Arthur Bourchier and Violet Vanbrugh were in excellent form in a short piece entitled *Dr. Johnson.* There were shooting parties and there were large dinner parties to which distinguished soldiers and various members of the Cabinet were invited so that the Kaiser could talk to them.

But nothing seemed to please him very much. Whenever he attempted to talk to the King's ministers about Anglo–German relations they were exasperatingly non-committal, while the King himself steadfastly declined to be drawn on the subject at all. If the Kaiser did not find the British congenial, they certainly did not find him so. They did not like the clothes he wore for shooting, which looked like a kind of uniform, though they had to admit that he shot well with the light gun he had to use because of his withered arm. They were appalled when some military members of his suite drew revolvers to shoot at the hares. And they were constantly irritated by his officious display of knowledgeability on every conceivable subject.

'What petrol do you use?' he asked on being shown the King's new car. The King did not know. Potato spirit was the best, the polymath informed him. Had he ever tried that? The King had never even heard of it. The conversation ended there. But a few days later the King was astonished to discover an extraordinary assortment of glass bottles, retorts and jars on his table together with various mineral and vegetable substances: the Kaiser had sent to Germany for them so that he could demonstrate to his uncle the method of manufacture of his favoured motor fuel. No one was surprised when, as the Kaiser boarded the *Hohenzollern,* the King was heard to murmur, 'Thank God, he's gone!'

Thereafter relations between the King and the Kaiser rapidly deteriorated, reaching their nadir in 1905 when, in an attempt to break the *entente cordiale,* the Kaiser, having spoken at Bremen of a 'world-wide dominion of the Hohenzollerns', made a bombastic speech at Tangier, asserting

Germany's 'great and growing interests in Morocco'. Castigating the Kaiser's speech, which had been made at the instigation of von Bülow, as 'the most mischievous and uncalled-for event which the German Emperor has ever been engaged in since he came to the throne', the King, who was himself cruising in the Mediterranean at the time, landed at Algiers where he took the remarkable step of asking the French Governor-General to send, on his personal behalf, a telegram of encouragement to Théophile Delcassé, who was reported to have resigned when pressed to show a more conciliatory attitude towards Germany. Delcassé had already been persuaded not to resign by Loubet when the King's message arrived; but as his country and Germany drifted close to war he was forced out of office, and French resistance to German demands for a conference on the future of Morocco collapsed.

The Germans badly mishandled the Morocco Conference, which not only left France the dominant power in the area, but also the prestige of the British, who had stood loyally by their partner, greatly enhanced. And the Kaiser, convinced that his uncle was plotting the destruction of Germany, was consequently more resentful of him than ever. 'He is a Devil,' he announced to three hundred guests at a banquet in Berlin. 'You can hardly believe what a Devil he is.' The King was no less uncomplimentary about the Kaiser. 'The King talks and writes about [him] in terms that make one's flesh creep,' Lord Landsdowne wrote, 'and the official papers which go to him, whenever they refer to His Imperial Majesty, come back with all sorts of annotations of a most incendiary character.' Nor did the King confine himself to comments about the Kaiser: von Bülow was 'badly informed'; the opinions of Baron von Holstein, head of the political section of the German Foreign Office, were as 'absurd' as they were 'false'; in negotiating with Russia, Germany was 'certain' to act behind England's back. In fact, the King was 'inclined to agree' with Francis Knollys that 'all public men in Germany from the Emperor downwards [were] liars'.

The King's displeasure with the Kaiser could be attributed to more than politics, the German Ambassador in London, Count Metternich, told von Bülow. 'It is said that the Kaiser talked freely in yachting circles about the loose morals of English Society, and in particular about King Edward's relationship with Mrs Keppel. King Edward is very touchy on this subject and this seems to have annoyed him especially.'

Nevertheless, in an effort to allay German suspicions about the *entente cordiale* and the Anglo–Russian *détente*, both of which the Wilhelmstrasse was endeavouring to break, the King wrote to the Kaiser on his forty-seventh birthday in 1906 to assure him that England 'never had any aggressive feelings towards Germany' and—less convincingly—that, since the sovereigns of the two countries were 'such old friends and near relations', the King felt sure that 'the affectionate feelings' which had 'always existed' would continue. The Kaiser replied in the same vein, reminding the King of the silent hours when they had both watched beside the deathbed of 'that great sovereign lady', Queen Victoria, 'as she drew her last breath' in her grandson's arms; and affirming that the King's letter, which 'breathed such an atmosphere of kindness and warm sympathy', constituted 'the most cherished gift' among his birthday presents.

When King and Kaiser met again the next year at Wilhelmshöhe both made an attempt to live up to these protestations of affection, the King—as Charles Hardinge told the Foreign Secretary, Edward Grey—'studiously avoiding all reference to political questions in which Great Britain and Germany [were] interested'. Afterwards the King wrote to tell Prince George how pleased with the Kaiser he had been. But 'although the King was outwardly on the best of terms with the German Emperor, and laughed and joked with him', Hardinge 'could not help noticing that there was no [such] real intimacy between them' as there was between the King and the old Emperor of Austria, whom the King described to Sir Lionel Cust as 'a dear old man'. As Frederick Ponsonby observed, 'there was always a feeling of thunder in the air whenever the King and the [Kaiser] were together . . . There were always forced jokes and the whole atmosphere seemed charged with electricity . . . Both were such big personalities that they each tended to dominate the conversation.' Ponsonby was thankful 'when the talk kept'— as the King always endeavoured to keep it—'on family topics and things that did not matter'.

The atmosphere during the return visit, which the Kaiser made to England the following year, was no less uneasy. At the last moment, either because he was offended by the reluctance of the English to accept an escort of German battleships at Portsmouth or because he feared that he might be embarrassed by remarks about the impending trial of his friend, Count Philipp Eulenburg, who was accused of homosexual offences, the Kaiser sent a telegram to say that 'bronchitis' and an 'acute cough' prevented him from coming. Persuaded to change his mind, the Kaiser arrived as planned on 11 November 1907, looking, as the King archly observed when proposing a toast to his guests at a banquet the next evening at Windsor, 'in splendid health'.

As usual, the King tried to avoid all political discussion with his nephew; but the Kaiser found audiences elsewhere and profoundly affronted many of them.

There were reports of savagely anti-Semitic tirades. There were even more alarming accounts of long monologues at the Hampshire house which had been rented for him, Highcliffe Castle, where he propounded the eccentric view that it was by adopting his strategic plan that the British army had saved itself from ultimate disgrace in the Boer War. The Kaiser also maintained that, out of family loyalty, he had vetoed proposals at the beginning of the war for an anti-British coalition; that he had stood almost alone in holding back the anti-British feelings in Germany; that he was England's best friend; and that the English were 'mad as March hares' not to recognize it. When the gist of these remarks appeared in the *Daily Telegraph* of 28 October 1908, the King expressed the opinion that 'of all the political gaffes' which the Kaiser had made this was 'the greatest'. Yet there was a worse one to come. A fortnight later the *New York World* provided a censored synopsis of an interview with the Kaiser which the *New York Times* had decided was 'so strong' that it could not be printed. And although he later repudiated the remarks attributed to him by the interviewer, W.B. Hale, the Kaiser was now on record as having said that war between England and Germany was inevitable, that the sooner it came, the better, that Great Britain was degenerate and her King corrupt. The King wrote in a profoundly aggrieved tone to Francis Knollys:

> I know the E[mperor] *hates* me, and never loses an opportunity of saying so (behind my back) whilst I have always been civil and nice to him . . . I have, I presume, nothing more to do than to accept [his emphatic denial]. I am, however, convinced in my mind that the words attributed to the G[erman] E[mperor] by Hale are perfectly correct . . . As regards my visit to Berlin, there is no hurry to settle anything at present. The Foreign Office, to gain their own object, will not care a pin what humiliation I have to put up with . . .

Had he been able to please himself, the King, who knew very well that the Kaiser, in Eckardstein's words, treated him 'as a subject for schoolboy jokes', would never have spoken to him again. But approached once more to meet him in an endeavour to smooth the path towards a better understanding between their two countries—and to halt competition in building up naval armaments—the King agreed to see the Kaiser on his way to Marienbad in 1908 and, on this occasion, to talk about important political matters rather than trivial family affairs. They met accordingly at Friedrichshof Castle one morning in August. The King had in his pocket a memorandum about naval expenditure which had been prepared for him by the Foreign Secretary. And as the morning wore on and the two sovereigns remained alone together, it began to be hoped that the basis for agreement was being prepared. Two hours passed, then three; and it was not until the early afternoon that the door was opened and the King and Kaiser emerged. All sorts of matters had been discussed, the King confided to Hardinge before luncheon, 'with the exception of naval armaments'. He had 'touched on the question and mentioned the document in his pocket'; but the Kaiser had 'neither asked to see the paper nor to know its contents', and the King had 'therefore considered that it would be more tactful on his part not to force upon [him] a discussion which he seemed anxious to avoid'.

Thankful, as always, to have an excuse not to risk a scene with his nephew, who would certainly in the course of it have shown off his detailed knowledge of British and German naval construction, the King then left it to Hardinge to have further talks with the Kaiser during the afternoon and evening. In the course of these talks the Kaiser 'made several satirical allusions to England's policy and her new friends', Hardinge reported to Edward Grey, 'and endeavoured to show what a good friend he had been to England in the past.' He again alleged that he had declined to enter a coalition against England, proposed by the Russian and French governments, during the Boer War and that he had, on the contrary, 'threatened to make war on any Power that dared to make an unprovoked attack on England'. He referred once more to the plan of campaign which his general staff had drawn up for the guidance of the British army after its early reverses in that war, a plan which 'had been followed by Lord Roberts in all its details'. And he complained that, whereas he was constantly sending his statesmen to London, no English statesman, with the exception of Lord Rosebery 'many years ago and Mr Haldane quite recently', was ever sent to Berlin.

Towards the end of the interview an aide-de-camp came to the Emperor and announced that the King was ready to leave for the railway station [Hardinge's report concluded]. As I somewhat hurriedly rose and asked permission to go to fetch my coat and hat, the Emperor stopped me and said in a very emphatic manner: 'Remember . . . the future of the world is in the hands of the Anglo–Teuton race. England, without a powerful army, cannot stand alone in Europe, but must lean on a continental Power, and that Power should be Germany.' There was no time nor opportunity to continue what might have been an interesting discussion.

So the British diplomats left Cronenberg with the subject of German naval armaments still in unresolved dispute.

The following year, in Berlin, the King apparently did bring himself to broach the embarrassing subject with the Kaiser when they were alone together. But he did so just before his departure and in an extremely diffident way. 'We are in a different position from other countries,' he explained. 'Being an island, we must have a fleet larger than all the other ones. But we don't dream of attacking anybody.'

The Kaiser agreed that it was 'perfectly natural that England should have a navy according to its interests and be able to safeguard them'. It was just the same with Germany, which also had no aggressive intentions.

According to the Kaiser's account of this conversation, the King immediately agreed with him:

He: Oh quite so, quite so, I perfectly understand it is your absolute right; I don't for one moment believe you are designing anything against us.

I: This bill was published eleven years ago; it will be adhered to and exactly carried out, *without any restriction.*

He: Of course that is quite right, as it is a bill voted by the people and their parliament, I know that cannot be changed.

I: It is a mistake on the part of some Jingos in England that we are making a building race with you. That is nonsense. We only follow the bill.

He: Oh, I know that is quite an absurd notion, the situation is quite clear to me and I am in no way alarmed; that is all talk and will pass over.

This conversation took place in the 'last minute before the King's departure'; and it was with evident relief that he brought the unpleasant discussion to an end and boarded his train. It had not been an enjoyable visit from the beginning. Two days previously, the King, unaccompanied by the Kaiser, had attended a reception at the Rathaus where he had delighted the city's businessmen and dignitaries by making a charming speech to the burgomaster's little daughter, who had offered him a gold goblet of Rhenish wine, and had consequently been given a warmly gratifying reception. But otherwise this visit to Berlin in February 1909 was characterized by a succession of minor disasters.

The Kaiser had done his best to make it a success; and had gone so far as to have Danish books and pictures of Copenhagen placed in the Queen's suite, as well as a concert piano, and, in the King's suite, a portrait of Queen Victoria and a large print of 'British Naval Victories'. But all his efforts were unavailing. On the outward journey the driver of the royal train had applied the brakes so suddenly that a footman serving dinner had lost his balance and upset a dish of quails over the Queen, leaving one bird suspended in her hair. She had made light of the accident and had kept Frederick Ponsonby and the rest of the suite 'in roars of laughter describing how she would arrive in Berlin *coiffée de cailles'.* But she had been able to do nothing to lessen the tension when the train arrived at the frontier town of Rathenow before the King was dressed. The bandmaster had been told to strike up 'God Save the King' as the train drew to a halt and to continue playing until the King appeared on the platform. 'For ten solid minutes' the band kept up the British National Anthem until the King's suite, standing to attention in full uniform, 'all nearly screamed'. At last the King appeared, looking flustered and cross in the uniform of a German field marshal. In order to make up for lost time, he walked at an unusually brisk pace as he inspected the guard of honour and a regiment of hussars and became in consequence very much out of breath, succumbing to a fit of violent coughing on re-entering the train.

At the Lehrter Bahnhof in Berlin it was the Kaiser's suite who were out of breath as they came 'running down the platform in a most undignified way' to greet the King, who appeared unexpectedly at the door of the Queen's carriage which was a hundred yards further down the platform from his own. There were even more undignified scenes when the visitors left the station for the coaches waiting to transport them to the palace. Frightened by the booming cannon, the cheering crowds and waving flags, some of the horses jibbed and refused to move, while others threw their riders and galloped away loose. The Queen and the Empress were obliged to change carriages, which entailed everyone else behind them doing the same and the occupants of the last carriage having to walk.

Neither the state banquet held that evening nor the court ball on Wednesday was any more successful. At the banquet the King, coughing constantly, found great difficulty in getting through a short speech which, breaking with his usual practice, he read from a prepared text; while the Queen, an unwilling guest at the Kaiser's table, did not endear herself to her host, who was picking at his food, by saying to him, 'You ride, you work, you take a lot of trouble. Why don't you eat? Eating is good for the brain.' At the subsequent ball, so Ponsonby reported, there was 'a proper row' when two of the Kaiser's sons and various princesses asked the band to play a two-step in defiance of the orders of the Kaiser, who, in accordance with his insistence that court balls were not held for amusement but to provide lessons in deportment, refused to allow any modern tunes to be played.

Throughout the ball, the King, in the uncomfortable uniform of the Stolp Hussars, looked tired and ill. Hearing his fearful cough and looking at his lined, drawn face, more than one of his fellow-guests feared that he might not have long to live.

19

The Final Months

We shall have some very bad luck this year.

'The King of England is so stout that he completely loses his breath when he has to climb upstairs,' the Controller of the Kaiser's Household noted during this visit to Germany in 1909. 'The Emperor told us that at the first family dinner he fell asleep . . . He has an amiable, pleasant manner and looks very shrewd . . . but he eats . . . and smokes enormously.'

After luncheon at the British Embassy on 10 February, the day of his visit to the Rathaus, he had been smoking one of his huge cigars and talking to the Princess of Pless when he had suddenly been seized with one of those choking fits which made Lady Cust think he was going to 'break in two'. As he fought for breath his face turned that alarming puce colour which his bouts of violent, bronchitic coughing had so often lately induced; the cigar fell out of his hand; and he fainted. 'My God he is dying,' the Princess of Pless thought. 'Oh, why not in his own country!' She tried to unfasten the stiff collar of his tight Prussian uniform, and as she struggled with it Queen Alexandra and Charles Hardinge hurried to help her. His doctor, Sir James Reid, was sent for, and the room was cleared. When the other luncheon guests returned, both the King and the doctor assured them that it was an attack of no consequence, Sir James Reid treating the incident 'in a very casual manner', according to Hardinge, 'and stating that it was simply a form of bronchial attack and in no sense dangerous'. But those who knew the King well could not disguise their concern.

The night before this attack he had gone to sleep at the opera where, at the Kaiser's command, a spectacularly realistic performance of the last act of *Sardanapalus* had filled the stage with fire and smoke. The King had woken up with a start. Thinking the whole theatre was in flames, he had demanded to know where the firemen were; and, much to his nephew's amusement, had with difficulty been reassured by the Empress Augusta.

For months now he had been looking tired and worn. Some days he coughed almost incessantly; he often complained of a sore throat; and he suffered from increasingly severe attacks of bronchitis which left him weak, lethargic and depressed. Yet he could not be persuaded to stop smoking those cigars which, when not in his mouth, were gripped between fat fingers resting on an ample thigh, and seemed almost as essential a part of his physical presence as his hooded eyes and whitening beard. His doctors warned him of their effect on his lungs; but, while he listened grumpily to their advice when he was ill, he did not always take it and refused to obey their orders when he felt well again. 'I really never can please you!' he once protested to Sir Felix Semon, who had advised him not to climb up hills at such a speed when deer-stalking in Scotland. 'First you torment me with your eternal warnings that I ought to take exercise, and now, when I do it, you scold me because I am overdoing it.'

As a younger man neither his excessive smoking nor his gargantuan appetite seemed to have affected his health unduly. His energy and zest for life had always been legendary. Rarely had he seemed tired. Once, after a particularly demanding week, he had been noticed by Charles Dilke at a requiem Mass for the Tsar Alexander II falling asleep standing up, his taper gradually tipping over and guttering on the floor. But normally he could stand a succession of late nights without showing the least exhaustion or abandoning his life-long habit of early rising.

He had only once been seriously ill since contracting typhoid fever in 1871. A painful attack of phlebitis in 1889 had subsided without complications; a fall downstairs at Waddesdon Manor in 1898 had resulted in nothing worse than a fractured knee-cap and a few weeks spent impatiently in bed. He had never been much troubled by his teeth: his dentist, called to Sandringham, had pulled one out after luncheon one afternoon in 1909, but the King had come down to dinner as usual and, on being asked if he had had gas, had replied, 'Oh dear no! I can bear pain.'

In the summer of 1902 however, shortly before the day fixed for his coronation, his doctors had been gravely concerned by a sudden deterioration in his condition. A severe chill had been followed by loss of appetite, then by eating even more food than usual and, for the first time in his life, drinking rather too much. He had become excessively irritable and edgy; and despite the extra work and activity which had been imposed upon him on succeeding to the throne and by the imminence of his coronation, he had put on so much weight that his waist measurement was found to be no less than forty-eight inches. He began to fall asleep in the evenings and even during meals. A violent pain developed in his lower abdomen.

Sir Francis Laking diagnosed appendicitis; but, rather than risk the major operation that this then entailed, he advised the King to stay in bed on a milk diet. In any case, the King, unaware of the gravity of his illness, was determined that the coronation must in no circumstances be postponed. He declared that he would be in Westminster Abbey with the Queen on 26

June even if he were to drop dead during the service: the hotels were already full of guests; crown princes and grand dukes had arrived from all over the world. It was given out that his Majesty was suffering from lumbago.

Even after the development of peritonitis, the King would not give way, continuing to work as hard as ever, insisting on attending to the most trivial details, worrying and fretting about every difficulty, even consulting a gypsy woman who much alarmed him by telling him that he would never be crowned and that her own imminent death—which, indeed, took place within a week—would very soon be followed by his own. Sir Francis Laking and Sir Thomas Barlow both warned him that an operation was essential; otherwise he might well die. The surgeon, Sir Frederick Treves, was ready to operate, they told him, and a room had been prepared at Buckingham Palace. Disregarding their urgent warnings, the King continued to insist that he could not disappoint everyone at the last moment like this: the coronation *must* proceed as planned. 'Laking, I will stand no more of this,' he burst out finally. 'I am suffering the most awful mental agony that any man can endure. Leave the room at once.'

Laking signalled to Barlow to leave; but he himself remained, begging the King to understand that obedience to his commands was out of the question. An operation must be performed immediately. The coronation could not possibly take place. Laking would not leave the room until the King agreed to see Treves. So the King at last gave way. At noon the next day he walked in his ancient dressing-gown to the operating table where he was given an anaesthetic. Queen Alexandra helped to hold him down as he struggled and threw his arms about, growing black in the face. When he was unconscious Treves waited for the Queen to leave the room, not liking, as he subsequently admitted, to take off his coat, tuck up his sleeves 'and put on an apron while the Queen was present'. Finally she had to be asked to leave, and the operation for perityphlitis began.

It was completed forty minutes later. As the effects of the chloroform wore off, the King opened his eyes and asked, 'Where's George?'

The Prince of Wales saw his father the following morning when the doctors and nurses announced that they had never seen 'such a wonderful man'. He was sitting up in bed, smoking a cigar. And he greeted his son cheerfully and with great affection. The frequent visits of the Queen were not so agreeable to him, as he had to talk so loudly to make her hear. Eventually he took to pretending to be asleep when he heard her coming. He made a rapid recovery, though, for which he warmly thanked Laking and Treves, both of whom he created baronets. In July, on boarding the *Victoria and Albert* at Portsmouth, Prince George found him eager to embark on a convalescent cruise, 'lying on deck and looking so well and delighted with the change'.

The King had returned invigorated from that cruise. But now that he was in his late sixties, he was increasingly prone to listlessness and to periods of the utmost depression when his problems and worries seemed insupportable. He talked even of abdication. He began to dread old age and loneliness; his bronchial trouble was chronic; his voice more gruff than ever; his digestion no longer so reliable; his bouts of lassitude alternated with spells of agitated restlessness; while his sudden violent rages were more frequent and alarming and less quickly overcome. When, for example, his visit to Russia was criticized in the House of Commons, and James Keir Hardie, the leader of the Labour Party, said that the visit was tantamount to condoning Tsarist atrocities, the King was furious. He refused to allow Keir Hardie, and another socialist who had attacked the Russian visit, to be invited to attend a garden party given at Windsor Castle for all Members of Parliament. And although he let it be known that they would be invited to future garden parties, he refused to have on any list of guests the name of Frederick Ponsonby's brother, Arthur—Liberal Member for Stirling and one of fifty-nine Members who had voted against the government's authorization of the visit —on the grounds that a son of a man who had been secretary to Queen Victoria ought to have known better.

The political discussions which appeared to cloud the horizon on every side made the King deeply despondent about the future. He was worried by the prospect of war; by the fear that Germany was getting ahead of England in the race for naval armaments; by the policies of social reform to which the Liberal government were committed and which he felt endangered the whole basis of society; by the quarrel between the two Houses of Parliament and the insistent demands for reform of the House of Lords.

He was, and had always been, as Charles Dilke said, 'a strong Conservative, and a still stronger Jingo'. Criticisms of the imperialistic policies of his mother's governments had never failed to infuriate him. At the time of the Afghan War in 1878-9 he had fiercely resented the attacks of the Liberal opposition on the conduct of the campaign and he told Sir Bartle Frere, 'If I had my way I should not be content until we had taken the whole of Afghanistan, and kept it.' He was equally insistent that England 'must for ever keep a strong hold over Egypt'. And after the death of General Gordon and the fall of Khartoum he had urged the annihilation of the Mahdi and the conquest of the whole of the Sudan. His open support of Dr Jameson's raiders was followed by his declared support of Cecil Rhodes, whom he invited to dinner, chiding the Prime Minister for refusing to receive him; by his sustained rejection of any suggestion that the Boer War was dishonourable, and his contention that it would be 'terrible indeed' if South Africa were 'handed over to the Boers'. He associated criticism of the British army with treason, and, while accepting that conscription would have to come and generally supporting Haldane, he viewed many suggestions for reform with scepticism: the proposal that the traditional uniforms of the army should be replaced by 'the hideous khaki' had at first dismayed him.

His firm objection to admitting natives to a share in the government of India was matched by his opposition to allowing women to have a say in the government of England. Having 'no sympathy at all' with female suffrage, he condemned the conduct of those 'dreadful women', the 'so-called "suffragettes" ', as 'outrageous'. He sternly admonished Campbell-Bannerman for having spoken in their favour, and told Campbell-Bannerman's successor that he deplored 'the attitude taken up by Mr Asquith on the Woman's Suffrage question'. Although he had agreed with Charles Dilke that Octavia Hill should have been appointed to the Commission on the Housing of the Working Classes, he 'hung fire', so Knollys told Sandars, when it was proposed that the aged Florence Nightingale should be awarded the O.M., being 'reluctant to give it to women'. And he was very cross indeed when the Home Secretary put forward the names of two women to serve on the Royal Commission for Divorce—on which, despite the King's protests, they did serve— since divorce was a subject which could not be discussed 'openly and in all its aspects with any delicacy or even decency before ladies'. 'He is quite unconvinced by the arguments brought forward in support of their retention,' his assistant private secretary, Arthur Davidson, told Asquith. 'The King considers it the thin edge of suffragettism and feels sure that its supporters will get stronger and more persistent in their demands when they see the principle, on which they base their claims, as partially recognised.'

He disapproved quite as strongly of ladies shooting. And as for the young: 'refinement of feeling in the younger generation does not exist in the nineteenth century . . . the age of chivalry has passed.'

He had not been blindly opposed to all change. He had been persuaded, for instance, by Lord Rosebery of the justice of the Third Reform Bill of 1884 which proposed to increase the size of the electorate by extending household suffrage to the country constituencies. And when the Bill had been rejected by the House of Lords and a demonstration organized by its supporters, he had gone to watch the procession from the Whitehall house of Charles Carrington, one of its principal advocates. Carrington had arranged for the demonstrators to turn their eyes to the right and take off their caps when they reached the Horse Guards, for the Prince and Princess of Wales would be standing on the balcony of the middle window opposite. As the huge procession approached, the Prince had begun to think that he had made a bad mistake in allowing himself to become involved with it. After all, as he had suggested to Rosebery at luncheon, attacks on a hereditary House of Lords were bound to harm a hereditary monarchy; and he had not appeared to be altogether reassured by Rosebery's contention that the Crown was above controversy and did not presume to resist the people's will as the Lords resisted the will of the Commons. The Prince's apprehensions had been immeasurably increased when the procession appeared at the bottom of Whitehall with red flags waving and bands playing the *Marseillaise*. 'Hey, Charlie!' he had said to Carrington. 'This don't look much like being a pleasant afternoon.'

Carrington had been right. As the procession had reached his house, all but three of the bands had changed their tune to 'God Save the Queen'; loud cheers had greeted the appearance of the Prince and Princess on the balcony; caps had been waved; and voices had been raised in singing 'God Bless the Prince of Wales'. After standing in the hot sun for an hour and a half the Princess had felt faint and had gone indoors to lie down on a sofa; but the vociferous protests from the crowd had brought her back and, propped up by a pile of cushions, she and the Prince had continued to receive an ovation which, as Carrington had commented, 'did one's heart good . . . The reception was something tremendous . . . In fact the day was a regular triumph for the royal family.'

Although the Prince had brushed off Conservative protests at his having been made use of by irresponsible radicals, any suggestion that he had ambitions to become a citizen-king in the style of Louis-Philippe would have horrified him. He had made friends with some republicans, but he had hoped by so doing to take the sting out of republicanism. He had shown himself in Birmingham, but he had intended by appearing there to do something to counteract the influence of Joseph Chamberlain and had been deeply gratified to hear the mayor declare that in England the Throne was 'recognized and respected as the symbol of all constitutional authority and settled government'. He had always done his best to show his sympathy with social reform by identifying the monarchy with the conscience of his people. He had always shown a sincere concern for their welfare, particularly for their housing; and he had not hesitated to condemn the 'perfectly disgraceful' conditions in which so many of the poor were forced to live. But he had no time for Socialists, never attempted to understand their ideals, and looked upon them in his last years as a dangerous threat to all that he held most dear.

It seemed to him in the summer of 1909 that some of Asquith's ministers, notably Lloyd George, the Chancellor of the Exchequer, and Winston Churchill, President of the Board of Trade, were behaving in the most irresponsibly inflammatory manner. On 19 July Knollys told Asquith that it was really painful for the King 'to be continually obliged to complain of certain of [his] colleagues'. And when, later on that month, Lloyd George, in one of his attacks on the House of Lords, made a speech in which he complained that a fully equipped duke was as costly to maintain as two dreadnoughts and less easy to scrap, the King, so Knollys said, felt constrained 'to protest in the most vigorous terms against one of his ministers making such a speech . . . full of false statements, of socialism in its most insidious form and full of virulent abuses of one particular class'. The King could not understand how the Prime Minister could allow his colleagues to make speeches which 'would not have been tolerated by any Prime Minister until within the last few years', which his Majesty regarded as being 'in the highest degree improper', and which he looked upon 'as being an insult to the Sovereign'.

Asquith made excuses which the King condemned as 'pitiful'. He acknowledged that Lloyd George had been greatly provoked by some 'foolish and *mean* speeches' by his opponents and was somewhat placated by a letter of explanation from him, yet he viewed the intensifying political crisis with the deepest despondency, telling Asquith that he thought party politics had never been more bitter. Distressed by attempts to 'inflame the passions of the working and lower orders against people who happen to be owners of property', he was equally upset by the intransigence of the House of Lords. He brought all the influence he could to bear upon them not to reject Lloyd George's budget as they were threatening to do in defiance of a rule that had not been broken for two hundred years; and he confided to Knollys that he thought the 'Peers were mad'.

Taking advice on the propriety of the Lords' intended action, he was told by some of his counsellors that rejection would be unconstitutional and by others that a budget which provided for revolutionary land taxes, as well as new income taxes and death duties, was a social measure that required the sanction of the electorate. Dreading an election fought on such an issue, the King renewed his efforts to reach a compromise, going so far as to ask Asquith to offer the Lords a dissolution of Parliament and a general election in three months' time if only they could be persuaded to pass the budget, unpalatable as it was. But despite the King's appeals, on 30 November 1909, playing into Lloyd George's hands, the House of Lords rejected the 'People's Budget'; and faced with the knowledge that he would now be required to dissolve Parliament so that there could be a general election, he confessed at Sandringham on 2 December that he had never spent a more miserable day in his life.

On New Year's Eve the customary ceremonies of 'first footing' were observed. The house was cleared of guests and servants just before midnight as usual, so that the King and Queen could be the first to open the front door in the New Year. On this occasion, however, they were forestalled by one of their grandchildren who, unaware of the importance that the King attached to such traditions, ran into the house by the back and flung the door open triumphantly as his grandparents approached it. The King looked at the child gravely and observed, 'We shall have some very bad luck this year.'

While the King was at Sandringham discussions were held in London about the possibility of either allowing the Prime Minister to assume the Sovereign's prerogative of creating peers or of curbing the power of the

Lords by framing a Parliamentary Bill whose passage through the House would be guaranteed by the King's giving a pledge to create enough new peers favourable towards it. The King, for his part, believed that if he were to create several hundred Liberal peers in order to limit the power of the House of Lords, as the government wanted him to do, he would not only fatally debilitate the Upper House but also abandon the political impartiality of the Crown to the ultimate ruin of its reputation. And as he again spoke gloomily of abdication, Asquith opened the Liberal Party's election campaign with the pledge that he would not assume office unless he could secure the 'necessary safeguards' for ensuring 'the effective limitation of the legislative powers of the Lords' as well as the Commons' 'absolute control over finance'.

After Christmas the King went down to Brighton with Frederick Ponsonby and Seymour Fortescue to stay with Arthur Sassoon during the forthcoming General Election. People who saw him there were shocked to discover how tired and old and ill he looked. At dinner time he sat silent and morose, while Mrs Sassoon tirelessly kept up the conversation with Fortescue and Ponsonby. Appalled by such electioneering slogans as 'Peers against People' and by the condemnation of the House of Lords as wreckers of the Constitution, and as an obsolete assembly of rich backwoodsmen trying to avoid paying taxes, he grew increasingly melancholy, grievously worried that the Crown, by being dragged into controversy, would be diminished in prestige. One day he was driven to Worthing where he fell asleep in his car on the seafront while a huge crowd gathered round, staring through the windows in sympathetic silence.

At Eaton Hall, where he went to shoot with the Duke of Westminster after leaving Brighton, his gloom was temporarily dispelled. He thought he saw a way out of his difficulties, and he asked Knollys to tell Asquith that if the Liberals won the election he would not feel justified in creating the number of peers that would be necessary to get the party's policies through the House of Lords until the country had been consulted at a second general election. Asquith, who was asked to treat this stipulation as strictly confidential, chivalrously agreed to do so and to undertake the delicate task of managing his party accordingly.

Nothing was said about the King's intervention in favour of the House of Lords during the election campaign which resulted in the government's retention of just enough seats to remain in office. According to Lord Esher this result 'caused great relief' at Windsor where it was felt that Asquith's slender majority would make it easier for the King to resist unwelcome demands.

In fact, the Prime Minister was preparing the way for an announcement that, distasteful as it would be to his more reformist supporters, would take a great weight off the King's mind. He could not accept a proposal, put forward by the King on his own initiative to the Lord Privy Seal, that the right to vote should be limited to a hundred peers of whom half would be nominated by the leaders of each of the two main parties; for this might well lead to the nomination of hacks selected because of their loyalty rather than their worth. But, on 21 February, Asquith made an announcement in the House of Commons virtually repudiating the pledge which he had made to his party before the election. He had neither requested nor received any guarantee about the creation of peers, he said. And he added that it was 'the duty of responsible politicians to keep the name of the Sovereign and the prerogatives of the Crown outside the domain of party politics'.

Gratified by these remarks, the King left for Biarritz by way of Paris for the holiday which his doctors had been vainly pressing him to take earlier than usual but upon which he had been reluctant to embark until assured that he was no longer needed in England. But although his mind was less ill at ease, he was still depressed and on edge. In Paris, at the Théâtre de la Porte St Martin, he attended a performance of the new play, *Chantecler*, an allegorical verse drama by Edmond Rostand, author of *Cyrano de Bergerac*. But he was 'dreadfully disappointed': he had never seen anything 'so stupid and childish'; while the theatre was so hot that he 'contrived to get a chill with a threatening of bronchitis'. He also suffered from an attack of acute indigestion followed by a shortness of breath and a sharp pain near the heart. Two days later he became so ill at Biarritz that Sir James Reid advised him to stay in bed. This he declined to do, though he agreed to remain in his room at the Hôtel du Palais where the Marquis de Soveral and Mrs Keppel were amongst his few visitors.

At the end of March he felt a little better; but he was still fretting about the political situation at home where Asquith's difficulties in getting his government's measures passed by Parliament were once again bringing into discussion the unpleasant topic of the King's creation of a complaisant majority in the House of Lords. The Queen begged him to join her on a Mediterranean cruise. The weather in Biarritz, as she had no need to tell him, was miserable that spring. There was thick snow in the hotel grounds on 1 April. And four days later, when the King sent home to Hardinge details of the arrangements he wanted made for the entertainment of ex-President Roosevelt in June, he still complained of 'snow, rain and constant wind'. But he did not want to leave for the Mediterranean while Mrs Keppel was in Biarritz. Besides, he felt he could not go so far away while it might be necessary at any moment for him to return to London.

So, excessively agitated by fear of being compelled to preside over the destruction of the House of Lords, by talk of a referendum, and by the possibility of the government's resignation, the King announced that he would remain at Biarritz until the end of the month.

On the evening before his departure, the town's authorities arranged a noisy and affectionate farewell, with sailors and soldiers, as well as the fire brigade, marching about below his balcony while fireworks exploded in the sky and bands played appropriate tunes in the courtyard. 'I shall be sorry to leave Biarritz,' he said the next morning, sadly gazing out to sea; 'perhaps it will be for ever.'

He returned to Buckingham Palace in the early evening of 27 April 1910, looking almost as exhausted as he had done before leaving for France. Yet he went to the opera that evening; received Asquith the next day; gave several other audiences on Friday before going to Covent Garden; and early on Saturday morning he left for Sandringham, having breakfast on the train. He arrived at Sandringham in time to walk round the garden with the agent and the head gardener before luncheon, looking at the alterations and the plantings which had been carried out in his absence. He was quieter than usual but seemed content; and in the evening, so Frederick Ponsonby said, 'he told stories of amusing incidents of former years'. The next morning he went to church as usual, though he did not walk across the park with the others but drove in a cab. And in the afternoon, despite rain and a biting wind, he again walked round the garden before settling down to some routine work with Ponsonby in the room that Francis Knollys used as an office.

On Monday afternoon he returned to London. It had been pouring with rain in the morning and the fields were sodden. The King looked out of the window, talking little. That evening he went to have a quiet dinner with Agnes Keyser, and on his return to Buckingham Palace it was obvious that he was about to have another serious attack of bronchitis. Yet when Ponsonby saw him the next morning, 'he seemed quite himself', apart from the cough and lack of appetite. After failing to eat any dinner, 'he smoked a huge cigar', Ponsonby recorded. 'Anything worse for a man with a cough I could not imagine, but curiously enough it seemed to soothe him . . . [Then] the King and I went into the Japanese Room where we remained silent. Presently in came Alice Keppel and Venetia James. We talked for a short time and then we played bridge, as he explained this prevented his talking.'

He had had 'a wretched night', he confessed the following morning, and could not eat any breakfast. Yet he insisted that he must carry on with all the audiences that had been arranged for him; and so he did, receiving his numerous visitors in his frock coat, which was *de rigueur* for such occasions, occasionally being seized, as he was when the American Ambassador called, with spasms of uncontrollable coughing.

On Thursday Ponsonby found him in his bedroom sitting at a writing table with a rug round his legs.

His face was grey and he appeared to be unable to sit upright and to be sunken. At first . . . he was like a man out of breath, but this gradually got better. He said he would sign what there was in the boxes, and I proceeded to open them and handed him documents for his signature . . . He seemed to like the work. Even the Foreign Office telegrams he read, but I kept back some documents that would have necessitated a discussion.

Ponsonby tried to leave more than once, but the King did not want to part with him:

I tried again to go, but he said in a gasping voice, 'You managed so well at Biarritz. I hope everyone was thanked.' I told him I had thanked them all. I said in as cheerful a voice as I could command that I hoped he would soon be better. He replied, 'I feel wretchedly ill. I can't sleep, I can't eat. They really must do something for me.' I was to be relieved next day by Arthur Davidson, and the extraordinary thing was that, ill as he was, he remembered this. He turned to me and said, 'In case I don't see you again, goodbye.' I shook him by the hand, but I do not think he meant anything more than what he usually said when I went out of waiting.

The King insisted on giving audiences as usual that day; and, as the well-informed Edward Marsh told Lady Gladstone, 'he was to receive Jack P [John Dickson-Poynder] as Governor of New Zealand, and somebody else [Major T.B. Robinson] as Agent General for West Australia [actually Queensland]. Lord Sheffield's mind set to work on these names and produced, "the Agent General for Newfoundland".' So when the Australian arrived the King made some comment about having been to his 'interesting colony'.

The Agent General, who knew he had never been anywhere near Australia looked bewildered. Hopwood [Permanent Under Secretary of State for the Colonies] saw what had happened and told the King who he really was. The poor King was so terribly upset at having made such a gaffe that he had a violent fit of coughing and turned quite black in the face—and this was really the beginning of the end. Jack P. said that when he got home he was sure he was a dying man.

The Queen had been sent for and, having left Corfu by way of Venice, she had arrived home that day. At Calais she had been handed a note from the Prince of Wales: 'His cough troubles him very much and he has slept badly the last nights. I cannot disguise the fact that I am anxious about him . . . I know Laking is writing to you and I will say no more but thank God you are coming home tomorrow to look after him. God bless you, darling Motherdear.'

The Prince and Princess and their two eldest sons were waiting to meet her at Victoria Station. Concerned that he could not meet her himself, as he had always done in the past, the King made all the arrangements for her reception at Buckingham Palace, ordering that all the Household should be ready to meet the Queen in the Grand Entrance Hall. The Prince of Wales, however, had decided that it would be better if his mother arrived without any fuss and gave instructions for her to be driven round to the garden entrance. She was profoundly shocked to see the King looking so ill. Up till then she had comforted herself with the belief that this was just another bronchial attack from which he would soon recover. He tried to reassure her, telling her that he had reserved a box for her that evening at Covent Garden.

At eleven o'clock the next morning Sir Ernest Cassel came to see him, but he was told that the King was too ill to be disturbed. Half an hour later, however, at the King's insistence, Cassel was summoned back to the Palace. He told his daughter:

> I found the King dressed as usual, in his sitting room, rising from his chair to shake hands with me. He looked as if he had suffered great pain, and spoke indistinctly. His kindly smile came out as he congratulated me on having you brought home so much improved in health. He said, 'I am very seedy, but I wanted to see you. Tell your daughter how glad I am that she has safely got home' . . . He then talked about other matters.

He tried to smoke a cigar but could not enjoy it. A light luncheon was brought to his bedroom; and having tried to eat it, he got up and walked towards the window to look at his canaries, whose cage stood by the curtains. While playing with them he collapsed and fell to the floor. Nurses ran towards him and helped him to a chair while Princess Victoria sent for the Queen.

It was clear now that he was dying, suffering from a series of heart attacks. The doctors examined him and could do nothing for him but allay his pain with morphia. Without much success, they had already given him oxygen to inhale and hypodermic injections of strychnine, tyramine and ether. He still sat in his chair, refusing to be helped into bed, protesting weakly, 'No, I shall not give in; I shall go on; I shall work to the end.'

Charles Hardinge went to 10 Downing Street and told Mrs Asquith that he had left Lord Knollys in tears. He suggested that a telegram should be sent summoning the Prime Minister home from the Mediterranean. Various friends called at the Palace to enquire after him, and some of the closest were allowed into his room to see him. The Archbishop of Canterbury was summoned; and the Queen herself, told that Mrs Keppel had seen the King the day before and was due to call again at five o'clock, said, 'It will be too late', and sent for her to return immediately. The Prince of Wales told his father that his horse, *Witch of the Air*, had won the 4.15 race at Kempton Park. 'Yes,' said the King, to whom the news had already been telegraphed. 'I have heard of it. I am very glad.'

These were the last coherent words he spoke. Twice he fainted, and soon lapsed into a coma. He was undressed and put to bed. The Archbishop was called in from the next room, and at a quarter to midnight on 6 May 1910 the King died without a struggle.

20
Drawn Blinds

How human he was! . . . What a splendour he was in the world!

'I have lost my best friend and the best of fathers,' the new King wrote in his diary, in an untidy hand bearing testimony of his distress, on the evening of the first day of his reign. 'I never had a [cross] word with him in my life. I am heartbroken and overwhelmed with grief.'

Queen Alexandra also confessed herself grief-stricken. She felt as if she had been turned into stone, she told Frederick Ponsonby, 'unable to cry, unable to grasp the meaning of it all, and incapable of doing anything'. It was not the biting cold of that wet afternoon at Sandringham that had killed him, she added as she took Ponsonby into the room where the King's body lay, but 'that horrid Biarritz'.

'She was most brave and touching, calm but breaking down now and again,' said Lord Halifax, who had accompanied the King on that walking tour in the Lake District over fifty years before and had asked if, as an old servant and friend, he might see him in death.

I was much touched by her taking up a prayer-book on a table by the side of the bed and saying, 'That is the prayer-book you gave him; he always had it with him.' . . . She took me again into the room and looked for a time, uncovering his face and said, 'Does he not look beautiful?' . . . He was lying on a little bed screened off from the rest of the room, just under a picture of Prince Eddie and his mother. He was not in the least altered and had that look on his face that death so often brings.

Lord Carrington was also shown into the darkened room; and as he looked down at the King's 'beloved' face which appeared 'quite happy and composed' above the collar of a pink shirt, he felt that he had lost the 'truest friend' that he had ever had. Charles Hardinge was taken in to see the King, too, and the Queen gave him the jade bell which he had so often seen on the King's writing-table and which Hardinge thereafter regarded as one of his 'greatest treasures'. 'I was deeply moved at seeing there, lying on a simple

bed, the dead man who had been so good to me and whom I really loved,'
Hardinge wrote. 'To me he was always the kindest of masters . . . I have
always missed him since.'

Ponsonby felt the same. He remembered what a 'lovable, wayward and
human' master the King had been. He recalled numerous acts of kindness:
how, for instance—unlike Queen Victoria, 'who rarely considered the feelings of her Household'—he would often, without being asked, suggest to
'some married man that he should go away and spend the week with his
family'. Ponsonby called to mind one particular example of 'that kindness
of heart which characterized all his actions'. It was a small incident but it
remained in his memory. It occurred during the King's continental tour in
1903. Aboard the royal yacht was Eduardo de Martino, a Neapolitan artist
who had been Marine Painter-in-Ordinary to Queen Victoria and had settled
in England in 1875. Ponsonby could not imagine 'anybody more inappro-
priate in the suite of an English King' than this Martino, who had taken the
place of Christopher Sykes as an ideal butt for the King's bantering jokes.
Yet Martino appeared so disappointed when he was given to understand
that he ought to remain on the yacht when the royal party went ashore, that
the King not only gave him permission to form part of the suite but took
pains to discuss with other less sensitive members of the party a rearrange-
ment of the order of precedence which would spare Martino's feelings by
ensuring that he did not rank last.

Numerous members of the King's staff recalled similar instances of his
kindness, tact and generosity; of his 'enviable gift', as Robert Vansittart, a
young temporary extra private secretary, described it, 'of making innocents
feel that he really wanted to see them'; of the pleasure they themselves derived from performing some service which made him momentarily happy
and brought forth that characteristic murmur of 'yes, yes, yes' like the
purring of a contented cat; of the enthusiasm he affected upon being offered
presents he did not really want, such as the stylographic pen given him by
Frederick Ponsonby. It was a 'wonderful invention', he declared, 'treating it
like a conjuring trick'. 'He used it for a short time simply to please me,'
Ponsonby recorded, 'but really hated it. Then mercifully he lost it and was
terrified lest I should give him another, but of course I had seen what a
failure it was and never alluded to it again.'

He was always punctiliously courteous to servants, prefacing his requests with 'please' and expressing his gratitude with 'thank you' and
delighting Lady Fildes's parlourmaid by the way he bowed and smiled at her
in the hall when he came to Melbury Road to have his portrait painted.

His own servants had to admit, though, that he was an increasingly
difficult man to work for as he grew older. Exacting, temperamental, impatient and irritable, he also had many foibles. One of the most tiresome was his
inordinate superstitiousness. He had a horror of crossed knives on a table

and kept an ever-watchful eye on the Master of Ceremonies at court levees to make sure that he wore his jewel of office correctly 'as any displacement was of evil omen'. His valets were expressly forbidden to turn his mattress on a Friday, and he would never allow thirteen people to sit down with him to dinner. Once when he discovered that he had accidentally done so three nights running at Friedrichshof, he was 'much upset' until he comforted himself with the thought that perhaps it did not matter as one of the company was pregnant. And Winston Churchill remembered how, as a young subaltern invited to dinner at Deepdene, he had arrived eighteen minutes late in the drawing-room where thirteen people, 'in the worst of tempers', were suffering from the King's steadfast refusal to lead such an unlucky number of people into the dining-room.

Sir Luke Fildes, who was asked to do a drawing of the King on his deathbed, was surprised to see a festoon of charms and keepsakes hanging from the head of the bedstead. He thought that each one must be 'a memento of some congenial entertainment'. But, as he was at work, Princess Victoria came into the room and enlightened him. 'I see you keep looking at those mascots of his,' she said. 'The old dear used to think they brought him luck.'

Unlike many highly superstitious people, however, the King never lacked courage. Lord Redesdale recalled how, once he had made up his mind to have the operation which necessitated a postponement of his coronation, he made not the least fuss about it, though he knew that he might die. Both in Ireland and in England he had been threatened with death by the Fenians; but this had never deterred him from visiting any part of either country, even though a strong escort of police was often considered necessary to protect him. When a man who had threatened to murder him was sentenced to ten years' penal servitude, he asked the Home Secretary to mitigate the severe sentence on the grounds that the man was probably mad. And when an anarchist student, who regarded him as responsible for 'killing the Boers', fired a pistol at him through the window of his carriage as his train was leaving Brussels in 1900, he behaved with the most perfect composure, never even changing colour, according to Charlotte Knollys, who was in the royal carriage, calling out to the people on the platform, who had grabbed hold of the would-be assassin, not to harm him. 'The King was the only man I ever met,' Lord Carrington noted in his journal after his friend's death, 'who did not know what moral or physical fear meant.'

Devoted as they were to the King when he was in one of his gratified and gratifying moods, his servants always held him in the greatest awe. For his forceful and formidable personality made him an extremely intimidating figure. 'Even his most intimate friends were all terrified of him,' Frederick Ponsonby wrote.

I have seen Cabinet ministers, ambassadors, generals and admirals absolutely curl up in his presence when trying to maintain their point. As regards myself, I varied. If I was quite certain of my facts I never minded standing up to him. In fact, I always noticed that he invariably respected people who stood up to him, and he carried this so far that he was always taken in by dictatorial and cocksure people. At times however I was perfectly terrified of him.

Ponsonby's daughter recorded that 'his angry bellow, once heard, could never be forgotten'.

All his staff dreaded these violent outbursts which suddenly erupted when his impatience and irritation could no longer be contained and which became more frequent and more terrifying as the King grew older. No one had more experience of them than Mr Chandler, the Superintendent of his Wardrobe, who would occasionally be summoned to come immediately to the King's room where his Majesty, pacing furiously up and down, would, as Sir Lionel Cust said, use the poor man 'as whipping boy or safety valve' and 'scold him unmercifully about something' as soon as the door opened. Yet Chandler, like the rest of the King's staff, was devoted to him and knew that once the storm was over every effort would be made to make amends for any feelings that had been hurt. As Lord Esher said, 'If the King assailed you, as he sometimes assailed me, vigorously, remorselessly, it was almost certain that within an hour or two he would send for you, or dispatch a few lines on a slip of paper, on some wholly different subject, in the friendliest manner, with no allusion to what had passed.' 'It was a pleasure,' Lord Fisher thought, 'to face his furious anger for the sake of the lovely smile you got later on.'

Stamper, the motor engineer, recorded:

Sometimes, if his Majesty were annoyed he would show his displeasure by assuming an air of the most complete resignation. Instead perhaps of upbraiding me, if I lost the way, he would question me quietly . . . gravely deplore the way in which Misfortune singled him out for her victim, and then settle himself gently in his corner, as if resigning himself to his fate. In his countenance there was written a placid acceptance of the situation and a calm expectancy of worse to come.

Sometimes, too, the King's anger would abruptly dissolve into laughter, as it did when, having decided to build a sanatorium with the £200,000 which Cassel had given him for a charity of his own choosing, the committee appointed to supervise its construction selected a site at Midhurst for which no adequate water supply could be found. The King's anger 'knew no bounds'. Refusing to listen to any excuses, he ended his assault upon Sir Felix Semon, the member of the committee with whom he was most often in contact, by declaring, 'I'll tell you something: you doctors are nearly as bad as the lawyers. And, God knows, that will say a great deal!' In the tense

silence that followed, Sir Felix felt constrained to laugh; and the King, surprised at first by such a reaction rather than the expression of contrition
which would have been more appropriate to his rage, began to laugh too.
The row was over.

It was not only his staff and intimate friends who had first-hand experience of the King's ungovernable, though fortunately brief rages. Prince
Christopher of Greece recorded in his memoirs the 'consternation stamped
on the faces of his guests' at a big dinner party when the King spilled some
spinach on his shirt. His face went red with fury as he plunged his hands
into the dish and smeared the spinach all over his starched white front. But
then 'he laughed in his infectious way, "Well, I had to change anyway,
hadn't I? I might as well make a complete mess of it." '

With his wife rarely—and with the Prince of Wales never—were there
any of these angry scenes which from time to time shattered the peace of
the Household. The Queen's unpunctuality continued to exasperate him to
the end; but, having completely failed to cure her, he had been obliged to
tolerate it. While waiting for her he would sit drumming his fingers on a
nearby table in that all too familiar manner, tapping his feet on the floor and
gazing out of the window with an expression which Frederick Ponsonby
described as being like that of a Christian martyr.

That alarming drumming and tapping could also be observed when he
was bored. Usually he contrived to hide his boredom in public and, when
duty required, could listen to the most tedious people with apparently rapt
attention. But there were occasions when he could not contain himself. Then
the agitated movements of his fingers and feet, growing more and more
rapid, would be supplemented by an icy, unblinking stare, or by a whispered
aside to an attendant to rescue him—as, one day at Longchamps, he had
whispered instructions to be saved from the all too oppressive proximity of
Mme Loubet sitting on one side of him and the equally unprepossessing and
no less stout wife of the Governor of Paris on the other.

This had been done with charm and courtesy, of course, for the King's
reputation for tactful behaviour with ladies was almost legendary. Stories
were told of occasional lapses, of his having, for example, discomfited the
American heiress, Mrs Moore, a rather absurd, importunate woman of whom
the King said there were three things in life one could not escape: '*L'amour,
la Mort et* La Moore.' Mrs Moore, having curtsied before the King 'almost to
her knees' in a flamboyantly theatrical gesture, was asked in a voice even
more penetrating than usual, 'Have you lost anything?' Such lapses with men
were more frequent. An American, who evidently wanted to be recognized
by the King and made a great fuss of bowing very low every time he saw
him, eventually got close enough at Homburg to observe, 'I guess, Sir, you
know my face?' 'I certainly seem to recognize,' the King is alleged to have
replied, 'the top of your head.'

There were also occasions when the King's laughter offended as much as his mocking words. On his return from Germany in 1909, impressed by the military atmosphere of the Kaiser's court, he decided that meetings of the Privy Council should in future be conducted in a more formal setting. Instructions were given that uniforms should be worn; and it was intimated that full ecclesiastical vestments would, therefore, also be appropriate. Cosmo Gordon Lang, the recently appointed Archbishop of York, a Scotsman with a keen sense of drama and a highly dignified manner, readily conformed to the King's wishes and attended his first Privy Council meeting in his splendid and commodious archiepiscopal robes. Having kissed the King's hand, he retired slowly backwards upon the diminutive figure of Lord Northcote, a former Governor-General of Australia, who was also attending his first meeting of the Privy Council. Northcote became entangled in the voluminous vestments from which he struggled unsuccessfully to emerge, while the Archbishop, evidently unaware of the foreign body within the folds of his cope, maintained his usual dignified composure. The King stepped forward to help; but, overcome by Northcote's ludicrous predicament, suddenly burst into laughter.

That irrepressible, infectious laughter was heard again a month later when the King was being driven in one of his motor-cars from Biarritz to San Sebastian to have luncheon with the King of Spain. The ridiculous sight of the slovenly Spanish soldiers lining the route, many waving and smiling genially rather than saluting, few standing to attention and some actually sitting down and smoking, was too much for him and, beginning to laugh, he could scarcely control himself before San Sebastian was reached.

Yet, although the King's laughter was often heard in private, the occasions when he was seen laughing in public were extremely rare. His customary public deportment was universally recognized, indeed, as being exemplary, combining, in a way that was considered unique, irreproachable dignity with easy affability, authority with charm. Scores of witnesses have given testimony to this. 'He was not a lover of the stage to no purpose,' wrote Sir Lionel Cust, 'and like a highly trained actor, he studied and learned the importance of mien and deportment, of exit and entrance, of clear and regulated diction and other details, which he absorbed quite modestly and without any ostentation into his own actions.' Other observers praised his ability to put people at ease with a few well-considered words, to move on from one person to the next with a remark that would draw them both into a conversation which they could enjoy while he went on to talk to someone else, to flatter them all with the help of his excellent memory. At a state banquet in Berlin he happened to catch sight of Mme de Hegermann Lindencrone, the American wife of the Danish Minister, whom he had met once briefly many years before. He went up to her and reminded her of that meeting which had taken place at Sommerberg where the King had gone to play tennis with Paul Hatzfeldt, a former German Ambassador in London.

' "Fancy your Majesty remembering all these years."

' "A long time ago. I was staying with the King and Queen of Denmark at Wiesbaden. I remember all so well. Poor Hatzfeldt! I remember what Bismarck said of him, 'Was he not the best horse in his stable?' " And he turned smilingly to greet another guest.'

He would try to talk to everyone and, unlike the Kaiser, to do so without a hint of patronage. A stickler for convention and the rules of precedence, he was so satisfied with the established order of society that he would not allow anyone to make disparaging remarks about any of its institutions. It was rarely suggested, though, that he was pompous. He would far rather sit down to a meal with an entertaining acrobat than a tedious duke. Nor did he have any religious or racial prejudices. Indeed, his tolerant attitude towards the Roman Catholic Church—emphasized by a visit to Lourdes, his insistence that Cardinal Manning as a Prince of the Church should rank after himself and before the Prime Minister on a Royal Commission, and his readiness to attend a Requiem Mass—led to absurd rumors that he was a secret convert, just as his friendship with so many Jews, and his resemblance to Sir Ernest Cassel, gave rise to equally ill-founded stories that he had himself inherited Jewish blood from a court chamberlain with whom his paternal grandmother had been in love.

Above all, as everyone agreed, the King had a strong sense of duty. Most of his time was spent in the pursuit of pleasure, and all of it was spent in comfort; yet even his sternest critics conceded that, when there was work to be done, sooner or later he brought himself to do it. There was, however, one notable dereliction. In April 1908 the King declined to return home from France when Asquith became Prime Minister on Campbell-Bannerman's death. 'I am *sure* he ought to return,' Francis Knollys told Asquith, 'and I have gone as far, and perhaps further, in what I have said to him than I am entitled to go.' But Asquith had to go out to Biarritz to kiss hands, and there was troublesome delay in appointments to the new Cabinet as it was impracticable for all the other ministers affected to cross the Channel. There were no embarrassing speeches in the House of Commons, where the King's failure to come home was nevertheless strongly deprecated. But some newspapers, rarely having occasion to criticize the King on such a score, condemned his selfishness. *The Times* suggested:

> It may perhaps be regarded as a picturesque and graceful tribute to the reality of the 'Entente' with our French friends that the King and the Prime Minister should find themselves so much at home in their beautiful country as to be able to transact the most important constitu-

tional business on French soil. Still, the precedent is not one to be followed, and everyone with a sound knowledge of our political system must hope that nothing of the kind will happen again.

It was suggested to the King that he might save himself from such attacks by emphasizing that he came to Biarritz for his health. But at the time the King felt 'perfectly well'. He would not say that he was not. He was not in the habit of lying. And he would not lie now. So nothing more was said to him about the matter. Soon it was forgotten; and, if the King remembered it with shame, he did not talk about it. It was better to remember the afternoons with Mrs Keppel, the drives into the country to Pau and Roncesvalles, the walks in the woods, the picnics by the road, the games of pelota at Anglet, the races at la Barre.

After dining with Lord and Lady Islington on the night of the King's death, Mrs Asquith had gone to see the Hardinges. Edward Grey was there, and both he and Charles Hardinge looked 'white with sorrow'. On returning to Downing Street, Mrs Asquith lay in bed with the lights turned on, 'sleepless, stunned and cold'. At midnight there was a knock at the door. 'The head messenger walked in and, stopping at the foot of the bed, said, 'His Majesty passed away at 11.45.' Mrs Asquith burst into tears. She had written earlier:

Royal persons are necessarily divorced from the true opinions of people that count, and are almost always obliged to take safe and commonplace views. To them clever men are 'prigs', clever women 'too advanced'; Liberals are 'socialists'; the uninteresting 'pleasant'; the interesting 'intriguers'; and the dreamer 'mad'. But, when all this is said, our King devotes what time he does not spend upon sport and pleasure ungrudgingly to duty. He subscribes to his cripples, rewards his sailors, reviews his soldiers, and opens bridges, bazaars, hospitals and railway tunnels with enviable sweetness. He is loyal to all his . . . friends . . . and adds to fine manners, rare prestige, courage and simplicity.

Lord Fisher would have agreed with her. He wrote:

He wasn't clever, but he always did the right thing, which is better than brains. I can't get over the personal great blank I feel in [his] death . . . There was something in the charm of his heart that still chains one to his memory—some magnetic touch . . . How *human* he was! He could sin, 'as it were with a cart-rope', and yet could be loved the more for it! What a splendour he was in the world!

The eulogies in the newspapers did not mention the sins, which struck Wilfrid Scawen Blunt as 'very absurd, considering what the poor King was'. 'He might have been a Solon and a Francis of Assisi combined if the characters drawn of him were true. In no print has there been the smallest allusion to any of his pleasant little wickednesses.' Yet it was these venial sins that had helped to make him the well-liked figure that he undoubtedly was and which largely accounted for the nation's 'sense of personal loss', a loss, so Lord Morley thought, that was 'in a way deeper and keener than when Queen Victoria died'.

King Edward was, in fact, a popular monarch because he was so obviously a human one. Lord Granville said that he had 'all the faults of which the Englishman is accused'. But it would have been more accurate to say that he had all the faults of which Englishmen would *like* to be accused. Also, he had many virtues which they are traditionally supposed to lack. He was not in the least hypocritical; he never attempted to disguise an unashamed zest for luxury and sensual pleasure. Yet, as Edward Grey put it, his 'capacity for enjoying life' was 'combined with a positive and strong desire that everyone else should enjoy life too'.

Mrs Keppel said much the same thing. She was prostrated by the King's death. Her daughter Sonia described how, 'at a few minutes' notice', the family moved from Portman Square to the Arthur Jameses' in Grafton Street where the blinds were drawn, the lights were dimmed and black clothes appeared, even for the little girl, with black ribbons threaded through her underclothes. Sonia could not understand why all this had to be so. She went to the room where her mother lay in bed. But Mrs James barred her way; and her mother looked at her blankly, 'without recognition, almost resentfully'. Sonia ran, frightened, to her father and burst into tears. 'Why does it matter so much, Kingy dying?' she asked him, sobbing on his shirt-front.

'Poor little girl,' he said. 'It must have been very frightening for you. And for all of us for that matter. Nothing will ever be quite the same again. Because Kingy was such a wonderful man.'

Colonel Keppel, like all those others who had grown fond of the King, felt conscious of the loss of a remarkable and irreplaceable character. It was difficult to become accustomed to his absence, to enter rooms where he had formerly been seen or to smell the pungent smoke of a Henry Clay cigar, to catch sight of a rakishly tilted Tyrolean hat, or a perky fox terrier, without remembering him.

Writing from Rufford Abbey where he was staying for Doncaster Races after the King's death, Lord Crewe remarked upon 'the sense of strangeness' that had come over all those places where his deep though penetrating voice and his gruff laugh were heard no longer in the corridors, where his 'intense and commanding personality' was felt no more.

Reference Notes

I am deeply indebted to the various owners of copyright material who have been kind enough to grant permission for extracts to be reproduced in this book. I am also most grateful to the authors and publishers of the following books, in which several of the royal letters and documents have already been printed: Philip Magnus, *King Edward the Seventh* (John Murray); Georgina Battiscombe, *Queen Alexandra* (Constable & Co.); Roger Fulford, *Dearest Child* and *Dearest Mama* (Evans Brothers); Cecil Woodham-Smith, *Queen Victoria: Her Life and Times* (Hamish Hamilton); Elizabeth Longford, *Victoria R.1.* (Weidenfeld & Nicolson); Giles St Aubyn, *The Royal George* (Constable & Co.); Mary Howard McClintock, *The Queen Thanks Sir Howard* (John Murray); and Theo Lang, *My Darling Daisy* (Michael Joseph).

Quotations from the diaries of Arthur J. Munby, the letters of Henry Ponsonby, the recollections of Frederick Ponsonby and the papers of Sir Edward Marsh are taken, with gratitude, from Derek Hudson's *Munby: Man of Two Worlds* (John Murray), Arthur Ponsonby's *Henry Ponsonby: Queen Victoria's Private Secretary* (Macmillan & Co.), Sir Frederick Ponsonby's *Recollections of Three Reigns* (edited by Colin Welch; Eyre & Spottiswoode), and Christopher Hassall's *Edward Marsh* (Longmans).

For extracts from the Macclesfield Papers I am indebted to Georgina Battiscombe and Messrs Constable & Co.; from the Campbell-Bannerman Papers to John Wilson and Messrs Constable & Co.; from the Soveral and Mensdorff Papers to Gordon Brook-Shepherd and Messrs Collins; and from the Edward Hamilton Papers to Dudley W.R. Bahlman and the Clarendon Press, Oxford.

p. 10 Sir George Combe's reports: National Library of Scotland (MSS. 7437). By June 1852 Combe had examined 'all the four Royal Children' and had found each one 'characterized by the organs of Self-Esteem, Love of Approbation, Firmness and Conscientiousness . . . greatly beyond the average of the general English brain. The same remark also applies to Concentrativeness; but above all Conscientiousness is largely developed. . . . This renders words spoken, or actions done to them greatly more felt than is the case with ordinary children.'

p. 11   Birch and Prince Albert: Londonderry Papers. Disraeli wrote to Lady Londonderry on 10 October 1851: 'You know or have heard of Mr Birch, the model tutor of the Prince of Wales and hitherto at the Chateau a prime favourite. It seems that Albert who has imbibed the ultra Lutheran (alias Infidel) doctrines and holds that all churches (reformed) are alike, etc., and that ecclesiastical formulares of all kinds ought to be discouraged, signified to Birch the other day that he did not approve of the Prince of Wales being taught the catechism, his Royal Highness not approving of creeds and all that. Conceive the astonishment and horror of Birch, a very orthodox if not very High Churchman, at this virtual abnegation of all priestly authority! He at once informed His Royal Highness that he must then resign his post. This could not on the instant be agreed to, as the Queen was devoted to Birch and Albert himself had hitherto greatly approved of him. After this there were scenes for a week, some very violent; it ended by Birch, who was unflinching, consenting to remain, the Prince of Wales being taught the Church catechism and the utmost efforts being made to suppress the whole *esclandre* which, if it were known, would, coupled with the connection and patronage of the National Exposition, complete, it is supposed, the Prince's popularity. He is already more than suspected by the Church [of] making the Queen, when in Scotland, attend the Kirk and not the episcopal church, to which he sends a lord-in-waiting, or a maid of honor, every Sunday, instead of the sacred presence.'

pp. 11-12   Birch's reports: Extracts on these and preceding pages are from Gibbs Papers; Philip Magnus, p. 7; also Cecil Woodham-Smith, pp. 335–36.

pp. 12-13   Gibbs's diary entries: *Cornhill Magazine*, p. 986, Spring 1951.

pp. 13-14   Becker's and Voisin's reports in Gibbs Papers, quoted by Philip Magnus, pp. 10-11.

p. 16   Wynn-Carrington on Prince Albert: Lincolnshire Papers (Bodleian MSS. Film 1120–21).

pp. 16-17   Prince's essay: Gibbs's report in Royal Archives quoted by Elizabeth Longford, p. 275.

p. 22   Lindsay's report: Royal Archives, quoted by Cecil Woodham-Smith, pp. 403-4.

pp. 23-24   Gladstone on Prince of Wales: Hawarden MSS., quoted by Philip Magnus, p. 27.

p. 30   Prince of Wales's lack of skill at tennis: Joseph Romilly's MS. Diaries, 28 January 1841 (Cambridge University Library, 6804-42.

p. 33   *New York Herald* reports: Press cuttings in the Royal Archives quoted by Woodham-Smith. Later quotations from *New York Daily Tribune* and *New York Times* are from Kinley Roby.

p. 38   Madingley Hall arrangements: King Papers, 12 June 1860 to 8 December 1861 (Cambridge County Record Office).

pp. 38-39   Prince at Cambridge: Acland Papers; Joseph Romilly's Diaries,

18 January 1861 to 21 May 1861. Romilly went to dinner with the Prince at Madingley on 24 January and afterwards recorded: 'The Prince did not wear a star or ribbon and we were all (as instructed) in an ordinary evening dress without gowns. . . . Whewell [William Whewell, Master of Trinity College] said Grace. The dessert was on the table at first: no viands on table: everything handed round. Wine was twice poured out for everybody without asking: seemed to be Sherry and Champagne. With the cheese Portwine was offered & cherry brandy. After dinner nothing but Sherry and Claret offered: no wine put on table. I think nobody tasted any part of the dessert except some little cakes which were handed round. . . . The ice after dinner was delicious.'

p. 39   Kingsley on the Prince: Desborough Papers, 5 May 1861 (County of Buckingham Record Office, D/86/32/40).

p. 48   Prince Albert at Madingley: Lincolnshire Papers, 25 November 1861.

p. 49   Prince at father's deathbed: King Papers, The Hon. Sir Charles Phipps to Lady King, 27 December 1861.

p. 52   Prince's letter to Wynn-Carrington: Lincolnshire Papers, 23 January 1862.

pp. 53-54   Stanley and Prince in Middle East: Acland Papers, as well as Prothero and Bradley.

p. 55   Prince's opinion of William Knollys: Knollys Papers (Kent County Record Office, U1186 C/47, undated [June 1883]).

p. 55   Queen Victoria's letter about William Knollys: Knollys Papers, 9 July 1862 (Kent County Record Office, U1186 C6/2). 'I know of *no* other person so fitted as General Knollys,' Queen Victoria added, 'for he possessed beloved Papa's great esteem and confidence, he is very amiable, particularly pleasant and agreeable and has great experience of the world. . . . He is besides very fond of young people.'

p. 57   William Knollys on Prince's happiness: Knollys Papers (U1186 C1/2, undated).

p. 59   Queen Victoria's horror of Princess Alexandra's mother's family: Paget Papers, quoted by Philip Magnus, p. 61.

p. 62   The ugly bridesmaids: Lady Geraldine Somerset's diary in the Royal Archives. This and other extracts quoted by Georgina Battiscombe.

p. 62   Prince's height: Archives of Messrs Henry Poole & Co. In 1860 the Prince's waist measured 39¾ in. and his seat 45 in. In 1905 his waist had expanded to 47 in. and his seat to 46½ in.

p. 63   Princess late for wedding: Lincolnshire Papers, 13 March 1863.

p. 65   Prince's contribution to Frogmore mausoleum: Knollys Papers (U1186 C38). Sir Charles Phipps wrote to Knollys on 3 May 1863: 'I think that the Prince of Wales can hardly realize all the expences that have fallen upon the Queen by the sad events of the last three years. . . . The Queen's expences have *far outgrown* Her income and were it not for a fund which I have with great care collected and set by she *could not get on. This in the STRICTEST CONFIDENCE.* . . . I hope that the expence of the Mausoleum will be spread over many years. I endeavour upon all occasions to advocate a very slow progress. I should be very sorry to pretend to interfere in any way in the financial arrangements of the Prince of Wales but I may hint to *you* that His Royal Highness has a very large *capital* still . . . which might be made available for this purpose. I have not hinted any of this to the Queen and I should earnestly hope it may not come to her knowledge for this is the point upon which she would be most tender.'

p. 66 Increase in Prince's income: Knollys Papers (U1186 C1/6). On 23 March 1865 General Knollys asked Phipps if there would be any objection to the Prince's going to see Gladstone 'on the subject of an increase to the £40,000 annuity. . . . It appears that several members of both Houses have told H.R.H. that there would be no difficulty now in getting his income increased, and that it would be better to ask for it while this feeling was warm.' Nothing came of the Prince's approach.

p. 67 Lady Macclesfield on Sandringham: Macclesfield Papers. This and other extracts quoted by Georgina Battiscombe.

pp. 68-69 Gladstone at Sandringham: Edward Hamilton's diaries, B.M. Add. MSS. 48, pp. 630-83. These have now been edited by Dudley W.R. Bahlman. This and all subsequent quotations from the diaries are taken from this edition. In May 1886 Queen Victoria made 'a devil of a row' about Gladstone and John Morley being asked to Sandringham (Rosebery Papers, 3 May 1886).

p. 69 The Bishop of Peterborough at Sandringham was William Connor Magee. The quotation is from Macdonnel's *Life*.

p. 75 Prince's request for information about 'present political crisis': Devonshire MSS. (340.527), 12 March 1873.

p. 82 General Knollys's excuses: Knollys Papers (U1186 C1/2), 17 October 1864. 'The parting at Copenhagen which took place on board the *Osborne* was painful to witness,' Knollys added, 'the King [of Denmark] particularly showing much distress.'

p. 88 Knollys on sailors' rude song: Royal Archives, quoted by Georgina Battiscombe, p. 89.

p. 91 Lady Carrington's complaints: Carrington MSS., 17 December 1865, 22 December 1865, 13 August 1866 (County of Buckingham Record Office, D/CN C5).

pp. 91-92 Parties at Wynn-Carrington's: Lincolnshire Papers, 20 February 1868.

p. 92 Prince and racing: The Queen's letters to Prince Arthur's governor, Sir Howard Elphinstone, are replete with warnings about the dangers of horse-racing: 'It is deeply regretted by *all* that *Ascot* should be *visited* THIS year [1872] by the Prince of Wales, and the Queen *has* done ALL she can to prevent it, but in vain. . . . It is not because the Queen thinks (and the Prince [Consort] still more) races the dullest things in the world, that she is so *anxious* that the Prince of Wales, and if he won't, that *Prince Arthur* should *discountenance* them *as much as possible* but on account of the horrible gambling, the *ruin* to hundreds of families and the heart-breaking of Parents caused thereby which lowers the higher classes *frightfully*.' (McClintock, p. 148.) Towards the end of her life the Queen's attitude softened, and for Christmas 1895 she gave the Prince of Wales two models of jockeys (Rosebery Papers, National Library of Scotland, MSS. 10016).

p. 92 Prince's letters to Filmer: Filmer MSS., Kent County Record Office (U120 C77). Energetic as the Prince was, even he was sometimes exhausted by his guests at Sandringham. 'The Bishop arrived here today and is in great force,' he once reported to Dean Wellesley; 'he played four rubbers of whist after dinner —then American Bowles with Dr Farre—and it is now 2 in the morning & he has just commenced a game at billiards with that eminent Physician' (Wellington MSS., 13 April 1871).

pp. 94-95 Farmer's description of Sandringham shoot: 'The Lady Farmer,' *Eighteen Years on the Sandringham Estate* (Temple Co., 1887).

p. 97 Foundation of Marlborough Club: Lincolnshire Papers. 'In 1917,' Lincolnshire added, 'the Marlborough Club was on its last legs. Sir Ernest Cassel (a German Jew) offered to finance it; but the members would not stand that; and King George V saved the club by producing £7,000.'

p. 98 Lord Carrington's advice to his son: Carrington Papers, 2 March 1863.

p. 99 Royal Buckhounds at Paddington: Lincolnshire Papers, Lord Carrington's journal.

p. 99 Queen Victoria's criticism of Prince at time of Phipps's death: Knollys Papers (U1186 C6/4), 26 February 1866.

p. 104 Princess Alexandra on happiness of her marriage: Downe Papers, 18 May 1869 (North Yorkshire Record Office, ZDS/W, 100).

p. 108 Disturbance at Olympic Theatre: Lincolnshire Papers, 2 March 1870.

p. 110 Prince at House of Lords: 'The Prince performed capitally yesterday in the House of Lords,' Lord Carrington told his son on 6 February 1863, 'not nervous and very dignified and well received' (Carrington Papers, D/CN C1/9).

p. 111 Mrs Francis Stonor on Prince in tears: Royal Archives, quoted by Georgina Battiscombe, p. 112.

p. 118 Appointment of Francis Knollys: Knollys Papers (U1186 C25/8). Queen Victoria was justified in her fears that, as a young man, Francis Knollys's morals were not above reproach. In April 1873 he accompanied the Prince to Vienna, where, 'before hearing that almost all the ladies of the town were reported to be poxed', he went with 'about as low a woman' as he had ever come across and afterwards confessed to his friend, Rosebery, that he was 'in a horrible fright' (Rosebery Papers, MS. 10016, 29 April 1873).

p. 119   Prince and Scots Fusiliers: Knollys Papers (U1186 C18/1), 13
          September 1870.

p. 119   Lord Granville on Prince: Henry Ponsonby's Papers, quoted
          by Arthur Ponsonby, p. 102.

p. 126   Princess Alexandra and India: Downe Papers, 21 March 1877.
          A letter from Lady Downe, written in India, made Princess
          Alexandra 'regret ten times more' that she was not allowed to
          'have a glimpse at least of that glorious East' which she feared
          she would never see (Downe Papers, 2DS/W/102).

p. 126   Queen Victoria's instructions about Indian visit: Salisbury
          Papers, 5 June 1875.

pp. 128ff Albert Grey's letters to his mother and his journal, quoted
          throughout this chapter, are in the Earl Grey Papers, Depart-
          ment of Palaeography and Diplomatic, University of Durham,
          MSS. pp. 216-17.

p. 129   Lord Carrington's comments on the tour are extracted from
          the Lincolnshire Papers, MS. 1120.

p. 131   Prince in Delhi: Grey Papers. A private soldier in the Eighth
          Regiment who formed part of the Prince's guard thought that
          his reception in Delhi was very subdued (MS. Letters of Private
          John Whitworth, Merseyside County Museum, Liverpool).
          'Any notion the natives may have entertained of the pomp and
          grandeur they were about to witness must have been quickly
          dissipated, as, riding with a lot of staff officers, the Prince was
          in no way conspicuous and was not I believe recognised by
          the majority of the natives. Slowly the procession wound its
          way thro the line of troops—the Prince conversing now with
          one now with another of the officers around him. Whether
          the natives testify their loyalty in a manner different to us or
          whether they were disappointed at the lack of show I know
          not. But certain it is that very few cheers greeted his advent.
          One "Champagne Charley" style of European tried by the
          force of example to call forth a hurrah from his black neigh-
          bours, but the effort was in vain. The attempt was, however,
          acknowledged by a graceful inclination of His Royal H's head.
          . . . The procession pursued its course, the Prince occasionally
          being called on to acknowledge the waving of handkerchiefs
          by European ladies. The whole affair did not last two hours,
          and the tameness of the reception was certainly the most no-
          ticeable feature in it.'

p. 133   Fights between wild animals: Lincolnshire Papers, MS. 1120.
          Carrington reported to his mother: '8 wild elephants tied by
          the leg at each end. 18 pairs of naked wrestlers. About a hundred
          naked spearmen yelling and dancing about and bolting through
          holes in the walls when the brutes got too close. . . . Then 2
          rhinoceros fought, then two bison—one broke the other's horn
          straight off and he got through the bars and escaped. An ele-
          phant being driven out seized a chain in his trunk and let drive
          right and left. . . . Then a tiger led by ropes appeared, rams
          fought, and carriages drawn by black bucks and stags galloped
          about—you can't imagine such fun. Just like a nightmare.'

p. 134   Prince commended by Lord Salisbury: Salisbury Papers, 13 May 1876.

pp. 136-39   Aylesford–Blandford scandal: Papers quoted in companion volume to Randolph S. Churchill's *Winston S. Churchill: Young Statesman*.

p. 140   Expedition to St Pancras: Lincolnshire Papers, Lord Carrington's journal.

p. 141   Prince and Wolseley: Devonshire MSS. (340.1528). The Prince wrote to Lord Hartington, at that time Secretary for War, on 17 September 1884: 'When I gave you the memorandum last week about the Adjutant-General of the Indian Army I knew nothing could be done in the matter but only wished you to have some proof how the "Wolseyites" get everything. I am quite aware that the present Adjutant-General did not fulfil the prescribed conditions but why should Sir T[homas] Baker simply because he is a "Wolseyite" have the same advantage. The whole matter resolves itself into this—however competent or able an officer may be, unless he belongs to the so called mutual admiration society, he has *no* chance of getting the "good things" in his profession.' Despite the Prince's protests, Sir Thomas Baker was nominated Adjutant-General on 10 October.

p. 146   Prince not kept informed: Knollys Papers. The situation did not improve. In 1899 the Prince was 'much incensed with Mr Chamberlain for not having kept him informed' on the Transvaal question (Salisbury Papers, 9 September 1899).

p. 146   Prince and Foreign Office Dispatches: Crewe Papers (C/30). 'My dear Rosebery,' the Prince was obliged to write soon after he had received the key (Rosebery MSS., 31 January 1893), 'I am sorry to say that my Cabinet Key has come to grief and I send you its remnants! Can you let me have another? I only hope the Cabinet is not as ricketty as the Key!'

p. 148   Everyone afraid of Queen Victoria: 'I was presented to Queen Victoria at Balmoral after dinner,' Lord Carrington wrote in his journal on 31 August 1866. 'As we were driving home [to Abergeldie] the Prince of Wales asked me, "Were you frightened?" I answered, "Well no, but I pretended to be as I thought the Queen would like it." '

p. 150   Princess Alexandra and Queen Victoria: Downe Papers (2DS/W/97), 8 April 1901.

p. 150   Princess Alexandra and Prince: Downe Papers (2DS/W/101), 10 August 1871.

p. 156   'I asked him to tea' and 'she had cooled off and become reasonable': *Pearson's Magazine*, October 1916, quoted by Margaret Blunden, p. 67.

pp. 157-58   Prince's protest about Adjutant-General to Duke of Cambridge: FitzGeorge Papers, quoted by Giles St Aubyn, pp. 289-90.

p. 158   Lord Hartington's advice about Tranby Croft: Devonshire MSS. (340.2385), 4 May 1891.

p. 159   Gordon Cumming sympathizers: Gordon Cumming Papers (National Library of Scotland, Box 172/2).

p. 160   Lord Salisbury's letter: Devonshire MSS. (2387), 16 June 1891.

pp. 160-61   Francis Knollys and the Archbishop: Devonshire MSS. (2389), 20 June 1891.

p. 161   Gordon Cumming's daughter: Information given to Anita Leslie's family.

pp. 161ff   Lord Charles Beresford's letter: Salisbury Papers, 12 July 1891. All the correspondence between the Beresfords and the Prince, as well as the letter from Lord Marcus Beresford, comes from the Salisbury Papers.

pp. 164-65   Prince's letters to Lady Brooke are quoted by Theo Lang.

p. 165   Lady Warwick to Frank Harris: *Pearson's Magazine*, quoted by Margaret Blunden, p. 91.

p. 167   Cleveland Street affair: Papers in Public Record Office (DPP 1/95/1-7). The Prince's emissaries were Sir Francis Knollys and Sir Dighton Probyn. The Deputy Director of Public Prosecutions reported to the Director on 16 September 1889 that Lord Arthur Somerset's solicitor was boasting that 'if we go on a very distinguished person will be involved (P.A.V.)'— Prince Albert Victor. 'I don't mean to say that I for one instant credit it,' the Deputy Director added, 'but in such a case as this one never knows what may be said, be concocted or be true.' This is the only reference to Prince Eddy in the whole of the huge file on the case, and in the opinion of the Director (17 September 1889) the solicitor concerned was 'a dangerous man' who was quite likely to make 'utterly *false* accusations against others'. Prince Eddy was certainly not a regular client at 19 Cleveland Street, as the police were watching the brothel over a long period of time, during which Lord Arthur Somerset was seen, shadowed and identified.

p. 167   Prince considers Somerset's involvement 'inconceivable': Lincolnshire Papers, 20 October 1889.

p. 167   Prince's verdict on Somerset: Salisbury Papers, 25 October 1889.

p. 169   Mrs Keppel 'much toadied' to: Lincolnshire Papers, MS., 1120. Lord Carrington attributed Princess Alexandra's dislike of Sir Ernest Cassel to Mrs Keppel's close friendship with him.

p. 170   Count Mensdorff diaries are quoted by Gordon Brook-Shepherd.

p. 170   Mrs Keppel and the Archbishop of Canterbury: Private information from the Earl of Crawford and Balcarres.

p. 172   Prince and Jaraczewski in Paris: Dossier du Roi Edouard VII, Bureau des Archives, Préfecture de Police, 150100, A.I.

p. 174   Cassel and G.C.B.: Asquith Papers, 18 December 1908.

p. 176   Marlborough House dinner for actors: Lincolnshire Papers.

p. 177   The Asquith, Sandars, Hardinge, Devonshire and Rosebery Papers all contain several requests from the Prince for favours and appointments for his friends. The requests on behalf of Ferdinand Rothschild and Canon Dalton are in the Salisbury Papers; that on behalf of Cassel in the Crewe Papers (C/58, 27 April 1901).

p. 177   Prince's plea to Rosebery to accept Foreign Office: Rosebery

Papers, 14 August 1892. 'Let me therefore implore you to accept office (if Mr Gladstone will give you a free hand in Foreign Affairs and not wish you to agree with him in *all* his Home measures) for the Queen's sake and for that of our great Empire!'

pp. 177-78 Letter from Revd H.W. Bellairs: BM Add. MSS. 44468, ff. 149-51.

p. 179 The Duke of Fife in Paris: Lincolnshire Papers, Lord Carrington's journal.

p. 180 Princess Victoria and Rosebery: Rosebery Papers. Knollys's correspondence with Rosebery is full of references to Princess Victoria. Lord Carrington was once asked at the French Embassy in London if it were true that the Princess was to marry the Marquis de Soveral (Lincolnshire Papers, Lord Carrington's journal).

p. 181 Dalton's reports on Prince Eddy: Royal Archives, quoted by Philip Magnus, p. 169.

p. 183 Queen Victoria's good opinion of Prince Eddy: Downe Papers (2DS/W/68-71), pp. 91-104.

p. 183 Prince Eddy at Aldershot: Lady Geraldine Somerset's diary, Royal Archives, quoted by Giles St Aubyn, p. 299.

pp. 185-86 Prince Eddy's treatment and last illness: Downe Papers, (2DS/W/68-71).

p. 186 Prince at son's funeral: Lincolnshire Papers.

p. 192 Munshi's letters from Queen Victoria: Minto MSS., 20 October 1909.

p. 193 Carrington on Esher: Lincolnshire Papers, Lord Carrington's journal.

p. 193 Installation of Carrington as K.G.: Lincolnshire Papers, Lord Carrington's journal.

pp. 194-96 King's clothes: Henry Poole & Co.'s records. After Henry Poole's death in 1876 the firm received few further orders from Marlborough House. Messrs Huntsman and Son, who received a royal warrant in 1865, became the favourite tailors.

p. 198 Queen Alexandra motoring: Londonderry Papers, Durham County Record Office (D/LO/F. 1127).

pp. 198-99 King on motor-racing: Chilston MSS., Kent County Record Office (U564. C9., 4 February 1903).

p. 200 King wins Derby for third time: Seth-Smith, pp. 261-64. *Minoru* was not owned by the King but had been leased to his Majesty with five other yearlings in 1907 by Colonel Hill Walker, later Lord Wavertree.

p. 201 Moneylenders outside French hotels: Préfecture de Police, Dossier 150100, A.I. The police reports contain many references to the Prince's alleged attempts to borrow money in France. One report (4 November 1885) asserts that he has been lent five million francs by the Duc d'Aumâle in exchange for a promise that one of his daughters will marry a princess of the House of Orléans on his coming to the throne. Another report (16 February 1889) refers to persistent rumours that the Prince is urgently in need of 200,000 francs, which he has tried to raise with the help of Mme Goblet, an antique dealer.

p. 202   Queen late for luncheon: The chef was Gabriel Tschumi—his memoirs, pp. 105-6.

p. 203   Felix Semon's memoirs are quoted by Sir Sidney Lee.

pp. 203-4   Lord Allington's daughter (Winifred Sturt) at Sandringham: Hardinge Papers, quoted by Magnus, p. 222.

p. 204   Evenings at Sandringham: Lincolnshire Papers, Lord Carrington's journal.

p. 207   King's slip in speech in Italy: Hardinge Papers, 30 April to 5 May 1909.

p. 208   King and Beresford: Lincolnshire Papers. In 1909 the King told Carrington that Beresford was 'one mass of vanity' and was 'not straight.' He seemed 'delighted' at Beresford's being 'snuffed out'.

p. 209   King's complaint about papers: Asquith Papers, 25 October 1908, 24 July 1909. Lloyd George was a particular offender. The King strongly objected to his writing 'Mr Lloyd George presents his humble duty . . .' instead of the more formal and customary 'The Chancellor of the Exchequer presents . . .'

p. 210   Balfour's rebuff: Haldane Papers, National Library of Scotland (MSS., 5907-8/41-3), 15 July 1908.

p. 211   Campbell-Bannerman's 'bad taste': Chilston MSS., Kent County Record Office (U564. C9, 3 March 1905).

p. 211   Winston Churchill talks 'simple nonsense': Ibid.

p. 211   Knollys's dislike of Churchill: Rosebery Papers, 20 January 1908. Knollys to Rosebery: 'Winston Churchill is to be asked to Windsor for a couple of nights. Personally I don't admire or care for him, but I think the King is quite right to take some notice of him.'

p. 211   Haldane 'always acceptable': Rosebery Papers, 14 December 1908.

p. 213   Band of Coldstream Guards in Germany: Haldane Papers, 8 October 1907. Haldane to Grey: 'The King feels that, though the German Embassy may be satisfied with the explanation given them by the Foreign Office, when the German Emperor hears of what has taken place, as he probably will, it will sound extraordinary to him that the Sovereign of this Country . . . cannot even send a military band abroad without the approval of the Foreign Office.'

p. 213   King's letter about Sinha: Minto MSS., 21 May 1909 (National Library of Scotland, 4E. 346).

p. 215   Balfour's letter about Shah: Royal Archives, quoted by Philip Magnus, p. 305.

p. 218   Princess Alexandra's memorandum on Heligoland: Devonshire MSS., 340. 2236. In sending the memorandum the Princess refers to it as having been written by herself.

p. 218   Queen Alexandra and Greece: Clarendon Papers, 1 May 1870.

p. 219   Prince George's reliance on father: Lincolnshire Papers, Lord Carrington's journal.

pp. 219-20   Prince George's fondness of father: *Lloyd George: Family*

Letters, 1885-1936 (9 May 1910): 'The King [George V] exceedingly nice. Talked a good deal about his father, of whom he was evidently very fond. His eyes, suffused with tears.'

pp. 226-27   The King's friend at the Paris Exhibition was Mrs Paget—letter quoted by Sewell, p. 81.

p. 228   'Poor old Buller!': 'Felix Semon's Memoirs'. In Lord Carrington's journal the difficult guest is not a bishop but the aged Lord Salisbury.

pp. 228-29   Duke of Devonshire's letter: Devonshire MSS., 4. 171, 15 November 1872.

pp. 229-30   King's entourage and his visit to Alnwick: Duke of Northumberland's archives.

p. 230   King's visit to Mount Stewart: Londonderry Papers, D/LO/F.1127.

p. 232   Entertaining royalty: Lincolnshire Papers. The King's hosts were sometimes rewarded with a K.C.V.O. Lord Iveagh received a G.C.V.O. with which he was 'hugely delighted' (7 January 1910).

pp. 235-36   King in France: Préfecture de Police, Dossier 150100, A.I. The King usually stayed at the Hôtel de Provence at Cannes. In February 1887, after he had attended the carnival at Nice dressed as Domino and masked, the police reported, '*Il s'amuse comme un jeune homme, rit de toutes les scènes grotesques et, de retour, prend grand plaisir à raconter les épisodes de la journée.*' Detectives often followed the King to the casino at Monte Carlo. He was usually unlucky, although a rumour that he lost 200,000 francs in April 1890 was described as '*inexact*'. He was once overheard by a detective remarking cheerfully to one of his companions, 'If you want to win, play with me. I always lose.'

p. 237   King in Denmark: Rosebery Papers, MS., 10016/66. Francis Knollys dreaded having to accompany the King, although the Queen thought that he enjoyed the visits. Knollys commented to Rosebery, 'How little she knows human nature!'

p. 244   'A cloud of bluebottle flies': The British visitor was Sir Henry Campbell-Bannerman. The quotations from the Campbell-Bannerman Papers on this and the following page are from John Wilson's biography, pp. 143-45.

p. 244   Sophie Hall Walker at Marienbad: Information from Anita Leslie.

p. 249   'Pawn in the game': Eyre Crowe's comment is quoted by Lord Vansittart, p. 46.

pp. 249-54   King's visit to Pope: Rampolla's, Sandars's, Balfour's and Bertie's letters and telegrams are in the Sandars Papers, Balfour–Edward VII Correspondence, 23 March 1903 to 29 April 1903. The other letters and Hardinge's reports are from the Hardinge Papers. Hardinge's description of his interview with Rampolla is in the Sandars Papers, 29 April 1903. Knollys remained persistently opposed to the visit. On 23 April he wrote to Hardinge from the Imperial Hotel, Exmouth: 'I shall be very sorry if it takes place. . . . The argument that the King when he was Prince of Wales called on the Pope is hardly to the point now, as an heir apparent can do many things which it is not advisable a Sovereign should.'

p. 254   Marquis de Soveral's letters are quoted by Gordon Brook-Shepherd.

p. 255   King's attitude towards republicans: Préfecture de Police, Dossier 150100, A.I. (11 February 1874).

pp. 256-59   King in Paris: Préfecture de Police, Dossier 150100, A.I., 1–8 May 1903.

p. 260   The Prince's reception in Cork in 1885: The equerry was Arthur Ellis. His description is quoted by Philip Magnus, p. 189.

p. 263   Letter from Knollys to Asquith: Asquith Papers, 5 June 1908.

p. 267   Bismarck 'hated the Prince of Wales': Rosebery Papers, 24 March 1889.

p. 267   Sir Augustus Paget's letter to Prince: Royal Archives, quoted by Philip Magnus, p. 209.

p. 270   Kaiser at Sandringham: Rosebery Papers, 26 November 1899.

p. 273   King on 'public men in Germany': Rosebery Papers, 19 February 1900.

pp. 274-76   Hardinge's reports to Grey (July 1916): 'Secret Cabinet Paper recording conversations which Lord (then Sir Charles) Hardinge had when Edward VII visited German Emperor and Emperors of Austria and Russia in 1906, 1907, 1908 and 1909'. Copy in Hardinge Papers.

p. 277   Kaiser's conversation with King in Berlin: *Grosse Politik der Europaischen Kabinette*, 28, No. 10260, quoted by Brook-Shepherd, p. 345.

p. 281   King consults gypsy: Lincolnshire Papers, Lord Carrington's journal.

p. 282   King and Arthur Ponsonby: Elibank Papers, National Library of Scotland. 'The King resents that Ponsonby, with his name, with his having been in the Diplomatic Service, and after having been Sir Henry Campbell-Bannerman's private secretary, should have voted as he did' (18 June 1908). The King ultimately relented, however, and gave instructions for Ponsonby 'to be invited to the Court Ball' on 10 July 1908 (Asquith Papers).

p. 283   King on suffragettes: Asquith Papers, 3 June 1908.

p. 283   Florence Nightingale and O.M.: Sandars Papers, 6 November 1903.

p. 283   Women on Divorce Commission: Asquith Papers, 5 September 1909.

pp. 283-84   Whitehall procession: Lincolnshire Papers, Lord Carrington's journal.

pp. 284-85   King's complaint about Asquith's colleagues: Asquith Papers, 19 July 1909.

p. 292   Carrington at deathbed: Lincolnshire Papers, Carrington's journal. As Lord Great Chamberlain, Carrington supervised the arrangements of the lying-in-state in Westminster Hall: '17 May 1910. I dressed and went into Westminster Hall. Everything in perfect order. . . . Then Big Ben began to toll, the Dead March

was heard and the procession filed into Palace Yard. . . . The
sight was most impressive. He lay there in the presence of the
royal family, high officials and the two Houses of the Lords and
Commons. The widowed Queen stood next to her son dressed
in the simplest way . . . no trimmings or ornaments of any
kind. She scarcely looked forty, so slim and upright and trim.
The new King wore naval uniform and the Garter. When the
service was over [his mother] knelt a few moments in prayer,
and then he took her by the hand and led her away. . . . Poor
Princess Victoria looked hopelessly miserable. Princess Christian, Princess Louise and Princess Beatrice, all old women now
. . . and my oldest and best friend stiff and cold in his coffin. . . .
The Hall looked magnificent, a silence that could be felt; and
the officers standing immovable at their posts. . . . It was a wet
night but the crowds stood patiently through the dark hours—
a forest of umbrellas and people shivering and stamping their
feet to keep warm. . . . Quite 25,000 were unable to obtain
admission when the gates were shut at 10 p.m. Yet all day [the
procession past the coffin] had gone on. . . . New carpets have
been put down as they were completely worn out. . . . At
eleven the King of Portugal came with Soveral [who was] terribly pale and upset. He held my hand for quite two minutes
saying over and over again, "This is too awful." He then knelt
and prayed before the coffin. . . . He feels the King's death
terribly. . . .

19 May 1910. We had a hard morning—many people trying
to get in who had no right. . . . At 1.45 we had notice that King
George and the Emperor of Germany were coming to Westminster Hall at 2.45 and that the Hall was to be closed for three
quarters of an hour. The police were aghast, and said they could
not be responsible for anything that might happen. So I got a
taxi and went off to Buckingham Palace and met Francis
Knollys coming out. He took me to the Household Dining
Room where the German suite were having luncheon and [I
arranged for the Emperor to go through the Star Chamber
Court so that he could lay his wreath] without any stoppage of
the crowd. . . . I received a telephone message from Probyn
saying that the Queen Mother desired me to take off the label
on her wreath and send it to her. . . . The inscription read, "For
my beloved husband from his broken-hearted and lonely wife,
Alix." . . . A curious thing happened last night. Just as Queen
Alexandra was momentarily expected, the Speaker and Arthur
James and some ladies in evening dress passed into the Peers'
enclosure. One of them was Mrs George Keppel . . . and the
Queen Mother expected every minute! An awkward situation.
[Lewis Harcourt, the First Commissioner of Works], to my
astonishment, volunteered to go and get rid of them, and so
saved the position. Mrs Keppel walked back into the Speaker's
House: and a very great difficulty was avoided. . . . Queen
Alexandra had her veil up and seemed perfectly calm: she
looked beautiful. . . . I then ordered the Palace to be shut up

and went to bed. Winston Churchill and a large party drew up: luckily Pom McDonnell [Sir Schomberg McDonnell, Secretary to the Office of Works] had not left and he absolutely refused them admittance. With this party was a brute of an American who pushed by and peeped round the screen, which was put to block the view, and came back grinning, saying, "I've seen him after all." The Beast! . . . The behaviour of the crowds has been simply marvellous. People waiting patiently for hours. Hundreds passed the night in the rain. They all went by from 6 a.m. to 10 p.m. quietly and reverently without intermission. Many curtsied, Catholics knelt and crossed themselves, children in arms were carried past. There was no noise, no pushing, no confusion. . . .

May 20 1910 . . . I was in the Hall by 7.45. It turned out a gloriously fine day. . . . The gun carriage and escort were waiting and everything ready about 9.15. The King, the German Emperor and eight kings rode into the yard [actually seven—of Denmark, Greece, Belgium, Bulgaria, Norway, Portugal and Spain]. They dismounted and Queen Alexandra, the Empress of Russia, the Princess Royal and Princess Victoria drove up. The Queen and the Empress got out and I took them into the Hall, where the Archbishop conducted a short service. The coffin was then . . . carried to the gun carriage. The equerries placed the pall on the coffin. The German Emperor kissed the Queen as he handed her into the carriage. The Queen patted the neck of the late King's charger and Caesar, the King's dog, which was led by the Highland Piper; and my duties were over.'

pp. 292-93 King's consideration: Knollys, Carrington, Hardinge Papers. The King had not always been so thoughtful as a younger man. Francis Knollys told Rosebery in 1885: 'April is [Harry Stonor's] month of waiting and he naturally expected to go to Ireland. Yesterday, however, the Prince told me he had been thinking it over and that he thought Ellis would be more useful. I am afraid Harry, though of course he will not say so or admit it, will feel it a little. I wish the Prince would not do these things, as people who are fond of him cannot but be a little "hurt" by them.' (Rosebery MSS., 16 March 1885.)

Bibliography

MANUSCRIPTS

Northumberland Papers (Alnwick Castle)
Grosvenor MSS (Grosvenor Estate Office)
Goodwood Archives (Chichester, County Record Office)
Romilly Diaries (Cambridge University Library)
Crewe Papers (Cambridge University Library)
Hardinge of Penshurst Papers (Cambridge University Library)
Dossier du Roi Edouard VII (Bureau des Archives, Préfecture de Police, Paris)
Wellington Archives (Stratfield Saye)
Henry Poole & Co. Records (Cork Street)
Lincolnshire Papers (Bodleian)
Gordon Cumming Papers (National Library of Scotland)
Rosebery Papers (National Library of Scotland)
Minto Papers (National Library of Scotland)
Haldane Papers (National Library of Scotland)
Combe Papers (National Library of Scotland)
Elibank Papers (National Library of Scotland)
Carrington Papers (Aylesbury, County Record Office and Bledlow·Manor)
Gibbs Papers (Oxford, County Record Office)
Cadogan MSS (House of Lords Record Office)
Acland Papers (Bodleian)
Earl Grey Papers (Department of Palaeography, University of Durham)
Manchester Collection (Huntingdon, County Record Office)
Downe Papers (Northallerton, County Record Office)
Londonderry Papers (Durham, County Record Office)
Devonshire Collections (Chatsworth)
Salisbury Papers (Hatfield House)
Filmer MSS (Maidstone, County Record Office)
Chilston MSS (Maidstone, County Record Office)

Knollys MSS (Maidstone, County Record Office)
King Papers (Cambridge, County Record Office)
Henniker Collection (Ipswich, County Record Office)
Cranworth Collection (Ipswich, County Record Office)
Wharncliffe Correspondence (Sheffield, Central Library)

PUBLICATIONS

Acton, Harold. *More Memoirs of an Aesthete*. Methuen, 1970.

Airlie, Mabell, Countess of. *Thatched with Gold: The Memoirs of Mabell, Countess of Airlie*. Edited by Jennifer Ellis Hutchinson, 1962.

Antrim, Lady Louisa. *Recollections*. 1937.

Arthur, Sir George. *Concerning Queen Victoria and Her Son*. Hale, 1943.

Asquith, Margot. *The Autobiography of Margot Asquith*. Edited by Mark Bonham Carter. Eyre & Spottiswoode, 1962.

Bahlman, Dudley W. R., ed. *The Diary of Sir Edward Walter Hamilton*. Clarendon Press, Oxford, 2 vols, 1972.

Bailey, John, ed. *The Diary of Lady Frederick Cavendish*. 2 vols, 1927.

Balsan, Consuelo Vanderbilt. *The Glitter and the Gold*. Heinemann, 1953.

Battiscombe, Georgina. *Queen Alexandra*. Constable, 1969.

Behrman, S. N. *Duveen*. Hamish Hamilton, 1952.

Bennett, Geoffrey. *Charlie B: A Biography of Admiral Lord Beresford of Metemmeh and Curraghmore*. Peter Dawnay, 1963.

Benson, E. F. *As We Were: A Victorian Peep-Show*. 1930.

———. *King Edward VII: An Appreciation*. 1933.

Beresford, Lord Charles. *The Memoirs of Admiral Lord Charles Beresford*. 1914.

Birkenhead, the Earl of. *The Life of Lord Halifax*. Hamish Hamilton, 1965.

Blake, Robert. *Disraeli*. Eyre & Spottiswoode, 1966.

Blumenfeld, R. D. *All in a Lifetime*. 1931.

Blunden, Margaret. *The Countess of Warwick*. Cassell, 1967.

Blunt, Wilfrid Scawen. *My Diaries*. 1919–20.

Blyth, Henry. *The Last Victorian Courtesan: The Life and Times of Catherine Walters*. Hart-Davis, 1970.

Bolitho, Hector. *Victoria: The Widow and Her Son*. 1934.

Bradlaugh, Charles. *George, The Princes of Wales, With Recent Contrasts and Coincidences*. 1870.

British Documents on the Origin of the War. Edited by G. P. Gooch and H. W. Temperley. 1926.

Broadhurst, Henry. *Henry Broadhurst M.P.: Told by Himself*. 1901.

Broadley, A. M. *Boyhood of a Great King 1841–1858*. 1906.

Brook-Shepherd, Gordon. *Uncle of Europe*. Collins, 1975.

Brough, James. *The Prince and the Lily*. Coward, McCann & Geoghegan, 1975.

Bruce, H. J. *Silken Dalliance*. Constable, 1946.

Bryant, Sir Arthur. *George V*. 1936.

Bülow, Prince von. *Memoirs*. Translated by F. A. Voigt. 1931–32.

Cecil, Lady Gwendolen. *Life of Robert, Marquis of Salisbury*. 1921–32.

Christopher, Prince of Greece. *Memoirs*. 1938.

Churchill, Randolph S. *Winston S. Churchill, Volume 1: Youth, 1874–1900*. Heinemann, 1966.

———. *Winston S. Churchill, Volume 2: Young Statesman, 1901–1914*, and companion volume 2. Heinemann, 1967.

Churchill, Winston S. *My Early Life*. 1930.

Cornwallis, Kinahan. *Royalty in the New World or the Prince of Wales in America*. 1860.

Cornwallis-West, George. *Edwardian Hey-Days*. 1930.

Corti, E. C. *The English Empress: A Study in the Relations between Queen Victoria and Her Eldest Daughter*. 1957.

Cowles, Virginia. *Edward VII and His Circle*. Hamish Hamilton, 1956.

[Cresswell, Mrs Louise]. *Eighteen Years on the Sandringham Estate by 'The Lady Farmer'*. 1887.

Crewe, the Marquess of. *Lord Rosebery*. 1931.

Cruise of H.M.S. 'Bacchante' 1879–82 compiled from the Private Journals . . . of Prince Albert Victor and Prince George . . . with additions by John N. Dalton. 2 vols, 1886.

Cust, Sir Lionel. *King Edward VII and His Court*. 1930.

Dangerfield, George. *The Strange Death of Liberal England*. 1935.

———. *Victoria's Heir: The Education of a Prince*. Constable, new edition, 1972.

Daragon, Henri. *Voyage à Paris de S.M. Edouard VII*. Paris, 1903.

Dixmier, Elisabeth and Michel. *L'Assiette au Beurre: Revue satirique illustrée*. Maspero, Paris, 1974.

Donaldson, Frances. *Edward VIII*. Weidenfeld & Nicolson, 1974.

Duff, David. *Whisper Louise: Edward VII and Mrs Cresswell*. Frederick Muller, 1974.

Eckardstein, Baron von. *Ten Years at the Court of St James's, 1895–1905*. 1921.

Edel, Leon. *Henry James: The Master, 1901–16*. Hart-Davis, 1972.

Edwards, H. *The Tragedy of King Edward VII: A Psychological Study*. 1928.

Erskine, Mrs Stuart. *Memoirs of Edward, Earl of Sandwich, 1839–1916*. 1919.

Esher, Reginald, Viscount. *Cloud Capp'd Towers*. 1927.

————. *The Influence of King Edward.* 1915.

————. *The Journals of Reginald Viscount Esher.* Edited by M. V. Brett. 4 vols, 1934.

Fildes, L. V. *Luke Fildes, R.A.: A Victorian Painter.* Michael Joseph, 1968.

Fisher, Lord. *Memories.* 1919.

Fitzroy, Sir Almeric. *Memoirs.* 1925.

Forbes-Robertson, Diana. *Maxine.* Hamish Hamilton, 1964.

Fulford, Roger. *Hanover to Windsor.* Batsford, 1960.

————, ed. *Dearest Child: Letters between Queen Victoria and the Princess Royal, 1858–1861.* Evans, 1964.

————, ed. *Dearest Mama: Letters between Queen Victoria and the Crown Princess of Prussia, 1861–1864.* Evans, 1968.

————, ed. *Your Dear Letter: Private Correspondence of Queen Victoria and the Crown Princess of Prussia.* Evans, 1971.

German Diplomatic Documents, 1871–1914. Translated by E. T. S. Dugdale. 1928.

Girouard, Mark. *The Victorian Country House.* Clarendon Press, Oxford, 1971.

Glyn, Anthony. *Elinor Glyn: A Biography.* Hutchinson, 1955.

Glyn, Elinor. *Romantic Adventure.* 1936.

Gore, John. *King George V: A Personal Memoir.* 1941.

Gower, Lord Ronald. *My Reminiscences.* 1895.

Greville, Charles C. F. *Memoirs, 1814–1860.* Edited by Lytton Strachey and Roger Fulford, 8 vols, 1938.

Grey, Mrs William. *Journal of a Visit to Egypt . . . in the Suite of the Prince of Wales.* 1869.

Grey of Fallodon, Viscount. *Twenty-Five Years.* 1925.

Guedalla, Philip. *The Queen and Mr Gladstone.* 1933.

Gwynn, Stephen, and Gertrude M. Tuckwell. *The Life of Sir Charles Dilke.* 2 vols, 1917.

Haldane, Richard Burdon, Viscount. *Autobiography.* 1929.

Hardinge of Penshurst, Lord. *Old Diplomacy.* John Murray, 1947.

Harrison, Michael. *Clarence.* W. H. Allen, 1972.

Hassall, Christopher. *Edward Marsh: Patron of the Arts.* Longmans, 1959.

Hegermann Lindencrone, L. de. *The Sunny Side of Diplomatic Life.* 1921.

Herbodeau, Eugène, and Paul Thelamas. *Georges Auguste Escoffier.* Practical Press, 1955.

Hetherington, John. *Melba.* Faber, 1967.

Holland, Bernard. *The Eighth Duke of Devonshire.* 1911.

Holmes, Sir Richard. *Edward VII.* 2 vols, 1910.

Hough, Richard. *First Sea Lord: A Life of Admiral Fisher.* Allen & Unwin, 1969.

————. *Louis and Victoria: The First Mountbattens.* Hutchinson, 1974.

Hudson, Derek. *Munby, Man of Two Worlds: The Life and Diaries of Arthur J. Munby, 1828–1910*. John Murray, 1972.

Huxley, Gervas. *Victorian Duke: The Life of Hugh Lupus Grosvenor, First Duke of Westminster*. Oxford University Press, 1967.

Jenkins, Roy. *Sir Charles Dilke: A Victorian Tragedy*. Collins, 1958.

Jullian, Philippe. *Edward and the Edwardians*. Translated by Peter Dawnay, Sidgwick & Jackson, 1967.

Kennedy, A. L., ed. *Letters to the Duchess of Manchester*. John Murray, 1956.

Keppel, Sonia. *Edwardian Daughter*. Hamish Hamilton, 1938.

King Edward VII: Biographical and Personal Sketches and Anecdotes. 1910.

Kurtz, Harold. *The Empress Eugénie, 1826–1920*. Hamish Hamilton, 1964.

Lang, Theo. *My Darling Daisy*. Michael Joseph, 1966.

Langtry, Lillie. *The Days I Knew*. 1925.

Lee, Sir Sidney. *King Edward VII: A Biography*. 2 vols, 1925–27.

Legge, Edward. *King Edward in His True Colours*. 1912.

———. *More about King Edward*. 1913.

Leslie, Anita. *Edwardians in Love*. Hutchinson, 1972.

Letters of Lady Augusta Stanley, The. Edited by A. V. Baillie and Hector Bolitho, 1927.

Letters of Queen Victoria, The. First series, edited by A. C. Benson and Viscount Esher, 3 vols, 1907; second series, edited by G. E. Buckle, 3 vols, 1926; third series, 3 vols, 1930.

Leveson Gower, Sir George. *Mixed Grill*. Frederick Muller, 1947.

Longford, Elizabeth. *Victoria R. I.* Weidenfeld & Nicolson, 1964.

Lutyens, Mary, ed. *Lady Lytton's Court Diary, 1895–99*. Hart-Davis, 1961.

Lytton, the Earl of. *Wilfred Scawen Blunt: A Memoir by His Grandson*. Macdonald, 1961.

McClintock, Mary Howard. *The Queen Thanks Sir Howard: The Life of Major-General Sir Howard Elphinstone*. John Murray, 1945.

MacDonell, J. C. *The Life and Correspondence of William Connor Magee*. 2 vols, 1896.

Mackay, Ruddock F. *Fisher of Kilverstone*. Clarendon Press, Oxford, 1974.

Madol, Hans R. *The Private Life of Queen Alexandra*. 1940.

Magnus, Philip. *Gladstone*. John Murray, 1954.

———. *King Edward the Seventh*. John Murray, 1964.

Manchester, the Duke of. *My Candid Recollections*. 1932.

Marder, Arthur J. *Fear God and Dread Nought: Correspondence of Admiral of the Fleet Lord Fisher of Kilverstone*. 3 vols, Cape, 1952.

Marie, Queen of Rumania. *The Story of My Life*. 1934.

Marie Louise, Princess. *My Memories of Six Reigns*. Evans, 1956.

Martin, Robert Bernard. *The Dust of Combat: A Life of Charles Kingsley*. Faber, 1959.

Martin, Theodore. *The Life of H.R.H. The Prince Consort.* 1875–80.

Maurice, Major General Sir Frederick. *Haldane, 1856–1915.* 2 vols, 1937.

Maurois, André. *King Edward and His Times.* Translated by Hamish Miles. 1933.

Mersey, Viscount. *Journal and Memories.* 1952.

——. *A Picture of Life, 1872–1940.* 1941.

Middlemas, Keith. *The Life and Times of King Edward the Seventh.* Weidenfeld & Nicolson, 1972.

Montagu of Beaulieu, Lord. *The Motoring Montagus.* Cassel, 1959.

Montgomery Hyde, H. *Henry James at Home.* Methuen, 1969.

Monypenny, William Flavelle, and George Earle Buckle. *The Life of Benjamin Disraeli, Earl of Beaconsfield.* Revised edition, 2 vols, 1929.

Morgan, Kenneth O., ed. *Lloyd George: Family Letters 1885–1936.* University of Wales Press, 1973.

Morley, John. *The Life of William Ewart Gladstone.* 2 vols, 1905.

——. *Recollections.* 2 vols, 1917.

Mossolov, A. A. *At the Court of the Last Tsar.* Edited by A. A. Pilenco; translated by E. W. Dickey. 1935.

Münz, Sigmund. *King Edward VII at Marienbad.* 1934.

Newton, Lord. *Lord Lansdowne.* 1929.

Nicolson, Harold. *King George V: His Life and Reign.* Constable, 1952.

——. *Sir Arthur Nicolson, Bart., First Lord Carnock.* 1930.

Noakes, Vivien. *Edward Lear: The Life of a Wanderer.* Collins, 1968.

Nowell-Smith, Simon, ed. *Edwardian England, 1901–1914.* Oxford University Press, 1964.

Ormathwaite, Lord. *When I Was at Court.* 1937.

Paget, Walburga, Lady. *Embassies of Other Days.* 1923.

——. *In My Tower.* 2 vols, 1926.

Paoli, Xavier. *My Royal Clients.* Translated by Alexander Teixera de Mattos. 1911.

Petrie, Sir Charles. *Scenes of Edwardian Life.* Eyre & Spottiswoode, 1965.

——. *The Victorians.* Eyre & Spottiswoode, 1962.

Pless, Daisy, Princess of. *From My Private Diary.* Edited by Major Desmond Chapman-Huston. 1931.

——. *What I Left Unsaid.* 1936.

Ponsonby, Arthur. *Henry Ponsonby: Queen Victoria's Private Secretary: His Life from His Letters.* Macmillan, 1942.

Ponsonby, Sir Frederick. *Recollections of Three Reigns.* Edited by Colin Welch. Eyre & Spottiswoode, 1957.

——, ed. *The Letters of the Empress Frederick.* 1928.

Pope-Hennessy, James. *Lord Crewe: The Likeness of a Liberal.* Constable, 1955.

——. *Queen Mary, 1867–1953.* Allen & Unwin, 1959.

Private Life of the King by One of His Majesty's Servants. 1901.

Prothero, R. E., and C. G. Bradley. *The Life and Correspondence of Dean Stanley.* 2 vols, 1893.

Read, Donald. *Edwardian England, 1901–15: Society and Politics.* Harrap, 1972.

Redesdale, Lord. *King Edward VII: A Memory.* 1915.

———. *Memories.* 2 vols, 1915.

Reminiscences of Lady Randolph Churchill, The. 1908.

Rhodes James, Robert. *Lord Randolph Churchill.* Weidenfeld & Nicolson, 1959.

———. *Rosebery.* Weidenfeld & Nicolson, 1963.

Roberts, Cecil. *The Growing Boy, 1892–1908.* Hodder & Stoughton, 1967.

Roby, Kinley. *The King, the Press and the People: A Study of Edward VII.* Barrie & Jenkins, 1975.

Rodd, Sir Rennell. *Social and Diplomatic Memories 1902–1919.* 1922.

Rose, Kenneth. *Superior Person: A Portrait of Curzon and His Circle.* Weidenfeld & Nicolson, 1969.

St Aubyn, Giles. *The Royal George, 1819–1904.* Constable, 1963.

Sanderson, Edgar. *King Edward VII.* 5 vols., 1910.

Sermoneta, the Duchess of. *Things Past.* 1929.

Seth-Smith, Michael. *Bred for the Purple.* Leslie Frewin, 1969.

Sewell, Lieut. Col. J. P. C., ed. *Personal Letters of King Edward VII.* 1931.

Shore, W. T. *The Baccarat Case.* 1932.

Sitwell, Osbert. *Great Morning.* Macmillan, 1948.

———. *The Scarlet Tree.* Macmillan, 1946.

Skinner, Cornelia Otis. *Madame Sarah.* 1967.

Somner, Dudley. *Haldane of Cloan: His Life and Times, 1856–1928.* Allen & Unwin, 1960.

Spender, J. A. *The Life of Sir Henry Campbell-Bannerman.* 1923.

——— and Cyril Asquith. *The Life of Lord Oxford and Asquith.* 1932.

Stamper, C. W. *What I Know: Reminiscences of Five Years' Personal Attendance upon . . . King Edward the Seventh.* 1913.

Stead, W. T. 'The Prince of Wales'. *Review of Reviews.* July 1891.

Stonor, Dom Julian. *Stonor.* R. H. Johns, 1951–52.

Stuart, James. *Reminiscences.* 1911.

Suffield, Edward Harbord, Baron. *My Memories, 1830–1913.* Edited by Alys Lowth. 1913.

Sykes, Christopher. *Four Studies in Loyalty.* Collins, 1946.

Thompson, F. M. L. *English Landed Society in the Nineteenth Century.* 1963.

Trevelyan, G. M. *Grey of Fallodon: The Life of Sir Edward Grey, Afterwards Viscount Grey of Fallodon.* 1937.

Troubridge, Laura, Lady. *Memoirs and Reflections.* 1925.

Trützschler, Zedlitz, Count. *Twelve Years at the German Court.* 1924.

Tschumi, Gabriel. *Royal Chef: Recollections of Life in Royal Households.* William Kimber, 1954.

Vansittart, Lord. *The Mist Procession: The Autobiography of Lord Vansittart.* Hutchinson, 1958.

Warwick, Frances, Countess of. *Afterthoughts.* Cassell, 1931.

———. *Life's Ebb and Flow.* 1929.

Watson, Alfred E. T. *King Edward VII as a Sportsman.* 1911.

Watson, Francis L. *Dawson of Penn.* Chatto & Windus, 1950.

Wechsberg, Joseph. *Red Plush and Black Velvet: The Story of Dame Nellie Melba and Her Times.* Weidenfeld & Nicolson, 1961.

Weigall, Lady Rose. *A Memoir.* 1913.

Westminster, Loelia, Duchess of. *Grace and Favour.* Weidenfeld & Nicolson, 1961.

Whitbourn, Frank. *Mr Lock of St James's Street.* Heinemann, 1971.

Who Should Educate the Prince of Wales? 1843.

Wickham Steed, Henry. *Through Thirty Years 1892–1922.* 1924.

Williams, Mrs Florence Hwfa. *It Was Such Fun.* 1935.

Wilson, John. *CB: A Life of Sir Henry Campbell-Bannerman.* Constable, 1973.

Windsor, the Duke of. *A King's Story: The Memoirs of H.R.H. the Duke of Windsor.* Cassell, 1951.

Woodham-Smith, Cecil. *Queen Victoria: Her Life and Times, Volume I. 1819–1861.* Hamish Hamilton, 1972.

Woods, Nicholas Augustus. *The Prince of Wales in Canada and the United States.* 1861.

Wortham, H. E. *Edward VII: Man and King.* 1931.

Wyndham, Hon Mrs Hugh, ed. *The Correspondence of Sarah Spencer, Lady Lyttelton.* 1912.

Young, Kenneth. *Arthur James Balfour.* Bell, 1963.

Zetland, Marquess of, ed. *The Letters of Disraeli to Lady Bradford and Lady Chesterfield.* 2 vols, 1929.

Index

King Edward VII is referred to as P of W and then, on his accession, as KE; Queen Alexandra successively as Alexandra, Pss of W and QA; and Queen Victoria as QV.

DATE DUE